FIDEL BETWEEN THE LINES

FIDEL

LAURA-ZOË HUMPHREYS

BETWEEN THE LINES

PARANOIA AND AMBIVALENCE
IN LATE SOCIALIST CUBAN CINEMA

DUKE UNIVERSITY PRESS *Durham and London* 2019

Printed in the United States of America on acid-free paper ∞
Cover designed by Matthew Tauch
Text designed by Aimee C. Harrison
Typeset in Minion Pro, Franklin Gothic, and Serifa Std
by Westchester Publishing Services

Library of Congress Cataloging-in-Publication Data
Names: Humphreys, Laura-Zoe, [date] author.
Title: Fidel between the lines : paranoia and ambivalence in late socialist
    Cuban cinema / Laura-Zoe Humphreys.
Description: Durham : Duke University Press, 2019. | Includes
    bibliographical references and index.
Identifiers: LCCN 2019006366 (print)
LCCN 2019012785 (ebook)
ISBN 9781478007142 (ebook)
ISBN 9781478005476 (hardcover : alk. paper)
ISBN 9781478006244 (pbk. : alk. paper)
Subjects: LCSH: Motion pictures—Cuba—History and criticism. | Motion
    pictures—Political aspects—Cuba. | Motion pictures—Cuba—History—
    20th century. | Motion pictures—Cuba—History—21st century.
Classification: LCC PN1993.5.C8 (ebook) | LCC PN1993.5.C8 H867 2019
    (print) | DDC 791.43097291—dc23
LC record available at https://lccn.loc.gov/2019006366

Cover art: View of the Monument to the Victims of the USS *Maine*,
Havana, Cuba. Illustration by Matthew Tauch.

Duke University Press gratefully acknowledges Tulane University's School
of Liberal Arts, which provided funds toward the publication of this book.

CONTENTS

ACKNOWLEDGMENTS

This book has taken me from Montreal to Chicago to Baltimore to Winnipeg to New Orleans and back and forth to Havana for more than a decade. Numerous people were essential in its making, both for their work on the book and for helping me keep it together in a sometimes too itinerant lifestyle. First and most importantly, I would like to thank the many Cuban filmmakers and intellectuals who generously gave me their time and their trust. Their stories and their passion for art and for life—their capacity both to dream utopian dreams and to be deeply self-critical—were what motivated me to take on this project. I cannot possibly name them all, but I hope they will see their imprints on these pages. My research in Havana would not have been possible without the support of the Escuela Internacional de Cine y TV (EICTV) and the Cinemateca de Cuba. At the EICTV, special thanks are owed to Maria Julia Grillo and Raúl Capote Rodríguez, who welcomed me into the EICTViano community and facilitated visas for numerous stays. The staff of the Cinemateca, especially Lola Calviño, Luciano Castillo, Mayda Ferrá, Manuel Herrera, Tony Mazón, Mario Naito López, Daymar Valdés, and Sara Vega, have been the best work colleagues I could have asked for. I am grateful for their help with archival research, their company, and for loaning me a desk and the air-conditioning in the summer of 2016, when I decided to finish the first draft of this book in Havana.

Thanks to the regulars at the Playita de 16 who kept me company during so many early morning swims. I learned much from them about life and politics in Cuba. Heartfelt thanks to Beatrix Berger, Esteban Bruzón, Claudia Calviño, Lisandra Díaz Moreno, Karel Ducase Manzano, David Fernández Borrás, Mayda Ferrá, Mayelin Guevara, Haroldo Jaen, Adriana Lord, Nathaniel Lord Romero (you are missed), Carlos Machado Quintela, Evelio Manfred Gay, Lianed Marcoleta, María Elisa Pérez Leal, Nery Romero Ferrer, Damián Sainz, Ebert Trujillo, Daymar Valdés, Rúben Valdés, Yan Vega, and Othón Yañez Troncoso. Their comments have been essential to this book and to the project I began while finishing this one. Most importantly, their friendship made Havana home and enriched my life through both my own and their moves to new countries.

This project found its first shape in the Departments of Anthropology and Cinema and Media Studies at the University of Chicago. There I owe a debt to William Mazzarella, Tom Gunning, Lauren Berlant, Michael Silverstein, and Stephan Palmié. Their faith in this interdisciplinary venture, the insightful questions they posed, and, most of all, their friendship and care over the years have been crucial in bringing this book to its final form. Anne Chien steered me through graduate studies and beyond, as she has for countless other students. Everything I know about Brecht I learned from Loren Kruger. Jim Lastra helped me think about international new cinemas. Miriam Hansen and Yuri Tsivian inspired me to take up film studies. I hope this book would have lived up to Miriam's high standards.

The current job market has been brutal to many of the most brilliant researchers and teachers I know. I am lucky to have found employment and am endlessly grateful to those who helped me in my own job searches and relocations. An Andrew W. Mellon Postdoctoral Fellowship in the Department of Anthropology at Johns Hopkins University provided me with two valuable years in which I began writing this book and started research on a second project. Special thanks go to Kristin Boyce, Anne Eakin Moss, Rachel Galvin, Yi-Ping Ong, Rani Neutill, Gabrielle Spiegel, and the members of the 2012–14 Andrew W. Mellon Seminar for their rich intellectual engagement and their incisive comments on early versions of two chapters of this manuscript. In Hopkins's anthropology department, I am particularly thankful to Andrew Brandel, Veena Das, Aaron Goodfellow, Jane Guyer, Clara Han, Niloofar Haeri, Richard Helman, Naveeda Khan, Neena Mahadev, Anand Pandian, Anaid Citalli Reyes-Kipp, Vaibhav Saria, and, most especially, my officemate and dear friend, Andrew Bush, for their support with this project and as I sought my first tenure-track position.

I am grateful to my colleagues in the Department of Anthropology at the University of Manitoba, where I held that first tenure-track position. Special thanks are owed to Kathy Buddle, Anna Fournier, Derek Johnson, Ellen Judd, Fabiani Li, and Greg Monks. They helped me strengthen my understanding of anthropology as a discipline and encouraged me to carve out an interdisciplinary path for myself. Also at the University of Manitoba, thanks to the members of the Humanities Institute's Latin American Power and Resistance Research Cluster for reading and to Jorge Nállim for crucial guidance on the logistics of bringing the book to press. The book took on its final form in my first years as an assistant professor in the Department of Communication at Tulane University. I could not ask for a more exciting and generative place from which to think the future of media and cultural studies. My colleagues are, to my mind, a model of the best sort of intellectual engagement and interdisciplinary collaboration. At Johns Hopkins, the University of Manitoba, and Tulane, finally, I owe a debt to all the students in my Cuban Cinema and my Media and the Public Sphere courses. Their curiosity and insightful questions did much to push the thinking that went into this project.

Over the years, many people have taken the time to talk me through my ideas or to provide comments on the conference papers, job talks, articles, and chapter drafts that have gone into the making of this book. Laurie Frederik, Susan Lord, and Paul Ryer helped orient me on my first trips to Havana and long afterward. Joao Felipe Gonçalves, Ariana Hernández-Reguant, Ana López, and Masha Salazkina pushed me to think in more sophisticated ways about Cuba, its cinema, and its politics. Conversations with Alex Boudreault-Fournier, Erin Debenport, and Cassie Fennell provided important provocations. Rachel Galvin, Eric Herhuth, Michelle Lelièvre, Sarah Luna, William Mazzarella, Hannah Rogers, Eli Thorkelson, and Jeremy Walton gave detailed and astute readings of individual chapters. Their care and labor were essential to helping me formulate and refine my ideas. I am forever indebted to Kenneth Brummel, Faizal Deen, Anna Fournier, Julie Gibbings, Ruth Goldberg, François Proulx, and Shayna Silverstein. I would not have made it to the finish line without their generous intellectual engagement, their friendship, and, in the case of Shayna, her presence throughout the years pushing me to write from the other side of social media or the library to the café table. Dan Morgan read so much and with such great care. Thanks also to him for always reminding me to finish.

Gisela Fosado at Duke University Press is an exemplary editor. Her enthusiasm, quick responses, and patience helped me write the book I wanted to write and, hopefully, one that others will enjoy reading. Emily Chilton, Lydia Rose Rappoport-Hankins, and Jenny Tan provided essential support at critical stages in my work on the manuscript. Liz Smith shepherded the manuscript through the editorial, design, and production process, and Sheila McMahon provided careful and detailed copyediting. I am grateful to the two anonymous readers for their painstaking attention to every level of the argument and writing and for their willingness to keep pushing for improvement over two rounds of reviews. I could not have asked for a more insightful reading. My gratitude also goes to David Sartorius and to two anonymous reviewers at *Social Text*. Their comments on an early version of chapter 2 pushed me to better articulate the broader stakes of this project.

The research for this project was made possible by generous grants from the University of Chicago, the Social Sciences and Humanities Research Council of Canada, the Fonds de recherche du Québec—Société et culture, and the Social Science Research Council. Earlier versions of chapters 1 and 2 first appeared as "Symptomologies of the State: Cuba's 'Email War' and the Paranoid Public Sphere," in *Digital Cultures and the Politics of Emotion: Feelings, Affect and Technological Change*, ed. Athina Karatzogianni and Adi Kunstman (London: Palgrave Macmillan, 2012); and "Paranoid Readings and Ambivalent Allegories in Cuban Cinema," *Social Text* 35, no. 3 (2017): 17–40. An analysis of Susana Barriga's *The Illusion* (2008), discussed in chapter 5, appeared as a film review in *E-misférica* 7, no. 1 (2010), http://hemisphericinstitute.org/hemi/en/e-misferica-71/laura-zoehumphreys-.

I am also grateful to the staff, faculty, and students of the master's program of the humanities at the University of Chicago for their support and company. Karin Cope and Miranda Hickman fostered my love for writing and creative thinking. Sam McGavin may well be right that it was her idea that I do research in Cuba in the first place. Her friendship has been invaluable during so many difficult moments. Thanks also to Mario Aranda, Diego Arispe-Bazán, Gláucio Augusto, Eleanor Bailey Little, Brian Brazeal, Justin Bur, Carolina Caballero, Nusrat Chowdhury, Brenda Cockfield, Will Eizlini, Paul Fagen, Dianna Frid, Julia Gibbs, Alayne Gobeille, Danny Gough, Elyn Humphreys, Paul Jenkins, Allan Lesage, Hillary Neeb, Stefan Reinecke, Phil Stalcup, Bill Toles, Dan Torop, Michael, Clare, and Evie Treberg, Nikola Tamindzic, Grete Viddal, Lonnell Williams, and Artemis Willis for helping me keep it all in perspective.

This project made an itinerant not just out of me. My thanks to Dziga, who has kept me company through two international moves and several annual migrations; to my mother, Suzanne Humphreys, who is an excellent copyeditor as well as the best long-distance driving, swimming, and canoeing partner I could ask for; and to my father, Glenn Humphreys, who helped take charge of the endlessly complicated logistical issues involved in jet-setting on a shoestring. My parents always believed in me even when I did not, and they never once hesitated to deliver indeterminate packages across international borders to unknown people. Their unwavering support has allowed me to live my life more richly, if, perhaps, not always all that sensibly. This book is dedicated to them.

CRITICISM FROM WITHIN

"For once I'd like to do an interview about cinema instead of talking about the same nonsense," a then thirtysomething Cuban filmmaker told me in February 2008 as he graciously showed me out of his apartment in Havana's middle-class Vedado neighborhood.[1] The "nonsense" to which he referred included questions about social criticism and censorship that I had introduced toward the end of our conversation, and which he had largely evaded. In the days that followed, this comment haunted me. From my first visit to Cuba in 2003, to full-time fieldwork from 2007 to 2009, and subsequent visits through 2017, my goal was to track how filmmakers were negotiating aspirations to produce films that depicted the nation's social and political realities with their dependence on broader structures for support: the socialist state as of the beginning of the Cuban Revolution and, following the collapse of the Soviet Union, the global market.[2] To the novice fieldworker that I was at the time, my interlocutor's resistance to my attempts to guide the conversation to these topics seemed to throw my entire project into doubt.

With time, however, I realized that it was precisely such resistances that needed to be explored. A year after our initial conversation, I returned to this same filmmaker's apartment to look over the transcript of our first interview together. A discussion of Susana Barriga's *The Illusion* (2008), a short first-person documentary about Barriga's painful and paranoia-imbued encounter with her exiled Cuban father in London, England (see chapter 5), soon led to a broader conversation about Cuban filmmaking and the lingering effects of Cold War divides on public debate in and about the island.[3] After detailing with some bitterness his encounters with censorship in Cuba, the film director recounted with equal rancor his experiences of being silenced by audiences abroad, who, he explained, often dismissed his statements about Cuban politics by saying that he would not be able to articulate such views on the island. "What freedom of expression are they talking about," he asked, "when they won't let me voice my opinions? I've found that the best way to survive in Cuba is to refuse to be part of either group."

This filmmaker was not alone in his wariness of a reduction of his work and beliefs to a binary view of Cuban politics framed, on one side, by staunch support for the Cuban government and, on the other, by the conviction that Cuba is a totalitarian regime that stifles all meaningful debate. Over the course of my fieldwork, I learned that politics and social criticism had become sources of both desire and anxiety for artists and audiences. In the post-Soviet era, a series of economic, political, and technological changes created new openings for public debate and representation. Artists and intellectuals celebrated the expansion of what could be articulated through cinema and other arts, while audiences crowded into theaters to see the latest controversial film or, in cases where state officials blocked these works from the big screen, circulated them informally over newly available digital technologies. But these openings also exacerbated the political paranoia that has long dominated the Cuban public sphere. While spectators argued about whether films harbored secret messages against the socialist state, veiled complicity with political leaders, or served as publicity stunts, filmmakers complained that these readings ignored the nuances of their depictions of Cuba and reduced their art to propaganda.

In the chapters that follow, I tease out the history and dynamics of this paranoid public sphere. Reading films against what artists and spectators say about them, as well as for how they rehearse and transform genres pervasive in art and in Cuban intellectual and political discourse, I show how Cuban filmmakers have historically turned to allegory to articulate an ambivalent relationship to the Revolution and how such attempts have repeatedly come up against paranoid readings of their work.[4] One of this book's central goals, then, is to explain the history by which nuanced political positions in Cuba have so often been reduced to Cold War binaries and to show how these divisions are increasingly out of step with the hopes and sentiments of many Cubans. This book thus also necessarily delves into themes with resonance beyond the island, exploring what happens to politics and public debate when freedom of expression can no longer be distinguished from complicity, how allegory and conflicts over textual interpretation shape the public sphere, and how textual analysis and ethnographic fieldwork can be brought together to better understand the broader social and political import of cinema.

Telling this story requires me to move back and forth in time across and within the chapters, in order to establish the precedents that set up the aesthetic and political positions and genres that play out in later debates. To make it easier for readers to follow these shifts, in the remainder of this introduction I provide a brief history of the major institutions, individuals, and events that have shaped Cuban cinema from the beginning of the revolutionary period in 1959 until 2017, then outline the book's major theoretical and methodological interventions. This introduction, then, provides an initial picture of how filmmakers working in a state socialist context have attempted to use their films to open up new meanings, the complexities and contradictions that have plagued these efforts, and what this can teach us about cinema, censorship, and the paradoxes of the public sphere.

Social Criticism, Censorship, and Cuban Cinema, 1959–2017

I take cinema as my focus because it has long been one of the sites where struggles over freedom of expression have been the most acute in Cuba.[5] Demonstrating both the importance granted cinema by the new revolutionary government and the political capital enjoyed by the Revolution's first generation of filmmakers, the Instituto Cubano de Arte e Industria Cinematográficos (ICAIC, Cuban Institute of Cinematographic Art and Industry) was one of the first cultural institutions to be established after the triumph against General Fulgencio Batista in January 1959. Following the nationalization of movie theaters and distributors in the early 1960s, the ICAIC dominated film production and distribution well into the 1990s. Artists and intellectuals on the island often praise the ICAIC for having safeguarded a broader margin for both aesthetic experimentation and public debate than other institutions, including, notably, state-operated journalism and television. As one of the ICAIC's most recognized directors, Tomás Gutiérrez Alea, once famously argued, Cuban filmmakers took on difficult issues in their films because "journalism . . . does not perform its mission of social criticism" (qtd. in Chanan 2002, 51; see also chapter 2). Much of the credit for the ICAIC's relative freedom is given to its longtime director, Alfredo Guevara, who headed the institute from 1959 to 1982, and again from 1991 to 2000, before taking over the leadership of the Festival Internacional del Nuevo Cine Latinoamericano (New Latin American Film Festival) until his death in May 2013. As is well known in Cuba, Guevara formed a close personal friendship with Fidel Castro during the 1940s, when the two were student activists at the University of Havana. It is also an open secret on the island that he was gay. Over the course of his career, Guevara drew on his personal ties to Castro to protect controversial films and filmmakers, including during the 1970s, the period of worst censorship in Cuba and an era when gay artists in particular came under attack.

Two of the institute's most important figures—Tomás Gutiérrez Alea and Julio García Espinosa—studied cinema at the Centro Sperimentale di Cinematografia (Experimental Film Center) in Rome in the 1950s, along with Néstor Almendros, who would soon leave the ICAIC and, eventually, Cuba, earning international recognition abroad as a cinematographer for the French New Wave and an Oscar for his work on Terrence Malick's *Days of Heaven* (1978). Other members came to the institute through their previous participation in local cinema clubs. They brought with them strong ties to and interests in Italian neorealism, international new cinemas, and the work of German playwright Bertolt Brecht and Soviet montage filmmakers such as Sergei Eisenstein. Leading leftist filmmakers from Dutch documentarist Joris Ivens to French Left Bank filmmakers Chris Marker and Agnès Varda visited the island, exchanging with the Cuban artists at the ICAIC and producing their own films inspired by the new revolution. And finally, in these first decades, the ICAIC also supported the production of films that challenged traditional gender roles and explored slavery and contemporary racial dynamics. Nonetheless, and in spite of the Cuban state's official objectives to combat gender and racial discrimination, the first generation of Cuban filmmakers typically consisted of white men from the middle or upper classes, with the notable exceptions of Afro-Cuban filmmakers Sergio Giral, Sara Gómez, and Nicolás Guillén Landrián.

Guevara was also by no means a straightforward champion of freedom of expression. Indeed, it was in response to his censorship of Saba Cabrera Infante and Orlando Jiménez Leal's short documentary about Cuban nightlife, *P.M.* (1961), that Fidel Castro famously delimited the boundaries of the cultural field in a speech that same year as follows: "within the Revolution, everything; against the Revolution, nothing" ([1961] 1980, 14). As I elaborate in chapter 1, this pronouncement gave rise to radically different interpretations. Some Cuban artists and intellectuals, including those associated with the weekly cultural supplement *Lunes de Revolución*, viewed Castro's declaration as the inauguration of a totalitarian control over the cultural field and eventually went into exile. For others, however, his statement was a guarantee of a freedom of expression within limits that they were willing to accept, and which they also fought to expand. In a performative play on Castro's phrase, the filmmakers associated with the ICAIC and other artists defended the right to "criticism from within." Over the course of the decades that followed, they worked to extend what could be articulated in public while remaining, on the whole, loyal to the values and ideals they associated with the Revolution, such as solidarity, social justice, national sovereignty, and commitment to public health care and education.

Allegory, understood here as an aesthetic mode in which the surface of a work suggests the existence of another meaning that needs to be decoded, played a crucial role in these attempts to articulate a critical but committed relationship to the Revolution.[6] Beginning in the 1960s, Cuban filmmakers adopted what I call modernist allegories. Drawing on modernist aesthetic techniques and open endings, filmmakers worked to create films they hoped would incite spectators to engage in critical reflection of social problems and take action to address them. Many of these works articulated an ambivalent take on socialism, smuggling in criticism of the state between the lines while nonetheless remaining true to revolutionary values and ambitions. For their part, spectators accustomed to such practices frequently responded to films with what, following Eve Kosofsky Sedgwick (2003), I term paranoid readings. By paranoid readings, Sedgwick means an allegorical mode of interpretation in which analysts strive to reveal the secret meanings and workings of power hidden beneath the surface of texts, often by mobilizing tautological arguments that unearth threats anticipated in advance by the critic.

In Cuba, the adoption of such paranoid interpretive tactics frequently led to the reduction of films to arguments for or against state socialism, leaving filmmakers struggling to shape perceptions of their work and their own politics. The efforts by Tomás Gutiérrez Alea to counter readings by some foreign critics of his film *Memorias del subdesarrollo* (*Memories of Underdevelopment*, 1968) illustrate these dynamics (see chapter 2), as does the 1991 censorship of Daniel Díaz Torres's bureaucrat comedy, *Alicia en el pueblo de maravillas* (*Alice in Wondertown*), which was pulled from theaters after only four days amid accusations on the island that it was "hyper critical," "defeatist," and even "counterrevolutionary" (see chapter 3).

While this book returns to the 1960s and the 1970s, the buildup from the mid-1980s to the censorship of *Alicia en el pueblo de maravillas* in 1991 marks the beginning of the late socialist era on which I focus, which itself can be roughly divided into three historical periods: the immediate post-Soviet era of the 1990s to approximately 2005, otherwise known as the "Special Period"; roughly 2006 to 2009, when the Cuban economy began to recover and Raúl Castro stepped in to take over from an ailing Fidel; and 2010 to 2017, when the economic reforms launched under Raúl Castro began to take on more distinctive shape.[7] The censorship of *Alicia* marked the rise to dominance of the second generation of filmmakers, those artists who were in their teens or early twenties in the 1960s, got their start as film critics and documentarists in that decade or in the 1970s, and were finally given an opportunity to make feature-length films when Julio García Espinosa took over as director of the ICAIC from 1982 to 1991. It also heralded the beginning of a new era in Cuban filmmaking and in Cuba more broadly. The collapse of the Soviet Union plunged the island into a severe economic crisis, which Fidel Castro denominated "the Special Period in Times of Peace," a moniker that referred to the government's adoption of wartime survival measures to survive the disappearance of the nation's primary trading partner. This economic crisis reached its peak in 1994, when thousands of Cubans took to boats and makeshift rafts in an attempt to make it to Florida.[8]

For all the desperation produced by a constant state of material shortages, however, the Special Period was also a time of hope and anticipation, as market reforms opened up new opportunities for individual entrepreneurship and suggested the possibility of political change. The state welcomed foreign investment, and a new influx of foreign visitors poured dollars not only into state coffers but also into the hands of individuals newly granted the right to operate as *cuentapropistas* (small business owners) in a limited range of activities, including running *paladares* (restaurants) and *casas particulares* (private homes that rent to tourists). In the realm of cinema, the loss of state funding slowed filmmaking to a trickle and led to a new dependence on international coproductions. These changes subjected filmmakers to market forces, but they also provided them with increased independence from the ICAIC, at least for those able to secure ongoing relationships with foreign producers. Finally, this era saw a new relationship to the diaspora. Whereas in previous decades leaving Cuba was a decisive juncture, in the 1990s state officials and artists alike began depicting the diaspora in a more conciliatory light. By the end of that decade, emigrants had begun traveling back and forth to the island with greater frequency, forming a new and more flexible diaspora than what had existed in previous years.

Citizens' growing dissatisfaction with an economy that, as many artists put it to me, was neither socialism nor capitalism but the worst of both combined, meanwhile, forced the state to grant new room for public expression. As the stories recounted in this book make clear, the state continued to censor works and to jail artists deemed political dissidents. But the 1990s also saw increasing attempts to contain dissent by giving it a limited outlet in the arts, including in cinema.[9] As I explore in this book's later chapters, economic crisis, emigration, the new relationship to the diaspora, a renewed emphasis on the personal, and the crisis in historicity provoked by the collapse of the Soviet Union all became dominant themes in films of the Special Period and the early twenty-first century, as filmmakers took advantage of their increased independence from the state to give voice to a growing disillusionment with the socialist state and its policies.

Yet at the same time, films fell prey to new forms of paranoid readings, as spectators debated whether the release of critical films represented wins in a battle for greater freedom of expression or were merely signs of more subtle tactics of power. The writings of German theorist Herbert Marcuse and Hungarian dissident Miklós Haraszti provide us with tools for understanding such mixed responses. In a 1965 article, Marcuse argued that, by the twentieth century, liberal ideals of tolerance were being used to stifle rather than to promote freedom. By burying news reports among advertisements or giving equal weight to progressive and regressive political views, he maintained, capitalist media conformed outwardly to demands for objectivity and plurality of debate while in reality ensuring that a population indoctrinated in the dominant ideology ignored real alternatives. Haraszti argued that a similarly paradoxical permissiveness was at work in late socialist Eastern European nations. By the 1980s, contended Haraszti (1988, 77–81), traditional practices of censorship in the Soviet Union had given way to a more permissive model in which an ever-greater range of artwork was allowed, provided that it did not challenge the system.

In the early decades of the Revolution, Cuban intellectuals criticized liberal notions of freedom of expression in terms that resonated with Marcuse's arguments (see chapter 1). But by the 1990s, Cuba seemed to many to be suffering from its own variant of what Marcuse described as repressive tolerance and Haraszti termed progressive censorship. The state's strategic relaxation of censorship and the increasing orientation of artists to the global market exacerbated paranoid readings of films, as artists and audiences worried that social criticism sacrificed aesthetic quality for political impact, bolstered the power of the socialist state by working as a safety valve or improving Cuba's reputation abroad, or served as a marketing stunt designed to appeal to spectators eager for images of socialism on the decline. As I elaborate in chapter 1 and throughout this book, these suspicions were often both reasonable and productive, drawing attention to changing strategies of power and pushing for greater freedom. But the constant return to the revelation of the other's political complicity also reinforced well-worn divides, thwarting the recognition of ambivalence and the emergence of alternative political positions.[10]

The work of a third generation of filmmakers was crucial both to the production of increasingly critical depictions of life under late socialism and to suspicions that such criticism reproduced state power and reinforced foreign stereotypes about the island. Born from the 1960s through the 1980s, these filmmakers got their start in filmmaking in the midst of the Special Period or in the first decade of the twenty-first century and are generally thought to be both more market savvy and more cynical, although they too often harbor lingering attachments to the Revolution, its ideals, and its materialities. In spite of the economic crisis, this is also a generation that enjoyed more—or at least different—professional opportunities than their predecessors. Many of the most successful of these artists, including several whose work is examined here, trained at Cuba's international film school, the Escuela Internacional de Cine y TV (EICTV, International School of Cinema and Television). Established in 1986 as a subsidiary of the Fundación del Nuevo Cine Latinoamericano (FNCL, New Latin American Cinema Foundation), the EICTV is located approximately one hour outside Havana and fifteen minutes outside the small town of San Antonio de los Baños, at the end of a narrow road that winds its way through citrus orchards. The self-contained complex includes classrooms, production studios, a movie theater, a café, a cafeteria, dormitories, apartments, an outdoor swimming pool, and a store renowned for its low prices and its ability to stock ready supplies of items from toilet paper to dish soap, even when these have been unavailable for weeks in Havana.

Reflecting the Third Worldist politics of its founders, the EICTV was originally dedicated to training young filmmakers from Latin America, Africa, and Asia. Though the majority of the school's students continue to come from Latin America, over the years the EICTV also developed strong relationships with Western Europe and Canada. By 2007, the school was also drawing students from Spain, Germany, and other countries for shorter seminars as well as for the school's core three-year intensive program, which is organized around one- to two-week workshops delivered by specialists from around the world. In addition to providing students with training and equipment to make short films during their studies, the EICTV promotes student works to international film festivals and sponsors alumni for exchange programs in cities including Paris and Montreal. Many of its alumni turn to the EICTV after graduation for employment, and the networks and friendships that they establish during their time at the school are often crucial to their careers and personal lives long after they have left the school, including, for several Cuban students, by serving as springboards to emigration.

Of course, not every aspiring young Cuban filmmaker has the privilege of studying at this elite institution. While the island's national arts university, the Universidad de las Artes (ISA, National Arts University), suffers from a relative paucity of funds and equipment compared to the EICTV, it also plays an important role in training and providing an alternate production center for young Cuban filmmakers.[11] In 1988 the ISA founded a part-time academic program for media workers. And in 2002 it began offering a full-time program with both theoretical and practical training components leading to a bachelor's degree through the Facultad de Arte de los Medios de Comunicación Audiovisual (FAMCA, Faculty of Art of Audiovisual Communication Media). A number of Cuban filmmakers earned a degree from the FAMCA either before or while studying at the EICTV. Other institutions on the island founded from the late 1980s into the twenty-first century—including, for instance, the German-Cuban nongovernmental organization Fundación Ludwig de Cuba (Cuban Ludwig Foundation) and, in more recent years, the Norwegian Embassy in Cuba—provide both economic resources and exhibition space to young Cuban filmmakers, further accelerating the decentralization of cinema.[12]

Perhaps the most significant threat to the ICAIC's dominance over cinema, however, is the increasing availability of digital technologies. As has been well documented, Cuba has one of the lowest rates of internet access in the world (see chapter 1). By the time I first visited the island, Cubans were already circumventing these limitations by circulating a wide array of international and local media, including Cuban films, hand to hand over flash drives and hard drives. These informal forms of exchange grew more elaborate over the years. Since about 2010, state control over media distribution has been displaced by the *paquete semanal* (weekly package): one terabyte of pirated digital media that is downloaded and distributed across the island over flash drive and hard drive on a weekly basis. The paquete's most sought-after contents are foreign or popular genres from South Korean television dramas and K-Pop music videos to national and international reggaetón. But its organizers do make explicit efforts to include Cuban cinema, from classic to more recent films, if only in an attempt to placate concerns on the island about the threat this new form of independent media distribution might constitute to the taste and values of Cubans.[13]

In addition to shifting control over distribution out of the hands of the state, the advent of digital technologies radically transformed production. From the early twenty-first century on, younger generations in particular purchased or borrowed increasingly inexpensive digital cameras and software editing programs, drawing on these tools to shoot and edit films with more independence from the ICAIC and other state institutions than ever before. Combined with changing social mores as well as the establishment of the film schools, digital technologies also helped diversify filmmaking, as some few more women and Afro-Cubans were able to obtain work, not just as editors or in other more traditionally accessible roles but also as directors, directors of photography, and sound engineers in what nonetheless remains an elite and male-dominated industry.

At the same time, the ICAIC worked to keep up with these developments. Under the leadership of Omar González, who took over from Alfredo Guevara in 2000, the state film institute established the Muestra Nacional de Nuevos Realizadores (National Exhibit of New Filmmakers), later renamed the Muestra Joven (Youth Exhibit), a yearly festival in which Cubans up to the age of thirty-five can show their films, compete for prizes, and take part in debates and workshops. Illustrating once again the ways in which new openings have gone hand in hand with new suspicions, the Muestra itself has provoked mixed reactions. While many artists praise the Muestra for providing young filmmakers with crucial exhibition opportunities, others criticize it as a strategy devised by the ICAIC to regain control over youth film production.[14]

These transformations in Cuban filmmaking went hand in hand with further economic and political developments on the island. As the state found more secure economic footing by the end of the 1990s thanks, in part, to new trade arrangements with Venezuela under Hugo Chávez, market reforms in Cuba slowed to a halt. Stricter regulations as well as restrictions on the number of licenses given out to operate small businesses slowed cuentapropismo, while also driving many seeking to make a living off self-employment as taxi drivers or in other professions back into the informal economy. In 2004 the American dollar, whose use was legalized in 1993 and subsequently became identified with the economic crisis, was replaced with Cuban convertible pesos (CUCs), while Fidel Castro himself suggested in 2005 that the Special Period might have come to an end.

As it turned out, even more radical changes were just on the horizon. In 2006 Fidel Castro withdrew from public office due to an illness that the government deliberately attempted to keep under wraps, and Raúl Castro stepped in to take his place. On February 24, 2008, Raúl officially acceded to the presidency amid promises to reform the economy and eliminate the dual currency. Two years later, the government announced plans to shift several thousand workers from the state sector to the private, reopening and expanding the categories in which individuals could apply for small business licenses in order to achieve this goal.[15] And on December 17, 2014, Presidents Raúl Castro and Barack Obama appeared on their respective nations' televisions to announce the renewal of diplomatic relations between the two countries after more than fifty years of Cold War enmity.

Filmmakers, for their part, scrambled to take advantage of these changes. While the ICAIC provided services to big Hollywood productions, artists fought for legal recognition of the independent production groups that had become increasingly integral to domestic film production on the island and to the provision of services to foreign filmmakers (see the coda). In the midst of struggles over the shape that filmmaking and the nation's economy would take, Fidel Castro passed away on November 25, 2016. When it finally took place, many felt that his passing arrived long after the transition that it might once have promised had already taken on whatever limited shape it was going to adopt. But his death also coincided with an unexpected historical twist. Only a couple of weeks earlier, to the surprise of mainstream media outlets and much of the American electorate, Donald Trump won the US elections against Hillary Clinton on a campaign platform that promised to roll back many of Barack Obama's policies, including the latter's efforts to normalize diplomatic and commercial relations with Cuba.

These promises would soon take effect. In the summer of 2017, the Cuban government put a temporary freeze on several categories of cuentapropista licenses in order to reorganize the system.[16] In the fall of that year, meanwhile, Donald Trump imposed new restrictions that limited American travel to Cuba and economic dealings with the numerous Cuban businesses owned or affiliated with the military and, amid accusations that the Cuban government had employed an unknown weapon to engage in sonic attacks on American diplomats, withdrew the majority of the staff from the only recently reopened American embassy on the island. In theory, at least, it will be up to the new Cuban president to navigate this political situation. On April 19, 2018, Raúl Castro stepped down as president while retaining his position as leader of the Partido Comunista de Cuba (PCC, Communist Party of Cuba), thereby passing the official leadership of the country to a non-Castro and to someone born after 1959—Miguel Díaz-Canel, born in 1960—for the first time since Fidel Castro officially took over the presidency in 1976.[17]

By the end of 2017 and the period that this book examines, then, Cuban filmmaking and Cuba were at a crossroads. The state's strategic relaxation of censorship, the growing influx of foreign funding for film production, and, as of the early twenty-first century, the increasing availability of digital technologies enabled filmmakers to produce films that were more openly critical of the nation's social and political problems and even, at times, of its highest political leaders than ever before. Yet these changes also rendered criticism itself suspect. Meanwhile, as 2016 came to a close, the island's political elites were partying with Hollywood stars and socialites from Vin Diesel to Paris Hilton while some Cuban Americans celebrated Fidel Castro's death by dancing in the streets of Miami amid Cuban flags and Trump signs. But by December 2017, Cubans were waiting to see what would happen to the reforms that seemed to have stalled just as soon as they began. Faced, on the one hand, with the threat that economic reforms on the island will turn into yet another version of postsocialist, authoritarian neoliberalism that benefits only a few and, on the other hand, with some Cuban Americans' willingness to embrace Trump's vision of a powerful America led by a strongman, especially if he makes good on promises to restore a "hard line" with Cuba, new political options are all the more important.[18] It is with the hope of making even a small contribution to this end that this book explores how Cuban filmmakers have, in the late socialist era, attempted to open up conversations about the meaning and significance of the Revolution in a context permeated by suspicion.

Autonomy and the Public Sphere

To take Cuban cinema as a site of significant public debate and representation is to tangle with the ideals of autonomy that have long subtended understandings of the public sphere. From the 1960s on, Cuban filmmakers have varyingly insisted that cinema should address social problems, reflect the everyday lives of Cubans, and incite spectators to critical reflection, feeling, and social engagement, all functions that have often been associated with the work of the public sphere. Yet, in the liberal imaginary, meaningful public debate and representation have historically been equated with an autonomy from the state and from the market to which Cuban artists are well aware that they and their work cannot lay claim.

In his seminal book *The Structural Transformation of the Public Sphere*, Jürgen Habermas ([1962] 1989) claims that the advent in eighteenth-century Europe of an art market and of new forms of subjectivity played key roles in the development of a literary and a political bourgeois public sphere. The production of art for the capitalist market freed works from the authority of the Church and the nobility, making them available for critical rational debate among citizens in which, at least in principle, social status and identity were bracketed. New forms of textual circulation, meanwhile, facilitated the public's inclusivity (36–37). At the same time, the rise of an intimate model of the family based not on economic necessity but rather on the free will and mutual love of its members helped foster a new perception of the individual as self-determining and autonomous, an ideal further cultivated through genres such as the domestic novel (46–49). Together, these developments provided a model for a political public sphere through which governance would be achieved not by dictate but rather by citizens coming together as equals to debate matters of public import.

This ideal of autonomy—whether at the level of art, politics, or individuals themselves—is cast into doubt by state socialism, which, as scholars have long pointed out, absorbs cultural production as well as large swathes of political, economic, and social life into its institutions. The growing role of the global market in Cuban arts in the post-Soviet era does not resolve these concerns. In their influential arguments about twentieth-century mass cultural production, Theodor W. Adorno and Max Horkheimer ([1944] 1987) maintain that the culture industry reduces art to commodities, eliminating the capacity that art supposedly enjoyed in earlier stages of capitalism to act as a critical reflection on the economic system on which it nonetheless depended. In line with this argument, Habermas concludes that, from the late nineteenth into the twentieth centuries, the arts were subsumed by market demands in ways that transformed public debate into passive consumption. In their efforts to cater to a mass audience, he argues, book producers lowered the "psychological threshold" of the works they sold while the emergence of new mass media such as radio, film, and television favored passive group reception over the critical debate that had shaped bourgeois engagements with art (163, 166–67, 170–71).

The translation of Habermas's *Structural Transformation* into English in 1989, nearly three decades after its original publication in Germany, gave rise to a new wave of scholarship on the public sphere. Numerous scholars queried the equation of the ideal democratic public with autonomy. Miriam Hansen (1990, 1991) argues, for instance, that early cinema opened up space to articulate what Oskar Negt and Alexander Kluge ([1972] 1993, 14–15) referred to as a "social horizon of experience" that incorporated the life contexts of individuals—women, people of color, the working classes—excluded from the bourgeois public sphere, even as such inclusion often worked in the interest of reproducing capitalism.[19]

Others have explored the existence of publics in state socialist and authoritarian contexts. In the Cuban context, Sujatha Fernandes (2006), Geoffrey Baker (2005, 2011), and Nicholas Balaisis (2016) demonstrate how hip-hop and cinema gave rise to new forms of public expression in post-Soviet Cuba. Of particular relevance to this book, Alexei Yurchak (2006, 116–18) argues that the "hypernormalization" of political discourse in Soviet late socialism fostered *svoi* or "deterritorialized" publics. As public speech and mass media became increasingly formulaic in late socialist Russia, citizens devised new strategies that allowed them to fulfill the formal requirements of political rituals while shifting the meanings of these activities. The advantage of such strategies was that they allowed Soviet citizens to adopt stances that went beyond political binaries, enabling individuals to hold onto those elements of socialism that remained meaningful to them while ignoring or making fun of the rest.[20]

These more expansive theorizations of publics are useful for considering how Cuban cinema works to involve spectators in a collective engagement with matters of general import to the nation. In the early decades of the Revolution, as I show here, Cuban intellectuals worked to establish an alternative public sphere, one that took political commitment instead of autonomy from the state as its basis, while nonetheless emphasizing the importance of citizen participation in debate.[21] In the late socialist era, criticism took on new valences as filmmakers used their work to reflect on the legacy of the Revolution and the crisis that followed the collapse of the Soviet Union. These films frequently reflected both the growing disillusionment of filmmakers and their ongoing attachments to revolutionary promises and values.

In Cuba as in late socialist Russia, in other words, the attempt to articulate an ambivalence that escapes well-worn political antagonisms became an increasingly important and even an explicit goal of many filmmakers. What Cuban late socialist public culture also reveals, however, is how political paranoia haunts such efforts. As Yurchak (2006) argues, life in late socialism cannot be reduced to binary oppositions between the state and citizens, surface and depth, oppression and resistance, freedom and complicity. But, as I show, such dichotomies nonetheless play an important role in citizens' imaginations of the state and other social actors, often to the detriment of attempts to move beyond them. Anxieties about autonomy further fuel suspicion and feed these dichotomies. Even early attempts in Cuba to theorize an alternative public sphere founded on revolutionary commitment were fraught with concerns about autonomy, as intellectuals worried both about the evanescence of the social energies they hoped might provide the basis for a revolutionary political order (see chapter 3) and about the threat that crowd affect might pose to individual capacities for critical reason (see chapter 2).

As artists and intellectuals grew increasingly disillusioned with the socialist state in the post-Soviet era, the ability to establish one's independence from both the state and the global market played an ever more important role in asserting one's credibility, but the allegiances and dependencies on which cultural production relied complicated such efforts. The broader points here are both, as scholars from Oskar Negt and Alexander Kluge through Miriam Hansen and Alexei Yurchak have pointed out before me, that a meaningful public sphere can exist in the absence of autonomy from the state and the global market and, less commonly recognized, that anxieties about autonomy shape public debate and representation. In the pages that follow, I show how aspirations to autonomy along with the inevitably heteronomous bases of artistic creation, debate, and subjectivity fueled a paranoid public sphere, limiting what arguments and experiences could be heard as participants and onlookers struggled to distinguish freedom of expression from complicity.

Allegory and Political Paranoia

Key to my discussion of paranoia and ambivalence in late socialist Cuba is also a claim about how allegory can both enable and constrain public debate and representation. In making this argument, I hope to encourage a shift in work on allegory from thinking about it as a mode whose meanings critics should (or should not) reveal to approaching it as a social practice involving not only texts but also people with often competing interests and goals. I am not, of course, the first theorist to find Cuba a particularly rich site from which to rethink the politics of allegory. In 1985 one of Cuba's foremost postcolonial theorists, Roberto Fernández Retamar, and Cuban essayist and screenwriter Ambrosio Fornet invited Fredric Jameson to hold the annual Marxist Literary Group's Summer Institute for Culture and Society in Havana at the Casa de las Américas, a cultural institution dedicated to fostering Cuba's relationship with Latin America, the Caribbean, and the world. Out of that meeting emerged Jameson's landmark essay "Third-World Literature in the Era of Multinational Capitalism," in which he makes the strong claim that "all third-world texts are necessarily . . . allegorical, and in a very specific way: they are to be read as . . . *national allegories*" (1986, 69).

Jameson bases this argument on three claims. First, he contends that, contrary to the West, where the political is always supplanted by the libidinal and personal, in the Third World, there is a more direct relationship between public and private, the collective and the individual. Second, he argues that the social and economic situations of Third World countries are defined by their struggle with First World cultural imperialism, prompting intellectuals to think of their work as political interventions. This struggle, finally, accounts for why the allegories of Third World texts are specifically national. Suggesting that a turn to the national might in other contexts be regressive, he maintains that, in the Third World, it is the properly revolutionary response to these nations' embattled position in the global system of capitalism.

Jameson's argument was subsequently taken to task by several scholars, including Aijaz Ahmad (1987), who criticizes the literary theorist for glossing over crucial differences between the diverse literatures and societies that the latter grouped together as Third World and for reinforcing a too-rigid dichotomy between so-called First and Third World texts. Importantly, however, Jameson's argument about Third World texts is only one instance of his broader theory that all texts are political allegories and of a particular sort. In *The Political Unconscious* (1981), Jameson contends that the task of the theorist is to uncover the hidden allegorical meanings of texts, which in the final instance are always imaginary resolutions of class conflict. The difference between First and Third World texts for Jameson is thus not so much one of kind but rather of degree: in First World literature the allegorical meanings that reveal the work's engagement with class and modes of production are concealed; in Third World texts, these meanings are evident, perhaps uncomfortably so (1981, 79–80).

It is Jameson's broader argument about texts and allegory that became the focus of controversy in later years. Eve Kosofsky Sedgwick (2003, 123–51) and other scholars contest the predominance in Jameson's oeuvre, as in critical theory more generally, of what they term "paranoid" or "symptomatic readings."[22] This work both builds on and departs from the analysis of political paranoia first advanced by Richard Hofstadter in his 1965 essay "The Paranoid Style in American Politics." For Hofstadter, as for later scholars, political paranoia might best be summed up as an interpretive style that weds a deep skepticism with the certainty that the "truth is out there"; that continuously scans events and objects for signs of hidden threats; that aspires to connect disparate events into totalizing narratives that themselves often remain worked through with gaps and uncertainties; and that sees politics and social life as struggles between opponents who are frequently cast in moral terms and determined in advance.

While Hofstadter was careful to distinguish political paranoia from its clinical counterpart, he nonetheless saw it as a deviation from the rational and even-handed debate that should characterize a healthy polity. Recent scholarship instead argues both that paranoia is a reasonable response to the often opaque and ambiguous workings of power and that it may be more central to dominant political and theoretical discourses than Hofstadter recognized. The question, then, as Sedgwick (2003, 124) puts it, is not whether paranoia is an accurate description of the world (it frequently is) but rather what effects such knowing has, what openings and what closures it might entail. If political paranoia, as some scholars show, can undermine and challenge dominant histories and systems of power, its repetitive recourse to predetermined enemies and narratives can also foreclose alternative takes on social and political situations.[23]

Sedgwick's (2003, 46–51) solution to this impasse is to propose that analysts undertake what she terms "reparative readings," focusing attention, as José Esteban Muñoz (2000, 257) puts it in an essay on Cuban art, on "building and potentiality" and how "individuals and groups fashion possibility from conditions of (im)possibility" instead of working to unveil "conspiracies and the secret." Here I take the debate over allegory and paranoia in a different direction, showing how both depth models of interpretation and criticisms of paranoid readings fail to fully capture the social and political dynamics of texts. Contrary to Jameson's and Sedgwick's arguments, I argue, allegory is neither immanent to texts nor an analytic tool that scholars can choose to take up or set down. Rather, paranoid readings, accusations thereof, and longings for meanings that might exceed reified political narratives are social processes that influence the production, circulation, and interpretation of texts as well as the social and political statuses of authors.

To understand how allegory shapes public debate, in other words, we must analyze how artists and spectators mobilize the mode, often to competing ends. This is especially—although not exclusively—true for Global South, state socialist, and authoritarian contexts. In these societies, long-standing traditions of political engagement through art, practices of skirting censorship through aesthetic indirection, and demands for depictions of the nation imposed by international art worlds often foster a search for hidden meanings in works that sometimes cooperate and sometimes conflict with artists' aesthetic and political goals.[24] Under such conditions, finally, questions of intention can become key sites for social contestation, as audiences impute strategies to artists who in turn struggle to clarify their political allegiances.

Reading Ethnographically

Over the years that I have worked on this project, I ran into different and often diametrically opposed sets of challenges from scholars in both of the disciplines in which I am trained and to which this work is indebted. While anthropologists complained that I focused too much on texts and spent too little time on people and social contexts, film scholars wondered why I was talking to the filmmakers in the first place. During one campus visit, for instance, a scholar who was interviewing me observed, not unsupportively, that artists lie or mislead audiences about what they mean all the time. If this is the case, then why use what they have to say about their work to understand the politics of texts?

While I take both sets of challenges seriously, my aim is to show how an interdisciplinary approach can challenge artificial divides between texts and contexts and shed new light on the social dynamics and effects of film. Achieving this goal has entailed interweaving the careful reading of films with archival and ethnographic research. I treat films not as self-enclosed and stable but rather as archives to be examined alongside other forms of data—film reviews; newspaper articles and editorials; personal letters and emails; interviews with filmmakers, cultural functionaries, and spectators; and participant observation at events and institutions key to the Cuban film community—for signs of the struggles and debates that went into a film's production, circulation, and interpretation.

Following preliminary field trips to Havana in 2003, 2004, and 2005, I conducted the bulk of my research for this project while living as a full-time resident in Cuba from October 2007 to August 2009, just after Fidel

Castro retired from active office and in the midst of Raúl Castro's first years in power. The EICTV generously accepted me as a foreign exchange student and I spent my first month at the school in San Antonio de los Baños where I attended classes with the students in the film direction and screenwriting streams of the school's regular program. After relocating to an apartment in Vedado, Havana, I continued to return to the school regularly on weekends to copy, watch, and discuss movies; hang out with friends; and catch up on the latest gossip. In Havana, meanwhile, I spent my days collecting and taking notes on films; scouring the archives at the Cinemateca de Cuba, an institution whose offices also served as an important site for gathering information about Cuban film history or the latest scandal; and attending and observing film production, press conferences, screenings, festivals, and academic conferences.

To take stock of the new economic and political transformations that got under way with greater force as of 2010, I returned to Havana in December 2011 to observe the release of the blockbuster hit *Juan de los muertos* (*Juan of the Dead*, 2011) at the New Latin American Film Festival. In the summer of 2014, I spent several weeks with Carlos Machado Quintela and Yan Vega as they worked on the editing of *La obra del siglo* (*The Project of the Century*, 2015). And in the summer of 2016 and in December 2017, I returned to Havana to follow up on recent controversies and observe the release of films—Alejandro Alonso's *El Proyecto* (*The Project*, 2017) and Ernesto Daranas's *Sergio y Serguéi* (2017)—relevant to the aesthetic developments tracked in this book. I also supplemented fieldwork in Havana with a trip to Miami to observe the release of *La obra del siglo* at the 2015 Miami International Film Festival and by keeping up through phone calls, social media, and visits with friends and interlocutors who remained in Cuba and those who subsequently emigrated and became part of the island's evermore-flexible diaspora.

Moving back and forth between the textual, archival, and ethnographic data gathered through the above activities has had several benefits. For instance, it often revealed tensions that I might not have detected had I only been focusing on one type of information. On more than one occasion, for instance, talking to spectators or reading between the lines of film reviews made me aware of controversies that had been provoked by films. Asking filmmakers about these debates in turn unearthed stories about their struggles to balance their own aesthetic and political inclinations with the demands and requirements of state officials, foreign contributors, and audiences, sometimes through aesthetic and narrative devices adopted during production and editing, and at other times through retroactive interpretations and defenses of their work.

Listening to what filmmakers have to say about their work is also important for political reasons. Part of my effort in this book is to refuse the temptation to dismiss artists' insistence on their own and their films' revolutionary allegiances as mere self-defense, behind which some other and truer political position might be discovered. Such arguments are often instrumental in ignoring the ambivalent relationship to the Revolution that filmmakers insist that they feel and that there is no real reason to doubt. Indeed, it is noteworthy that several of the artists with whom I worked were quite open with me about the jokes about important political figures, including Fidel Castro himself, that they had included in their films, demonstrating both how meanings that might once have been considered heretical have become run of the mill and, at least in some cases, how such jokes went hand in hand with attachment to the revolutionary project.

At the same time, I do not reduce the meanings of films to what either spectators or artists have to say about them. There are, of course, many reasons for which an artist might be reluctant to openly admit to the meanings that they may or may not have deliberately included in their works, ranging from fears of political repercussions to, more simply, a desire to let audiences make their own meanings out of their films. Perhaps even more importantly, as any person who has ever participated in the making of a creative—or, for that matter, scholarly—work knows, those who get attributed with the authorship for a work neither operate alone nor are they always cognizant of the social and political patterns and habits that inform what they produce, and which in turn may play a role in the ways in which audiences interpret these works.

Indeed, there is no reason to treat what artists and spectators tell the ethnographer as any more or any less unmediated or free from broader social patterns than the films themselves or any other form of expression. As readers of this book will soon discover, in many cases I make my arguments by bringing together analyses of the aesthetic tactics and narrative patterns of films with discussions of the discursive strategies adopted by Cuban artists, political leaders, and spectators. In so doing, this book also suggests how an interdisciplinary approach to genre might help us better understand the social lives of films. As Christine Gledhill (2000) observes, studies of genre in cinema studies have repeatedly run into at least two key problems: first, taxonomic efforts to identify specific genres are often confounded by the actual hybridity of films; second, while film scholars turned to genre in an effort to think about the social effects of the cinema, the question of how such categories relate to broader social patterns is often left undertheorized or reduced to more or less sophisticated versions of arguments that films "reflect" the social.

Here, I instead follow linguistic anthropologists in defining genre more broadly as a set of norms according to which texts ranging from verbal utterances to films are constructed and interpreted by both authors and audiences, and which are subject to contestation and transformation.[25] This more flexible and socially oriented definition owes much to the work of Mikhail Bakhtin, who theorizes genres as "relatively stable types of . . . utterances" that could range from "the single-word everyday rejoinder" to "novels, dramas, [and] all kinds of scientific research," which, he argues, themselves often rework simpler, primary, genres (1986, 60–62). From this perspective, then, genres may be linked to particular media and contexts but can also move between them, with some artistic and other works deriving their meaning at least in part from the ways in which they draw on, refer to, and remediate speech genres with specific social and political resonances.[26]

Building on these arguments, I show how filmmakers pick up on genres key to everyday conversation and intellectual and political discourse and incorporate these into their films, just as audiences and filmmakers some-times incorporate narrative patterns from films into their own life stories and speech. Importantly, every adoption of a genre can either stay close to its conventional use or push at its limits in ways that open up new mean-ings, while spectators' familiarity with these intermedial genres influence the debates to which films give rise. By reading individual films both against what is explicitly said about them and in relation to the broader genres that they engage and transform, I shed light on how these works serve as nodal points for debates about life, politics, and art.

Finally, let me say a word about the films I address. *Fidel between the Lines* draws on new ethnographic and archival information about the pro-duction and reception of several canonical Cuban films that served as key points of conflict or transition in Cuban cultural production. These include Tomás Gutiérrez Alea's *Memorias del subdesarrollo*, Daniel Díaz Torres's *Alicia en el pueblo de maravillas*, and Alejandro Brugués's *Juan de los muertos*. This book also examines lesser-known films by younger Cuban filmmakers, such as Laimir Fano's *Oda a la piña* (*Ode to the Pineapple*, 2008), Susana Barriga's *The Illusion*, Carlos Machado Quintela's *La obra del siglo*, and Alejandro Alonso's *El Proyecto*. I do not claim to present a com-prehensive history of Cuban cinema; indeed, there are many key filmmakers whose work I have not had the space to consider. With the exception of Yan Vega's *Memorias de una familia cubana* (*Memories of a Cuban Family*, 2007), discussed in chapter 5, I have also chosen to focus on films produced on the island, thus emphasizing works that reflect changing institutional politics and dynamics within Cuba while also situating them in the context of debates between Cubans on the island and those in the diaspora. By moving between canonical and lesser-known films, this book aims to shed light on how changing practices of social criticism and censorship, conflicts over allegory and authorial intention, and recurring genres—modernist and modern allegory, criticism of the bureaucracy and bureaucrat comedies, stories of staying and fighting for an improved nation—have shaped Cuban filmmaking and public debate on and about the island.

Title and Outline of This Book

The title of this book, *Fidel between the Lines*, is meant to invoke a number of interpretations. First and most obviously, it refers to the pervasiveness of allegorical methods in the production and the interpretation of Cuban cinema and, especially, the importance of such tactics in a context shaped by censorship. This is a meaning implicit in the phrase in Spanish, "entre líneas," and its English translation, "between the lines," which my interlocutors sometimes used to invoke efforts to convey controversial meanings through films and other artwork. Second, the title is also a play on the name "Fidel." In the context of Cuba, Fidel most readily invokes the Revolution's charismatic political leader, who, as I show, has often been the butt of more or less veiled jokes in Cuban films. Also significant is the fact that the Latin word *fidelem* from which this name is derived means faithful. Ironically, then, the common use of the term *fidelista* to describe those Cubans who are loyal to Fidel might more creatively be interpreted to refer to those who are faithful to faith itself. In a similar sort of separation of affective orientation from its supposedly original referent, many of the intellectuals and artists whose work this book describes have continued to hold on to the ideals and values of the Revolution in part by becoming increasingly critical of the Cuban state, its policies, and even its top political leaders. Finally, *Fidel between the Lines* also invokes the fading importance of this leader toward the end of the period under examination in this book. While I do not pretend to predict what lies in store for the island, it is my hope that this book's analysis of intellectuals' attachment to revolutionary values and ideals, their growing dissatisfaction with the socialist state and its policies, and the way in which political paranoia complicates public debate and the articulation of a collective horizon of experience will contribute something to the efforts to feel out the shape of this new era.

Chapter 1 shows how new openings facilitated by digital technologies and the state's strategic relaxation of censorship exacerbated the political paranoia that has long shaped public debate in Cuba. It takes as its case study what was commonly referred to as the "email war," a 2007 debate about censorship that took place among Cuban intellectuals on and off the island shortly after Fidel Castro first fell ill and retired from public office. To many of those involved, this debate seemed to showcase the potential of digital technologies to enable a public sphere free of state control and open to all Cubans, regardless of geographic or political affiliation. Yet such hopes quickly ran aground on political paranoia as participants in the debate struggled to discern the contours of state powers or exile agendas that they suspected were operating just behind the scenes. In recounting this debate and the history that led up to it, the chapter also shows how, in the early years of the Revolution, Cuban intellectuals worked to establish an alternative public sphere that took political commitment as its foundation, and how new aspirations to autonomy in the post-Soviet era went hand in hand with suspicion.

Chapter 2 expands on this analysis of repressive tolerance and its consequences, demonstrating how new openings for the representation of social problems in the post-Soviet era complicated paranoid readings of Cuban films. In the early decades of the Revolution, I contend, Cuban filmmakers turned to allegory both to produce socialist spectators who could think for themselves and as a way of incorporating controversial meanings into their work as open secrets, there for "sophisticated" spectators to see but opaque enough to be undetectable by censors, or at the very least easy to deny. In many cases these strategies suggested a political ambivalence that exceeded binary takes on state socialism. Yet spectators accustomed to directors who expressed controversial positions between the lines all-too-often reduced these veiled allusions to stances for or against the Revolution, leaving Cuban filmmakers struggling to shape perceptions of their work and their politics. To track how these dynamics changed over time, I begin by revisiting one of Cuba's most renowned films, Tomás Gutiérrez Alea's *Memorias del subdesarollo*, on the basis of new ethnographic information about its production. I then analyze the reception of Alea's final two films—*Fresa y chocolate* (*Strawberry and Chocolate*, 1993) and *Guantanamera* (1995), both codirected with Juan Carlos Tabío—as well as reactions to contemporary digital and film shorts, including Eduardo del Llano's *Monte Rouge* (2005) and Laimir Fano's *Oda a la piña*. The strategic relaxation of state censorship, the growing orientation of filmmakers to the global market, and, as of the twenty-first century, the rise of digital technologies, as I show in this chapter, have both enabled filmmakers to produce ever-more-openly critical films and rendered criticism itself suspect.

The remaining chapters of this book take up specific case studies and genres to examine how paranoia and ambivalence shaped late socialist Cuban cinema. Chapter 3 takes as its central case study one of the most important censorship scandals in the history of Cuban cinema, the controversy over Daniel Díaz Torres's *Alicia en el pueblo de maravillas*. A play on Lewis Carroll's *Alice's Adventures in Wonderland*, the film tells the story of a naïve but enthusiastic theater instructor whose attempts to rally the apathetic inhabitants of a town to address their problems are thwarted by the autocratic bureaucrat in charge of the local sanatorium. Party officials argued that the bureaucrat in the film was a satire of Fidel Castro and that the film itself was counterrevolutionary. My reading of these events instead takes seriously Daniel Díaz Torres's claims that the film was founded on revolutionary ideals. I argue that the scandal over *Alicia* reveals both the centrality of criticism of the bureaucracy to political and intellectual discourse under state socialism and the ideological precariousness of this genre. Criticism of the bureaucracy normally contains tensions within state socialism by deflecting blame for the corruption of revolutionary energies from top political leaders onto mid- and lower-level administrators. But as disillusionment with state socialism set in, Cuban intellectuals began mobilizing the genre to criticize Fidel Castro's rule as itself a reification of the vitality that ought to animate the Revolution, a strategy that *Alicia en el pueblo de maravillas* anticipated.

Chapter 4 shows how, from the Special Period into the twenty-first century, bureaucrat comedies were combined with a critical version of nationalism and endings in which characters choose to stay in Cuba and fight to improve the nation. Reading these endings against intellectuals' use of this genre in their own life narratives, I argue that such stories were often mobilized to articulate political ambivalence; specifically, they articulated a commitment to challenging state policies combined with an ongoing attachment to revolutionary values or, more simply, to Cuba. Yet these endings also provoked suspicion. In order to avoid accusations of counterrevolution, filmmakers have always had to be careful that the open endings of their films suggested that social problems were ongoing but could eventually be resolved within the context of state socialism. In the disillusioned post-Soviet era, however, filmmakers also confronted suspicion of endings deemed excessively optimistic or too proximate to official state ideology. To show how filmmakers worked to navigate this quandary, I draw on film analysis and participant observation of the Havana premiere of *Juan de los muertos*, Cuba's first zombie comedy and the first major commercial success by independent filmmakers. I contextualize the reception of *Juan de los muertos'* ending through analyses of two key post-Soviet bureaucrat comedies—Arturo Sotto's *Amor vertical* (*Vertical Love*, 1997) and Juan Carlos Tabío's *Lista de espera* (*The Waiting List*, 2000)—as well as new ethnographic and archival information about the production, censorship, and reception of *Lista de espera*.

Chapter 5 takes films themselves as a significant site of reception, examining how a new generation of filmmakers explored the legacy and significance of revolutionary filmmaking for an uncertain present. In this chapter, I turn my attention to a series of films by young Cuban filmmakers working outside the ICAIC that focus on another theme that dominated post-Soviet filmmaking: the crisis in historicity that accompanied the collapse of the Soviet Union and the loss of certainty in the socialist future. Produced between 2005 and 2017, the films examined in this chapter demonstrate how the sense of living in a historical impasse or parenthesis lasted well into Raúl Castro's presidency, in spite of the hopes for change that initially accompanied this political transition. They also show how a new generation of filmmakers turned to the montage experiments of the 1960s and 1970s to criticize the teleological certainty that shaped early revolutionary filmmaking and to find tools with which to make tangible the uncertainty of the late socialist period. Paying homage to the work of Afro-Cuban filmmaker Nicolás Guillén Landrián, whose films were long censored on the island, as well as to French filmmakers Chris Marker and Agnès Varda and Afro-Cuban director Sara Gómez, these films challenge the classificatory impulses of Cold War politics and of filmmaking itself by revealing the difficulty and violence involved in producing meaning out of an ambiguous reality.

The coda considers key political events from 2014, when Barack Obama and Raúl Castro announced the normalization of relations between the United States and Cuba, to Donald Trump's election in 2016 and the imposition of a new chill on relations between the two countries in 2017. The events described in this chapter—including several new censorship scandals, Cuban filmmakers' efforts to secure a cinema law, and Hollywood's first big-budget ventures onto the island—revealed ever-more-forceful demands for political and economic reform on the part of artists and intellectuals on the island. But they also suggested a nascent nostalgia for older forms of political patronage. Documenting filmmakers' involvement in and reaction to these events through participant observation and ethnographic interviews, the coda shows how, in the 2010s, Cuban artists grew increasingly resistant to state censorship, even as they worried about what change might bring in a context where legal status for independent producers was slow in arriving and the cultural institutions that had once supported and protected critical and experimental art—if always within limits—appeared to have lost the political power that they had once held. In the midst of this renewed historical and political impasse, this book unfolds the story of how Cuban artists and intellectuals have historically attempted to negotiate a more nuanced relationship to state socialism and the Cuban Revolution, one that, at its best, aspired to a democratic and participatory public, while also refusing the impoverished political options produced by binary approaches to the Revolution and its promises.

CHAPTER ONE

SYMPTOMOLOGIES OF THE STATE

The Return of the Censor

On January 5, 2007, not long after Fidel Castro withdrew from public office due to illness, a Cuban TV show celebrated the lifetime achievements of an elderly poet by the name of Luis Pavón Tamayo. Cuban intellectuals would tell you that, as an artist, Pavón was nothing to write home about. But as a censor, he had acquired extraordinary levels of notoriety. As head of the Consejo Nacional de Cultura (National Cultural Council) from 1971 to 1976, Pavón oversaw national cultural policy during a militant period referred to by Cuban intellectuals as the *quinquenio gris* (five gray years), the *decada negra* (black decade) by the more pessimistic, or even, in dubious homage to Pavón, as the *Pavonato*.[1] This was an era when gay and otherwise "problematic" artists were fired from their jobs, relegated to obscure workplaces, and denied opportunities for publication and exhibition; when officials carefully monitored the appearance of young men and women for suspiciously long hair or risqué hems; when Beatles records were smuggled in and youth listened to them in secret. Ushered in by the 1971 imprisonment of poet Heberto Padilla, this militant form of censorship began to wane in 1976, when the Ministry of Culture replaced the National Cultural Council under the more lenient leadership of Armando Hart. The quinquenio gris gave a final sign of life during the Mariel boatlift in 1980, when 124,700 Cubans left for the United States, including many Afro-Cubans, gay men, Jehovah's Witnesses, and others deemed troublesome by the state, while Fidel Castro led mass rallies denouncing the emigrants as "scum" and "lumpen" and mobs threw eggs at their homes.[2]

To the horror of Cuban intellectuals, no mention of Pavón's role as director of the National Cultural Council was made on the television program. The following morning, writer Jorge Ángel Pérez sent an email denouncing the television appearance to a handful of established intellectuals on the island, who in turn forwarded the scandalous news to their own lists of contacts. More emails followed quickly on the heels of this initial missive, fueled by fears that Pavón's return might represent a secret conspiracy to restore a more militant cultural policy at a time of political uncertainty. Within a few days, intellectuals on and off the island were engaged in a heated debate about censorship in Cuba both in the past and in the present. In what came to be known as *la guerra de los emails*, or the email war, what began as an exchange among a group of friends and colleagues suddenly held out the promise of a new Cuban public sphere, one that would be open to dialogue among all Cubans, irrespective of geographic location, politics, profession, or age. Yet as new participants and, in particular, exiles and younger intellectuals joined the fray, many raised concerns that the limited reach of email on the island and the very terms in which criticisms were framed might reduce the debate to a safety valve that secured rather than challenged censorship. When the exchanges slowed to a trickle toward the end of January 2007, participants were ultimately left uncertain as to whether the email war signaled new freedoms or more subtle tactics of state control.[3]

In this chapter, I turn to the email war to show how new openings in the post-Soviet era, facilitated in this case by digital technologies and the strategic relaxation of state censorship, exacerbated the political paranoia that has long shaped Cuban society and politics. While paranoid responses to the email war were both reasonable and strategic, I argue, they also reinforced the political divides that some Cubans, at least, hope to overcome. The dynamics that I examine here are firmly rooted in island and diasporic Cuban histories. Indeed, one of the goals of this chapter is to provide a more in-depth introduction to the people, institutions, events, texts, phrases, and political positions that have historically shaped the Cuban cultural field and to outline how they played out in a debate that subsequently served as a key reference point for ongoing conflicts over censorship in Cuba. But this local story also speaks to issues that go beyond the island, demonstrating how a public sphere can thrive in the absence of autonomy from the state—and, more specifically, how intellectuals under socialism fought for an alterna-

tive public sphere that would take political commitment as its foundation—
and how anxieties about the attenuation of autonomy can themselves shape
and limit public debate.

Paranoid Traditions and "Palabras a los intelectuales"

Born in the midst of the Cold War, the Cuban Revolution was characterized from the start by conspiracy thinking.[4] Faced with the real threats of
rebels in the Escambray Mountains and invasion by Miami-based exiles,
political leaders called on citizens to scan everyone and everything for signs
of enemy activity. The establishment in 1960 of the Comités de Defensa
de la Revolución (CDRs, Committees for the Defense of the Revolution),
neighborhood organizations entrusted with social welfare programs and
the task of rooting out "counterrevolutionaries," helped establish suspicion
and surveillance as everyday parts of life.[5] Even the terms with which the
enemy was designated—*el imperialismo* (imperialism), in reference to the
United States' nineteenth-century expansionist policies and twentieth- and
twenty-first-century interventions in Latin American and world politics;
and *gusanos* (worms), for Cubans who actively opposed the Revolution or
went into exile—suggested a far-reaching plot carried out by morally corrupt and inhuman adversaries. Such conspiracy thinking and Manichaean
divides also quickly came to characterize cultural politics. In May 1961, six
weeks after Fidel Castro declared the socialist nature of the Revolution and
Cuban military forces fended off a group of exiles backed by the CIA in the
Playa Girón (Bay of Pigs) invasion, the head of the ICAIC, Alfredo Guevara,
denied an exhibition license to *P.M.* (1961), a short documentary directed
by Saba Cabrera Infante and Orlando Jiménez Leal that used a free cinema
style to record Havana nightlife.

Many Cuban intellectuals argue that this act of censorship was part of
an effort to secure the ICAIC's control over cinema.[6] Saba Cabrera Infante
was the brother of author Guillermo Cabrera Infante, who at the time directed the weekly cultural supplement *Lunes de Revolución*. One of the outcomes of the confrontation was the closure of *Lunes de Revolución* and the
eventual exile of the intellectuals associated with this project. More broadly,
the censorship of *P.M.* also ignited a debate over freedom of expression in
the Revolution.[7] As tensions over the incident rose, a three-day conference
was organized at the Biblioteca Nacional (National Library) in June 1961.
Historically, few records of the interventions made by the intellectuals and

artists who gathered for those three days were made public, and secondary accounts of the exchanges are often in flagrant disagreement over what transpired.[8] Fidel Castro's closing remarks, however, were released under the title "Palabras a los intelectuales" (Words to the Intellectuals) and subsequently became one of the Cuban Revolution's most frequently cited and hotly contested sources of cultural policy. Explaining that his opinion was only one among many, Castro opened his speech by gesturing toward a climate of dialogue between politicians and intellectuals on the question at hand: "the freedom of writers and artists to express themselves" ([1961] 1980, 10). But he quickly moved on to assert a threat that trumped this question. As he listened to the intellectuals express their concerns over the course of the three days, he explained, he frequently had the impression that "we didn't have our feet on the ground." If there was one fear that everyone should share, it was the survival of the Revolution itself.

> What should be the primary concern of every citizen? The concern that the Revolution will surpass its limits, that the Revolution will asphyxiate art, that the Revolution will asphyxiate the creative genius of our citizens, or should we not all be concerned for the Revolution itself? The real or imaginary dangers that might threaten the creative spirit or the dangers that might threaten the Revolution itself? It is not a matter of invoking this danger as a simple argument, we are merely pointing out that the state of mind of all citizens of the country and the state of mind of all revolutionary writers and artists, or of all writers and artists who understand and justify the Revolution, must be: what dangers threaten the Revolution and what can we do in order to help the Revolution? ([1961] 1980, 10)

Protecting and fostering the Revolution, he concluded, must therefore be the guiding principle in managing all other questions, including that of freedom of expression.

At the same time, Castro insisted that the Revolution was not simply a negative limit but was also a positive horizon for artistic production. Intellectuals should not fear the asphyxiation of creativity by the Revolution, noted the political leader, because the Revolution "defends liberty" and "by its very essence can't be the enemy of liberty" ([1961] 1980, 11). More concretely, he reassured his audience that one of the goals of the Revolution was to "develop art and culture, precisely so that art and culture will become a true patrimony of the people" (15). To prove this point, he went on to elaborate at length the various material and institutional supports the government was in the midst of constructing to achieve this goal, including the establishment of the Unión de Escritores y Artistas Cubanos (UNEAC, Union of Cuban Artists and Writers), which continues to act as one of the most significant institutional groupings of artists on the island (22); the transformation of a country club and golf course into a national arts university (the ISA) where working-class students would have the opportunity to study while residing in what were once the "mansions of millionaires" (29); and even the construction of an artists' retreat on the Isle of Pines, which was later renamed the Isle of Youth (25).

Castro also offered reassurance to the numerous artists and intellectuals who feared the imposition of socialist realism.[9] Endorsed in 1934 as the official style of the Soviet Union and under some revision by the 1960s, by the time of the Cuban Revolution socialist realism was associated in Cuba as elsewhere with excessive restrictions on aesthetic form and an idealized and impossibly heroic vision of reality. Everyone was in agreement, Castro insisted, that artists should enjoy absolute freedom of form; it was only when it came to content that the question became more complicated ([1961] 1980, 11). And while the Revolution's objective must be to ensure that "cultural goods reached the people," this did not mean that artists had to sacrifice quality or aesthetic complexity. Rather, every effort should be made not only to make sure that "creators produced for the people" but also that "the people elevated their cultural level in order to close the distance with creators" (16). If protecting the Revolution from its enemies took precedence over an absolute freedom of expression, then this was because true freedom—including the freedom to create formally sophisticated art for the people with all the necessary material and institutional support—would be provided through the Revolution.[10]

The challenge remaining was to determine the appropriate parameters for content. Castro engaged this question by asking for whom freedom of expression in the new society was a concern. The artist or writer who was a revolutionary could never fear for his creative liberty, he declared, because such a person would place the Revolution and its needs above all else, including his own creative vocation. The question was also "not a problem" for counterrevolutionary artists or writers because they knew "where they should go." It was only those intellectuals who "don't have a revolutionary attitude before life but who, nonetheless, are honest people" for whom the Revolution could pose a threat.[11] To this group, Castro provided questionable reassurance. "The Revolution cannot renounce having all honest men and women march alongside it," he declared. "The Revolution has to aspire to converting everyone with doubts into a revolutionary." In a phrase that governed Cuban cultural policy well into the twenty-first century, he concluded that all artists should be guided by the dictate "dentro de la Revolución, todo; contra la Revolución, nada" (within the Revolution, everything; against the Revolution, nothing) ([1961] 1980, 12–15). With the preservation of the Revolution as an absolute limit, Castro thereby guaranteed those intellectuals and artists who were neither revolutionaries nor counterrevolutionaries the dubious freedom of continuing to create while revolutionaries worked toward the anticipated day when the entire citizenry would line up behind their ideals.

"Palabras a los intelectuales" thus cast artistic production in the shadow of the enemies of the Revolution and made determining the difference between allies and foes a question of detecting intellectuals' interior political beliefs and allegiances. Despite his distinction between form and content, artistic works themselves were not the principal objects of concern in Castro's speech. Rather, as evidenced by his description of artists as "honest" or "dishonest," "revolutionary" or "counterrevolutionary," it was the political intentions of artists that were to be put on trial. Making political belief the basis for deciding which art and artists counted as "within" the Revolution, "Palabras" instituted an anxious symptomology as its measure.[12]

The Limits of Tolerance

This speech and its subsequent citations, however, also ensured a paranoia that cut both ways. In a divide that has played an important role in Cuban cultural politics ever since, interpretations of Castro's speech split into two dominant positions: those who viewed Castro's declaration as the establishment of a totalitarian control over the Cuban cultural field; and those who saw in his words and in the Cuban Revolution a guarantee of freedom of expression within limits that they accepted and that, especially in later decades, they fought to expand. For those who adopted the first position, Castro's speech confirmed the Cuban government's adoption of a system of censorship antithetical to meaningful debate. From this perspective, any effort to foster change that fell short of directly challenging Castro's rule could only be complicit with state repression.

The second position, by contrast, grew out of efforts by Cuban intellectuals in the 1960s to theorize an alternative public sphere, one that would preserve a significant role for criticism within the Revolution while calling attention to the ideological nature of liberal aspirations to autonomy. In a 1965 essay, Herbert Marcuse argued that, in twentieth-century capitalist societies, efforts to guarantee tolerance in fact only stifled dissent and reinforced power and exploitation. By burying news reports among advertisements or printing progressive and regressive views side by side, capitalist media paid lip service to freedom of expression while ensuring that a population indoctrinated in the dominant ideology reproduced the status quo. In his essay "El socialismo y el hombre en Cuba" (Socialism and Man in Cuba), also published in 1965, Che Guevara decried the hypocrisy of art under capitalism in similar terms. Under capitalism, argued Guevara, artists were free to express alienation through their work, provided that they avoided turning art into "a weapon of denunciation and accusation." Artists who respected "the rules of the game," he concluded, obtained "all honors—the honors that might be granted to a pirouette-creating monkey" ([1965] 1967, 635).

Roberto Fernández Retamar echoed such arguments in a 1969 conversation among Cuban intellectuals about the role of the intellectual in the new society.

> The intellectual who fulfills or believes himself to have fulfilled the "function of the permanent critic" in the heart of capitalist society considers himself ideally dissociated from society. In practice, he frequently remains integrated within the system, which retains and uses him through its editorials, magazines, and in some cases prizes, and jobs, etc. His criticism remains merely ideal; it is lacking in practical efficacy. For this reason, so long as he does not go beyond certain limits . . . the system tolerates him and even encourages him, and the supposed critic can rest easy in his conscience pretending to exercise a virulence that doesn't really go beyond the verbal. (Dalton et al. 1969, 59–60)

By contrast, Fernández Retamar continued, revolutionary intellectuals "know themselves to be integrated into revolutionary society." This did not, however, mean that they should "applaud [the errors of the Revolution] like seals." Rather, the duty of the intellectual was to "criticize" these errors, but to "criticize [them] *desde adentro* [from within], as our own errors" (Dalton et al. 1969, 60).[13]

This revolutionary mode of criticism resonated with the alternative Marcuse offered to repressive tolerance, and for which he used Cuba as a tentative model. To restore tolerance to its initially progressive stance, argued the theorist, individuals must begin tolerating only those positions that would advance society toward truth, peace, and social justice while suppressing regressive viewpoints that would only benefit the capitalist elite. But such a solution also raised its own quandaries. In the aforementioned 1969 debate, Ambrosio Fornet echoed Fernández Retamar's insistence on the intellectual's necessarily critical adherence to the Revolution. "The revolutionary criticizes, must criticize—in this we are all in agreement—in the name of the Revolution and its goals; he must criticize as a revolutionary for revolutionaries in order to serve revolutionary interests," he insisted (Dalton et al. 1969, 40). But he also invoked Che Guevara's dismissal of bureaucratic efforts to resolve the question of what art should look like in the new revolutionary society. Citing Guevara's arguments in "El socialismo y el hombre en Cuba," Fornet highlighted the dangers that plagued attempts to identify which art was acceptable within the Revolution. "We have always advocated for a critical literature," Fornet explained. "But in practice this problem becomes complicated, because critical literature operates with a margin of ambiguity that makes it disturbing, which is precisely its virtue. And then it becomes very easy, as Che would say, to seek simplification: 'what everyone understands, which is to say, what functionaries understand'" (Dalton et al. 1969, 40).[14]

This group of intellectuals thus both insisted on the integral role of debate in ensuring the health of the new society and accepted the imposition of limits on the forms that criticism could take. As the above statements by Fernández Retamar and Fornet suggest, this position frequently involved a performative play on Castro's speech. Mikhail Bakhtin argues that authoritative utterances present themselves to speakers as distant, powerful, and unalterable (1981, 342–43). Yet, as Richard J. Parmentier contends, speakers often redeploy such utterances in new contexts in order to grant legitimacy to their own positions (1994, 70–73). In a similar move, Cuban intellectuals argued that Castro's injunction, "within the Revolution, everything; against the Revolution, nothing," included what they termed *critica desde adentro* (criticism from within). The difficulty, they claimed, was that by leaving unclear what counted as "within the Revolution," Castro's speech opened the door for functionaries and "dogmatics" who, out of erroneous political conviction, *oportunismo* (opportunism), or *doble moral* (double morality), sought out signs of counterrevolution where there was only revolutionary criticism to be found.[15]

By 1969, Fornet's warning about the slippery slope by which semiotic polysemy might be deemed counterrevolutionary was not merely theoretical but reflected growing concerns, even among the Revolution's staunchest supporters, about the direction that revolutionary and cultural politics were taking. From roughly 1965 to 1968, Jehovah's Witnesses, gay men, delinquents, and others declared unfit for obligatory military service, among them several artists and intellectuals, were sent to the Unidades Militares de Ayuda a la Producción (UMAPs, Military Units to Assist Production), work camps in which internees were obligated to carry out long and arduous hours of agricultural labor. Several internees ended up in psychiatric wards; others committed suicide; a smaller number died of torture. The UMAPs were finally shut down in 1968 as a result of both international and domestic pressure, including interventions by the UNEAC (Casal 1971, 459). In October 1967, Che Guevara was executed by the Bolivian army while leading a guerrilla revolution in that country, dashing hopes for a continent-wide revolution. In April 1968, the Cuban state embarked on what was known as the Ofensiva Revolucionaria (Revolutionary Offensive), closing down all remaining private businesses and leaving Havana and the country at large lacking in goods and services.[16] Hopes that the Cuban Revolution would carve out a unique path for socialism crumbled further that year when, in August, Fidel Castro endorsed the Soviet invasion of Czechoslovakia, which put an end to that country's experiment with a more open form of socialism and confirmed Cuba's alliance with the Soviet Union. Finally, these events were compounded when two major agricultural projects—a plan to render Havana agriculturally self-sufficient (Cordón de la Habana [Havana Greenbelt Project] in 1968) and a project to harvest ten million tons of sugarcane (Zafra de los Diez Millones [Ten Million Ton Sugar Harvest] in 1970)—both of which involved a significant investment of resources and volunteer labor, ended in failure.[17]

In this political context, the arts saw a closing of ranks, focused in particular around what is commonly referred to as the "Padilla Affair." Cuban poet Heberto Padilla first sparked controversy in 1967, when he defended a novel by Guillermo Cabrera Infante in a survey conducted by a Cuban literary supplement. At the time, Cabrera Infante, who had previously been the director of the cultural supplement *Lunes de Revolución* and was involved in the censorship scandal that sparked Fidel Castro's "Palabras a los intelectuales," was already living in Europe. A few months later, Cabrera Infante gave an interview in which he made clear his opposition to the Cuban Revolution. As Lourdes Casal puts it, Padilla thus found himself in the "dangerous position of having defended a 'traitor'" (1971, 7). In 1968 Padilla ran into worse trouble. That year, a jury granted his book of poems *Fuera del juego* (*Out of the Game*, 1968) the UNEAC's prize for poetry, while Antón Arrufat's play *Los siete contra Tebas* (*Seven against Thebes*, 1968) won in the category of theater. Even before the prizes were decided, however, cultural functionaries, including, according to some, Luis Pavón, approached jury members to persuade them to change their minds (Gallardo 2009, 172–73).

In the end, the prizes were maintained and both books were published accompanied by a note from the UNEAC executive committee making clear their objections to the works' politics. Further demonstrating what many felt was an attack not only on Padilla and Arrufat but also on Cuban cultural production at large, an author who some believe may have been Pavón published a series of articles in the military's journal, *Verde Olivo*, under the pseudonym Leopoldo Ávila. These articles lambasted Padilla, Arrufat, and Cabrera Infante and argued more broadly that Cuban intellectuals, fearful of the "specter of the pamphlet," a term often used in Cuban cultural politics to refer to the reduction of art to propaganda, had neglected their duty to record the revolutionary efforts of the Cuban people (Casal 1971, 35). Tensions in Cuban culture finally came to a head three years later. On March 20, 1971, Padilla and his wife, poet Belkis Cuza Malé, were arrested. Cuza Malé was held for three days, but Padilla was detained for more than a month. He was finally released on condition that he deliver a public self-criticism at an assembly held at the UNEAC.

Around the time of his release, Cuban officials gathered for the Primer Congreso de Educación y Cultura (First Congress of Education and Culture). In keeping with the growing militancy suggested by Padilla's arrest, this conference formalized government restrictions on the arts and education, resulting, for instance, in injunctions to "take into consideration the political and ideological conditions" of workers assigned to "universities, mass media, and literary and artistic institutions" and warnings about fashion, religion, homosexuality, and foreign intellectuals (Casal 1971, 105–6). So began what Cuban intellectuals frequently refer to as the *parametración* of the Cuban cultural field, or the restriction of employment and opportunities to publish and travel to those who met a highly restrictive set of political and social parameters.

The ICAIC was clearly not immune to the political environment of the 1970s. As I discuss in chapter 5, at least one of the institution's employees—Afro-Cuban documentarist Nicolás Guillén Landrián—was fired during this period, while others saw their work censored and detained. Nonetheless, alongside the Casa de las Américas, the ICAIC is often thought to have escaped the worst consequences of the quinquenio gris, thanks in part to Alfredo Guevara's revolutionary credentials and close ties to Fidel Castro.[18] This theory is emblematized in a story about the 1971 Congress that one filmmaker recounted to me as follows: "Armando Quesada [who was responsible for theater and dance in the National Cultural Council] was in charge in this Congress with delivering the critical pronouncements on cultural institutions. And on the day that he was to criticize cinema, Fidel arrived and put his arm around Alfredo, or so goes the legend. In these things in history there always remain certain obscure zones that one day will be known."[19]

This account speaks to the symptomologies in which Cuban artists and citizens engage as they struggle to decipher the meanings of the obscure signals on which socialist state officials often rely.[20] It also suggests ongoing belief that some definitive truth about Cuban history might yet be revealed, if only the right documents could be produced. The debates that broke out over Luis Pavón's reappearance in 2007 both repeated and complicated such strategies and hopes, revealing profound disagreements among Cuban intellectuals not only over assignations of guilt and heroism in the 1970s and beyond but also over what counts as freedom of expression.

Chance Has No Chance against Censorship

Seven months after the email war came to a close, echoes of these events could still be heard in the hallways of Cuba's international film school, the EICTV. Over dinner in the school's cafeteria or hanging out in the windowed hallway that opens onto the school's lush yards, students speculated about potential links between the email war and recent rumors that the University of Havana planned to restrict its students' and faculty's access to the internet. They analyzed the emails that they had most appreciated, told stories about their attendance at the youth conference that was prompted by the debate, and spoke with excitement about the spontaneous airing of criticism and demands that were too frequently silenced. But they also expressed the disappointment they felt when it seemed like the energy fomented by the email exchange was all too quickly dissipated and even, they suspected, deliberately contained by the state.

A meeting with an older Cuban intellectual who had been a key player in these events gave me new insight into their contradictory nature. As we sipped Cuban-style espressos in the school's open-air El Rapidito café, the television transmitting the school's satellite connection chattering in the background, I brought up the subject of the email war. He rushed to correct me: "That's just a pejorative name invented by the officials. It wasn't a war; everyone who participated was on the same side." Yet as I spoke with other intellectuals and read through the hundreds of pages of emails archived on the website of the online dissident magazine *Consenso*, to which he directed me, it struck me that the invocation of war bore some accuracy. The letters revealed a general outrage against Pavón's television appearance and a consensus that Cuba was badly in need of a more open public sphere. But this consensus was woven through with paranoia as intellectuals found in both the original event and in subsequent interventions signs of secret plots fomented by an enemy on whose name they could not agree.

In a paranoid worldview, chance or coincidence seems impossible. Rather than viewing history as a series of unintentional forces, Richard Hofstadter (1965, 32) argues, the political paranoid discovers links between disparate events and finds at their origin the secret actions of an enemy bent on destroying entire ways of life. As Eve Kosofsky Sedgwick (2003, 130, 131–32) elaborates, the political paranoid anticipates the enemy's presence. Preferring to locate the principle they dread rather than risk being taken by surprise, they read everything as a sign of this enemy's presence, even when the events or texts in question might yield other meanings.

From the beginning, a similar paranoid symptomology fueled the reactions of Cuban intellectuals to Pavón's appearance. By all accounts, Luis Pavón had disappeared from public view after the Ministry of Culture replaced the National Cultural Council in 1976. Many linked his sudden reemergence on a program that portrayed him as a national hero to another morbid thought that was on everyone's minds in January 2007: the seemingly imminent possibility of Fidel Castro's demise. Only a few months before, Castro had withdrawn from public office due to serious health problems, leaving his brother serving in his stead. The deliberate secrecy surrounding his illness fed speculation that the founder and emblem of the Revolution might soon be gone forever and, indeed, that he might already be dead. Compounding these concerns, other ghosts from the past had also recently returned to the Cuban political scene. In the months leading up to January 5, Jorge Serguera and Armando Quesada, responsible, respectively, for the censorship of radio and television and for the decimation of theater during the 1970s, appeared as special guests on national television shows.

A group of intellectuals with established positions in national cultural organizations was the first to respond to these events. They did so by invoking defenses of criticism from within and arguments about dogmatists, anxiously detecting in the confluence of these events signs of secret political maneuvers to restore militant cultural policies or at least whitewash the censors' histories. One of the first to write was Desiderio Navarro, editor and translator for the Cuban critical theory journal *Criterios*. Acknowledging that Pavón was only one player in the generally repressive cultural bureaucracy of that era, Navarro nonetheless accused him of carrying out his orders with an excessive zeal.[21] "How many erroneous decisions were taken 'higher up' on the basis of . . . Pavón and his allies' diagnostics and prognostics of the supposedly grave threats emerging from the cultural field?" he demanded. Where other cultural functionaries at the time had done their best to protect intellectuals and keep cultural forums "as little closed as possible," Navarro argued, Pavón's actions were responsible for the "irreversible damage to the lives" of those who were censored or "'parametered,' in one way or another," the "self-censorship" that dominated those years, the influx of the worst cultural works from Eastern Europe, and the emigration of "many of those artists who were neither revolutionaries nor counterrevolutionaries whose concern Fidel had tried to dissipate in *Palabras a los intelectuales*."[22]

Making an ominous pattern out of the recent TV appearances, Navarro demanded to know "why this sudden glorious media resurrection of Luis Pavón . . . occurred precisely at this moment in the history of our country, a moment when the entire nation is waiting to know the outcome of the convalescence of our Commander in Chief, and this only a few days after the equally sudden television reappearance of Jorge Serguera."[23] Cuban author and screenwriter Arturo Arango wrote to Navarro with equal confidence that mere coincidence could not explain these events or their timing. "Although it seems like the product of chance," he argued, "the appearances of Jorge Serguera and Luis Pavón Tamayo on Cuban television only a few days apart from one another have to be interpreted as a symptom."[24] "It's better to be taken for paranoid than it is to seem an idiot," added architect Mario Coyula, approving the call to action. "Let's hope that it's only a coincidence."[25] Other artists who had been embroiled in scandal alongside Heberto Padilla and censored throughout the 1970s only to be restored to favor in the post-Soviet era, including, for instance, playwright Antón Arrufat, added their support.

As the emails snowballed, the minister of culture, Abel Prieto, called two meetings with this group of intellectuals, inviting the president of the Instituto Cubano de Radio y Televisión (ICRT, Cuban Institute of Radio and Television) to the second of these encounters. The ICRT president tried to quell the intellectuals' suspicions. The failure to mention Pavón's history had been pure coincidence, he argued, the chance outcome of his selection through regular channels as a guest for the show and the young script researcher's unfamiliarity with this historical era. But the intellectuals were having none of it. Ambrosio Fornet, who attended both encounters, insisted that he never believed that the television appearances represented an effort by Pavón and others to retake their former positions of power: "I wasn't afraid that this was an attempt to rescue the quinquenio gris and now they're going to bring in Pavón to substitute for Abel Prieto, not at all. That never occurred to me because it was impossible. After everything, after all the development that [the field of] culture has had, after the policies that have been carried out over the course of so many years, the presence of Abel [Prieto] and all of us in directorial positions within the UNEAC, it was totally impossible that this would take place."[26] But the young script researcher's claim that she did not know about Pavón's past as head of the Cultural Council was equally implausible, he insisted: "Either the people in television were being underhanded or their level of ignorance was unusually high." For Fornet, the television appearances thus revealed an urgent need to discuss censorship in the 1970s in order to ensure that this historical "memory was not lost" and "things were left clear."

The convergence of the television appearances with Fidel Castro's illness added to the sense of urgency felt by many intellectuals. Explained Arturo Arango:

Everybody feared something different. There were two things that drew my attention. First, that we were in a moment of obvious change in the structure of power in Cuba [with] Raúl taking over from Fidel. I didn't really think that [Pavón's appearance] was a central action of the government, but I did think that that group was trying to retake the positions that they had lost. And on the other hand, it seemed to me that we were in a period of change in which it was necessary to speak and to establish your point of view and your opinion. At a time like that you can't sin by staying silent. That is, you can't let it be the case that tomorrow something happens and you feel guilty because you didn't do something to provoke the opposite reaction. There are moments in which one knows that things are quiet and more or less foreseeable; for better or for worse what is coming is inevitable. And at other moments you have to take a stand and try to influence the course of events. It seemed to me that that moment was of that second sort.[27]

Suspicions of conspiracy thus provided Cuban intellectuals with an opportunity and even, some felt, a moral obligation to address censorship not only in the past but also in the present at a moment of critical political change and uncertainty. Yet, as the email war unfolded, many worried that calls to denounce censorship and to revisit the country's history might only contribute to limiting public debate and reinforcing state power.

When Open Is Closed

From the beginning of the email war, intellectuals called for an open transparent debate that would include Cuban artists and intellectuals on and off the island, youth, and the general public. The appearance of email responses from a handful of Cuban writers overseas, observed Arturo Arango in one early missive, raised the question of "who should participate in the debate, or who has the right to participate in the debate?" Don't those who live outside of Cuba already belong within the corpus of Cuban culture? Wouldn't excluding them go against the spirit of everything that has been done to reincorporate all those aspects of Cuba and its culture that are dispersed throughout the world?" he asked, referencing post-Soviet efforts to forge new relationships with the diaspora.[28] "Wouldn't saying that this problem only concerns those who lived through those years be equivalent to saying that it is a problem of the past, with no bearing on the present or the future?" he continued, insisting on the importance of youth participation in the debate. Finally, he concluded that the debate ought to extend beyond the cultural field to include all Cubans: "Even though those of us who are participating [in the debate] work in literature and the arts, the era of dogmatization that we call the Pavonato affected the entire country. Although my mother, mother-in-law, and my neighbors didn't know Luis Pavón, they were also damaged by him."[29] From abroad, author Amir Valle endorsed this call for inclusivity. "Thanks for pointing out something very important," he wrote in an email addressed to Arango. "There are many young writers (and others who are not so young, such as myself) who also have a right to opine, support, and dissent. I myself have received emails from a few who should be listened to." He signed off: "*Abrazos* [hugs] from a cold Berlin."[30]

The debate's reliance on email gave many hope that the discussion might succeed in acquiring this broad reach. As Michael Warner (2002) notes, the constitution of publics and the forms that they take rely, among other factors, on the rhythms according to which texts circulate and the modes of address and styles used in texts. The "concatenation of texts" over time as they circulate along regular pathways and establish intertextual relations with one another provides the sense of an ongoing social space. The speed at which texts circulate, meanwhile, a factor in which medium plays a key role, affects the proximity to or distance of a given public from political action. Finally, the modes of address and the styles used in texts work to describe and performatively bring into being a public of a particular sort, a project that is also always open to failure and contestation (Warner 2002, 62, 82).

A curious doubling of address in many early missives in the email war suggested how email's sender/receiver model combined with its copy, paste, and forward functions to enable what might otherwise have been experienced as private exchanges to suddenly take on a public dimension. In more than one instance, intellectuals marveled at or, conversely, reflected with dismay on how emails they had written to one or a few acquaintances ended up circulating further than they had anticipated. At other times, they deliberately fostered this extended circulation. In an email addressed to author and film scholar Reynaldo González, who was among the first of the intellectuals to react to Pavón's appearance, writer Ena Lucía Portela observed that she had at first intended to "send this little message to you privately, only for you, in part because I am not accustomed to shouting in the agora and in part because, if memory serves, you and I don't know one another personally." In the end, she explained, she had decided to copy her message to others because "if one is going to manifest support and solidarity with someone who has shouted, one shouldn't do it in a low voice."[31]

Some worried that this doubling of the personal with the public would transform the debate into an emotional airing of grievances. In one early missive, Havana-based art critic and curator Orlando Hernández commented that "the fact that the forum for these debates is email . . . may convert it into the gossip of resentful and pained old writers and artists." But others (including, eventually, Hernández himself) celebrated the debate's reliance on email, arguing that digital media enabled the exchanges to bypass state control and bring an open public into being. "Certain figures of the government tried to close down the debate," recalled Havana-based film critic Gustavo Arcos. "Because it had been produced in a spontaneous, independent, and alternative way, they were overwhelmed by it and couldn't control it as they had in other eras. What sense is there in trying to control information if we live in a world in which information flows everywhere? The state still acts with the outdated mentality that they control the media when the opposite is true and the proof is this situation with the emails."[32]

As Warner (2002, 75) observes, however, while the self-constitution of publics through discourse enables us to imagine them as autonomous and indefinitely open, in practice the realities of circulation, address, and style impose constraints. Likewise, in the case of the email war, fantasies of information flowing everywhere soon ran up against both material and discursive limitations. Access to the internet gradually increased after Raúl Castro officially acceded to the presidency in February 2008. In 2008, the government legalized the sale and purchase of DVD players, personal computers, and cell phones. In 2015, the state telecommunications company, ETECSA, launched Wi-Fi hotspots in select parks and other locations across the island and, in December 2018, rolled out a 3G data service for smartphones. These services remain prohibitively expensive for many, but have greatly expanded opportunities to access the internet. As of 2010, meanwhile, the *paquete semanal* (weekly package), one terabyte of pirated digital media that is downloaded and circulated hand to hand over flash drive and hard drive across the island, has also helped circumvent state control over distribution and the island's still limited internet access.[33]

But in 2007, when the email war took place, these improvements seemed lightyears away. According to a 2009 Cuban government survey, only 2.9 percent of Cubans had regular access to the internet while a slightly larger number, 5.8 percent, used email (ONE 2010). These numbers are most likely low even for that period, since Cubans often accessed the internet or email through informal or illegal methods they would be unlikely to report. In terms of legal methods, some Cubans had access to the internet or email at work, while others were granted dial-up accounts from home through their workplaces. These accounts, however, were largely restricted to a national intranet service that provided email and a limited range of state-curated websites. Supplementing these official means of access, Cubans also used flash drives and hard drives to share articles, emails, and other digital information in a method of circulation that preceded and has continued to operate alongside the paquete semanal. Finally, while only foreign residents were legally allowed to purchase dial-up connections from home without institutional permission, a rampant business in the piracy and sale of codes to these accounts provided some Cubans with another means of getting online. In sum, while some Cubans found ways—legal or otherwise—to access the internet or at the very least email, obstacles to connectivity were significant and well known.

Awareness of email's limited reach on the island combined with wariness of how texts were framed to exacerbate suspicions of attempts to move the debate to other forums. On January 18, 2007, a week after the meeting between intellectuals, Abel Prieto, the ICRT president, and staff from the TV show where Pavón made his appearance, the leadership of the UNEAC published a letter responding to the controversy in the Communist Party's newspaper, *Granma*. The authors expressed their support for the "just indignation of a group of our most important writers and artists," noting fears that the three television shows might "respond to an intentionality and express a tendency that is alien to the cultural policy that has guaranteed and continues to guarantee our unity." "From the first moment, it was of the utmost importance to have the most complete support from the leadership of the Party," the letter proclaimed, reassuring readers that the meeting with the ICRT president had revealed that the programs did not represent "the organization's policy" but rather were the result of grave errors. "The Martí-inspired, anti-dogmatic, creative, and participatory cultural policy of Fidel and Raúl founded with 'Palabras a los intelectuales' is irreversible," it concluded.[34]

Intellectuals on and off the island responded with outrage. The UNEAC's declaration was the only information on the debate to emerge in official state media. But, in keeping with state socialist tendencies to communicate through ambiguous signals, while the letter named the three television shows, it did not explain what had happened on these shows to spark the intellectuals' outrage. "That people receive a gray cloud instead of information, that at the end the nation says '*oye*, something big has happened, I don't know what it is but it seems like it was something to do with the artists,' is an act of informational irresponsibility," wrote author Félix Sánchez.[35] Intellectuals complained of having to explain what had happened to friends and neighbors left bewildered by the UNEAC's vague references. "The opaque and minimal Declaration left the nation in limbo. Many neighbors and friends have asked me what happened, why this Declaration was published," protested Eddy E. Jiménez Pérez. "In sum, the immense majority doesn't know the true causes that provoked the declaration."[36] In a strategy repeated in subsequent controversies, the letter's failure to provide a complete context for the events it referenced ensured that it could be understood only by those already "in the know," frustrating intellectuals' desire to open up their debate to the general citizenry.

To make matters worse, the UNEAC document gave ample space to the assertion that this was a "debate between revolutionaries," warning that while "some intervened with honesty in the polemics from outside Cuba, others, obviously working in the service of the enemy, have tried to manipulate and take advantage of the situation." Whether this assertion was meant to reassure Cuban political leaders who might be alarmed by the intellectuals' activities, to remind intellectuals that there was always a limit to what form of criticism would be tolerated, to take a stand against the more vocal criticisms delivered by Cubans abroad, or, as is likely the case, to accomplish a mix of all three, the UNEAC's reference to the enemy infuriated many participants.

Havana-based musician Pablo Menéndez declared:

It seems to me that this discussion strengthens us in all senses. I think it's good that the UNEAC's Declaration came out, but like many others I feel that it is base and cautious. . . . Of 5 paragraphs, it dedicates 2 to discussing the "enemies of the Revolution" (nobody cares what they do or don't say about all of this). The very fact of engaging in an ample discussion without fear is a triumph over those who deny the possibility that this type of democratic and revolutionary debate can take place in Cuba. Why speak of them and even less to them? The Martí-inspired, anti-dogmatic, creative, and participatory cultural policy of course permits ample debate and allows us to move forward, not backward like those who invited these characters to our television. "Irreversible" doesn't mean static or stagnant. To negate progress is to negate the Revolution.[37]

Menéndez's criticism of the UNEAC's declaration took for granted its exclusion of counterrevolutionaries from public debate in Cuba. But his resistance to references to counterrevolutionaries and his association of the Revolution with debate, progress, and change suggested an expansive definition of who and what type of interventions might fall into the category of an acceptable intervention from within the Revolution.

Others took such objections further. Octavio Miranda wrote:

The famous "Palabras a los intelectuales" (1961) represented by the government as proof of democracy and liberty cannot be clearer: "within the Revolution, everything; against the Revolution, nothing." Who establishes these limits, what are they? Why can't one be against the Revolution? Aren't these words equivalent to saying, "either you're with me or you're against me?" . . . Let's not accuse every person who expresses opinions that oppose or simply differ from those of the government of "working with the enemy," as the "Declaration of the UNEAC's Secretariat" has affirmed, or of having an "annexationist agenda."[38]

Suggesting how accusations of working with the enemy served to polarize politics, Miranda queried not only the limits of what criticism could be counted as within the Revolution and who would set these boundaries but also the existence of these limits in the first place and, with it, the exclusion of those deemed counterrevolutionaries from Cuban public life.

Yet in spite of pervasive criticism of the UNEAC declaration, many intellectuals found it significant that the cultural institution had felt it necessary to publish the document in the first place. One of Cuba's most internationally well-known novelists, Leonardo Padura, observed: "For those who weren't aware of the debate (that is to say, the majority of the island's inhabitants), the declaration only let them know that something had happened about which they had no other information or antecedents. For those who did know what was happening, even when we weren't entirely satisfied with the tone and breadth of the UNEAC document, it nonetheless made it clear that silence and indolence are no longer possible: wounded memory does not allow new manipulations."[39]

Exiled author Jorge Luis Arcos also acknowledged the significance of the UNEAC letter. But whereas for Padura its publication signaled a concession to intellectuals on the part of authorities, for Arcos it merely indicated new strategies for repressing dissent.

> I have to acknowledge that the publication of such a text in *Granma* is an unusual occurrence. It seems that the magnitude of the discontent was so great that [the UNEAC] had no choice but to publish it if they wanted to repair the error that had been committed in a moment as singular as the one that our country is currently experiencing. But as we know, image is what counts—whether it is image for the exterior or image for the interior. And it is in the name of that image that truth, passion, memory, as well as the infinite contradictions that are inherent to life will be buried.[40]

If the UNEAC declaration was an acknowledgment of the intellectuals' outrage and an attempt to repair the damage wrought by the television appearances, argued Arcos, this was an effort whose goal was primarily to defend and improve the domestic and international reputation of the government while restoring politics as usual in a country in which, he went on to declare, "it has been so many years since there was democracy (more than half a century) that it is now possible to declare with complete naturalness that there is democracy in Cuba."

For those Cubans without easy access to the internet and email or personal ties to Cuban intellectuals, the UNEAC's declaration was their only sign of the email debate. By leaving out the essential details of the contemporary and historical events that had sparked the controversy, the letter left the vast majority of the Cuban population with only a vague and confused impression of controversy in elite circles. By invoking the threat that enemies of the Revolution had tried to infiltrate and take control of the exchange, the declaration mobilized paranoia to reestablish the limits to the Cuban public sphere that at least some intellectuals who participated in the email war hoped to overcome. And while its publication, to some, suggested that Cuba's cultural institutions were increasingly finding it necessary to bend to intellectuals' growing resistance to censorship, others saw in such concessions new strategies for preventing any meaningful debate or political change on the island. Reactions to the UNEAC declaration made clear how the adoption in the 1960s of practices designed to tolerate only those interventions deemed within the Revolution eventually gave rise to what could just as easily be dismissed as repressive tolerance or progressive censorship, to borrow, respectively, Herbert Marcuse's and Miklós Haraszti's terminology. As even intellectuals who supported the Revolution grew increasingly dissatisfied with the state and its policies, they worried that the state's seemingly more liberal tactics might themselves be a ploy to reproduce the status quo.

Suspicions that protests against censorship might simply mask new strategies of state power can also be seen in reactions to a series of conferences on the quinquenio gris organized by Desiderio Navarro in response to Pavón's television appearance and the ensuing debate. As mentioned earlier, following the meeting with Prieto and the ICRT, many of those in attendance argued that a public discussion of censorship in the 1970s was necessary both to ensure that younger generations were aware of what had occurred and to avoid a repetition of such tactics in the present. "Some people had lived through these events but others only knew of them from what they had overheard," Navarro explained. "There had yet to be an analysis or a text published on these years."[41] The conferences he sponsored were intended to address that gap, but they also sparked a new series of difficulties. Given the initial furor that accompanied the debate, Navarro feared that the auditorium of the Casa de las Américas, where the first conference was held, would not be able to accommodate everyone who might wish to attend. Reluctant to hand-select guests himself, Navarro told me, he therefore delegated responsibility for distributing invitations to the island's state cultural institutions and announced that he would circulate the full texts of the conference presentations via email the day after the event.

Intellectuals soon began to argue that these arrangements had been devised not by a single intellectual and his organization but rather by state officials who plotted in secret to contain the debate. "It's very difficult to accept that in the end everything is cooked up behind closed doors and the rest of us have to accept an edited version of reality (as has always occurred)," objected one correspondent, signed only as "Betty." "I imagine that it isn't your idea but in the same way that you didn't accept Pavón on TV, you shouldn't now permit that they choose the public for you. It's a concession that goes against what you defend."[42]

If there was not sufficient space in Casa de las Américas, exclaimed Orlando Hernández, then the conference should be moved to a baseball field or a pasture.

Maybe I'm being too suspicious or mistrusting. But I believe that the conference has been converted into a meeting, a meeting that wasn't called, but where the Minister [of Culture] will probably assist and speak alongside the presidents of the sections of the UNEAC and a few *compañeros* selected from institutions that are themselves selected, etc. . . . It will be a meeting (with the Minister) masked as a conference. And this is what worries me or bothers me: that this conference (and *Criterios* as a result) will be converted into a fire extinguisher or a safety valve that avoids or postpones a more ample convocation.[43]

Francis Sánchez, a younger author from the provinces, expanded on Hernández's objections.

Criticisms as strong or stronger than what has been said in these messages have been published in Cuba, in *La Gaceta de Cuba*, and what has happened? What tremendous truths have been published in the [Cuban political science] journal *Temas* only to end up at the bottom of trunks or wells? It's not a question of reeling off a bunch of truths and telling tales; these have already emerged in more than a few essays, poems, short stories, articles, interviews, etc. . . . Desiderio justifies this effort on the basis that "this period and the phenomena of this period that have survived or been revived in subsequent eras remain unknown or unexplained for many generations." Let's set aside this nonsense. Don't ask us to be quiet and listen to the venerable elder. Don't convoke didacticism in the false hope of finding the missing link. Everyone here already knows what is essential and necessary to know about those years. . . . That certain politicians, functionaries, etc. haven't realized what happened? I believe their mode of "not knowing" builds on another type of wisdom that isn't that of the game planted in academic salons. They don't want to know the future that we desire. They refuse to learn from the future. When has someone as intelligent as Desiderio, for instance, had the good fortune of having one of his incisive analyses spark a dialogue with those who "know" or "don't know" but decide?[44]

The first of these conferences left many with a bitter taste in their mouth. A crowd of youth excluded from the invite-only gathering protested outside the doors of the Casa de las Américas to the sound of the refrain "¡Desiderio, Desiderio, oye mi criterio!" (Desiderio, Desiderio, listen to my opinion!). When he learned of this protest while browsing the internet from his home connection later that evening, Navarro quickly arranged for a conference to be held specifically for youth at the ISA with the original panelists and Abel Prieto in attendance. A microphone was made available for audience members to voice their questions and opinions. One friend and film student at the EICTV who attended this meeting told me that while many youth spoke out against ongoing censorship in the present, most felt that their concerns were inadequately addressed and left the conference deflated. After this event, attendance at the conferences dropped. Navarro attributed this diminishing interest to a combination of factors: the challenge many faced in reaching the new conference location at the ISA, located on the outskirts of Havana; his distribution of the talks over email; and the focus of panelists on censorship in the past rather than in the present.

With their academic style, their selective guest lists, and their initial exclusion of youth, many intellectuals feared that the conferences would add another dead body to the pile of ghosts resurrected by the ICRT: that of the email debate itself and its potential to foment a more open public sphere. Most intellectuals dismissed arguments that Navarro's organizational decisions were, as "Betty" implied, the outcome of secret state plots. But many concurred with the concerns raised by Orlando Hernández and Francis Sánchez. Like the UNEAC declaration, the conferences reproduced a familiar dynamic in which state officials placated the nation's sometimes troublesome intelligentsia by providing them with a forum while the majority of the Cuban population remained ignorant of the debates taking place in elite spheres.

Absolute Enemies

As the previous discussion makes clear, intellectuals' hopes that the email war might lead to an open and inclusive public sphere were hindered both by the material limitations of email in Cuba and concerns that those few manifestations of the debate in other forums—the UNEAC letter and the conferences on the quinquenio gris—would merely function as a form of repressive tolerance, allowing intellectuals to let off steam while continuing to ensure that public debate remained limited in both content and reach. The ways in which intellectuals interpreted Cuban history and politics further complicated aspirations to forge a new public. Whereas participants who defended the possibility of criticism from within recounted the history of censorship in Cuba as a struggle to establish a true, critical Revolution, those who equated the Cuban Revolution with a repressive totalitarianism argued that such efforts only served to entrench a regime under whose rule meaningful debate was by definition impossible. The adoption of one or the other of these two positions continuously set intellectuals at odds with one another, resurrecting the political divides that some, at least, claimed to want to overcome, as participants scanned one another's statements for signs of political complicity and opportunism.

Desiderio Navarro's first email was a catalyst for a debate that soon became as much a conflict over how to interpret the causes of censorship in Cuba as an assessment of the 1970s. Recall that Navarro drew on "Palabras" to establish Pavón's guilt. Insisting that the functionary's decisions had in many ways contributed to the censorship, self-censorship, and exodus of intellectuals during the 1970s, Navarro contrasted Pavón and his repressive tactics to other functionaries, who, he argued, had struggled to protect artists and cultural production. Here we have the key elements of Cuban history viewed as an ongoing battle against dogmatism: the militant and repressive bureaucrat is contrasted to the cultural functionary who does his best, while censorship and repression are cast as deviations from the critical commitment that constitutes the true principle of the Cuban Revolution.

This interpretation of Cuban cultural politics characterized other key texts in the email war. In his presentation at the first of the quinquenio gris conferences, for instance, Ambrosio Fornet declared the email war a "battle" won in an ongoing "war" against "a vision of the world based in suspicion and mediocrity" (2008, 25). In an email circulated after this conference, Reynaldo González elaborated on this position. From the beginning of the Revolution, he argued, the cultural field had been dominated by a "struggle for power" between proponents of the "aberrant and abortive Soviet cultural practices, theories, and propaganda" and another group who "responded to the artistic conceptions operative in the country." This first group acquired dominance over the cultural field during the 1970s, leading to "the destruction of institutions that were the pride of our culture and, above all else, a criminal rejection of everything that was different." After the 1970s, the second group restored its dominance over the cultural field, but the first survived the setback, engaging in a "devious struggle," whether "in front stage or camouflaged," and resurfacing in this latest attempt to "contradict . . . a cultural line that is procuring a new type of dialogue." Accusing Pavón and his allies of imposing Soviet socialist realism and Stalinist cultural policies on a Cuban culture that was, at its core, "vanguardist and Western," González's account cast dogmatic functionaries as the real counterrevolutionaries, representatives of a foreign policy that threatened national taste and morality.[45]

For those who viewed Cuba as a totalitarian regime, by contrast, all the fuss about Pavón and his cronies was at best naïve and at worst cynical. How could the TV appearances signal the threat of a takeover of the cultural field, they demanded, when these figures merely represented trends inherent to state socialism and were acting on the orders of those who had truly governed cultural production from the 1960s on, Fidel Castro or, in his absence, his brother? "How can we allow ourselves to imagine that we are now faced with the revival of 'those errors' [of the 1970s], precisely at the moment when the country is being run by the person who was directly behind many of those disasters and who operated the strings of the sad puppets that Pavón, Aldana, and company, actually were?" asked Amir Valle, reminding his readers that, as director of the military journal *Verde Olivo* in the late 1960s, Pavón had begun his career under the leadership of Raúl Castro, who served as commander-in-chief of the armed forces.[46]

"As one of the messages says, it is crucial to find out who gave the order to air those television programs," Valle continued, in reference to Navarro's original email. "But, I would add, it is even more important to discover what political strategy orders such as these correspond to. And here we would find a clear answer: the political strategy has always been the same, with some nuances and slight modifications according to the intelligence or stupidity of the Pavón in charge."[47] "Everyone in the cultural field in the 1970s knew that Luis Pavón and others were only responding to Fidel Castro's policies. Nothing happened in Cuba that didn't have his approval and wasn't one of his orders," observed Belkis Cuza Malé, as she recalled her experiences of censorship alongside her husband, Heberto Padilla. To demand reparations for Pavón's public appearance while avoiding naming the true culprits behind Cuban cultural policy—the Castros—was thus to remain complicit with a repressive regime, a tactic that could only be motivated by opportunism or fear. "The majority of those who are now writing agitated messages of protest have climbed to high-ranking positions in the official Cuban cultural hierarchy," concluded Cuza Malé. "All of a sudden, all of this is in danger, and fear makes its appearance."[48]

The key mistake of intellectuals on the island, argued other Cuban emigrants, was that they continued to believe that socialism could allow for debate and dialogue. "The limits of [Desiderio Navarro's] position is essentially that of all those who continue to insist at this stage in the game that the freedom to criticize and Cuban socialism are compatible," wrote Cuban scholar Duanel Díaz from his home in the United States. Acknowledging that Pavón had earned the ire of Cuban intellectuals, Díaz insisted that by "placing most of the blame on the functionary . . . Navarro largely freed the revolutionary government from responsibility." "The truth is exactly the opposite of what Navarro says," Díaz observed. "The very existence of socialism, before and after the fall of the [Berlin] wall, depends on repressing in-depth criticism, because this would melt it like a piece of ice exposed to the Cuban midday sun."[49] Writing from Mexico City, José Prats Sariol likewise insisted that island intellectuals' objections to Pavón's appearance betrayed a deeper political complicity. "What isn't clear in the Aristotelian rhetoric of those who denounce the homage to Pavón is whether or not they have at last lost the little faith that they retained in the political leadership," he argued. "This, it seems, is what still eludes them."[50]

For other intellectuals, however, it was these self-styled heroes of freedom who were the true opportunists. They accused emigrants of denouncing socialism from comfortable positions, arguing that many exiles had never risked openly protesting censorship while they still resided in Cuba. Writing from the Dominican Republic, Cuban sociologist Haroldo Dilla Alfonso dismissed the more vitriolic of the email responses from exiles as an "arrogant libel" that betrayed their authors' tendencies to "consider themselves virtuous and uncompromising warriors." "Putting the test case of opposition" to intellectuals on the island, continued Dilla, "is immoral," both because "the majority of people who I have seen expressing such disdainful and arrogant opinions in truth never defied the system while in Cuba beyond a few private conversations with slightly raised voices" and because intellectuals everywhere "are always calculating what is and isn't judicious to say, whether this be for political, ethical, or economic reasons." "Let's be frank," he concluded. "Protecting ourselves is a professional infirmity."[51]

From his home in Mexico City, author and screenwriter Eliseo Alberto, known, for instance, for his work on Tomás Gutiérrez Alea and Juan Carlos Tabío's 1995 film, *Guantanamera* (see chapter 2), argued that missives such as those written by Duanel Díaz and José Prats Sariol would only get in the way of the struggle in Cuba to protect the "spaces of relative intellectual freedom" that island writers and artists had won in recent years, thanks to the "value of their works and also to their personal positions, which are progressively more autonomous and independent." Taking up Prats Sariol's rhetorical question as to whether island intellectuals had at last lost faith in Cuba's political leadership, Eliseo Alberto retorted, "Who knows? Revolutionaries can 'lose faith' [in political leaders] without, for that reason, ceasing to feel committed to what has, until now, been the motivating force of their lives."[52] Disillusionment with the state, its policies, and political leaders, to rephrase this position slightly more forcefully, often went hand in hand with ongoing faith in the Revolution and its promises, a precarious balancing act and expression of political ambivalence that intellectuals abroad missed when they suggested that any position short of open opposition to the state was merely complicit.

Demonstrating this point, some missives that circulated later on in the debate struck a balance between histories of the Cuban cultural field as, on the one hand, structured by a war between dogmatists and critical revolutionaries and, on the other, as a totalitarian regime tightly controlled by the Castros. In one much-discussed email, film critic and documentarist Enrique Colina invoked a defense of criticism from within to denounce the censorship of Cuban films by state television and to demand public accountability from Cuban political leaders. From 1968 well into the 1990s, Colina directed *24 por Segundo* (*Twenty-Four Frames a Second*), a weekly television show in which he presented and analyzed national and world cinema. Insisting that "for many years, ICAIC signified in this country a more open, tolerant, and anti-dogmatic cultural policy," Colina noted that as host of this show he had often found himself at a crossroads between the ICAIC's more liberal practices and the militancy of state television.

He had had to defend the show or suffer its cancellation for a variety of reasons over the years, Colina observed. But by far the most controversial area of programming was that related to national cinema. "Many Cuban films were and remain prohibited from TV because they do not conform to an ideology . . . that rejects the essential principle that keeps a Revolution alive and allows it to endure: dialectics—recognition of contradiction and the need for change." Closing his message with a list of films that had yet to be shown on television, Colina called for these films' immediate airing, the publication of the emails that had been circulating, and the televised appearance of political leaders before journalists who would ask them "difficult questions on those themes whose resolution rests on . . . the practical solution of problems . . . and the recognition of the fundamental right of citizens to demand accountability from their representatives."[53]

Colina's message indicates the ways in which arguments for criticism from within were mobilized in the late socialist era for an increasingly far-reaching challenge to the state in part by defining the Revolution itself in ever-more-flexible ways—as dialectics, change—or, as Colina described it elsewhere in his email, the "Revolution that [intellectuals] have in their heart and in their thinking, what remains valid and recoverable from what has been built." In later chapters of this book, I will expand on how intellectuals mobilized such flexible definitions of the Revolution and an ambivalent attachment to its promises to criticize state policies and Cuba's highest political leaders. For now, however, I want to explore a different dilemma that threaded its way through the email debate, one indicated, for instance, by some key differences between Eliseo Alberto and Haroldo Dilla's comments. Note that whereas Alberto argued that intellectuals had won ever greater "spaces for intellectual freedom" through their growing efforts to be "autonomous and independent," Dilla observed more cynically that the work of intellectuals everywhere is always limited by economic, political, and ethical constraints, even if these took on, he insisted, particularly stringent forms in Cuba. These comments suggest how a growing desire for intellectual autonomy alongside an awareness of the social and institutional dependencies that make cultural production possible fueled the accusations of complicity that flew back and forth between Cuban intellectuals. In the next section of this chapter, I explore this tension by way of stories of censorship and intellectuals' changing relationship to the ICAIC, then turn in the final section to conclusions about the email war.

Autonomy, or That Impossible Object of Desire

Earlier I noted how, in the 1960s, Cuban intellectuals who subscribed to the Revolution attempted to bring into being an alternative public sphere that would preserve social criticism while challenging liberal understandings of autonomy. This position, I explained, was justified in part through arguments that intellectuals' aspirations to act as autonomous critics of state and society under capitalism merely ended in a repressive tolerance that ensured the reproduction of the status quo. Commitment to the Revolution was thus a necessary first condition for social criticism and public debate that would lead to truth and social justice for all. Similar arguments about the constraints placed on cultural production under capitalism could still be detected in the statements of Cuban intellectuals in the twenty-first century. On more than one occasion, my interlocutors responded to my queries about censorship by insisting on the limits placed on expression in any society or by noting that economic pressures—decisions as to whether to fund the production of a film, for example—were as effective a form of control as any political censorship. In a typical statement of this sort, one film director commented, "The artist never escapes censorship. There was censorship in the Renaissance, censorship today. Hollywood film directors become producers to try to escape censorship and even then censorship persists—the censorship of the public." "You can't make another movie or live off of prestige," he noted as he recalled specific instances where American film directors had made films praised by critics that nonetheless lost money at the box office.[54]

Others argued that the motivations for and the effects of censorship were often more complex than simple repression. The ICAIC leadership, one filmmaker observed, sometimes engaged in censorship "because they are highly aware of how the work might be read by people outside of the cultural field and the consequences these reactions might have for the ICAIC. So they'll advise [artists] to edit some scene or other so that there are no obstacles to the film's release." Acknowledging the fact that such edits "always entail a mutilation of the work," this director nonetheless insisted that these strategies worked to ensure the survival of the ICAIC, its artists, and even their capacity to create polemical films. Film editor Nelson Rodríguez adopted a similar position in his recollections of how Alfredo Guevara blocked the release of *Un día de noviembre* (*One Day in November*), which he had worked on with his life partner at that time, director Humberto Solás. "At the time, we were really upset and angry" he told me. "But afterward we realized that Alfredo had managed the situation very intelligently." Completed in 1972, the film was a pessimistic view of Cuban reality in the aftermath of the events that closed the 1960s. Had it been released during this period of increased censorship and institutionalized homophobia, Rodríguez surmised, he and Solás, two high-profile artists whose romantic relationship and gay identities were well known, would have been kicked out of the ICAIC. "He took care of him!" Rodríguez exclaimed. "That was his [Guevara's] way of taking care of him [Solás]."[55]

In this case, the passage of time allowed an intellectual to retrospectively interpret the censorship he had previously resented as a form of care and protection—a cultural functionary's efforts to do the best he could in less than desirable circumstances. By the early twenty-first century, however, such compromises had become increasingly distasteful to many. In one instance, an older filmmaker asked me to redact the name of an official who had censored his script. My interlocutor's justification for his request was that he wanted to preserve the reputation of this official, who, my interlocutor argued, had himself only been acting under pressure by political leaders. But when I recounted this story, withholding all names, to a young filmmaker friend of mine, he responded with outrage, insisting that censorship and those responsible for it must be openly denounced. It would be fair to wonder, as did my young friend, if my interlocutor's request were a form of self-censorship designed to keep him in the good graces of the cultural functionary in question. Yet my interlocutor's explanation of his motive seems equally plausible. The request suggests an acute awareness of the ways in which engaging in censorship for any reason increasingly came to be seen as shameful in later years.

As it turned out, however, young filmmakers had their own embarrassed loyalties. One of the most important forums for the work of young Cuban filmmakers is the Muestra Joven (Youth Exhibit). Hosted annually by the ICAIC, the event provides youth under the age of thirty-five with an opportunity to exhibit their work and to attend workshops with established filmmakers. In spring 2009, a young filmmaker who had trained at the ISA and the EICTV and competed in the Muestra in previous years denounced the event in an interview published in the Miami-based newspaper *El Nuevo Herald*. "What unites [youth] is the desire to put our finger on what's important and to address themes that have been silenced in official media," the *Nuevo Herald* quoted the young filmmaker as saying. "But political and cultural functionaries have worked to ensure that this movement doesn't gain momentum." "The Muestra is nothing but a desperate attempt to control film production when this was escaping their control and to impede the emergence of a true movement of independent artists," he concluded (Cancio Isla 2009).

Far from simply presenting youth with the opportunity to show their work and engage with other artists, in this statement the Muestra provided another example of repressive tolerance, an attempt to curtail the work of emerging filmmakers by encouraging them to comply with the norms of an official institution. Events at the time gave some validity to the young filmmaker's argument. Just a year previously, the ICAIC had recruited five young filmmakers whose short films had earned recognition for their critical treatment of taboo social themes to produce an omnibus documentary about Cuban literacy programs throughout Latin America, *La dimensión de las palabras* (*The Magnitude of Words*, 2008). Many of those who participated in the making of this documentary insisted that they had attempted to go beyond the propagandistic depictions of such programs common to state television. But even they acknowledged that the project may well have been intended to win youth over to more positive representations of the Revolution, in part by providing them with a rare opportunity to travel and work abroad.[56]

Still, dismissals of the Muestra and those who worked there did not sit well with many Cubans on the island. "To stay in the United States, you have to speak ill of Cuba in the manipulative media of Miami and someone with his education shouldn't have allowed himself to fall into that trap," commented one teacher at the EICTV. "Did he get paid to give that interview?" asked a friend of mine when I told him the story, before inquiring whether what the young filmmaker had said about the Muestra was true. Another young director argued that, in giving the interview, the filmmaker had proven himself as opportunistic as the artists who went from directing critical documentaries to participating in *La dimensión de las palabras*. It did not matter if the ICAIC hoped to use the Muestra to "control" youth, he argued; what mattered was that the exhibit was one of the few places where their work was shown. Those who worked at the Muestra often fought to screen controversial works, he added; interviews such as this one would only make their job more difficult.

When arguments for criticism from within were first made in the 1960s, intellectuals asserted their difference from the "dogmatic bureaucrats" they argued were trying to reduce artistic work to propaganda, while nonetheless accepting the limit placed on criticism by Fidel Castro. In the disillusioned post-Soviet period, by contrast, artists increasingly attempt to distance themselves from censorship of any sort. Endeavoring to assert their autonomy from the state, intellectuals of all generations, on or off the island, present themselves as heroic intellectuals speaking truth to power. Yet as the stories recounted above indicate, in a context where the state—and exiles—court intellectuals not only with trips abroad and material resources but also by providing them with a forum, it is often difficult to distinguish freedom from complicity, criticism from repression. This gives new meaning to intellectuals' insistence throughout the email war on narratives that placed blame for censorship on either the Castros or on figureheads—Pavón, Quesada, Serguera—whose political clout lay long behind them. Both tactics allowed intellectuals to call out the complicity of others while asserting their own autonomy. Such finger pointing reveals as much as it conceals intellectuals' anxieties about their own inevitable ties to power, the ways in which state institutions or exile politics enable them to voice criticism and engage in public debate if only as a means of cooptation.

As the flow of emails slowed, participants in the debate were left with mixed feelings. Intellectuals attributed a number of "wins" in a battle for greater freedom of expression to the email war: the release on state television of several of the ICAIC films listed by Enrique Colina as having previously been censored from that medium; Raúl Castro's organization of forums where the government heard people's complaints in the summer of 2007; and the growing movement of Cuban bloggers.[57] Subsequent acts of censorship have been met both with email exchanges and, as access to the internet has improved over the years, blog posts and collective letters posted to social media. In many cases, these later instances cite the email war as an important precedent, linking these events together into an ever-more-insistent demand for an open and inclusive public sphere, made possible in part through the growing availability of digital technologies.[58] But the paranoia that wove through the email war begs the question of whether it would ever be possible to create a public sphere that would feel open and transparent to all Cubans. Given both the long-standing political fault lines and the new strategies of power that characterize the Cuban cultural and political fields, every intervention can always potentially be dismissed as complicit with state power, exile politics, or, as we will see in the next chapter, the global market.

These paranoid interpretations are, of course, often reasonable and productive. By scanning even interventions denouncing censorship for signs of complicity, intellectuals draw attention to the changing strategies of cultural functionaries and political leaders while insisting on the right of citizens to be heard. But the repetitive recourse to totalizing accounts of Cuban politics and the denunciation of predetermined enemies can also close down opportunities for the production of new political alternatives and meanings. Faced with the often complicated and messy motivations, loyalties, and dependencies that characterize Cuban cultural production, reducing the cultural field to a war between dogmatists and "true" revolutionaries or to a totalitarian regime governed by the Castros can provide a treacherous relief. While the paranoid search for dogmatist functionaries or the workings of a totalitarian apparatus transforms every text and action into a potential sign of hidden political conspiracy, it also provides the certainty of answers: Guevara defended his artists while Pavón executed repressive orders with excessive relish and disastrous consequences; Pavón was a puppet and the Castros were the puppet masters. These are poor comforts for the many Cubans who would like to dismantle the enduring standoff between revolutionaries and dissidents—those who continue to believe that the Revolution contains the seeds for a society that would value social justice and collective welfare; and those who denounce the current political regime in the hopes of building a more inclusive democracy.

CHAPTER TWO

PARANOID READINGS
AND AMBIVALENT ALLEGORIES

Monte Rouge

Let us begin with a film: as Nicanor prepares coffee, taking a lingering whiff of the brew, he hears a knock at the door. He looks reluctantly at his steaming cup. When he answers, two serious-looking men introduce themselves as Rodríguez and Segura and explain that they are there to install the microphones. In response to the many complaints they received, the government is launching a new plan, Rodríguez elaborates. Rather than spy on people in secret, from now on they will bug the apartments of their "clients" openly, thereby making their work more "participatory." When an astonished Nicanor asks why he, of all people, has been chosen for this pilot program, Rodríguez explains that his complaints about the government are more "creative" than the average. "Your analyses of our migration policies have really been very insightful," notes the secret agent. "In reality, you have helped us a lot." Besides, he adds, a colleague of theirs took the only car and Nicanor's place was in walking distance. Adding to this tale of material woes, the agents soon determine that the only room in the house in which their outdated equipment will work is the bathroom. As Nicanor contemplates with consternation the agents' demand that he accommodate his criticism to this awkward situation, Rodríguez specifies further parameters: "The other day you spent fifteen minutes explaining to that musician friend of yours why, in spite of everything, you prefer to live here." Nicanor nods eagerly, perhaps looking for a reprieve as reward for his nationalism. This hope is quickly disappointed. "The good things about the system don't interest us," Rodríguez observes. "Stick to yours."

These are scenes from Eduardo del Llano's *Monte Rouge*, a fifteen-minute independent short that in 2005 spread from flash drive to flash drive in Cuba and went viral over the internet abroad, sweeping its creators in controversy. In the months following the release of the short, Luis Alberto García, who played Nicanor, and Néstor Jíménez, who performed the role of Rodríguez, were blocked from working as actors in state television. Ironically, Luis Alberto García told me, this ban began just after he had informed a CNN reporter with some pride that he had suffered no consequences for his participation in the short.[1] Exaggerating this actual censorship, rumors circulated that del Llano and the rest of his team had been thrown in jail or worse. And in the midst of the controversy, *La Jiribilla*, an online Cuban state cultural magazine, published an interview in which del Llano insisted, "It would never occur to me to attack the Revolution" and "everyone knows how important the work of the Cuban state security has been" (Acosta 2005).

Some Cuban exiles dismissed the interview as made under duress, arguing that it was designed to protect the careers of those involved in the short's production while allowing *Monte Rouge*'s subversive message to speak for itself. "It's a film that is totally critical of repression," declared Miami-based Cuban film critic Alejandro Ríos. "If, out of fear, the filmmakers have to resort to certain declarations to protect themselves, so be it" (qtd. in Leyva Martínez 2005). Others were less convinced. On the one hand, rumors circulated in Miami that the short was a deliberate attempt to improve the state's international image by making it seem as though it tolerated dissent (Prieto 2005). On the other hand, a young island-based sound engineer told me that filmmakers like del Llano and others worked in anticipation of being censored. "It's as if for them the fact that the film was censored means that it was good, that it was very critical," he observed.[2]

The film itself, however, can also be read as providing more ambivalent political commentaries than those unearthed by some of its spectators. Rather than serving as a veiled attacked on an all-seeing and all-controlling state apparatus, the material obstacles the agents face might just as easily be interpreted as a joke that the government is as hard pressed to make ends meet as its citizens. Rodríguez's praise for Nicanor's "creative" criticism, meanwhile, transforms surveillance into a perverse form of democracy, an exaggerated version of repressive tolerance in which the state strives to listen in on citizens' complaints and even takes them into account, if only to prevent more drastic forms of dissatisfaction. Finally, Rodríguez's injunction to

Nicanor to "stick to yours" suggests a comic send-up of what many Cuban artists feel is the constant reduction of their art and political stances to binary political positions for or against the Cuban Revolution.

This latter frustration is one in which, in the aftermath of the controversy stirred up by the short, del Llano shared. "I made this film to criticize things that bug me in this society, but from within this society and not to destroy this society," he told me. "People on both sides tend to go to extremes and I don't like the extremes." Not only did the polarized reception of the film work against his efforts to express a more ambivalent take on life in Cuba, del Llano noted, but they also reduced *Monte Rouge* to politics. "I tried to make a work of art, not a political pamphlet," he complained as he recounted how journalists who interviewed him asked him not about the film but about what he thought would happen after Fidel Castro died. "It might be good art or bad art, but it's art."[3]

Debates such as these were a repeat occurrence throughout my fieldwork with Cuban filmmakers. While spectators argued about whether films harbored secret messages against the socialist state, veiled complicities with political leaders, or served as publicity stunts, filmmakers complained that these readings ignored the nuances of their depictions of Cuba and reduced their art to propaganda. In the pages that follow, I unpack the history and consequences of such paranoid readings through a discussion of key films and developments in revolutionary Cuban cinema. I begin by revisiting one of Cuba's most iconic films, Tomás Gutiérrez Alea's *Memorias del subdesarrollo* (*Memories of Underdevelopment*, 1968), drawing on new ethnographic information about its production. I then turn my attention to the reception of Alea's final films—*Fresa y chocolate* (*Strawberry and Chocolate*, 1993) and *Guantanamera* (1995), both codirected with Juan Carlos Tabío—as well as digital and youth filmmaking. I close with a reading of Cuban filmmaker Laimir Fano's graduating short from the EICTV, *Oda a la piña* (*Ode to the Pineapple*, 2008), analyzing this film's critical take on allegory in Cuban cinema.

By telling this history, I show how allegory, paranoia, and ambivalence shaped the production and reception of Cuban cinema from the earliest years of the Revolution on, and how these dynamics have become increasingly fraught in the post-Soviet era. In the 1960s, I argue, Cuban filmmakers adopted what I term modernist allegories both in an effort to construct new socialist citizens who could think for themselves and as a means of communicating controversial messages between the lines. When such messages were picked up by high-profile spectators steeped in Cold War dichotomies, artists often found themselves struggling against politically polarized interpretations to defend their work as criticism from within, loyal to the Revolution but critical of its failings. As the reception of *Monte Rouge* reveals, such paranoid readings only became more complex in the post-Soviet era. The state's adoption of repressive tolerance, the growing influence of the global market, and, as of the early twenty-first century, the rise of digital technologies enabled filmmakers to articulate more open criticisms of the state and its policies than ever before, but they also multiplied the reasons for which such works could be deemed suspect. Filmmakers thus found themselves in a bind, facing accusations of complicity whether their films were viewed as daringly critical or as not critical enough, as supporting the state by making it seem "as if" it tolerated debate, or as playing to the market by offering images of socialism on the decline. These dynamics make clear how allegory in Cuba, as in other contexts, can both enable and constrain public debate, at once bringing into view issues that might not otherwise be articulated in public and fostering a search for hidden meanings in artworks that risks reducing them to well-worn political interpretations.

A New Aesthetics for a New Man

If allegory, ambivalence, and political paranoia have long played dominant roles in the production and reception of Cuban cinema, this is due in no small part to the international context that shaped the early years of the Cuban Revolution. As my reference to the debates over form and socialist realism in the previous chapter suggests, with the triumph against Fulgencio Batista in 1959 and Fidel Castro's official declaration of the socialist nature of the Revolution in 1961, Cuban artists went from immersion in Western avant-garde movements to questioning the role of art under socialism just as canonical approaches to this issue were thrown into turmoil in Eastern Europe. Nikita Khrushchev's denunciation of Stalin's "cult of personality" in his 1956 speech to the Soviet Union's Twentieth Party Congress inspired artists in Eastern Europe to rebel against the aesthetic values of the Stalinist era.[4] Leftist artists and intellectuals in Western Europe and North America, meanwhile, trained their hopes for a nontotalitarian socialism on Cuba and traveled to the island to take part in debates over aesthetics and politics that raged throughout the 1960s.[5] Inspired by these developments, as well as the explosion of "new cinemas" around the world, Cuban filmmakers denounced socialist realism for infantilizing spectators and idealizing reality, arguing instead for a critical cinema that would represent society in all its complexity, engage in formal experimentation, and foster public debate.

One of the debates that best exemplifies Cuban filmmakers' resistance to socialist realism was sparked by a 1963 newspaper editorial by Blas Roca, who had previously been the leader of the prerevolutionary Partido Socialista Popular (PSP, Popular Socialist Party) and who went on to become an important functionary in the revolutionary government.[6] After the chilling of relations between the United States and Cuba in 1961, the ICAIC filled the newly nationalized movie theaters with films donated from Eastern Europe and old movies from its archives. While many spectators found the Soviet bloc films unconscionably boring, others clearly preferred their straightforward moral principles. When the film institute was finally able to import movies in 1963, Roca wrote an editorial denouncing the exhibition of Federico Fellini's *La dolce vita* (*The Sweet Life*, Italy, 1960), Pier Paolo Pasolini's *Accatone* (Italy, 1961), Luis Buñuel's *El angel exterminador* (*The Exterminating Angel*, Mexico, 1962), and Lautaro Murúa's *Alias Gardelito* (*Alias Big Shot*, Argentina, 1961).

Admitting that he himself had not seen these films, Roca cited the objections of a well-known radio personality and various workers who argued that the films "show[ed] the corruption or immorality of some countries or social classes without resolving anything." Thanks to its realistic images and its mass spectatorship, asserted the functionary, cinema enjoyed a more immediate and direct influence on spectators than the other arts: "The image in movement, the dialogue, the sensation of reality that the screen is capable of presenting penetrates the spectator easily, impresses him, provokes his reactions, awakens his feelings, moves his reason." Revolutionaries, argued Roca, must therefore take care to exercise the seductive power of cinema in the service of socialism by showing films that either directly stimulated "the desire to work, the elevated ideal, valiant heroism, fraternity, *compañerismo*, self-sacrifice," or served as light entertainment that "aided in rest, provided new energy for work, and new strength for action" (Roca [1963] 2006, 145–46, 148).

The ICAIC filmmakers were not immune to concerns that the cinema might exercise a dangerous sway over the masses. As part of a continent-wide resistance during the 1960s and 1970s to efforts by US government agencies and private corporations to influence Latin Americans through media, Cuban film critics, filmmakers, and cultural functionaries denounced the distorting ideological effects of Hollywood, the old commercial Latin American cinemas, and other popular media.[7] In a 1969 article, for instance, Alfredo Guevara argued that the United States had colonized the minds of Latin American spectators and blocked the development of these nations' "intellectual autonomy" not only by taking over major media industries but also through the "invasion of comics, radionovelas, and tele-novelas" whose "themes" and "simplifying, facile, [and] schematic language have served through many years to condition not only the taste but also the reader, radio-listener, and spectator's capacity for comprehension" ([1969] 1998, 41–42).

At the same time, Guevara ([1963] 2006) resisted Roca's solution for harnessing the affective power of cinematic images. "We know what this is about, and it's not the first time that we've heard this 'siren song,'" objected the ICAIC director in an editorial, decrying Roca's comments as a demand for "the positive hero, the need for a happy end, constructive morality, the elaboration of archetypes, so-called socialist realism." The trouble with socialist realism, elaborated Guevara, was that it transformed art into pro-paganda—an "*arte-opio*" (opium-art), as he put it. By substituting "typical supermen" with equally "abstract archetypes," socialist realism "reduce[d] the public into a mass of 'babies' to whom maternal nurses administer[ed] the perfectly prepared and sterilized 'ideological baby food'" (171–73).[8] For Guevara and for the ICAIC filmmakers, the imposition of socialist realism would only ensure that the masses remained in the stupefied and intellectually dependent state to which US cultural imperialism had re-duced them.[9]

The goal of the truly revolutionary intellectual and artist, by contrast, should be to produce "not a domesticated and satisfied doll but rather that new man liberated at last from his alienation," as Ambrosio Fornet put it in a 1968 speech ([1968] 1980, 318–19). This objective in turn required an art that revealed reality in all its complexity, engaged in formal experimen-tation, and provoked critical reflection among spectators. Since "even so-cialist society" was neither "a paradise nor a limbo" but included "moral and psychological deterioration," artists must be allowed to depict not only the triumphs of the Revolution but also its contradictions, insisted Alfredo Guevara ([1963] 2006, 171). Representing a complex reality in turn required a constant search for new aesthetic forms: "The truly revolutionary artist is the artist who, by renewing the means of expression, delivers new elements of reality" (Guevara [1963] 1998, 32). A handful of ICAIC directors involved in the debate with Roca gave an even more directly activist spin to this vi-sion of an experimental and realist cinema. "As an art, cinema cannot be reduced to mere entertainment or a didactic pharmacopeia," they argued. "We believe that a work of art is valid insofar as it stimulates the specta-tor's consciousness and makes him see the necessity of finding solutions, of changing reality, of transforming the world" (Trejo, Canel, and Colina [1963] 2006, 160).

It was only by engaging in formal experimentation and representing the complexities and contradictions of everyday life, in other words, that art could stimulate the reflexive activism needed for the Revolution. If the link between these points was left largely implicit in these early debates, one truth emerged as indisputable for the ICAIC filmmakers: revolutionary cinema would be art, not politics. In a 1962 speech, Guevara acknowledged the importance of creating genres that would fulfill the Revolution's immediate pedagogic needs but insisted that artistic documentaries and feature films must be protected from "all didactic intentions." He elaborated: "Art educates, but we can never accept that art has education as its end goal. . . . We sincerely believe that if we demand of the artist or artistic work a 'revolutionary' message of the sort that a political speech or a philosophical or social essay could contain, we will only achieve one objective: the spiritual assassination of the creator and the asphyxiation of art" ([1962] 1998, 47).[10]

Like the Third Cinema and political modernist filmmakers with whom they were in conversation, Guevara and the ICAIC filmmakers took for granted that art had a role to play in the construction of new revolutionary subjectivities and the new society. But while their international colleagues worked to disrupt capitalist forms of entertainment, in the wake of Stalinism, Cuban artists argued that a truly revolutionary art, one that would act as the foundation for a liberatory rather than a totalitarian socialism, must also avoid being subsumed by what they viewed as the transparent referentiality of politics. As art and not politics, the aesthetic revolution would be indirect—or to an extent.

Directed Indirection and Modernist Allegories

All sides of the debates that raged throughout the 1960s, at least among artists committed to the Revolution, were in agreement that art for art's sake had no place in the new society. The question was how to put the aesthetics that Cuban filmmakers and their allies valued—an aesthetics of indirection—to work in the direction of producing the new society. Modernist allegories provided one solution. As Angus Fletcher ([1964] 2012, 306–16) observes, artists can draw on a variety of techniques to introduce more or less indeterminacy in allegorical works. Cuban filmmakers strove to strike a balance between didacticism and indeterminacy by rendering their messages through modernist techniques.[11] The assumption at work here was that, by grappling with modernist aesthetic forms and open endings, spectators would independently work out the socialist values and meanings posted by Cuban films. Modernist allegories would train spectators to become new men and women who thought for themselves, guaranteeing a socialism that preserved individual freedom instead of reducing citizens to a mass of "babies" or "dolls" who took orders from on high.

Attempts to produce critical revolutionary subjects through modernist aesthetic techniques can be seen at work in a number of films from the 1960s. The film most frequently cited as an example of allegory in early revolutionary Cuban cinema, Humberto Solás's 1968 *Lucía*, recounts three Cuban revolutions in three vignettes: the first tells the story of an upper-class woman during Cuba's final war for independence from Spain; the second imagines a middle-class woman's involvement in the fight to overthrow President Gerardo Machado during the 1930s; and the third depicts amateur actress Adela Legrá as a *mulata* (mixed-race) *campesina* (peasant) who, in rural Cuba in the 1960s, learns to read and joins a collective work brigade against her husband's wishes. Each story is presented in a different aesthetic style and centers on a female protagonist named Lucía.[12]

Lucía's merging of gender, racial, and national narratives was further consolidated by the release of the film in 1968, which marked the one-hundredth anniversary of the nation's first war against Spain. By abstracting the characters from their specific historical contexts and linking them together through their shared name, *Lucía* both draws attention to the changing social status of women in Cuban history and, in keeping with the revolutionary government's own self-mythologization, uses these stories to represent the 1959 Revolution as the fulfillment of Cuba's century-long struggle for independence. Importantly, however, the film's open ending tempers this triumphant message, albeit in ways also in keeping with official revolutionary ideology. The film closes with the third Lucía fighting with her *machista* husband on a beach while a young girl looks on laughing in an open ending meant to remind spectators that the struggle over machismo is ongoing and to invite them to fight for a future in which this conflict too might be resolved.[13]

It is a different film from 1968, however, that best exemplifies the aesthetic ideology of directed indirection. While not as well received at the time of its release as *Lucía*, Tomás Gutiérrez Alea's *Memorias del subdesarrollo* (*Memories of Underdevelopment*, 1968) has since become one of Cuba's most renowned films and is frequently cited by Cuban filmmakers as a model for contemporary critical cinema. *Memorias del subdesarrollo* tells the story of Sergio, a bourgeois intellectual who stays behind in Cuba when his wife and family leave the country at the onset of the Revolution. Early on in the film, Sergio meets Elena, an attractive lower-class girl of seventeen. When she expresses her desire to become a film actress, he arranges for an audition with his "director friend," a character played by Alea himself, then takes her to his apartment, where he offers her his ex-wife's clothes and seduces her aggressively. Soon after this encounter, Elena returns to Sergio's apartment happily singing love songs, a stark contrast to her previous vacillations between accepting and refusing his advances and her worries about what to tell her mother.

At this point, the film cuts to a series of freeze-frames of Elena and documentary-style shots of Cuban women, accompanied by Sergio's voice-over:

> One of the things that most disturbs me about people is their inability to sustain a feeling, one idea, without getting distracted. Elena proved to be totally inconsistent. It's pure inconsistency, as Ortega would say. She doesn't connect things. This is one of the signs of underdevelopment: the inability to connect things, to accumulate experience, and develop oneself. It is difficult to produce a woman shaped by sentiments and culture here. It's an indulgent environment. Cubans waste all their talent adapting themselves to the moment. People aren't consistent. And they always need someone to think for them.

Sergio's allusion here to José Ortega y Gasset is significant. In the 1939 essay to which Sergio refers, the Spanish philosopher argued that European societies on the brink of World War II had regressed to an animal-like existence. Individuals had lost the properly human quality of autonomous reflection, succumbing instead to the influence of demagogues and the world around them.[14] Reinforced by this intertextual allusion, at first glance the sequence thus appears simply to express Sergio's growing skepticism of his lover and the revolutionary masses. Like all Cubans, he argues, Elena is incapable of integrating her experiences and developing knowledge.

To stop at this reading, however, would be to privilege narrative over film form. In his 1982 theoretical treatise, *Dialéctica del espectador* (*Dialectics of the Spectator*), Alea devised a theory of cinema that also served as a retrospective theorization of *Memorias del subdesarrollo*. As the ICAIC filmmakers had done in previous debates, Alea dismissed both capitalist forms of entertainment and Soviet socialist realism. Hollywood's "happy end" was an "effective ideological weapon," he observed; the typical "light comedy or melodrama" worked by introducing conflicts that threatened "society's established values" only to restore the status quo, leaving spectators with the "feeling that everything is very good and it isn't necessary to change a thing." Efforts to adapt such tactics to the socialist cause by "replacing Tarzan with a revolutionary hero" would only instill a similar conformism.

Yet he also dismissed the "happenings" of the 1960s, arguing that while these avant-garde tactics elicited the active involvement of spectators, such effects ultimately remained contained "within spectacles" that were only entertaining "for those who can give themselves the luxury of looking at things from above" without "changing anything." While a truly revolutionary work of art must be "open," he concluded, it must also avoid being "ambiguous, inconsistent, eclectic, or arbitrary." The revolutionary work of art should "launch [the spectator] along the path of truth" and serve as a "guide for action" by "signal[ing] to the spectator the route that he must take in order to discover for himself a higher level of understanding" (1982, 30–33).

Alea found inspiration for such work in the aesthetic theories and practices of German playwright Bertolt Brecht and Soviet filmmaker Sergei Eisenstein. Brecht (1977, 82) ultimately advocated for the adoption of the aesthetic tactics best suited to specific contexts. However, he is best known for his theorization of techniques such as the "separation of elements," in which music works as a commentary on action, title cards draw out the "social points" of scenes, and the parts of a play relate to one another as separate "play[s] within the play," such that the "knots" between scenes are clearly evident. For Brecht, such strategies were meant to disrupt spectators' absorption into plot and character, encourage them to adopt a critical stance on the events depicted onstage and, ideally, prompt them to take up revolutionary action in their own milieus (1977, 82–85; [1930] 1992, 37–41; [1949] 1992, 201). In *Dialéctica del espectador* (1982), Alea drew on Eisenstein's work with montage to argue that cinema's capacity to produce new juxtapositions between images and sounds provided a film-specific means of achieving such Brechtian distantiation effects. He also, however, synthesized Eisenstein and Brecht's theories, arguing that moving back and forth between affective or bodily aesthetics and appeals to spectators' reason might itself have revolutionary potential (1982, 38–39).

Viewed in light of Alea's arguments, the sequence from *Memorias del subdesarrollo* described above can be read as a metatextual moment designed to teach the spectator how to read the film. As Alea observes in a brief cameo as Sergio's director friend in the film, *Memorias del subdesarrollo* is a "collage," combining fiction, documentary, found footage, and freeze-frames into six titled segments. To get at its meaning, spectators must succeed at synthesizing events where Elena and, it turns out, Sergio himself have failed, in this case by grappling with the film's form and connecting its segments to one another. At different points in the film, Sergio contemplates the foreign luxuries with which he showered his ex-wife; drags Elena through an art gallery and Hemingway's house in an attempt to "culture" her; dwells on the relationship between Hemingway and his Afro-Cuban servant, René Villarreal, whom, he muses, Hemingway attempted to "mold to his necessities" in a typical relationship between "el gran señor y el criado fiel" (master and faithful servant); and waxes nostalgic about the blonde, German lover of his youth.

Eventually, he rejects Elena, only to be confronted by the girl's family, who demand first that he marry her and then take him to court on charges of rape. Elena's family's concern for her virginity emphasizes their attachment to a vision of femininity that, the film suggests, stands in stark contrast to the values of the new society. A shot that follows soon after the court trial conveys this point, showing two young women with rifles strapped to their shoulders lingering in front of a shop window filled with wedding dresses. But when we read across the film's different scenes, Sergio appears even more inconsistent and underdeveloped than Elena. The aggressiveness of Sergio and Elena's sexual encounter suggests rape, regardless of the court outcome. His efforts to remake the Cuban women in his life in the image of his lost German lover, meanwhile, establish an analogy between Hemingway and Sergio that reveals the latter's alienation: unable to integrate himself into the European world to which he aspires, Sergio is also incapable of relating to the new revolutionary society in which he is immersed.[15] By the end of the film, Sergio is left alone and isolated, anxiously pacing his well-appointed apartment while the nation prepares for invasion during the Cuban missile crisis.

At least according to the filmmakers, reading the film in this way would train spectators to be critical revolutionary subjects, capable of thinking for themselves in the direction suggested by the film. In the coda to *Dialéctica del espectador*, Alea noted that by repeating whole sequences while changing key elements, the film established a dialectical movement between Sergio's "subjective" and the filmmakers' "objective" vision of reality. Through such techniques and the overall montage structure of the film, spectators who at first identified with Sergio, the filmmaker theorized, would gradually distance themselves from the character, until they finally left the theater ready to do battle with their own lingering bourgeois values (1982, 71).

The trouble with this aesthetic ideology of directed indirection, of course, is that spectators often have ideas of their own. Like all genres and aesthetic modes, allegory is not immanent to textual form but is a set of historically and culturally specific expectations according to which authors compose texts and audiences receive them. While Cuban filmmakers counted on spectators' ability to read between the lines, the resulting allegorical interpretations therefore sometimes came into conflict with their aesthetic and political goals. This was especially likely when audiences engaged with complex films such as *Memorias del subdesarrollo*, which aimed to produce critical but committed spectators not only through modernist aesthetic techniques but also through the inclusion of illicit meanings as "open secrets," accessible to "sophisticated" spectators but also easy to deny. Alea's decades-long efforts to shape interpretations of his film demonstrate the difficulties that these allegorical strategies can pose for artists.

Shortly after Sergio concludes that Cubans "always need someone to think for them," the film cuts suggestively to a billboard illustrated with the words *Playa Girón* and Fidel Castro's face, seen fleetingly through the window of the character's car as he drives his bourgeois friend Pablo to the airport (figure 2.1). Years after I first wondered about the political significance of this moment, the film's editor, Nelson Rodríguez, told me a story that transformed this cut into the scene's central meaning. In place of the sequence that appears in the finished film, he recounted, he and Alea (affectionately known in the Cuban film world as Titón) had originally mounted a reel that intercut still photos of Fidel Castro delivering a speech with shots of the gathered masses. They then overlaid the whole with an African song in which a choir repeats the lines sung by a soloist. Rodríguez explained:

> Mario García Joya . . . was a very good still photographer and a good friend of Titón's. In one of those demonstrations with Fidel in the Plaza de la Revolución that were hours and hours long and where there were thousands and thousands of people and Fidel talking, Mayito had taken a number of photos of Fidel, close-ups of Fidel at the podium with the microphone and making his usual gestures. He climbed up the tower, the monument [of José Martí], and filmed the masses from up there.
>
> And so Titón came along and chose some photos of Fidel and some of the masses. He sent the photos to be filmed in cinema and added an African tribal song as soundtrack. The soloist would sing a verse and then the

chorus would repeat it. And so it was Fidel as the soloist and the masses as the chorus. We edited the sequence and laughed a lot and had a lot of fun and when we finished it and we saw it we said, this isn't going to fly. [Titón explained], "No, no, I just wanted to see it. I knew that it would be really strong." With the billboard on the highway you already know, you can see the intention. [The choral version of the sequence] filled out something that was already said and reinforced it in a way that was complicated. And so Titón picked up his reel and took it home with him.[16]

Rodríguez's story illustrates both the playful ways in which Cuban filmmakers sometimes engaged the rules of censorship and the anxiety that imbued perceptions of the revolutionary masses even among the most committed of Cuban intellectuals. For the editor, Sergio's contemplation of the consequences of underdevelopment was a secret message, a wink that the savvy spectator could decipher to get the joke that Cubans were in danger of letting Fidel Castro "do their thinking for them." The filmmakers' association of intellectual vulnerability with a generic Africa, meanwhile, bespeaks a concern about the effects of the crowd on individual capacities for reason, a concern that was also marked by racism.[17]

In spite of the sequence's allegorical criticism of Fidel Castro and the Cuban masses, however, from Rodríguez's perspective, it only confirmed Alea's status as a critic from within the Revolution.[18] While a number of intellectuals with whom I spoke detected traces of Alea's own life experience and bourgeois class background in the fictional Sergio, the editor insisted on their difference. If Sergio was a stand-in for any of the artists involved in the project, it was Edmundo Pérez Desnoes, the writer on whose novel the film was based, he contended. Like Sergio, argued Rodríguez, Desnoes never fully comprehended the Revolution and eventually ended up migrating to the United States. Alea, by contrast, "integrated himself into the process. He always had a critical attitude, but he integrated himself." "He was always very courageous and protested. Every time things weren't clear for him he spoke up," Rodríguez concluded.[19] When the film was released some years after its completion in the United States, several American film critics, including, notably, Julianne Burton (1977), concurred with this assessment of the essentially prorevolutionary if critical stance of the film and its director, insisting on the importance of separating the perspective of the film and its creators from that of its protagonist (see also Amaya 2010, 118–22).

Some spectators on the other side of the Cold War, however, saw the sequence in a different light. American film critic Andrew Sarris asserted that

Figure 2.1 The billboard featuring Fidel Castro as seen through the window of Sergio's car in Tomás Gutiérrez Alea's *Memorias del subdesarrollo* (1968).

the National Society of Film Critics had awarded *Memorias del subdesarrollo* a $2,000 prize because the judges were impressed by its "very personal and very courageous confrontation of the artist's doubts and ambivalences regarding the Cuban Revolution," then went on to imply that Alea had been censored for this work by the Cuban state. He hoped that "the award might help the development of Gutiérrez Alea's career, as he hasn't, to our knowledge, made another film in five years" (qtd. in Gutiérrez Alea 1982, 61–62). This appraisal took on even more pointed political connotations given that it was made in part as an objection to the US government's decision to deny Alea a visa to the United States so that he could receive the prize in person. By suggesting that *Memorias del subdesarrollo* and Alea were at odds with the Revolution, Sarris recovered the director and his work for American Cold War politics.

British film critic Don Allen made an even stronger claim for the antirevolutionary politics of *Memorias del subdesarrollo* and its director. "It seems as improbable that Tomás Gutiérrez Alea's *Memories of Underdevelopment* . . .

should have been approved for export by the Cuban authorities as that Buñuel should have made *Viridiana* under Franco's nose," wrote Allen in his 1969 review of the film published in *Sight and Sound*. "Both films in their different ways undermine, or significantly question, the cultural values of the country that sanctioned them." Sergio's dilemma, argued the critic by way of explanation of this initial claim, is that he is caught between two equally unviable alternatives—his "bourgeois formation" and "the over-facile, ready-made alternative—unquestioning acceptance of the Castro Revolution." If this description of the two unviable extremes presented by the film resonates with Alea's own understanding of his work, the remainder of Allen's analysis takes the film to different political ends. Invoking Edmundo Desnoes's explanation of the character's dilemma—that he failed to recognize the need to become involved in the construction of the Revolution—Allen noted that "Alea's direction" nonetheless "evokes sympathy for Sergio's plight." The film critic based this argument through reference to the film's "close-ups of sad faces (joyless, post-revolutionary Cuba!)" and, notably, to the billboard sequence: "Sergio's contention that people always need someone to think for them is given point by a close-up of a poster of Castro and Play Girón" (Allen 1969, 212–13). Rather than serving as evidence for Alea's status as a valiant critic from within, as Rodríguez would have it, for Allen, the billboard sequence was an attempt to smuggle an attack on the validity of the Revolution itself past the watchful eyes of censors.

Faced with such responses, Alea worked to render transparent the revolutionary meanings spectators were supposed to have discovered for themselves. He insisted on the film's revolutionary politics in articles and interviews that he began publishing even before the film's release, suggesting, as Hector Amaya argues (2010, 110–11), that he himself was anxious about how the film might be interpreted. His interventions both prior to and following the release of the film also clearly indicate efforts to manage its reception. In the coda to *Dialéctica del espectador*, for instance, Alea argued that reviewers such as Andrew Sarris and Don Allen suffered from an excessive identification with Sergio prompted by their own political and class backgrounds (1982, 62–63). This was, he acknowledged, a manipulation to which the form of the film lent itself: "We believe that all work made within the Revolution, especially in the difficult phase of the construction of socialism in which we are presently living, can be used to an extent by the enemy if it takes a critical look at reality. Especially if it is a work like this one where the problems depicted are not resolved with the final image that appears on the screen but rather extend themselves beyond the theater, a work where the eventual conclusion of the problematic rests in the consciousness of the spectator who is invited to think" (71). The strength of *Memorias del subdesarrollo*, allowed Alea—the fact that it did not dictate conclusions but prompted spectators to engage in critical reflection—was also its vulnerability.[20]

As the reception of *Memorias del subdesarrollo* reveals, allegory has historically served a number of purposes in Cuban filmmaking. For artists who rejected socialist realism as propaganda, directed indirection guaranteed the aesthetic and political value of their work while also enabling them to articulate illicit criticisms between the lines. Yet such tactics could also leave filmmakers vulnerable to interpretations that conflicted with their political allegiances and threatened their social standing. When readings that insisted on the counterrevolutionary meaning of Cuban films or other works took on a high profile in the hands of critics, functionaries, and political leaders, they could have grave repercussions for the careers of both artworks and artists. It is here that allegory reveals its third function. As Alea's defense of *Memorias del subdesarrollo* indicates, the invocation of hyperallegorical spectators provided filmmakers with an alibi. Pointing to polysemy and the contextualized nature of interpretation, Cuban artists shifted responsibility for the text's political meanings onto audiences. Such tactics can justifiably elicit suspicion that authors are denying their "true" intentions to protect their careers while counting on films to communicate meanings that they cannot express openly. Indeed, while Alea responded at length to Andrew Sarris's and Don Allen's comments about *Memorias del subdesarrollo* in the coda to *Dialéctica del espectador*, he avoided any reference to the billboard sequence, an omission that can only be read as significant.

Still, Rodríguez's insistence that the sequence demonstrated Alea's critical adherence to the Revolution suggests that something gets lost if we equate allegory with a mask designed to conceal even as it communicates counterrevolutionary meanings. Anne-Lise François contends that open secrets may exceed a hermeneutics of suspicion, functioning not as an invitation to expose a hidden truth but as a "license to take the revealed for granted" (2008, xvi). Something like this nonemphatic revelation can be seen in Rodríguez's recollections of the sequence's creation as a pleasurable diversion indulged in by two artists who essentially adhered to the Revolution but protested its instantiations. As long as debates about secret messages in films and what directors "really meant" remained the stuff of rumor, laughing and playing with images of Fidel Castro and seeking out allegorical criticisms of the state were just part of what it meant to be a knowing socialist citizen: the type of person who was ready to make fun of the system's failures but was also eager to improve socialism or, at the very least, was not very much against it.

Criticism as Complicity:
Coproductions and the Special Period

This relationship between aesthetics and politics, ambivalence and paranoia grew more complex in the post-Soviet era. The loss of state funding for cinema in the midst of the economic crisis of the Special Period increased filmmakers' dependence on international coproductions and their independence from the ICAIC, especially for those directors able to secure ongoing relationships with foreign producers. Combined with the state's adoption of repressive tolerance and growing political disillusionment in the midst of the failing economy, these changes fostered the production of ever-more-critical allegories of the nation while also exacerbating the paranoid reception of Cuban films. While exiles and dissidents argued that critical films were a ploy to strengthen state power, intellectuals on the island worried that they played into stereotyped depictions of life under late socialism. In both cases, criticism itself came under suspicion.

Concerns that critical allegories were designed to secure the hegemony of the socialist state can be seen in the reception of one of Alea's last and most successful films, *Fresa y chocolate* (*Strawberry and Chocolate*, 1993), which was picked up by Miramax for distribution in the United States and was the first Cuban film to be nominated to the foreign-language category of the Oscars. Codirected with Juan Carlos Tabío, the film recounts the friendship between Diego, a gay intellectual, and David, a university student from the provinces, in 1979, just before the 1980 Mariel boatlift. After first agreeing to spy on the older man, David eventually sides with Diego's criticism of state-sanctioned homophobia and censorship; loses his virginity to Diego's neighbor, Nancy; and matures as a writer thanks to Diego's tutelage. At the end of the film, Diego is forced to flee the country and the two embrace, having arrived at a new understanding that doubles as an allegorical reconciliation between state-approved intellectuals and those marginalized by censorship, as well as between Cubans on the island and in the diaspora.

At the time of *Fresa y chocolate*'s release, Cuban artists were still reeling from the censorship scandal over a 1991 film, Daniel Díaz Torres's *Alicia en el pueblo de maravillas* (*Alice in Wondertown*) (see chapter 3). In this context, intellectuals on the island interpreted the film as a watershed event heralding the triumph of a more liberal political current. They praised Alea and Tabío for their courageous indictment of state censorship and institutionalized homophobia and lauded Alfredo Guevara for the "intelligent" manner in which he managed the film's release. One filmmaker with whom I spoke noted how Guevara arranged for *Fresa y chocolate* to premiere to an international audience at Havana's New Latin American Film Festival, where it won a variety of awards, and then took advantage of the film's success to immediately place it in theaters throughout Havana. "Who was going to tell him no?" my interlocutor speculated. "The people from the festival were still in Havana, and it would have caused a scandal."[21]

Exiles and dissidents, however, were less convinced that the film's release signaled a triumph for freedom of expression. Almost a decade earlier, Alea had been embroiled in a public debate in the New York magazine the *Village Voice* over *Mauvaise conduite* (*Improper Conduct*, 1984), a documentary directed by exiled Cuban artists Néstor Almendros and Orlando Jiménez Leal that denounced state-sanctioned homophobia and censorship in Cuba.[22] Acknowledging the horrors of the UMAPs, Alea observed that this error was in the past. Homophobia, he argued, was a cultural problem that had both preexisted the Revolution and had been exacerbated by the need to militarize in response to US aggression against the island. "In the middle of a battle, you cannot discuss aesthetics or homosexuality," Alea observed to an interviewer for the *Village Voice*. "You have to pick up the gun and receive orders" (Goldstein 1984, 44). If Almendros had made a successful career for himself after leaving Cuba, Alea concluded in a follow-up letter also published in the *Village Voice*, it was "obvious that most of these people have nothing better to sell and that they try to make a career out of their anti-Cubanism" (Gutiérrez Alea 1984).[23]

In light of this debate, *Fresa y chocolate* can be seen as part of an ongoing dialogue with Almendros, who passed away in 1992, shortly before the film's release. Alea himself sometimes supported this interpretation (Chanan 2002, 47–49; Schroeder 2002, 103–6). For exiled intellectuals and dissidents, however, *Fresa y chocolate* represented a sudden about-face that was doubly suspicious given the film's release shortly after the collapse of the Soviet Union and in the midst of Cuba's new economic and political isolation. "This same person who is now pretending to be the defender of Cuban homosexuals persecuted by the regime denounced Néstor Almendros when the latter screened his actually true documentary, *Improper*

Conduct, which showed the horrific reality of homosexuals under Castro," wrote Guillermo Cabrera Infante in a letter published in the Spanish newspaper *El País*. After a brief account of Alea's arguments in the *Village Voice* debate, he concluded:

> Now, the soldier on the attack has converted himself into a valiant defender. His vaunted defense of sexual liberty is nothing more than a *política castrista del dialogueo* [a Castro policy of supposed dialogue] by other means. Everyone (from the boss [Alfredo] Guevara to the *máximo líder* [maximum leader]) is trying to show that a democratic Fidel Castro who pardons and forgets even his own offenses is possible. *Fresa y chocolate* is nothing more than a product of that factory of lies. It's as though Hitler had ordered Leni Reifenstahl, via Goebbels, to film *Schindler's List* (Cabrera Infante 1994).

Others concurred with this assessment of *Fresa y chocolate* as propaganda for the Cuban state. One Havana-based dissident told a foreign reporter that the film was "in line with the position of Cuban officials" and that it gave "the impression that there have been changes." "That's important for economic reasons," he concluded, since "other countries want to see changes" (Cavanaugh 1995).

Arguments that the film was dictated by political leaders clearly overstate their case. Still, the suspicions of exiles and dissidents were not without grounds. In a letter sent to Fidel Castro shortly before the release of *Fresa y chocolate* at the New Latin American Film Festival, Alfredo Guevara reassured the leader that the film "didn't have political problems." He specified, "Better stated, it treats political themes but these are resolved in the behavior, words, actions, and development of the protagonists." In case this was not sufficient to confirm the film's revolutionary sympathies, Guevara offered a stronger motivation for tolerating its release: "Fidel, by accepting this film and without saying a word, we close internationally that horrible moment that some called chapter and that I prefer to call a 'parenthesis' that was the UMAP" (2003, 493–94). Guevara may well have felt strongly the horror of this period. Not only was Guevara himself gay, but he had also provided work and protection to some gay artists who found themselves vulnerable in the militant era of the 1970s. Nonetheless, Guevara's letter also reveals how political leaders can capitalize on critical films in an effort to save political face and put to rest a difficult past.

Alea and Tabío thus found themselves in the uncomfortable position of defending a film that decried state oppression not against political leaders but against those who detected in the film complicity with that state's own attempt to improve its international image. When a Spanish reporter asked the directors why they thought the government had allowed their film to be released, Tabío recognized that the film's message was in keeping with Cuban political leaders' current needs. "With rigid positions on both sides nothing will be achieved and Castro knows this," Tabío explained. "There has to be a change that leads to understanding because the situation in Cuba is unsustainable, especially economically." Then he added hastily, "This doesn't mean that we are part of the regime's propaganda apparatus, charged with transmitting to the world the image of a new Cuba" (qtd. in Casadevall 1994). These anxious assertions reveal, once again, both how establishing one's status as an artist in the disillusioned post-Soviet era became increasingly tied to the ability to demonstrate one's autonomy from the state and how the state's adoption of repressive tolerance complicated such efforts. In a context where the ability to release politically daring works often depended on the protection of state officials who worked to convince political leaders that criticism of state policies was in the best interest of the political hierarchy, artists and audiences found it increasingly difficult to distinguish between freedom of expression and complicity, criticism and repression.

At the same time, filmmakers' growing orientation toward the global market in the 1990s contributed to a different set of suspicions. The success of *Fresa y chocolate* helped spark a global interest in Cuban cinema and in the work of Alea and Tabío in particular, which they were quick to take advantage of. According to Tabío, the duo began work on their final film, *Guantanamera* (1995), after Alea was approached by the Spanish production company Tabasco Films, which was looking to build on the reception of *Fresa y chocolate*. The filmmakers resurrected a screenplay that they had begun working on in the 1980s, adapted it to reflect 1990s Cuba, and recast most of *Fresa y chocolate*'s principal actors in new roles.[24] The resulting film depicts the adventures of a group of characters traveling across the island to deliver a corpse to Havana. This journey provides a pretext to depict an economically depressed country overrun with propaganda, roadside cafeterias that are always out of food, a transportation system in shambles, and a thriving black market.

The project's clear commercial ambition, however, contributed to suspicions that the filmmakers were capitalizing on global stereotypes about the island. Cuban film critic Rufo Caballero (1996), for instance, disparaged *Guantanamera* in a review of a different Cuban movie. "Lucid consideration of ... social context should not be reduced to showing *guajiros* [peasants] selling bananas for dollars by the side of the highway," he observed wryly in implicit reference to a scene from *Guantanamera*. Joel del Río was even more direct. "*Guantanamera* aspired to be so popular that it didn't forget any of the clichés that, for those who don't know any better, could be identified with Cubans," he wrote. "Here we find a compendium of *santería*, Don Juan–style machismo, the most crude sexism . . . and let's not forget swear words, the exaltation of the 'inventive' spirit, and other clichés" (qtd. in García Borrero 2001, 160–61). Two years later, *Guantanamera* famously stirred up more controversy when Fidel Castro accused it of making "light of the nation's tragedies" (qtd. in del Valle 2010, 90) while intellectuals rushed to defend Alea, who had succumbed to cancer shortly after the release of the film.[25] Castro's disapproval of *Guantanamera*, for which he eventually tacitly apologized, demonstrates how artists have continued to contend with limits to official tolerance in the post-Soviet era. But the controversial receptions of *Fresa y chocolate* and *Guantanamera* also show just how complex paranoid readings became in the late socialist period as, in addition to navigating official state censorship, films also fell suspect to arguments that criticism only reinforced the power of the Castro government or catered to spectators eager for images of socialism on the decline.

Criticism and Digital Filmmaking in the Twenty-First Century

As demonstrated by the responses to *Monte Rouge* with which I began this chapter, digital cinema has been subject to similarly anxious searches for signs of complicity with state and market. As the tacit ban placed on hiring Luis Alberto García and Néstor Jíménez as actors in state television that followed the release of *Monte Rouge* makes clear, digital technologies alone are not enough to provide artists with immunity from state censorship. Nonetheless, in the twenty-first century, the growing availability of digital technologies worked alongside foreign funding and the state's adoption of repressive tolerance to increase filmmakers' independence from state institutions. *Monte Rouge*, for instance, was shot in del Llano's own home using a borrowed mini-DV camera and five hundred Cuban convertible pesos, omitting the need for state funding or shooting permits.

Digital technologies have also allowed filmmakers to sidestep state-controlled methods of distribution. Because of the US embargo on Cuba, as of 2019 there was still mutual disregard for copyright on the part of both nations. While the Cuban government freely showed pirated copies of the latest Hollywood blockbusters in movie theaters and on state television, Miami TV channels screened digital copies of films made in Cuba, including independent shorts produced by youth. Cuban films were also sold abroad through dedicated eBay stores or distributed through YouTube and Vimeo. Given the ongoing difficulties involved in accessing the internet from the island, meanwhile, Cuban films circulated on the island either informally through flash drives and hard drives or, as of 2010, via the paquete semanal.

In 2007–9, the artists I worked with worried that these digital forms of circulation might remain limited to intellectual circles in Havana. None-theless, in my travels across Cuba, I encountered several students and art-ists who had seen independent shorts. Informal distribution also clearly extended beyond elites. In 2011 a middle-aged man who lived in a lower-income neighborhood in Havana and worked painting car parts at a state factory told me with enthusiasm about how he shared digital Cuban films with his neighbors over the local area network they had improvised in their apartment building to play video games. He was a particular fan of the Nica-nor series that Eduardo del Llano went on to create using *Monte Rouge*'s ac-tors and characters. Laughing as he described with relish his favorite scenes, he observed, "It's a way of criticizing things that really happen." "And how do you get these shorts? Always under the table," he concluded.

As comments such as this reveal, the unofficial means by which indepen-dent films circulate are themselves at times an important part of the plea-sure they provide. Indeed, criticism and censorship can sometimes drum up interest in a film. After *Monte Rouge* was rejected by Havana's New Latin American Film Festival, it was shown simultaneously at an off-film festival that was excitedly advertised to me by two young filmmakers as censored. At least in one instance, a foreign film professional also appeared to advo-cate appealing to spectators' desires for the illicit. At a workshop for young filmmakers at the 2008 New Latin American Film Festival, a British sales agent told the audience that they should use Cuba as a hook to sell their films because "this is kind of a closed shop here." In this statement, it was not Cuba as an exotic tropical island that could be sold to foreign markets, another stereotype that plagues Cuban-made films and coproductions, but Cuba as politically isolated and censored.

Yet these strategies also provoked mixed reactions among intellectuals. In an interview after the release of *Fresa y chocolate*, Gutiérrez Alea ex-plained that Cuban filmmakers took on the role of social critics "because there are no other voices. Journalism, for example, does not perform its mission of social criticism. In spite of this, people talk in corridors, in cafés, on the street, on sidewalks, in lines, but the problems of society are not discussed in the press. This is a great frustration, and one feels the need to speak out" (qtd. in Chanan 2002, 51). In this statement, the drive to compensate for Cuban state journalism's inadequacies was a positive quality, a tactic through which filmmakers took on the role of heroic intellectuals by resisting state censorship and giving public voice to citizens' dissatisfactions.

For others, however, the proximity of cinema to journalism provoked distaste. "Havana is full of shorts that circulate from hard drive to hard drive, but this doesn't mean that they have a cinematic value. Maybe they have a journalistic value, maybe a different kind of value, but not necessarily cinematic," filmmaker Pavel Giroud told me. "As a thirty-six-year-old I want to see work that demonstrates cinematic bravery from somebody who is twenty-five years old, and the bravery is almost always in what they say while the way in which they say it is direct and basic. This has an explanation. In Cuba, journalism doesn't do the work that it should and so there is a demand that the filmmaker do the work of the journalist." The digital revolution compounded this threat to aesthetic quality, Giroud concluded, encouraging individuals to style themselves as artists simply because they had access to the means of production.[26]

Others worried that the drive toward criticism in digital cinema contributed to polarizing politics. Some of the young filmmakers with whom I worked tacitly acknowledged their appreciation for the publicity that Miami TV shows gave their work and defended the right of critics to interpret films as they pleased. But many complained that Miami film critics manipulated their works for their own political ends. "Youth make these documentaries not with the intention of attacking the government but rather to criticize and to reflect on reality so that we can improve," insisted filmmaker Alejandro Ramírez, whose short documentary *DeMoler* (*Destruction*), which addressed the 2003 closures of sugar mills in Cuba, was screened by Cuban film critic Alejandro Ríos on his show on Miami TV. Another young filmmaker with whom I spoke wondered how these shorts were making their way so quickly from the island to Miami television. Speculating that "somebody" from the ICAIC must be selling the films, he mused that he "would like to know who it was, so that at the very least he could invite me for a beer." But then he quickly assured me that even if Miami's Channel 41 were to pay him to talk about communism, he would refuse, "because I don't want to be used for that type of propaganda."[27]

Finally, some young filmmakers complained of fatigue with the drive to represent the nation and social problems. Arturo Infante, a younger director and screenwriter known for his satirical send-ups of life on the island, commented:

> I often ask myself why my shorts always reflect in some way on my reality, on what is around me. This is sometimes a bit tiresome. Sometimes I find myself saying, I want to tell a story and that's it, *ciao*, that doesn't have anything to do with Cuba or with the reality that is around me. But at the same time, I feel like it's something that I have to do. On the one hand, I would like to detach myself from this reality and tell a story and that's it, a story about whatever, and on the other hand I also feel if not a duty at least a tendency to talk about the absurdities that are around me. But I don't think that cinema has to be critical. It's critical when you have something to criticize. For me, cinema has to be entertaining before anything else.[28]

Pavel Giroud was even more adamant in his resistance to the equation of Cuban cinema with national realities. "I understand that Cuba has its particularities but artists are artists in Cuba and in Japan," noted Giroud when I asked why he focused on the early revolutionary period in his first two films. "I'm interested in universal dramas, in films that can be understood and enjoyed in any part of the world. I don't want to close myself off in a national framework."[29] Analysts and artists alike have long recognized how demands for supposedly "universal" aesthetic qualities can serve as a means to impose artistic standards from the Global North on artists from other nations (Franco 2002, 35–36; Winegar 2006, 176–77). Arturo Infante's ambivalence about his own tendency to critically represent his reality and Pavel Giroud's aspirations to the universal, however, show how young artists in the Global South can feel equally constrained by what they experience as the international art world's stereotyped and restrictive demands for the national.

Cuban cinema, it seems, has undergone a strange new twist. In the early decades of the Revolution, filmmakers turned to depictions of the nation to resist what they saw as the colonization of Latin America by US media. Criticism, meanwhile, worked alongside directed indirection to guarantee that cinema would be art, not propaganda, even as it exposed films to readings that were sometimes in tension with artists' aesthetic and political goals. In the post-Soviet era, the state's strategic relaxation of censorship and the increasing availability of foreign funds and digital technologies contributed to what many celebrated as a growing tide of criticism in cinema and other arts, but these dynamics also exacerbated the anxieties surrounding such work. While most Cuban filmmakers continue to use their films to reflect on the reality around them, they also worry that criticism and the paranoid readings to which it contributes might betray their desires to convey more nuanced representations of life under late socialism and for their films to be viewed, first and foremost, as art. In the remainder of this chapter, I show how one young filmmaker attempted to navigate these dilemmas, then turn to some conclusions about the politics of allegory and its role in public debate in Cuba and beyond.

The Unbearable Burden of Allegory

A week or so after I arrived at Cuba's international film school, the EICTV, in October 2007, a debate over the social function of cinema broke out in a class on film direction that I was sitting in on. When the British instructor asked the students what they hoped to learn from their studies, several argued for a cinema that would be at once political and nondidactic in terms that echoed arguments for early revolutionary Cuban and Latin American cinema. "Films can criticize the world but can't change it," commented one. "I want to make entertainment that is intelligent." A second student argued for an even more active social function for cinema. "I think films can change people's attitudes," he argued. "They can take risks and show what is not often shown." A third student proposed a version of directed indirection. "I want to show tendencies in the world so that the film can indicate possible solutions to problems without telling spectators what these solutions should be," he noted.

Yet the sole Cuban in the room rejected even these tempered associations of art with politics. "I'm not interested in transmitting ideas or in making a thesis film but rather in provoking physical responses in spectators," insisted Laimir Fano. "I want to make a cinema that is physical and sensual." The next day, Fano clarified his comment as we ate lunch together in the EICTV cafeteria. Acknowledging that his films would always be "social" because he was a "social being," he nonetheless insisted that the sensual should precede ideas in cinema. "As a Cuban, I am disgusted by how they are always trying to feed ideology to us through television and other media," he observed. "Cinema, I think, should try to convey other things, things that can't be said in words." Even early revolutionary films such as *Memorias del subdesarrollo* posed a threat to film's aesthetic specificity, he noted, risking the reduction of cinema to reason at the expense of feeling and the sensual.

Despite his protests, however, by the end of the academic year Fano had proven himself to be, as one of his colleagues referred to him, "the most political of us all." Through the story of a mulata cabaret dancer who loses her rhythm, his graduating thesis, *Oda a la piña* (*Ode to the Pineapple*, 2008), criticizes the marketing of Cuba for the foreign gaze and denounces Cuban intolerance for those who are different. The allegorical dimensions of the short are present from its opening images. As a narrator's voice intones the first lines of "A la piña" (To the Pineapple), an eighteenth-century poem widely considered to be one of the first expressions of *criollo* nationalism, the pineapple itself comes into view: a close-up hones in on a large, artificial pineapple bobbing against a cement wall grayed with faded paint, then the camera tilts down to reveal the mulata in skimpy cabaret outfit upon whose head the adornment is perched. As the young woman awkwardly practices her dance moves, a smile of visible frustration flickering across her face, an old man reflected in the mirror beside her beats out the rhythm on the urine bag attached to his wheelchair. Behind her, a tourist poster advertises Cuba's beaches.

Evidently, all is not well in paradise. Cuba is not the tropical Eden the canonical poem and tourist poster proclaim it to be, and the sultry mulata who has long figured the nation stumbles in her attempt to market herself as such. The second sequence reveals the tragedy behind her frustration. Joined by a chorus line sporting oversized fruit on their heads, the Pineapple walks ineptly through her steps at a rehearsal performed for two German executives (figure 2.2). When the foreigners object to her continued awkwardness, the off-screen voice of the group's Cuban manager asks in a staccato rhythm with postproduced echo, "Ven aca, chica. ¿Que carajo te pasa? ¿Dónde está tu ritmo?" (Look here, girl. What in hell is happening to you? Where is your rhythm?). Her voice answers—"Lo perdí" (I lost it)—while her lips remain still, a confession that provokes the vocal protests of the Germans and the disembodied laughter of her fellow dancers. Underscored by the sequence's nonrealist use of sound, lighting, and color, this answer brings the short's allegorical drama to the fore: the mulata's body involuntarily rejects the burden of producing the national stereotype for foreign consumption.

The sequence that follows adds a more local level to the short's allegorical meanings, emphasizing the Pineapple's inability to keep step with a rhythm regimented not just by foreign stereotypes but also by domestic expectations. As the narrator intones the poem's next stanza, the dancer walks out

Figure 2.2 The Pineapple dancing in the cabaret in Laimir Fano's *Oda a la piña* (2008).

of the cabaret and onto the streets of old Havana, trailing her frothy skirt behind her. "¡Pinga! ¡Cojones!" (Fuck!), shouts a car driver as he leans on his horn and comes to a sudden halt, narrowly missing her. "¿Tu estás sorda, chica?" (Girl, are you deaf?), shouts a bicycle taxi driver a few minutes later as he narrowly misses her, ringing his bell loudly. The problem, however, is that she hears too well. As she makes her way through the dense neighborhood, the city's iconic sounds—the rocking of an old chair, the moans of a woman astride a man, the clinking of a spoon stirring a mojito—coalesce into a bombardment of noises and images that at last overwhelm her. In the closing sequence, the camera cuts rapidly between the Pineapple's tear-streaked face and close-ups representing the city's sounds until she collapses into a heap on the ground. As the narrator intones the closing lines of "A la piña," a conga line forms around her fallen form, feet shuffling to the rhythm of the insistent rumba refrain, "¿Dónde está Teresa? ¿Dónde está Teresa? Teresa, Teresa" (Where is Teresa?).

Did Fano cede to the national stereotypes he had initially set out to undo, using cinema to convey ideas and to appeal to spectators' desires for criticism? At times he himself seemed to entertain such a notion. "I feel as though we just participated in a ritual to kill Fidel," he told me one evening. We were sitting in Old Havana's Central Park, discussing a play we had just seen in which two characters wait anxiously for the death of the old woman who lives next door. Fano's allegorical reading of the play soon led to a conversation about politics in Cuban art and in his own work. He had intended to make a film where social criticism would be present but would take second place to the short's story and sensual dimensions, he explained. But he was frustrated by how quickly many spectators reached for political interpretations. Viewed from this perspective, the film acquires a third allegorical meaning: the dilemma of the artist who sells Cuba as the site of politics while longing for aesthetics.

Fano's explanation, however, also invites an alternative reading of his film, one that keeps its sensual dimension in view. *Oda a la piña* uses allegory both to convey political meanings and to reflect on the history of the mode in Cuban cinema. After the Pineapple confesses to having lost her rhythm, her Cuban manager warns her not to mess around. "There are plenty more pineapples in this country," he cautions as the film cuts to an image of Afro-Cuban women of every age gathered morosely around a table, sporting pineapple headdresses. Just visible is a poster announcing a 1964 Cuban documentary by Rogelio Paris about the nation's musical traditions, *Nosotros la música* (*We Are the Music*). The Pineapple's imminent substitutability in a nation of impoverished women waiting for their opportunity to fulfill the national stereotype is here directly tied to the nationalist efforts of early revolutionary cinema.

The complicity of Cuban cinema in the perpetuation of reductive images of the nation is further reinforced through the short's closing sequence, which comments on and reworks the opening images of *Memorias del subdesarrollo*. Alea's film begins with handheld shots of a crowd that ignores a shooting in its midst, dancing itself into a frenzy to the "Teresa" chorus while soldiers recover the body. The sequence closes in a freeze-frame of a black woman's sweat-streaked face as she stares defiantly into the camera. In *Memorias del subdesarrollo*, these images are used to criticize Sergio's incapacity to comprehend the reality around him; later in the film we see a new version of the same sequence, this time showing a bewildered Sergio in the crowd as dissonant, nondiegetic music accentuates his confusion. For Alea (1982, 45), the repetition of the sequence suggested a metaphorical link between the death of the anonymous man in the crowd and Sergio's own uncertain future in the new revolutionary society.[30]

In *Oda a la piña*, by contrast, it is the mulata who faces destruction. Significantly, *Memorias del subdesarrollo*'s opening sequence was shot with the assistance of Nicolás Guillén Landrián, an Afro-Cuban filmmaker whose work was rediscovered in Cuba in the early twenty-first century after being censored for decades.[31] *Oda a la piña*'s closing sequence both evokes this historical elision and implies that Alea's depiction of a black woman is complicit with the reduction of the mulata to an abstraction. This point, moreover, is delivered through a carefully cultivated aesthetic. If the Pineapple has lost her rhythm under the pressure of domestic and foreign expectations, Fano's short recounts her dilemma by celebrating cinema's sensual potential through an exquisite use of lighting and color that culminates in a veritable city symphony. These aesthetic techniques are arguably as much object as vehicle for the short's political meaning. Equating Cuban cinema's reliance on allegory with the marketing of national stereotypes, *Oda a la piña* suggests that to open up new meanings, filmmakers must resist the reduction of art to a reified politics.

Aesthetic Longings

Scholars have long maintained that artists and audiences working under conditions of censorship draw on allegory and other forms of aesthetic indirection to communicate illicit meanings and to contest dominant ideologies. This has certainly been true in Cuba. In the early decades of the Revolution, Cuban filmmakers turned to allegory both to avoid what they saw as the reductive propaganda of socialist realism and as a strategy for incorporating controversial meanings into their works as open secrets. Allegory continued to exercise importance in post-Soviet Cuban cinema, as the state's strategic relaxation of censorship and the growing availability of foreign funds and digital technologies allowed filmmakers to produce and circulate more overtly critical films than in previous decades.

Yet, as I have demonstrated, allegory can also place important constraints on public debate. Spectators trained to read between the lines often reduced Cuban films to politically polarized interpretations, reading what filmmakers insisted were more ambivalent takes on the Revolution as arguments for or against socialism. In the post-Soviet era, such paranoid readings grew increasingly complex, as criticism itself came to seem complicit with state power or the global market. Theodor Adorno (1977) once argued that Bertolt Brecht's politically "committed" theater was both bad art and bad politics; by reducing works to a superficial and distorted account of social problems, Adorno claimed, Brecht's oeuvre sacrificed the potential of art to serve as a protest of the current state of affairs (183–84). In the disillusioned post-Soviet era, Cuban filmmakers began to express similar concerns, worrying that overt criticism risked prioritizing politics over aesthetics while also delivering a reductive vision of life in late socialist Cuba.

The broader point here is that it is only by approaching allegory as a contested social process that we can shed light on the crucial role it plays in cultural politics. Struggles over the meanings of films and the intentions of authors shape public debate and influence the social standing of artists, as filmmakers, spectators, and critics take up works in ways that sometimes reinforce long-standing political divides and at other times hold out the elusive promise that aesthetics might yet open up room for play with new meanings. In the next chapter, I elaborate on these points by examining how conflicts over allegory shaped the reception of Daniel Díaz Torres's *Alicia en el pueblo de maravillas* (1991), transforming a film that its creators insisted was born out of a commitment to and an attempt to revive revolutionary ideals into a censorable attack on the Revolution.

CHAPTER THREE

FAITH WITHOUT FIDEL

In Which Alicia Goes to Wonderland
and Meets a Bureaucrat . . . or Was It Fidel?

"I don't know why every time one depicts a *dirigente* [apparatchik] everyone imagines he represents Fidel," Daniel Díaz Torres laughed dismissively.
"For me, the character was a bureaucrat."[1] The character in question was
from Díaz Torres's own *Alicia en el pueblo de maravillas* (*Alice in Wondertown*), a film that, when it was released in 1991, provoked one of Cuba's most
significant censorship scandals. My encounter with Díaz Torres in the lobby
of Havana's Charlie Chaplin Cinema that afternoon in late March 2008 was
serendipitous. I had spent the morning scouring reviews of the film in the
Cinemateca's archives at the ICAIC's main building next door and was curious to get his take on the authors' damning references to the film's allegorical subtext. "The lack of political debate in Cuba means that spectators are
always ready to look for a second meaning in films," the director concluded,
dismissing these interpretations of his film along with their intimations of
his counterrevolutionary intent. "Artists aren't trying to make crossword
puzzles for spectators to figure out."

Accounts of post-Soviet Cuban cinema often begin with the controversy
over *Alicia en el pueblo de maravillas*, thus ironically linking a period that
saw a relative relaxation of censorship with censorship. Based on a screenplay
written by Eduardo del Llano in collaboration with the comedy group Nos
y Otros (Ourselves and Others), the film tells the story of Alicia, a naïve but

enthusiastic theater instructor who is sent for her first assignment to the fictional and, as it turns out, dystopian town of Maravillas de Noveras.[2] A play on Lewis Carroll's *Alice's Adventures in Wonderland*, Díaz Torres's film is at once an absurd satire and an explicit allegory. "Pueblo" means both "town" and "people" in Spanish, inviting readings of the film's events and characters as a commentary on the Cuban nation.

This invitation to allegory soon proved the film's downfall. Met with enthusiasm when it first screened at the Berlinale Film Festival in February 1991, in the months leading up to the film's Cuban premiere in June of that same year, rumors flew about its potential meanings. As bootleg VHS copies began to circulate on the island, the ICAIC held private screenings with select intellectuals in an attempt to stem the mounting controversy. But by the time *Alicia* was released on the island, both foreign and local spectators were eager to read the corrupt director of the local sanatorium as Fidel Castro, and a Chinese chef, who keeps showing up at inopportune moments with a knife in hand, as Raúl. Alicia's eventual escape from the town across a small stream, meanwhile, was interpreted as a call to abandon socialism or, more metonymically, as her flight to Miami. Finally, Alicia and Omar Rodríguez, the town's cultural director and Alicia's eventual love interest, were decried as stand-ins for Cuban intellectuals' own aspirations to political power. Denounced as an assault on socialism in its time of crisis, the film was pulled from movie theaters after only four days, while Alfredo Guevara, who had been replaced in 1982 by Julio García Espinosa as head of the ICAIC, was called in to help mediate the growing confrontation between Cuban filmmakers and political leaders.[3]

The timing of the film's release and political struggles within Cuba's cultural bureaucracy clearly played a role in the scandal. Work on *Alicia* began in 1988, two years after Fidel Castro announced a campaign to "rectify errors and negative tendencies," encouraging criticism of many of the topics addressed by the film: bureaucracy, corruption, inefficiency in production, and workplace theft. But due to difficulties in production, the exhibition of *Alicia* ended up coinciding with the collapse of the Soviet Union. In the face of Cuba's sudden economic and political isolation, Cuban intellectuals told me, what would have been a controversial film a few years earlier suddenly became explosive. Power plays within the Cuban state bureaucracy further compounded this accident in schedule. According to filmmakers, Carlos Aldana, the head of the Communist Party of Cuba's Department of Ideology, used the occasion to mount an attack on the ICAIC. During the few days the film was shown, the party ordered its membership to attend screenings in a concerted effort to stifle positive reactions to the film. One Cuban intellectual with whom I spoke recalled witnessing party members shouting insults at the screen or even hitting audience members who dared to laugh at the film's jokes, while another remembered applauding the film in a youthful gesture of rebellion.[4] Compounding suspicions of a power struggle, in the months between *Alicia's* Berlinale screening and its official release in Havana, a plan was announced to dissolve the ICAIC and fuse it with the state television and radio institute, the ICRT. While state functionaries justified the merger as a cost-saving measure, the ICAIC filmmakers viewed it as an attempt to put an end to the relative freedom they had historically been afforded by the film institute's more liberal policies.

These contextual factors have been well documented by several scholars.[5] As I read through Cuban reviews of the film and talked to the artists and intellectuals who had been involved in the scandal, however, what struck me was the central role that debates over allegory, authorial intention, and textual interpretation played in the controversy. Díaz Torres's complaint about spectators who reduce films to crossword puzzles is, on one level, a description of how spectators approached the film, reducing signs that might have been taken up as broader social metaphors to metonyms for specific individuals and acts in ways that stoked the controversy. It also clearly worked as a strategy of self-defense, deflecting responsibility for the film's meanings onto spectators. Indeed, as in the controversies over *Memorias del subdesarrollo* and *Monte Rouge* discussed in chapter 2, the gap between authorial intention and interpretation figured importantly in efforts to quell the controversy. Also as in these other conflicts, however, this line of defense cannot simply be dismissed as a mask designed to hide the artists' "true" counterrevolutionary intentions. Rather, as I show in this chapter, the controversy over *Alicia en el pueblo de maravillas* demonstrates, once more, how Cuban filmmakers have historically turned to allegory to convey ambivalent criticisms of socialism, and how such efforts have often been reduced to arguments for or against—in this case, against—the Revolution.

In the case of *Alicia*, to make this argument requires exploring a genre pervasive both in Cuba and in other state socialist contexts: criticism of the bureaucracy. As Díaz Torres's comments to me make clear, one allegorical slippage in particular played a key, if sometimes implicit, role in arguments about the film and its creators' political designs: that between the bureaucrat in the film and Fidel Castro. While Díaz Torres vehemently and repeatedly denied the resemblance, other artists with whom I spoke insisted that the reference was clear. Even more curiously, I soon discovered that this particular equation extended beyond a single film to a speech genre pervasive among artists. Whether in response to my queries about the place of bureaucracy in Cuba or in reference to other topics, older intellectuals in particular often moved from criticism of bureaucracy to arguments that Fidel Castro and his government represented the bureaucratization of the Revolution. Faced with such discursive tactics as well as the centrality of themes of bureaucracy, corruption, and workplace inefficiency in several comedies from the 1980s—bureaucrat comedies, as I call them here—I soon found myself pondering a series of conundrums. Why is criticism of the bureaucracy so pervasive in Cuba and, for that matter, in other state socialist societies? What made it so easy for my interlocutors to move from such talk to questioning Fidel Castro, and yet also made it plausible for Daniel Díaz Torres to deny charges of counterrevolution by explaining his film as a criticism of the bureaucratization of the Revolution? And finally, how do slippages between bureaucrats and Fidel Castro square with intellectuals' insistence on their commitment to the values of the Revolution?

In this chapter, I take up these questions by exploring how criticism of the bureaucracy unfolds in three discursive contexts: speeches and writings produced by Cuban political leaders in the 1960s and the 1980s; bureaucrat comedies, a genre that came to the fore in Cuba in the 1980s; and twenty-first-century Cuban intellectual discourse. Situating *Alicia* in this intertextual context, I argue that the scandal of the film was not that it harbored secret counterrevolutionary messages but rather that it unsettled a tension in state socialist ideology: that between revolution as an ideal of transformation and collective effervescence that promises to make social demands and the political order feel immanent to individual needs and desires; and the everyday demands of governance, which rely on the state as a set of hierarchical institutions and administrative organs. Criticism of the bureaucracy normally contains this tension, deflecting complaints against failures to achieve energetic unity from top political leaders to the bureaucracy. But *Alicia*'s adoption of the genre tipped it into a more far-reaching satire of state authoritarianism, one that for some spectators, at least, went too far. In so doing, *Alicia* also proved prescient, anticipating the ways in which intellectuals would later take up criticism of the bureaucracy to challenge Fidel Castro's rule as itself a distortion of revolutionary energies. By the twenty-first century, in other words, faith in the Revolution and its values often went hand in hand with opposing Fidel (and Raúl) Castro, even as hopes for reform and wariness of the alternatives kept many intellectuals attached to existing structures of governance.

The ideological tension to which criticism of the bureaucracy is a response is not unique to Cuba or to state socialism. Rather, it is linked to a broader dilemma that has long plagued both liberal and state socialist imaginaries—namely, the question of how to manage affect so as to bind citizens to the social order while also guaranteeing individual freedom. Terry Eagleton (1990) frames this quandary as follows. No political order can survive without "tak[ing] account of 'sensible' life," he writes. Governance does not typically thrive on repression or, for that matter, political cynicism alone but instead aims to appeal to the desires, sentiments, habits, customs, and material experiences of individuals. The effort to tie citizens to the dominant political order through such affective or aesthetic resonances becomes all the more urgent under capitalism and liberal democracy.[6] To achieve a society where self-determining citizens will govern themselves, individuals who face one another as competitors in the marketplace must be made to comply with the laws and requirements of the social order all while, at least ideally, experiencing such compliance not as external compulsion but as a response to their own desires and needs. Affect and aesthetics resolve this dilemma by encouraging citizens to internalize social demands (Eagleton 1990, 20). As Jean-Jacques Rousseau puts it in *The Social Contract*, the most important law is not that "graven on tablets of marble or brass, but on the hearts of the citizens," which "replaces authority by the force of habit" (2001, 94).[7]

As I have shown in the previous two chapters, political leaders and intellectuals under state socialism challenged liberal ideals of autonomy, but they nonetheless took seriously the problem of individual freedom. As this chapter elaborates, the crowd and its energies played a key if often tenuous role in demonstrating how state socialism might guarantee a social order that felt immanent to individual needs.[8] This conception of the crowd took on one of its most poignant formulations in Che Guevara's essay "El socialismo y el hombre en Cuba" (Socialism and Man in Cuba).[9] Responding to criticisms that the Revolution was sacrificing individuals "on the altar of the state," Guevara argued that political leaders had developed what he termed "an almost intuitive method of sounding general reactions to problems." He explained: "In the large public concentrations, one observes something like a dialogue between two tuning forks whose vibrations provoke new ones in the interlocutor. Fidel and the masses start to vibrate in a dialogue of increasing intensity until they reach a climax in an abrupt finale, crowned by our war and victory cry" ([1965] 1967, 629). In Guevara's provocative image, revolutionary governance is direct and immediate. Bypassing political campaigns, legislative bodies, and even the mass media, the masses and their political leader, physically copresent in the public square, explode in collective effervescence. Fidel Castro does not merely represent the people; he vibrates with their desires and needs. ———

As the works of social theorists from Max Weber to Émile Durkheim suggest, however, maintaining such a resonant unity is a treacherous project. Weber's concept of charisma, explains Edward Shils, refers to the perception of a proximity to "the vital force which underlies man's existence" and which is often given the name of God, whether it is achieved through scientific inquiry, artistic pursuit, or political action (1965, 201). Numerous scholars have theorized Fidel Castro as just such a charismatic leader, noting, for instance, the religious overtones that some Cubans granted his leadership when white doves, which are sacred in Afro-Cuban religion, landed on his shoulder during a speech shortly after the triumph against Batista's forces.[10] Yet, at least according to Weber, such charismatic authority is doomed to fade, becoming a "mere component" of institutions "when the tide that lifted a charismatically led group out of everyday life flows back into the channels of workaday routines." While the charismatic leader calls on followers "to maintain the purity of the spirit, the charismatic message inevitably becomes dogma, doctrine, theory, reglement, law, or petrified tradition" ([1922] 1968, 1121–22).

Che Guevara's image of the Cuban crowd and its charismatic leader also bears an unmistakable affinity with Émile Durkheim's theory of collective effervescence in *The Elementary Forms of Religious Life* ([1912] 1995).[11] In his most emblematic description of collective effervescence, Durkheim claims that participants in Australian Aboriginal coroborees transported themselves into a state of ecstasy as they ran, shouted, collided with one another, and brandished their weapons: "Once the individuals are gathered together, a sort of electricity is generated from their closeness and quickly launches them to an extraordinary height of exaltation" ([1912] 1995, 217). For Durkheim, this religious ecstasy is, at heart, a palpable experience of the social. Unlike later religious and social orders, argues Durkheim, "primitive societies are not Leviathans that overwhelm man with the enormity of their power and subject him to harsh discipline." Rather, "each individual carries the whole [of society] in himself. It is part of him, so when he yields to its promptings, he does not think he is yielding to coercion but instead doing what his own nature tells him to do" (226).

In Durkheim's work, however, such collective intensities are, as William Mazzarella (2017, 1) puts it, "chronically unstable and leaky," always at risk of either exceeding their original containers or fading into the background. Thus, for instance, Durkheim notes that efforts to preserve the collective intensities of the French Revolution, which he takes as a modern example of collective effervescence, ultimately failed: "revolutionary faith" faded as "disappointments and discouragements quickly replaced the first enthusiasm" ([1912] 1995, 216, 430). Durkheim concludes his book with a lament about how, in his own era, the old rituals that had once aroused passions had either faded into custom or were no longer suited to present need, leaving early twentieth-century France in a "state of uncertainty and anxiety" that, he claimed, must eventually give way to new efforts to stoke collective energies (429–30).

We should be wary of taking Weber and Durkheim's arguments and, especially, their stark divides between supposedly premodern and modern societies at face value. Indeed, their work is arguably more a reflection of concerns that shaped their own twentieth-century European contexts than an analysis of the small-scale societies they purported to describe. As a result, however, their arguments do succeed in highlighting concerns that also shaped Cuban political and intellectual discourse. Guevara's own writings betrayed a pervasive concern about the durability of the collective energies he otherwise praised. In "El socialismo y el hombre en Cuba," Guevara insisted that more formal institutions were needed to ensure consistent communication between political leaders and the people ([1965] 1967, 632–33). Yet, in an earlier essay, he complained that attempts to establish such mechanisms had only ended in an excessive centralization that impeded revolutionary energies.

Acknowledging that bureaucracy preexisted the Revolution, Guevara suggested that it had become a more endemic problem under socialism than it had been under capitalism, where the bureaucracy had been subordinated to the bourgeoisie. Whether because they suffered from a "lack of revolutionary consciousness" and "conformism with what was wrong," or because they had become increasingly "desperate faced with repeated problems that couldn't be solved," he elaborated, many individuals took refuge in "bureaucracy, filling out papers and excusing themselves from responsibility through written excuses that allow them to continue vegetating." This absence of what Guevara termed "an internal motor" led to increasing *papeleo* (the filling out of forms) and *reunionismo* (endless meetings to discuss issues that are never resolved), which, in turn, put a "brake on the flow of information from the base and the communication of instructions or orders from the central organizations" ([1963] 1967, 546–47). In this argument, then, bureaucracy was both fed by a dangerous diminution in collective effervescence and threatened to spawn an excess of perverted energy.[12]

Armando Hart elaborated on this criticism in a series of editorials published in 1967 in the Communist Party newspaper, *Granma*.[13] Like Guevara, Hart insisted both that bureaucracy predated the Revolution and that the Revolution had contributed to the problem. The nationalization of production, he observed, meant that bureaucratic agencies that, under capitalism, had been "fragmented and dispersed, were reorganized . . . into a vertical structure" while bureaucrats themselves achieved an unprecedented degree of power. Unlike their capitalist counterparts, socialist functionaries "occupied decisive positions with regards to the means of production and politics." This, in turn, led to the production of a "special stratus of citizens at the heart of the bureaucratic apparatus," a "new class" oriented toward the protection of its own interests and divorced from the masses and productive work (Hart Dávalos 1967, 174, 183).

What was worse, bureaucracy risked infecting both the Communist Party itself and Cuban citizens (Hart Dávalos 1967, 175). Bureaucracy, elaborated Hart, was like a "corrosive acid." It spilled over from "alienated" bureaucrats who "diluted" their energies among "forms, memorandums, orientations, and plans" to workers who see "problems that [they] understand and know how to resolve . . . remain unsolved or badly handled." As a result, workers lost their "faith and confidence in the Revolution," and, finding themselves "crushed by a deluge of memos, models, and other manifestations of the bureaucratic spirit," were themselves "converted into bureaucrat[s]" or "machine[s] carrying out orders, circulars, and instructions." Bureaucracy's contagious perversion of revolutionary energies, Hart concluded, posed an even bigger threat than US imperialism. Whereas "imperialism is an external enemy who is out in the open," he cautioned, "bureaucracy corrodes us from within" (180–81).

Notably, Hart advised political leaders seeking to stop the spread of bureaucracy to look to Fidel Castro as model. "We know from experience that there is no better control than that provided by a capable man . . . impregnated with the spirit of the Revolution," observed Hart. Castro exemplified this "new style" of leadership, one that involved intensive "work on the terrain, [going] from barn to barn, analyzing every problem to its last detail, orienting, debating, and conversing with the workers, living their problems and difficulties" (1967, 182). In Guevara and Hart's writings, bureaucracy threatened to transform government into a veritable Leviathan, corrupt, hierarchical, and out of touch with citizens, who, in turn, lost their desire to solve collective problems. This, they suggested, was a dilemma that could only be solved through more immediacy. As we shall see, however, this solution would prove particularly "leaky."

The Bureaucrat and the New Man under Rectification

Criticism of the bureaucracy thus expressed anxieties about the utopian dream of a society organized by collective effervescence and an adaptable and resonant connection between individuals and the political order. By giving voice to these concerns, it also frequently contained them. This strategic use of the genre came to the fore in the late 1980s during a period denominated by Fidel Castro in 1986 as the "Rectification of errors and negative tendencies." Rectification was Cuba's answer to the Soviet Union's glasnost and perestroika, but it also differed from Soviet strategies in important aspects. Whereas Mikhail Gorbachev combined a relaxation of state censorship and openings for public debate with market reforms, Fidel Castro's parallel call to engage in criticism of social problems was made in the name of an increased economic and political centralization that strengthened the authority of the Communist Party.[14] Arguing that the construction of socialism was a political and revolutionary task, Castro declared that the party must take back the planning and management of the economy from a growing class of corrupt administrators and bureaucrats, a process that required cultivating citizens' socialist consciousness and renewing the direct bond between political leaders and Cuban citizens.

By the 1980s, Hart's warnings had come true; while an administrative class had become firmly entrenched, national enterprises continued to underperform. In the 1970s, the Cuban government introduced limited market reforms, allowing industries, for instance, to retain a percentage of their profits and legalizing private-sector work in occupations such as carpentry, plumbing, and private housing construction. While these reforms were generally popular, they also created new problems. Workers seeking to increase their income through private-sector employment had new incentives to filter materials from state workplaces and to absent themselves from their state centers of employment, while Cuban political leaders argued that managers were often deficient in their punishment of such activities (Eckstein 2003, 45–46, 55–56).

These market reforms also led to new economic distinctions, exacerbated by the first trips back to the island in the late 1970s by Cuban Americans. Cuba was a very "closed off and homogeneous society in the 1970s," commented one of my interlocutors, but as the island began "opening up in the 1980s . . . a certain class started to become very visible." He recalled: "In those years, there was an administrative class that was basically the one that had cars. The phenomenon of *'tití mania'* started. This was a tendency among men who had economic resources and were roughly between the ages of forty and fifty to recycle their wives for women who were much younger. Of course, there was also the counterpart, which was that these young girls sold themselves to lovers or husbands with cars out of desire for economic improvement."[15] Far from leading to the egalitarian society promised by the Revolution, then, by the 1980s, efforts to stimulate the economy had already begun to promote social and class differences, which were themselves accompanied by new social anxieties about gender and the relationship between romance and financial gain.

Rectification was meant to combat these growing class differences, as well as related problems of workplace theft, the informal or black market, and inefficiencies in production, which political leaders blamed on the market reforms of the 1970s.[16] In a speech delivered at the 3rd Congress of the Communist Party in 1986, Castro claimed that the Revolution had gone astray by relying too heavily on "economic mechanisms." Market reforms, he explained, had plunged the country into economic and moral confusion. State administrators and functionaries had abused their newfound powers by behaving like capitalists in disguise. But whereas capitalists sought efficiency and quality in goods, socialists who aped their ways provoked only chaos in production. By trying to resolve problems with money or by seeking only their own personal profit, these administrators had bred problems ranging from inefficiency to outright corruption. Insufficient homes were being built, constructions of hospitals and other buildings were left unfinished, enterprises were unprofitable, and payrolls had been inflated by retaining unneeded workers, a tactic that "degenerat[ed]" and "corrupt[ed]" people by "teach[ing] them not to work." In some cases, functionaries and employees had robbed and resold state resources on the black market to line their own pockets (Castro Ruíz 1986).

To counter such corruption, Fidel Castro and other political leaders called for a restoration of revolutionary ethics as emblematized by Che Guevara and the revolutionary new man. But this invocation of the new man introduced a new set of complications. On the one hand, the new man exemplifies discipline and self-sacrifice. According to this model, to be a revolutionary means to obey the party completely, which in turn will directly manage all of the nation's affairs. Yet from the first, the myth of the new man also emphasized citizen initiative and action from below. In a speech delivered to the Unión de Jóvenes Comunistas (UJC, Communist Youth League), Guevara praised the gathered youth for their spirit of self-sacrifice, discipline, and duty but also cautioned them against excessive docility and obedience. The young communist must be resolutely nonconformist, continuously alert to all problems and injustice, quick to question things that were not clear, and ready to protest "every time something occurs that is wrong, no matter who has said it," argued Guevara. Resisting the reduction of the Revolution to "formalism," the new man must instead serve as an example for older people who had "lost a certain juvenile enthusiasm, who had lost their faith in life" ([1962] 1967, 364).

Cuban political leaders thus found themselves facing a difficult ideological problem. How was the state to reconcile the rebellious and critical nature of the new man with citizen obedience to the Revolution's aging political hierarchy? Bureaucracy or, to be more precise, the faulty morals and practices of mid- and lower-level bureaucrats here ceased to be a stumbling block and instead became a solution. At one point in his 1986 speech to the Communist Party, Fidel Castro recalled visiting a hospital construction site where only pillars of a sterilization room had been built as workers sat idly by, waiting for supplies from the Ministry of Construction. With the direct approval of their *comandante* and material support from the party, the maintenance workers finished the construction of the room. "They are going to invent something new there," Castro exuded. In a similar move *Granma* discussed the case of a Santiago woman who had been fired from her job as an accountant for denouncing bookkeeping and payroll inconsistencies. After reviewing her situation, the Communist Party restored her to her position and dismissed her bosses (Pérez-Stable 1999, 162–63). In these instances and others, citizens who stood up to corrupt mid- or lower-level functionaries were presented as acting in unison with the nation's top leaders.

Key to these images of spirited new men and women working alongside political leaders was what might be termed a fantasy of benevolent surveillance. As one film director told me: "In Cuba, a phrase became popular in which people said, 'When Fidel finds out he'll fix this. This is happening because Fidel hasn't found out yet. Fidel doesn't know.' That is to say, the sewage flows over and Fidel doesn't know about it so it can't be fixed?! This was a way that

Cubans justified the immobility of the state, the failure to solve problems—because Fidel didn't know about it."[17] Viewed from the perspective criticized by my interlocutor, abuses of power and ineffective state services were not the fault of state socialism or top political leaders but were provoked by a glitch in communication: news of these problems had yet to percolate to the highest levels of power. Paired with this fantasy of benevolent surveillance, criticism of the bureaucracy held out the hope that social problems could be amended and the effervescence of the Revolution restored if only citizens could bypass corrupt administrators to secure the comandante's attention.

Bureaucrat Comedies in the 1980s

Bureaucracy thus provided the perfect enemy for both the spirited new man dedicated to combating the reification of the Revolution and for a state whose claim to legitimacy rested on its energetic bond with the people, neatly providing an outlet for social dissatisfaction while preserving faith in top political leaders. In cinema, worries about the evanescence of revolutionary energies came to the fore in a series of bureaucrat comedies with precedents in the Noticiero ICAIC Latinoamericano (ICAIC Latin American Newsreel); Sergio Giral's drama about racism and workplace corruption, Techo de vidrio (Glass Ceiling, 1981); and Tomás Gutiérrez Alea's 1966 film, La muerte de un burócrata (The Death of a Bureaucrat).

Observers often argue that ICAIC filmmaking took a turn to historical and militant topics in the 1970s, which they link both to the preferences of filmmakers and to the difficult political climate of that decade.[18] By the end of the 1970s, however, criticism and contemporary concerns returned to the fore. Film critic and director Enrique Colina explained:

> There was a lot of popular discontent. Many things were not working well: services, the streets, garbage collection. Taxis didn't stop when you called them. If you went to an optometrist, you would find frames for your glasses, but not temples, or, if they were there, they'd be the wrong color. Every time there has been a palpable level of discontent in the population because things aren't working well, [the government] has created openings so as to allow things that are poorly done to be criticized through the media. In 1977 such an opening was created. The Revolution was no longer a dream, it was a fact, and many important things had been achieved, but mistakes had also been made. Bureaucracy had grown enormously. One of the reasons that they created this opening was to combat bureaucratic deformations.[19]

In cinema, this early relaxation of state censorship of the media found its first results in the *Noticiero ICAIC*. Under the leadership of Santiago Álvarez, film directors such as Daniel Díaz Torres, Fernando Pérez, and Rolando Díaz began producing monothematic newsreels dedicated to problems in transportation, housing, and production, while cartoonists took up similar themes in Cuban humor magazines such as *Dedeté* and *Palante*.[20]

As the 1980s progressed, these themes made their way into fiction film. The first feature-length fiction film to adopt criticism of the bureaucracy as its organizing genre was a drama directed by a filmmaker who had already made his mark in Cuban cinema. The son of an American mother and a Cuban father, Afro-Cuban director Sergio Giral grew up between Havana and New York. While waiting tables as an aspiring visual artist in Greenwich Village in the late 1950s, Giral met and befriended Néstor Almendros, who regaled the younger Giral with stories of cinema and the Cuban Revolution and, when Giral went to visit his parents in Havana in the early 1960s, facilitated an introduction to the ICAIC. Excited by the possibility of using cinema to explore "Cuban culture, especially questions of race," Giral decided to stay in Cuba and joined the state film institute, where he established his reputation through a trilogy of films on Cuban slavery, including *El otro Francisco* (*The Other Francisco*, 1974), *Rancheador* (*Bounty Hunter*, 1976), and *Maluala* (1979).

With *Techo de vidrio*, Giral directed his interest in race in Cuba to the contemporary for the first time. The film tells the story of a white engineer and a black manager, who are both caught taking construction materials for their own or others' personal use. The lower-ranking black manager is swiftly brought to justice, despite the fact that he took the materials to help a friend whose house was in danger of collapsing. But at first it seems that the higher-ranking white engineer, who was motivated by the desire to build a larger study in his already ample home, will evade consequences. By the end of the film, the engineer chooses to confess to his misdeeds, thus bringing a happy resolution to the story of racism, class privilege, and corruption. Giral told me that he made the film out of a desire to "help" the Revolution, by "showing that there were people living the '*dulce vida*' among a certain class of functionaries—nothing like what [the Revolution] was supposed to be like."

But *Techo de vidrio* proved controversial from the outset. According to Giral, the screenplay for the film came under scrutiny by the Ministry of the Interior, after which Alfredo Guevara organized a commission to review it. This commission "censored two or three things" and gave the green light to the film, but the production of *Techo de vidrio* took place under surveillance and it was ultimately blocked from theatrical and festival release. Contextual circumstances may well have played a role in the censorship of the film. By the time *Techo de vidrio* was completed, Alfredo Guevara had been reassigned to a position as Cuba's ambassador to the United Nations Educational, Scientific and Cultural Organization (UNESCO) and Julio García Espinosa had taken over at the helm of the ICAIC following a scandal over Humberto Solás's megaproduction, *Cecilia* (1981).[21] When Giral inquired about getting *Techo de vidrio* shown, he recounted, Espinosa told him that he had "better forget about it because it is not such an important film anyway." "He couldn't take responsibility for the film because he was not Alfredo [Guevara]," Giral observed, reflecting the widespread sentiment among Cuban intellectuals that Guevara's political and social capital often allowed him to protect controversial films and filmmakers in ways that others could not. For his part, Giral decided to wait ("not just me—anyone who had something like that happen to them stayed quiet," he observed) only to find himself unable to get approval for another screenplay for the following five years.[22]

The bureaucrat comedies of the 1980s, finally, also have a direct precedent in Tomás Gutiérrez Alea's 1966 film, *La muerte de un burócrata*. In *Muerte*, a young man discovers that his aunt cannot receive her widow's pension unless they can provide the identity card that was buried with her deceased husband. The hapless and naïve protagonist is soon swept up in the cogs of a bureaucracy constituted by both corrupt, materialistic functionaries and rubber-stamping officials, impassively executing byzantine rules with no regard to real-life problems. *Muerte* also satirizes reductive and "bureaucratic" solutions to art. As the film's first sequence reveals, the deceased man's claim to the status of model worker is made on the basis of his invention of a machine that pops out identical busts of José Martí, thus transforming sculpture and commemoration into a mechanical expression that, in the end, proves its inventor's own undoing. In a nod to a sequence from Charlie Chaplin's *Modern Times* (1936), the worker dies when he is caught up in the cogs of his own machine and is reduced to a cement bust.[23] Bureaucracy, meanwhile, is comically shown to have infected even the film's own narration. The film's credits are presented in the form of a contract laden with official language, accompanied by the sounds of a typewriter and pompous music.

The bureaucrat comedies of the 1980s retained *Muerte*'s self-reflexive play as well as its two-pronged characterization of bureaucracy as at once involving hierarchical corruption and an impassive execution of illogical rules.[24] To these elements, they added a more extensive focus on the problems in infrastructure and social services, such as housing and transportation, that dominated political discourse and the *Noticiero ICAIC* of the late 1970s and 1980s, as well as a more directly activist dimension. In these films, the young hero or, increasingly, the young heroine is a revolutionary new man or woman who struggles to institute creative solutions to collective problems in solidarity with her fellow Cubans. Corrupt or rule-obsessed bureaucrats, meanwhile, stand in the way of the protagonist's efforts to help society toward the communist utopia.

The first two bureaucrat comedies of this decade were directed by Juan Carlos Tabío, who was promoted in the early 1980s by Julio García Espinosa to fiction filmmaking alongside other directors, including Daniel Díaz Torres, who had previously worked in the *Noticiero ICAIC* or in documentary filmmaking. Both of Tabío's bureaucrat comedies met with a happier fate than did *Techo de vidrio*. This may suggest an increasing tolerance for criticism of the bureaucracy among political leaders as the 1980s progressed and the genre began to play a more central role in state rhetoric. It also demonstrates the compatibility between Tabío's films and the ways in which criticism of the bureaucracy was deployed in official state discourse. To differing degrees, both Tabío's first film, *Se permuta* (*House for Swap*, 1985), and his second, *¡Plaff! O demasiado miedo a la vida* (*Plaff! Or Too Much Fear of Life*, 1988), focus discontent on mid- and lower-level bureaucrats, holding out hope that freeing up the channels of communication between citizens and top political leaders may yet lead to the restoration of collective effervescence.

In *Se permuta*, it is an excess of deviant social energies that gets the story going. Based on an idea by Tomás Gutiérrez Alea, the film takes as its central device the improvised system of *permutas* (house exchanges) that Cubans developed in lieu of the sale and purchase of homes that, under state socialism, were severely constrained by the state.[25] When Gloria witnesses her daughter, Yolanda, pocket a love letter from an Afro-Cuban car mechanic, she embarks on a quest to upgrade their home in the lower-income Guanabacoa neighborhood for one in a more upscale area, where she hopes her daughter will find a more "suitable" suitor. To realize this aspiration, she pieces together a complicated series of housing exchanges, arranging for a family with multiple children to move into a large but decaying home while the couple who occupied that house moves into Yolanda and Gloria's apartment. The latter, meanwhile, take up abode in a two-bedroom apartment in the middle-class Vedado neighborhood, where Gloria's hopes for her daughter soon bear fruit. When a full bus drives past the stop where Yolanda was waiting for it, a clear jab at the state of public transit, she accepts a ride from Guillermo, a midlevel functionary, in his Lada, the ownership of which indicates his privileged status.

Guillermo soon seduces Yolanda—or perhaps, more precisely, Gloria—through his willingness to employ his personal contacts to improve his own life and impress those around him. He works his connections to get tickets for a sold-out play for Yolanda, secures a telephone for Gloria, courts foreigners at a fancy bar, and fantasizes about buying luxury goods on a work trip abroad. His misuse of his position is given its most succinct formulation in an image that emblematizes the idea of a social energetics gone wrong. When a subordinate suggests a less expensive and less-energy-consuming billboard than the one with a thousand light bulbs and neon lights planned by Guillermo, Guillermo insists that this is a "very important campaign" and they have to design something that will "impact people . . . even if it costs a little more." "This has everything!" he exclaims as he holds up the more expensive version he prefers. As the camera cuts to a close-up of the design, he reads out the slogan with some satisfaction: "Economic rationalization means savings." As this scene makes clear, Guillermo is the spitting image of the socialist disguised as capitalist denounced by Fidel Castro in his 1986 speech, eager to throw excessive amounts of money and resources at all problems, even in a campaign for efficiency.

The film treats this excess energy not only as immoral but, more importantly, as repetitive and alienated. In his classic essay on comedy, Henri Bergson ([1900] 1924) theorizes laughter and the comic in terms that resonate interestingly with the work of Weber and Durkheim. Here, he maintains that we laugh at individuals who are unable to adapt to changing circumstances and instead pursue a set idea or behavior in a "mechanical" and "rigid" manner. As Bergson puts it, "the comic is that side of a person which reveals his likeness to a thing, that aspect of human events which, through its peculiar inelasticity, conveys the impression of a pure mechanism, of automatism, of movement without life" ([1900] 1924, 87). Such automatism not only betrays individual alienation; it also gets in the way of social cohesion. A well-functioning society, Bergson elaborates, requires that its members engage in a continuous process of "adjustment of wills which will fit more and more perfectly into one another" (19). Laughter, in his model, therefore serves as a social corrective, calling attention to behaviors that threaten this ideally flexible and adaptive relationship.

In *Se permuta*, this corrective version of laughter combines with a Brechtian-inspired self-reflexivity in an effort to restore the collective social energies that, as we have seen, have gone awry in the film. After announcing his desire to marry Yolanda, Guillermo convinces Gloria to piece together new and ever-more-elaborate housing exchanges in order to secure the couple a more luxurious home. When the first of these exchanges falls apart, Gloria embarks on a second. At this point, the film interrupts the fictional story with a scene in which Enrique Colina discusses *Se permuta* on the TV show dedicated to cinema he in fact hosted at the time, *24 por Segundo* (*Twenty-Four Frames a Second*). In a close-up of a blue-lit TV screen, Colina explains that Gloria's machinations, which at first struck us as funny, have now grown "repetitive." As the camera moves back to reveal Yolanda herself watching the show, Colina continues, explaining that Gloria has at last found the "ideal housing exchange to secure her daughter, Yolanda, and Guillermo's happiness." But Yolanda, it seems, has her doubts about this solution. As melodramatic theme music starts to play, the young woman stands up abruptly and leaves the room. Taking note of this action, Colina calls for the next sequence to be played.

Drawing attention both to the film as a film and to the mechanical and alienated nature of Gloria's behavior, this scene finally leads to *Se permuta*'s happy socialist ending. While Gloria and Guillermo were becoming increasingly engrossed in their individualistic pursuit of a well-heeled home, Yolanda for her part was falling in love with Pepe, a poor, Afro-Cuban civil engineer. After watching Colina discuss her predicament, Yolanda finally reaches a decision. She breaks off her engagement with Guillermo and follows Pepe to Cuba's Isla de la Juventud (Isle of Youth), where together they will create inexpensive, prefabricated homes to solve the housing problem. In the closing images of the film, the young couple reveals what a truly adaptive and collectivist energy looks like, jokingly moving the door to their new prefab home about an empty lot as they attempt to find the perfect location. Guillermo, meanwhile, gets what is coming to him. Called in by his boss for a meeting that he hopes will lead to a trip abroad, he is met instead with a boardroom filled with disapproving faces. This dénouement suggests a version of the fantasy of benevolent surveillance recounted earlier: when news of Guillermo's abuse of his position and ineffective managerial tactics reaches a higher level of power, his superiors intervene. *Se permuta*'s criticism of the bureaucracy thus preserves faith in the state hierarchy and in collective effervescence, reducing the problem of bureaucracy to the errant energies of a few individuals. As Tabío himself told me, "*Se permuta* is a bit naïve; it's a Manichaean take on reality. In that era, we were all a little naïve. We saw things in an idyllic way."[26]

Juan Carlos Tabío's second bureaucrat comedy, *¡Plaff! O demasiado miedo a la vida*, takes these themes of bureaucracy and the struggle to harness social energy to the Revolution one step further. Through the use of an open ending and a circular narrative structure, the film presents the struggle with bureaucracy as an ongoing problem that will not be easily resolved. In *Plaff*, even more so than in *La muerte de un burócrata*, bureaucracy has taken over the production and narration of the film itself. *Plaff* begins with an intertitle explaining that the film was made in record time so that it could be released on the "Día del cineasta" (Day of the Filmmaker). This effort at speed, however, has evidently resulted in a fair deal of what was often derided at the time as *chapucería* (shoddy work).[27] When the film's first image appears, it is shown upside down, then cuts to white, while the voice of a projectionist announces over the loud clicking of a movie projector that the film's first reel arrived damaged and will be sent back to the ICAIC for repairs. Viewers are then left to begin the film with its second reel. This criticism of bureaucracy is further elaborated in the film's narrative, which tells the story of Concha, a middle-aged woman who objects to the marriage between her baseball player son, José Ramón, and Clarita, an engineer. As the conflict between the two women unfolds, Concha finds herself the target of eggs thrown repeatedly at the side of her house and eventually dies of a heart attack, while Clarita struggles with the bureaucracy to get a polymer that she has invented developed.

The tense relationship between Concha and Clarita is highlighted in an early scene that takes place at the watch shop where Concha works as a manager. When an elderly man arrives seeking compensation for a defective watch that is still under warranty, Concha explains that he can either exchange the watch for a new one or get his money back. The client chooses exchange, only to discover that he will receive just five days of warranty on the replacement watch, the time remaining to him on his original contract, instead of the six months granted a new purchase. The gentleman objects, but when Concha tells him to present his complaints to the management, he acquiesces forlornly. At this point, Clarita, who has witnessed the entire exchange, intervenes. Instructing the man to ask for his money back for the broken watch, she then tells him to use this money to purchase the new watch, which will now come with the full six months' guarantee. Concha, meanwhile, becomes increasingly irate with Clarita. After José Ramón arrives and drags Clarita out of the shop, Concha complains to the client that everything for the young woman is "absurd" or "poorly done" in spite of the fact that "the Revolution has given her everything." "Youth are very ungrateful," the elderly gentleman concurs, transforming the scene into what Guy Baron describes as a scathing "criticism of . . . administrative ineptitude and its tacit acceptance by a population dulled by irrationality of this type" (2011, 57).

While Concha, as depicted in this scene, adopts a bureaucratic mentality, prioritizing rules and regulations over solving problems, Clarita embodies the new woman, quick to challenge everything that is wrong. Like Guillermo in *Se permuta*, Tabío explained to me, Concha is a person "who sees life in a mechanical manner: things are as they say they are, not as they really are." Indeed, throughout the film, Concha epitomizes that older generation that Che Guevara argued had not only reduced the Revolution to a nonproductive "formalism" but had also "lost their faith in life" ([1962] 1967, 364). In one of the film's two central plots, Concha struggles to discover who has been throwing eggs at her, an act that, according to Afro-Cuban religion, brings bad luck to its target. Over the course of the film, Concha becomes increasingly distraught as possible suspects are cleared of guilt, or at least so it seems, and yet the eggs continue to be thrown. As her anxieties mount, Concha finally succumbs to a heart attack when she hears what she thinks is yet another egg (but which turns out to be a baseball) hit the side of the house. The film, meanwhile, disrupts any empathy spectators might feel for Concha by accompanying her collapse with the nondiegetic sound of a heart monitor flat lining.

In the film's final scenes, the mystery of the eggs is resolved. When Concha's *madrina* (godmother) runs into José Ramón and a now-pregnant Clarita at the cemetery, she invites them back to her house along with several of the film's other characters.[28] Here she reveals that each of the characters had thrown an egg in the hopes of scaring Concha into leaving her home and moving in with her kindly suitor, Tomás. In a satirical send-up of the plots of the telenovelas Concha consumes, while Concha loved Tomás, she had resolutely refused his offer of marriage, afraid that he would turn out to be a philanderer like her deceased husband. Concha, her madrina concludes, was "too afraid. Too afraid of life." Mikhail Bakhtin argues that the body and its "lower" functions—"defecation and copulation, pregnancy, and birth"—often play a "regenerating" role in grotesque forms of humor, standing in for the possibility of renewing the collective (1984, 19–21). In *Plaff*, Concha's death by eggs suggests just such a rebirth, killing off the member of the older generation most fearful of change in the film to make room for the new, vital energies of youth, as emblematized by Clarita, José Ramón, and their soon-to-be-born child.

Refusing the easy ending of Tabío's earlier film, in *Plaff*, however, bureaucracy does not die with Concha. Making the grotesque aspect of the film even more evident, the film's second central plot pits Clarita against a seemingly endless bureaucracy, as she struggles to get permission and resources to develop an inexpensive polymer she has invented out of pig manure. Clarita's efforts are first thwarted by her boss's preference for foreign technologies, which she angrily dismisses as motivated by a desire "to travel abroad and waste money." But even after the polymer is proven to extract metals from water and the young woman is granted an award for her invention, her efforts to see her invention developed continue to be blocked. Bureaucrat after bureaucrat cites rules and regulations, demands that paperwork be filled, and refers the case to the "proper" authority until the proposal at last reaches the head of the "Institute for the Development of Excrement," who in turn only demands more paperwork, dismissing the pretensions of so-called inventors when this is where the "highly qualified specialists are."

Comically emphasizing the labyrinthine nature of this bureaucracy, meanwhile, every one of the bureaucrats in the film is played by the same actor, Jorge Cao, including one female bureaucrat whom Cao plays in drag. All the bureaucrats are named Contreras; and each carries on an ongoing battle with an outsized filing cabinet that blocks the doorway to their office, causing them to hit their head against it every time they walk through the door. Yet when his secretary announces to Contreras, this time in his role as director of the Excrement Institute, that the filing cabinet has finally been taken away, his joy is dampened by the pile of papers left in its wake. These are his memos about the filing cabinet, explains the secretary, as well as the responses, the replies to the responses, and the responses to the replies. She proposes that they clean up the mess by throwing out the papers. Contreras protests, "I need a written record of everything I do!" and leaves his secretary to find a solution, which she does by ordering a filing cabinet exactly like the one just removed.

If Clarita attempts to advance the Revolution by literally recycling refuse into new energy for the collective, in other words, the bureaucracy's obsession with *papeleo* (paperwork) stops up her efforts to get the collective's energies flowing. Nonetheless, things begin to look up for the young inventor when José Ramón makes a public appeal on her behalf. Toward the end of the film, José Ramón gives an interview on national television in which the baseball star explains that he is sad not because he has been benched due to an injury to his arm (obtained offscreen earlier in the film) but because of the obstacles confronting his engineer wife, whose "polymer is not being produced nor, from what we can see, will it be produced, because of the idiocy of the bureaucracy, the stupidity and the stinginess of a group of functionaries from a ton of different places." "It's because of this type of person that the country can't advance!" he concludes.

Shortly after this scene and Concha's death, a final Contreras appears on Clarita and José Ramón's doorstep and announces that the polymer will, after all, be developed. Not only is baseball Cuba's national sport, but Fidel Castro himself was famously a baseball fan and was even known to provide interviews about national matters (including egg production) while playing the game.[29] Perhaps, then, we are meant to assume that work on the polymer finally advances because José Ramón's televised plea has reached the ears of the comandante himself. Regardless, this deblocking of bureaucracy proves short-lived. The final Contreras announces that Clarita must rush production for Chemist's Day, suggesting that the bureaucracy's dedication to formalities over practical reality will once again impede progress. Bringing the film full circle, *Plaff* then closes with the reel that had initially arrived damaged. Turned right-side up and running smoothly, this reel reveals that it was Concha who threw the first egg in an attempt to frighten Clarita. Truly, as Armando Hart might have put it, Cuba's worst enemy lies within.

The Bureaucratization of the Revolution

By deflecting dissatisfaction onto lower- or midlevel administrators and bureaucratically minded citizens, criticism of the bureaucracy thus enabled a far-reaching depiction of social problems and state practices, while holding out hope that collective effervescence might yet be restored through the concerted efforts of revolutionary new men and women working in cooperation with the nation's top leaders. This strategy for containing dissent, however, was also inherently volatile. Stripped of its veneer as a rational system of decision-making, argues Claude Lefort, bureaucracy reveals a hierarchical structure focused on its own reproduction (1986, 103, 106, 111–12). As we have already seen, Cuban political leaders such as Che Guevara and Armando Hart themselves viewed bureaucracy in a similar light, even as they exempted top political leaders from this criticism. But by the twenty-first century, arguments tying bureaucracy to a reified and authoritarian system of power took on new force in Cuba, as intellectuals mobilized criticism of the bureaucracy to denounce Fidel Castro and other top officials for standing in the way of revolution as an ideal of change and collective effervescence.

The older filmmakers and intellectuals with whom I worked often described their relationship to the Revolution in its early years as one of collective effervescence. Ambrosio Fornet, for instance, recalled how, when he returned from Spain in 1959, Cuba seemed to him to have been transformed into a paradise on Earth.

> There was a sense of community in which one would say, "Let's go collect raw materials," cardboard, bottles, this and that. It was part of *"el baño del pueblo"* [immersing yourself in the people], your way of learning how to be communitarian, of identifying yourself with others, enacting solidarity. "They don't have to come and sweep the streets; we can sweep." When I returned from Spain in September 1959, all the doors were open everywhere. And I felt, "This is what I want, this is what I aspire to, this is the world that I love." Maybe it was a question of religion. My mother was Baptist and I had been to the Dominican school and I knew my Bible and my gospels and it seemed to me that we had already reached paradise. How marvelous![30]

Filmmaker Gerardo Chijona remembered the early years of the Revolution in similarly romantic terms.

> It was a romantic era. Everyone absolutely wanted to be doing what they were doing. There was a project that, especially at that age, gave you the opportunity to participate—it was a collective project, but you knew that you had your little space to interact with it. For all the material needs, for all the political tensions, it was fundamentally a romantic moment in the country. It was very easy to fall in love with a process like that, especially at the age that we were, when we were starting our lives, and there were opportunities for all of us to become involved. It was something that we all shared.[31]

Juan Carlos Tabío argued that when Eastern European socialism collapsed in the early 1990s, it was this collective commitment that held the Cuban Revolution together.

> What happened in Poland or in Hungary where socialism was established by the Soviet army didn't happen in Cuba. In Cuba, the Revolution was a process that was completely popular and in which one participated. There was a relationship, let's say of love, with the revolutionary process, and which was,

nonetheless, anguished, because you're in love but, at the same time, you start to see the defects, the fissures or things that shouldn't be. It's not like in the case of Eastern European intellectuals where socialism was imposed by the Soviet boot. These are totally different cases. This was a revolution that was absolutely popular and that had deep roots. And so everything happened differently.

As these stories suggest, many older intellectuals were attracted to the Revolution by promises of personal fulfillment in a society striving for collective solidarity, social justice, and national autonomy. Yet, as time wore on and economic difficulties and inequalities persisted and worsened, they became increasingly exhausted by exhortations to self-sacrifice for the sake of a future utopia that never seemed to arrive. Tabío elaborated: "At first you say things are like this but it will get better, we're making sacrifices in order to accomplish things. But when those goals get farther and farther away and aren't achieved, you say, 'What are we doing?' You have to rethink things. And that's what happened, I think, with Cuban intellectuals."

Even in the face of this growing disaffection, however, many were reluctant to abandon the promises they had long associated with the Cuban Revolution. Explaining wryly that he was "becoming more and more of a pessimist," Tabío insisted that there were values in the Revolution that must be saved. "I believe that the seeds for a better future are in Cuban society," he explained. "There are elements of social justice in Cuban society, in this concept of the Revolution." Enrique Colina summarized the sentiments of his generation in similar terms: "I can say that, like many *compañeros* of the ICAIC, I agree with the principles of the Revolution: social justice, the need to preserve our national sovereignty, dignity, respect for individuals, respect for diversity, respect for rights. This is revolution. But we are in disagreement with the way things have been done."

Intellectuals' uses of criticism of the bureaucracy in the twenty-first century reflected this ambivalent attachment. Rather than divorcing themselves from the social project that had long served as a mainstay of their lives, older intellectuals in particular criticized the state and its practices as themselves a betrayal—or, more precisely, as the bureaucratization and stagnation—of the Revolution and the vital energies that it had initially unleashed. When I asked Enrique Colina to explain what he meant by bureaucracy, he responded:

Bureaucracy is the crystallization of the vitality of the Revolution and the deformation of this process of change. All societies need an administration—

functionaries and politicians—who are those who give structure to the state. But a lot of the time, this structure becomes an end in itself. And on top of it, [in Cuba] this end in itself is happening in a state that is so totalitarian that it inserts itself into every aspect of life. Mixed up in this are also the interests of those who are within that state structure, who want to keep their positions in order to enjoy a certain privilege in an economic context in which there are no private businesses, where people can't make their living any other way. In a system that is supposedly egalitarian, they have certain privileges and opportunities that the majority of the population doesn't have.

At first things were different here, because the young guerrillas were more westernized and questioned the stagnation of Marxism. They wanted a fresh and more vital interpretation; also, this emerged from Third-Worldism. Previously socialism had been theorized for developed countries but here they were talking about socialism in underdeveloped countries. But when all of that vitality that the Revolution had took on institutional form and the years passed, the urgency of this need for change and this desire to avoid stagnation started to wane. Those who are in charge started to stagnate. And, in the case of Cuba, they got used to having an absolute power. They started to believe that they know the truth because they are the ones who started the Revolution and so everything they say and do must be revolution, which is a bureaucratization of the concept. There is no more revolution here. That is already over.

Colina's account of bureaucracy as a blockage of revolutionary energies at first follows the conventions of the genre as established by Cuban political leaders. In Colina's statement, as in Armando Hart's 1967 editorials, concerns about the bureaucracy translate into worries about the growth of a privileged class of administrators who seek only their own self-interest at the expense of efficiency and collective energies.

Yet where Hart proposed to solve this problem through the promotion of revolutionary consciousness among leaders, holding up Fidel Castro as an example to be followed, several decades later, Colina argued that it was revolutionary leaders themselves who had begun to "stagnate." Insisting that Fidel Castro was not "corrupt" but a "man who believes in his principles and is honest with his ideas," he nonetheless noted that he had begun to feel increasingly impatient with and critical of tendencies in Cuba to displace blame to lower-level functionaries. "When they blamed the technocrats during rectification, this, to me, was unacceptable," he explained, referencing the execution of top officials, including General Arnaldo Ochoa

Sánchez, on charges of drug smuggling and treason in 1989. "It was an easy way to avoid responsibility. It is never the fault of the *maximum dirigencia* [maximum leadership]. It's always others who are responsible."[32]

In other cases, intellectuals mobilized an ideal of revolution as a continuously adaptable process of change to question Fidel Castro's authority. In this vein, art director Erick Grass observed:

> Revolution is progress; it's constant development; it's a constant struggle so that things will change. You can't stay stuck with what we are used to thinking about as the Revolution: Fidel and all his team, the old revolutionaries and the old communists. To be truly revolutionary one has to recognize all of our defects, recognize them and work to change them. We can't entrench ourselves in the idea that if one speaks ill of these problems one is a counterrevolutionary. The real counterrevolutionaries are those who defend official images of bonanza when, in reality, the country is in crisis.[33]

Statements such as these take Che Guevara's call to speak up against everything that is wrong "no matter who said it" further than Guevara himself likely intended. Here, the real counterrevolutionaries are the aging political leaders who continue to protect a status quo gone wrong, while to be a revolutionary means revealing difficult realities and fighting for change. As such comments make clear, if criticism of the bureaucracy once promised reconciliation between citizens and their political leaders, by the twenty-first century, intellectuals were drawing on this genre to reclaim the ideals and promises of the Revolution against authoritarianism and even Fidel Castro himself.

Alicia, the Bureaucrat, and the Trouble with Open Endings

Reading *Alicia en el pueblo de maravillas* in these discursive contexts sheds new light on how the film could at once be defended as revolutionary and denounced as an attack on socialism. Anticipating the ways in which intellectuals would deploy criticism of the bureaucracy in the twenty-first century, *Alicia*'s use of the genre moved beyond criticizing the bad morals of a few administrators and citizens to challenge state authoritarianism more broadly. From the time I first interviewed him about the scandal over *Alicia* in 2003 through conversations in 2009, Daniel Díaz Torres repeatedly insisted that his film was inspired by the political atmosphere of glasnost, perestroika, and rectification and aimed to restore revolutionary energies.

"The film was based on principles that I defend, principles that for me are authentically revolutionary," he told me. "It was a criticism of a bureaucratic deformation of power, of a loss of civic-mindedness, and a reminder that, as revolutionaries, people needed to act, to question, to engage in positive criticism."[34]

At the level of plot, this call for renewed revolutionary activism is conveyed through Alicia's efforts to engage the townspeople in the creation of socially relevant art that will counter citizen apathy and the paternalism that perpetuates it. Maravillas, as Alicia discovers upon her arrival in the town to take up her role as a community theater instructor, is plagued by the sort of workplace inefficiency and corruption criticized by Fidel Castro in the late 1980s. From Candido, the truck driver who was seduced by a voluptuous woman into illegally selling state cheese; to Pérez, the functionary driven mad by anonymous messages that proclaim his virtues after he sells out a colleague to climb the company ranks—the townspeople have all been sent to Maravillas to be rehabilitated for misdemeanors in their state workplaces. But life in Maravillas only exacerbates these problems. The medicine cabinet in Alicia's hotel room opens directly onto another resident's bathroom due to "construction"—or so explains Omar Rodríguez, the town's cultural director, who introduces himself with some embarrassment when she opens the cabinet to find him shaving and flirting with a lover. Like Juan Carlos Tabío's *Plaff* before it, *Alicia* also makes ample use of the grotesque to depict a social energetics gone wrong: pipes make wretched gurgling noises, a large metal tube seems to come alive, rotating to chase Alicia and spew mud at her, and a speaker vomits grimy liquid, while a sign below it advises that "open ears" are best accompanied by "closed mouths."

Compounding these ills, the head of the local sanatorium, the acronym for which, significantly, spells SATAN, rules the town through a combination of surveillance, intimidation, and propaganda. Throughout the film, citizens pause to listen in on Alicia's conversations, while makeshift spy equipment—mini-megaphones mounted on sticks, to be precise—follow her every move. In one early scene, workers haphazardly toss buckets of asphalt off the back of tractors, causing clouds of floating papers to stick to the feet of passersby, while a cheerful voice explains the disaster over a loudspeaker as part of the "Pig Plan" to improve the city's streets. Monuments in the city square, meanwhile, spell out PRODUCTION and CONSCIOUSNESS in enormous stone letters—all caps—while nearby park benches built to disproportionate sizes force the townspeople to sit with their feet dangling off the ground. The "charismatic message," to borrow

Max Weber's terms, has, quite literally, become "petrified tradition," while "paternalistic" governance, as Díaz Torres put it to me, infantilizes citizens and prevents their "authentic participation." Even the film's art direction is mobilized to emphasize the conformism that pervades Maravillas. Characters wear clothing made out of identical material—a print depicting fried eggs on a yellow background—which one Cuban friend interpreted as a reference to the paucity of goods available in state stores in the 1980s, and which Díaz Torres explained as a criticism of efforts to "impose uniform thinking" on Cuban citizens, efforts that, he insisted, were a "negation of the meaning of revolution."[35]

For her part, however, Alicia is not content to stand idly by. Partway through the film, she learns that the townspeople have been hard at work on producing a play in which a worker refuses to accept a fan so that, as one of the amateur actors explains to a perturbed Alicia, "we will all be equal in the heat." Why don't they write a play about the actual problems of the town's inhabitants, she asks Omar in a later scene set in the city square, after he finishes telling her yet another of the townspeople's stories. As they talk, an old man seated on one of the square's oversized park benches surveils the couple, laughing convulsively as his feet dangle childlike off the ground (figure 3.1). Omar at first dismisses Alicia as "naïve" and suggests that they instead take romantic refuge in one another. But Alicia refuses to be cowed by either surveillance or cynicism. "I may be naïve, but I'm not cynical," she proclaims, turning abruptly to the old man and demanding to know what he is laughing about. Omar, meanwhile, agrees to join her in her efforts to rally the townspeople.

Alicia's struggle to make a new kind of art comes to a head during a screening of a short cartoon animation about a bird stuck in a pile of cow dung whose defeatist moral goes: when you are buried in shit, it is best to stay still for fear of attracting worse trouble. "How can you say that this is good? What does this mean?" Alicia demands when the animation comes to an end, interrupting the townspeople's applause. Her second question might equally refer to the significance of the film or to the townspeople's approval of it. But the children in the audience take up the first version of her query, providing an exegesis of the animation, while the director of the animation sneers, "Don't you realize, *compañerita*, that even children understand the meaning of my work?" A heated debate ensues, only to be interrupted by ominous music and a flashing red light as the sanatorium director descends in a grille-covered elevator into the dank basement in which the townspeople are gathered.

Figure 3.1 Alicia tries to convince Omar to join her in combating the apathy of the Maravillenos in Daniel Díaz Torres's *Alicia en el pueblo de maravillas* (1991) while an old man seated on a nearby park bench looks on and laughs cynically, his feet dangling childlike off the ground.

He had overheard their "stimulating" conversation from his office, the director explains in a statement that is at once comic and chilling, reminding spectators of the surveillance pervasive throughout the film. "This has always been our policy," he intones, raising one index finger in the air, "to give voice to the people" (figure 3.2). Belying this claim to democracy, the film cuts to a point-of-view shot from the director's perspective, showing his finger in the forefront of the frame as he points toward each character one by one. "It didn't matter to us if Rodríguez, to give an example," he says, indicating Omar, "had a previous situation in his workplace and now a few small personal problems." As the director draws attention to the characters' troubled histories in a doublespeak to which everyone in the room is attuned, Alicia's allies abandon her from fear. "I want to say that the *compañera* theater instructor's intervention seems somewhat superficial," pronounces one of her allies nervously when the director asks him if he has anything to add. Alicia makes a final attempt to rally the courage of the

It has always been our policy

Figure 3.2 The all-seeing director of the sanatorium in Maravillas calls attention to the failings of individual characters to frighten them into compliance in *Alicia en el pueblo de maravillas* (1991).

townspeople. "I don't know if you are all ruined, but I do know that you are alive!" she exclaims, asserting the citizens' rights to their opinions in spite of their previous mistakes. But she is met only with the feeble query of an old man whose inability to hear her speaks for the others' refusal to follow her lead. "Cowards!" she proclaims. Then she storms out of the basement, as a riff on the theme song from *Star Wars* and a flash of lightning accompany her departure in an ironic crescendo.

As I have shown, criticism of the bureaucracy typically contains dissatisfaction by holding out the fantasy that social problems could be resolved if only citizens could bypass the bureaucracy to communicate directly with Fidel Castro. But as this scene demonstrates, in *Alicia*, there is no sign of a higher power to which citizens might appeal, surveillance is far from benign, and even the film's depiction of the activism of the new woman (Alicia) seems to vacillate between sincerity and hyperbole. The townspeople's reluctance to stand up for social change clearly has a source greater than the errant morals of a few mid- or lower-level functionaries: fear of an all-seeing authority whose pretense at democratic inclusion only barely masks totalitarian control over their lives. The use of point-of-view shots as the sanatorium director singles out his targets, meanwhile, suggests that blame does not rest solely at the feet of those in positions of leadership. Aligning spectators with the director's tactics of intimidation, the film both implicates citizens themselves in this "bureaucratic deformation of power" and calls on them to overcome it. In *Alicia*, this is clearly a task whose resolution requires something more than firing a few functionaries to free up the channels of communication between Fidel Castro and the masses.

The film's use of criticism of the bureaucracy to criticize a hierarchical and authoritarian use of power already suggests one reason for which the film might have been viewed as a condemnation of Cuban state socialism, in spite of Díaz Torres's insistence that it was meant to restore revolutionary energies. Such a reading was given further fuel by the film's modernist narrative structure and open ending. Following the screening of the animation, as I have just noted, the schoolchildren and the director of the short film make fun of Alicia for what they perceive as her failure to understand an allegory that is so transparent that even children can interpret it. But the film, in turn, makes fun of the townspeople for their taste in art. If the cartoon is horrible, as Alicia claims, then this is as much because of its style and the excessively transparent nature of its meaning as because of its defeatist message.

Alicia en el pueblo de maravillas, by contrast, takes a more nuanced approach to the construction of its meaning. In a twist on *Plaff*'s missing first reel, *Alicia* begins with what at first appears to be its ending. A young woman, who we will only later learn is Alicia, makes her escape across a stream and waves down a passing truck. When she climbs aboard, however, she is confronted by a character dressed in a Darth Vader–style cape, who will later be revealed as the sanatorium director. She throws him over the side of the bridge, where he falls, presumably, to his death. The rest of the film is then presented as a flashback designed to explain this odd murder.

When these events are repeated toward the end of the film, however, their status as reality is drawn into question. Following her outburst during the screening of the animation, Alicia is made prisoner in the town sanatorium. She makes her escape with the help of Omar and the schoolchildren, who turn the animation and its defeatist moral on its head, substituting manure for mud in the sanatorium's baths and smuggling Alicia out by hiding her in the hollow center of a statue of a schoolgirl in uniform.[36] Alicia then disguises herself as a man to compete in a town race whose prize, an announcer explains, will be departure from Maravillas so as to "spread" the town's "initiatives" to "other provinces" and the "entire country." As the riff on the *Star Wars* theme plays, the sanatorium director finally recognizes Alicia among the crowd, calls for his Darth Vader cape, and sets out after her. Her escape then leads to a repetition of the film's opening images: we watch her run across the small stream, flag down the truck, and throw the sanatorium director off the bridge. This time, however, the body of the sanatorium director explodes, leaving behind only a puddle of bubbling, yellow mud. In the scene that follows, Alicia wakes up to find herself back in the broken-down bus station from whence she first began her journey to Maravillas. When a waitress brings her a bottle of water, reminiscent of the sulfuric water used as treatments in Maravillas' sanatorium, she pours it out onto the ground. Spectators, meanwhile, are left to ponder whether, as Alicia puts it in a direct address to the camera, the preceding events "were or were not a nightmare" and to make sense of the enigmatic moral with which she closes the film: "With warm, fizzy, water without a label, you won't reach your goal."

In interviews after *Alicia*'s release, Daniel Díaz Torres repeatedly insisted that Alicia's rejection of the bottle of water stood in for her refusal of "an apathetic and conformist attitude." The invocation of the dream, meanwhile, was meant to blur the line between fiction and reality and invite spectators to look for parallels between social problems and their hyperbolic depiction in Maravillas (West 1993). According to this argument, far from condemning the Revolution, the film's open ending was meant as a Brechtian incitement to action. Like Alicia, the spectator is supposed to "wake up," recognize the problems that surround them in their everyday reality, and work to resolve them so that Cuba does not become Maravillas or, in the language of the film, so that the town's "initiatives" are not spread to the "country."

For many of the film's Cuban reviewers, however, this ending confirmed *Alicia*'s condemnation of the Cuban Revolution in its moment of crisis. "Alicia doesn't want adjustments or improvements under a sky so gray," observed Bernardo Callejas in a review published on June 16, 1991, in the Cuban newspaper *Trabajadores* (*Workers*). "She also doesn't admit the possibility of change. She simply wants to start from zero, after escaping in a stampede from the Maravillenos and everything they have been able to create." Callejas linked *Alicia*'s supposed call to abandon state socialism to contemporary events, comparing Alicia and Omar to dissident playwright Václav Havel, who acceded to the presidency of Czechoslovakia in 1989, and implying that the film represented Cuban filmmakers' aspirations to power: "If an expert in representations can become the president of Czechoslovakia, why shouldn't this new crème de la crème guide those humble and poorly oriented townspeople of Maravillas who can't see beyond their own noses down the right path?" In a review published a couple of days later in *Granma*, Roxana Pollo concurred with his assessment of the film as an attack on the Revolution. "In *Alicia en el pueblo de maravillas*, the therapeutic effects of satire, the attack on and proclamation of our deficiencies, leaves no room for hope," she wrote. "Hell doesn't merit salvation. The alienated characters of Maravillas . . . have only one choice: to flee."

Lea Jacobs (1988, 1997) argues that one of the norms regularly applied by censors to Hollywood cinema under the Hays code was the "rule of moral closure": films could represent morally dubious situations, provided that these problems were resolved by the end of the film in socially normative ways. From the 1960s on, as we have seen, Cuban filmmakers rejected Hollywood's "happy endings" as ideologically suspect, opting instead for open endings meant to incite spectators to address the social problems depicted in films. Yet as reactions to *Alicia* demonstrate, filmmakers were not entirely free of the strictures applied under the Hays code or in other contexts shaped by censorship. Rather, they engaged in a delicate balancing act, working to ensure that the problems they depicted in their films appeared resolvable within and through state socialism. As Tomás Gutiérrez Alea cautioned in *Dialéctica del espectador*, the "open work of art" must not be "ambiguous, inconsistent, eclectic, or arbitrary" (1982, 33; see also chapter 2). In one plausible reading, then, *Alicia* draws on the revolutionary activism of the new man and modernist aesthetic techniques to call on citizens to combat corruption, apathy, bureaucracy, and bad art, in order to restore the Revolution to its true effervescence. But in the fragile political circumstances that accompanied the collapse of the Soviet Union, the filmmakers' attempts to walk the delicate line between criticism from within and counterrevolution, directed indirection and excessive openness, came undone.

Hyperallegorical Spectators Strike Back

Demonstrating once more the central role that conflicts over allegory, interpretation, and authorial intention play in shaping public debate in Cuba as in other contexts, arguments not only about what *Alicia* meant but also about who was responsible for the production of these meanings permeated the controversy that surrounded the film. After he was called back from his position at the UNESCO to manage the scandal, one of the tactics that Alfredo Guevara used to try to put an end to the debate was to screen *Alicia* at the December 1991 New Latin American Film Festival, preceded by an introduction by both himself and Daniel Díaz Torres. This was a plan to which Díaz Torres initially objected. In a letter addressed to Guevara on September 20, 1991, the filmmaker recalled the positive reception the film had received at the Berlinale. The film and its initial acclaim, he insisted, reflected "favorably not only on Cuban cinema, but also on the Revolution" by demonstrating the Cuban state's openness to criticism and public debate. It was the scandal over *Alicia* and not some characteristic inherent to the film itself, continued the director, that had ruined *Alicia*'s ability to work in favor of the Revolution. Noting that Miami's Cuban exile community was beginning to take an interest in the film, Díaz Torres insisted that this reaction was one that had been facilitated by denunciations of *Alicia* as counterrevolutionary on the island and which would then be used as further evidence of the filmmakers' counterrevolutionary intentions. "It seems like an inevitable and almost diabolical circle is closing," he wrote. With the favorable reception of *Alicia* in Miami, "people will say 'here is the ideal spectator for this film. What were the hidden intentions of this film, that it is now celebrated by the enemy?'" (qtd. in Guevara 2008, 484–85).

To some degree, Alfredo Guevara agreed with Díaz Torres's argument that the denunciations of the film as counterrevolutionary were themselves responsible for the controversy. In a note included in a 1992 press release about the film, Guevara insisted that "the film . . . belongs to Daniel Díaz Torres, a Cuban revolutionary from Cuba and for Cuba, who won't let himself be pushed into dispirited or counterrevolutionary positions, nor will he allow counterrevolutionaries to use the film against his intentions." If *Alicia* had been construed otherwise, then this was due to the "ambiguity" inherent in all art. "Fortunately, there always remains a margin for the imagination of the receiver" in interpretation, declared the ICAIC director. "Every spectator should ask himself (and also explain to himself) the reasons for his own reactions," concluded Guevara (2003, 480–81). Transferring responsibility for readings of the film from its creators to the audience, Guevara implied that those who found counterrevolution in *Alicia* should look to their own consciences.

But the ICAIC director also clearly placed blame for the controversy on what he viewed as the film's excessive ambiguity. In a private letter responding to Díaz Torres's 1991 letter, Guevara insisted that he believed in Díaz Torres's "sincerity and pain" but also objected to the filmmaker's characterization of the plan to present *Alicia* at the New Latin American Film Festival as "hypocritical." "You are not willing to recognize that the film has a potential double reading," noted Guevara. "But it does."

> The conflict didn't begin with the measures [taken against the film,] regardless of how excessive or offensive these might appear to you. It began with the film, with its potential double reading, and, as a result, with its conception and creation. . . . I do not reject the critical spirit, or the necessity and convenience of its exercise. But I am aware of the fact that different degrees of disenchantment with the Revolution, with the revolutionary project and its leadership, and sometimes—you insist that this is not your case and I do not doubt it—with its leader, have become mixed up with this critical spirit. (Guevara 2008, 488–89)

If *Alicia* had proven controversial, then this was because its creators had failed to take sufficient care to ensure that their modernist allegory would work to improve the Cuban Revolution, a project that Guevara here carefully distinguished from challenging Cuba's political hierarchy.

For their part, those who denounced the film in the Cuban press dismissed arguments that they should look to themselves for the origins of the counterrevolutionary meanings that they detected in *Alicia*. "Only those who are suspicious believe that we are demoralized by the 'errors in interpretation'" to which the film lent itself, declared one reviewer with transparent sarcasm. "If you are not a 'dogmatic,' you should understand that [the filmmakers] don't mean to describe our democracy or attack our political system" (Rodríguez Parilla 1991). "These are ambiguous elements in a film replete with signs that don't abide by an entirely recognizable code and for that reason admit all sorts of interpretations," observed another, as he drew out some of the meanings he believed could be found in the film. Yet if spectators could not establish their interpretations with certainty, these readings also could not simply be denied. "In these zones of uncertainty, the filmmakers will be able to claim that, instead of what one has seen or believes to have seen, they meant to say one thing or another," he noted. But then he quickly asserted the rights of spectators against such strategies: "Those who have watched the film have an equal right to read its contents" (Callejas 1991).

While Daniel Díaz Torres and Alfredo Guevara turned to arguments about aesthetic polysemy and the role of spectators in producing meaning to defend *Alicia*, as such exchanges make clear, spectators insisted on the legitimacy of their own interpretations. Díaz Torres's attempts to deny the controversial readings, meanwhile, were themselves often dismissed as a subterfuge designed to protect his work and his career. Well into the twenty-first century, Díaz Torres continued to insist that there was no connection between the head of the sanatorium and Fidel Castro. Acknowledging that the sanatorium director is "the *dirigente máximo* [maximum leader] of the town," he nonetheless maintained that it was "an absurd and, in some cases, opportunistic comparison to say that [the film] referred to Fidel. Not once have I seen Fidel with [the sanatorium director's] attitude. He can be a controversial figure, from many perspectives he is a complex figure. But I have always seen him as passionate and dedicated to his ideas, which he defends with vehemence. And for me this character is cold, sibylline. He's nothing like Fidel."[37] Others, however, were equally adamant about the opposed reading. "The character who is the mayor of the town is Fidel and everybody knows it. The gestures and everything, because it's him who makes all of the decisions and is the leader of the town," insisted one Cuban filmmaker when I inquired about the scandal over *Alicia*. "It's a different issue if someone doesn't have the courage to tell you this."[38]

As with other such controversies, however, to dismiss Díaz Torres's claims that *Alicia* was founded on revolutionary ideals would only resurrect the binary view of state socialism and the Cuban Revolution that his work, like that of other filmmakers, might otherwise go some distance in undoing. As I have shown in this chapter, by the twenty-first century, Cuban filmmakers were drawing on criticism of bureaucracy and a vision of revolution as constant change and collective effervescence to argue that Fidel Castro himself represented the stagnation and bureaucratization of the original spirit that had fueled the Cuban Revolution. Regardless of what Díaz Torres and those involved in making *Alicia* did or did not intend to mean, from this perspective, caricaturizing and criticizing Fidel Castro can be compatible with faith in revolutionary values and ideals of solidarity, social justice, and national sovereignty. Indeed, to some, taking on the existing political hierarchy and, at minimum, demanding greater accountability from political leaders began to seem necessary for revivifying the Revolution.[39]

If the controversy over *Alicia* can thus be linked to growing criticisms of the state and political leaders on the part of intellectuals in the twenty-first century, it did not lead to wholesale political change. Thanks to the intervention of Alfredo Guevara and the concerted efforts of Cuban filmmakers, the ICAIC survived the scandal over the film and the proposed merger with state television and radio intact, only to run into financial problems as Cuba plunged into the economic crisis that followed the collapse of the Soviet Union. And while the distribution of *Alicia* remained restricted for years to select international film festivals and bootleg VHS copies, Daniel Díaz Torres and the other artists involved in the project maintained their careers and went on to make several other films.

In spite of his ongoing rancor over how the reception of *Alicia* was handled, for his part, Díaz Torres insisted that the controversy had had a generally positive outcome. It gave rise, he told me, to "a discussion between Cuban filmmakers and political leaders, which led to a more complex understanding of art and culture on the part of political leaders, and, on the part of artists, to a greater awareness of their responsibility in a changing context." This, he elaborated, meant both that art must reflect even difficult realities and that artists needed to remain aware and wary of the repercussions of their work for a country where the "United States was at the same distance from Havana as Varadero." Acknowledging that conflicts between political leaders and artists continued to arise, Díaz Torres insisted that a new and improved understanding between the two groups could be seen in the numerous critical films that had followed on the heels of *Alicia*, including Tomás Gutiérrez Alea and Juan Carlos Tabío's *Fresa y chocolate* (1993) and Fernando Pérez's *Madagascar* (1994).[40]

By the time I spoke with him, Díaz Torres thus seemed to have fully absorbed and taken on Guevara's admonishment in 1991 to his distressed, younger self: if criticism within the Revolution was important, so was the need to ensure that such criticism did not lend itself to dismantling the Cuban political system. We need not view this settlement as either cynical or naïve, as Alicia and Omar described her two options in the face of corruption and apathy in Maravillas. Rather, hope that artists and political leaders might well have reached a new accord, as well as fears of what would replace the Castros were they to fall, kept many Cuban intellectuals attached to the existing political system, even as they grew increasingly skeptical of political leaders and worked to expand the boundaries of what could be articulated in public. The economic crisis of the 1990s, however, only exacerbated this disillusionment. In the next chapter, I discuss how, in the 1990s and the twenty-first century, growing resistance to dominant revolutionary ideology and state calls for self-sacrifice came into conflict with ongoing limits to official tolerance and a new orientation to the global market, further complicating the production and interpretation of a new series of bureaucrat comedies made by and about a younger generation.

CHAPTER FOUR

STAYING AND SUSPICION

Troubled Endings

The first time I saw Alejandro Brugués's *Juan de los muertos* (*Juan of the Dead*, 2011) was with a friend and fellow scholar of Cuba in Chicago, a month after its release at Toronto's International Film Festival in September 2011. By then, the film had already raised a flurry of international media attention, provoked in part by its timing. Work on the screenplay and efforts to secure foreign investment began as production of Brugués's first feature-length film, *Personal Belongings* (2006), was being completed and, hence, prior to Fidel Castro's official withdrawal from power. But by the time the film was released, the Cuban government, under the new leadership of Raúl Castro, had embarked on an ambitious program to reform the economy. Just a year earlier, in September 2010, the government had announced plans to expand the categories in which individuals could apply to work as small business owners, or *cuentapropistas*, as part of an effort to shift several thousand workers from the state sector to the private. And in May 2011, following several months of debate, the Communist Party of Cuba's Congress officially adopted new guidelines for economic and social reform—the "Lineamientos de la política económica y social" (Guidelines for Economic and Social Policy). As Cuba's first zombie comedy and the largest commercial feature to be produced independently of the ICAIC since 1959, *Juan de los muertos* anticipated how Cuban filmmaking, too, might be transformed by economic decentralization. The film heralded the arrival of a new and irreverent generation of filmmakers, willing and eager to take on the socialist state not only through satire more openly critical of top political leaders than in previous Cuban films but also, and perhaps even more significantly, through market-savvy production and promotional strategies.

In spite of its innovations, however, like many other Cuban films before it, *Juan de los muertos* combined criticism of the state and of the difficulties of life in late socialist Cuba with an insistence on values long associated with the Revolution. Merging the conventions of the Hollywood zombie movie with those of the Cuban bureaucrat comedy, *Juan de los muertos* tells the story of Juan, a fortysomething ne'er-do-well whose first reaction to the zombie apocalypse is to turn it into profit. "Juan of the Dead, we kill your loved ones" becomes the new slogan of his zombie-killing business in which he is soon joined by his sex-obsessed best friend, Lázaro; Lázaro's son, Vladimir California, whose main desire is to live somewhere where no one has ever heard of Fidel Castro; La China, a mixed-race *travesti* with an equal knack for the slingshot and for stealing radios; China's friend, El Primo, a mountainous black man with the unfortunate habit of toppling over at the first sight of blood; and Juan's daughter, Camila, who was taken to Spain as a child to escape Juan's immoral ways.[1] Comedy ensues as the gang demonstrates their dedication to making money over saving lives while the state takes refuge in propagandistic platitudes. Yet at the end of the day, nationalism and solidarity win out. Faced with the option of leaving for Miami with his friends and daughter or staying behind, Juan opts for the latter, taking on the zombie horde out of love for Cuba and a desire to help his fellow citizens.

As the film's credits began to roll, my friend stormed angrily out of the theater. "Why does the hero always have to stay in Cuba?" he protested when I caught up with him outside. Not only could Juan's decision to take on the zombie horde be read as suicide, he argued, but messages such as these slighted those who chose to emigrate, especially when their destination was Miami. Indeed, the ending of *Juan de los muertos* rehearsed what by 2011 was a well-worn genre in Cuban cinema. From the early 1960s on, leaving Cuba was treated as a betrayal of the nation, one often cast in personal and familial terms, and punishable through state appropriation of the emigrant's property and belongings. But in the midst of the economic crisis that followed the collapse of the Soviet Union, thousands of Cubans fled the island, often motivated more by financial and material necessity than by political reasons. The loss of the island's socialist allies, meanwhile, increased the economic importance of remittances and the political goodwill of the Cuban diaspora.

In this context, the dynamics of emigration and the question of whether to stay or to go went from playing a marginal role in select Cuban films to becoming one of the most dominant preoccupations of the island's cinema.[2] Many scholars observe that post-Soviet films treated emigration and emigrants with greater empathy than in previous years, challenging the revolutionary state's long-standing vilification of exiles (Díaz 2000, 2001; Johnson 2014). Others, however, argue that even these more conciliatory depictions often worked in harmony with state goals (Saavedra 2005). By celebrating Cubans who chose to stay in Cuba or depicting emigrants as forced to leave against their will, these scholars argue, films reinforced state ideology while working to bridge the divide with moderate expatriate communities whose support had grown essential to the nation's survival.[3]

Here I take these arguments in a slightly different direction, showing how cinematic representations of staying in Cuba and fighting for the nation contributed to the dynamics of ambivalence and paranoia that shape the Cuban public sphere. In the previous chapter, I argued that, from the 1980s on, intellectuals turned to criticism of the bureaucracy to hold onto the promises of the Revolution while distancing themselves from political leaders and state policies, even as official tolerance for criticism in art— the state's adoption of repressive tolerance or progressive censorship, as I have been terming this strategy throughout—kept many artists attached to existing institutional structures and modes of governance. This chapter explores how, in the post-Soviet era, filmmakers turned to stories of staying and fighting to communicate a similar ambivalence. In intellectuals' own life stories, as well as in a new series of bureaucrat comedies by and about younger generations, choosing to stay in Cuba and fight for the improvement of the nation came to signify commitment both to addressing social problems and to challenging state policies, including, importantly, state demands for citizen self-sacrifice.

A new emphasis on love plots worked alongside this genre, meanwhile, to reimagine the relationship between the personal and the collective. In the bureaucrat comedies of the 1980s, love played a central but ultimately supporting role in stories that revolved around the hero or heroine's struggle to improve the collective. In post-Soviet bureaucrat comedies, by contrast, love itself became the object of such quests, as the action was moved along by the protagonists' efforts both to consolidate personal romance and to build a nation capable of sustaining that love. In "El socialismo y el hombre en Cuba," Che Guevara argued that true revolutionaries were motivated by a love for the collective so strong that they were willing to sacrifice their own well-being and that of their families for the sake of the Revolution ([1965] 1967, 637–38). The protagonists of post-Soviet bureaucrat comedies, by contrast, stayed in Cuba to fight for a nation that could satisfy the material needs and ensure the personal fulfillment of all citizens. Stories of staying and fighting thus combined with love plots to articulate a demand for greater attention to individual needs and desires as well as an ongoing commitment to the nation and revolutionary values and ideals. But this genre also provoked new forms of suspicion. As the reception of *Alicia en el pueblo de maravillas* demonstrates (see chapter 3), Cuban filmmakers have always had to be careful that the open endings of their films suggested that ongoing social problems could be resolved within the framework of state socialism. But in the disillusioned post-Soviet period, artists also found themselves confronting skepticism of endings deemed uncomfortably proximate to official state ideology.

Juan de los muertos provides a particularly interesting twist on this dilemma. My friend's reaction to the film stayed with me when I traveled to Havana in December 2011 to observe its release at the New Latin American Film Festival, the first time the film was screened in Cuba. Through conversations with the Spanish producer and Cuban artists behind the film, as well as through participant observation of screenings and interviews with spectators, I paid attention to how different individuals and social groups interpreted the film and its politics. While many older Cuban spectators identified with Juan's decision to stay and take on the zombie horde, others dismissed the ending as an effort to placate state officials. Like my friend, they objected to the aspersion the ending cast on emigration and to what they viewed as its suicidal tone. These reactions speak to the ways in which the ending of the film seemed, to some spectators, uncomfortably closer to canonical state mythology than to post-Soviet challenges to citizen self-sacrifice. Yet ironically, as I learned, Juan's kamikaze leap into the zombie horde was inspired as much by the filmmakers' aspirations to deliver Hollywood and crossover-inspired spectacle and entertainment as by their efforts to convey a social message. Read against stories of staying and fighting in filmmakers' personal life narratives and in other post-Soviet bureaucrat comedies, the mixed reactions to the ending of *Juan de los muertos* thus encapsulate the challenges that confronted Cuban filmmakers in the post-Soviet era. From the 1990s on, filmmakers found themselves caught between the often-contradictory demands of state censors, on the one hand, and politically disillusioned audiences, on the other, while, in the 2010s, a new generation began producing films where social criticism was often at once a means of fomenting debate and just part of the fun in a new, entertainment-forward cinema.

The Special Period

On more than one occasion, Alejandro Brugués noted that the character Juan was based on his older brother, Juan, who was in his thirties when the Soviet Union collapsed. The character stood in for, as Brugués observed, "that generation who lived the best of socialism, of the Soviet Union, only for that world to fall apart." "It's a generation that is filled with sadness and nostalgia," he concluded.[4] In addition to speaking to economic changes under Raúl Castro's new government, *Juan de los muertos*, like the bureaucrat comedies of the 1990s and the early twenty-first century that preceded it, can thus also be read as an allegory of the Special Period and its aftermath. To understand these references in post-Soviet bureaucrat comedies, then, we must begin with an account of the Special Period and the mixed feelings it provoked, as citizens struggled to survive in a context that many described to me as "the worst of socialism and capitalism combined."

It is difficult to locate the end of the Special Period with any definitiveness. Some point to the crisis over Elián González, the young boy who, in 2000, was returned to his father in Cuba after his mother died en route to Florida and her family attempted to gain custody over him. Others note the withdrawal of the US dollar from legal use on the island in 2004 and Fidel Castro's reference to "the extremely hard special period, which we are now leaving behind" in a speech given on International Women's Day in 2005 as the decisive endpoint.[5] Yet as late as 2007 to 2009, many of the artists and intellectuals with whom I worked insisted that Cuba was still in the Special Period. And in July 2016, well into the economic reforms launched by Raúl Castro, rumors circulated that the nation might be plunged into a new Special Period as a result of deepening crisis in Venezuela, which, in the early twenty-first century, became one of Cuba's primary trading partners.[6] These uses of the term suggest how the Special Period has come to stand in not only for a specific historical period concentrated in the 1990s but also for a broader economic, moral, and ideological crisis inaugurated by the collapse of the Soviet Union.

If the end date of the Special Period is debatable, however, its onset was decisive and traumatic. "In the Special Period," explains Ariana Hernández-Reguant, "there was a 'before,' which was stable, perhaps purer in its altruism and high ideals, a 'now', which was confusing and unsettling, and a future that was, for many, another country" (2009c, 2–4). With the collapse of the Soviet Union in 1991, the Cuban government lost its primary trading partner and was forced to adopt severe economic measures. Chinese bicycles flooded the streets as public transit ground to a halt in the absence of fuel and spare parts; newspapers published articles about how to make meals out of fruit peels in the face of chronic food shortages and rising malnutrition; and Cubans took to prostitution and other forms of hustling as political leaders opened up the country to tourism in an effort to keep the economy afloat. *Inventar* (to invent), *resolver* (to resolve), and *luchar* (to struggle) became the watchwords of the Special Period, describing the *bricoleur*-style ethos by which citizens took advantage of the resources and opportunities at hand in order to make ends meet in the midst of material scarcity.[7] These economic difficulties in turn sparked mass migration. The Special Period reached its crisis point in 1994, when more than thirty thousand Cubans took to rafts and improvised crafts ranging from floating cars to windsurfers to make the dangerous ninety-mile journey to Miami. This exodus in turn led to the wet-foot/dry-foot policy, a new interpretation of the Cuban Adjustment Act in which Cubans who reached land were allowed to remain in the United States and apply for residency while those who were intercepted at sea were returned to the island.[8]

The collapse of the Soviet Union is often thought to have been particularly difficult for older Cubans. Film director Manuel Herrera, who was born in 1942 and founded a cinema club in Santa Clara, Cuba, before moving to Havana and joining the ICAIC in the 1960s, recalled: "Personally, the change hit me hard. It caught me at a moment when my youth was over. I had been committed to a project that all of a sudden disappeared."[9] For Julia Yip, an editor who worked on the *Noticiero ICAIC Latinoamericano* (ICAIC Latin American Newsreel) from 1973 until this project was suspended due to lack of resources in 1990, the transition was deeply distressing.

> Ever since I started to work, I always had a very intense life, because alongside work there was volunteer work and guard duty; one's everyday life was very intense. It was as though you were running and suddenly you were stopped cold. I was earning a salary without working and that made me feel awful. Finally, [an ICAIC administrator] told me, "Look, you're going to drive yourself crazy, calm down, this isn't your problem. They're paying you because there is a situation in the country. You're not to blame for it. Now if you want to work I'll bring you here to the ICAIC and set you to picking up

papers." He spoke to me very firmly because, truthfully, I was out of it, I was taking pills for nerves and everything, until finally I assimilated that it wasn't my problem but rather a national issue, that at least my salary was guaranteed. But it was very hard, and for a lot of people it was very hard, because on top of it [the crisis hit us] at a difficult age, which was neither young nor very old but rather at an age that you said well, what is the future?

For Yip, as for many older filmmakers, the Revolution entailed both a set of political ideals and an everyday way of life that had governed the majority of their adult lives. Overwhelmed by the disruption of these ideals and routines, Yip scrambled to restore something like her old life (getting paid for working, being plugged into any form of collectivity rather than being isolated at home) until, at last, she was supplied with a narrative that made the loss manageable, less "crazy" making—it's not you, it's the nation—and a new normal started to take hold.[10]

Yet if older Cubans arguably had the most difficulty adapting to new realities, it was the generation that followed them who came to emblematize the crisis and its ideological and economic disorientation. Born between 1960 and 1990, this generation is referred to by some as *la generación de los muñequitos rusos* (the generation of the Russian cartoons) because of their shared love and nostalgia for the Eastern European cartoons on which they were raised and which disappeared with the collapse of the Soviet Union. To others they are known as *la Generación Y* (Generation Y), because of the predominance of names that begin with this letter among children born from the 1970s through the 1980s.[11] These were the first and the last of the revolutionary new men and women anticipated by Che Guevara, the youth who, born into actually existing socialism, were supposed to grow up "free of the original sin," the failure to be "authentically revolutionary," which Guevara argued had tainted their predecessors ([1965] 1967, 636). But while their childhoods were imbued with confidence in the immortality of socialism, their early adulthood was shaped by disillusionment and mass emigration.

The disorientation provoked by this sudden transition is particularly notable among the older members of this generation, those who, born in the 1960s, launched their careers in the midst of the crisis. Eduardo del Llano, who got his first break in filmmaking in 1991 as the screenwriter for *Alicia en el pueblo de maravillas*, recalled how the collapse of the Soviet Union shocked a generation raised to believe that socialism would eventually triumph over capitalism.

You have to understand that the fall of the socialist camp surprised us, us and the whole world. Until that moment, we really believed that development was on the side of socialism. The Soviet Union was the first to send rocketships to space. The Vietnam War was a crime committed by the United States—that was really clear. In that era, the first Cuban astronaut also went to space. And so, it seemed to us that we were on the right side. That there were problems, but that in ten, twelve years, capitalism was going to come to an end. Then, all of a sudden, the Berlin Wall fell. It was a terrible change to our way of seeing the world. We lived in a country where we didn't have certain freedoms but where there was sufficient food and one could live fairly well. It seemed like we were on the right side—that capitalism and imperialism were the bad guys and that we were on the side of good. And all of a sudden, in three years, all of that changed. From 1989 to 1991, all the socialist countries disappeared. Not only did capitalism not disappear; it was stronger than ever. Socialism vanished as an alternative and Cuba, a country where there had been a certain abundance, all of a sudden fell into incredible misery.[12]

Like del Llano, director Arturo Sotto remembered growing up with certainty in a socialist future: "I was born with the Revolution, and that is like a mark, a stamp that they put on you. I remember when I was eleven or twelve years old that the year 2000 seemed really far away and we imagined what Cuba would be like. Socialism was the system of the future, and capitalism, like the Marxist manuals tell you, was in perennial crisis. We waited every day for capitalism to stop existing because if it's in crisis and is so sick and is digging its own grave, when will it be buried?" With the collapse of the Soviet Union, Sotto added, his generation's dreams of a triumphant future ran aground on the realities of underemployment and mass emigration: "My generation studied and had expectations, but then these were blocked. The majority of those who went to school with me have left Cuba. There is a whole generation that isn't in Cuba."[13]

As these comments suggest, the crisis of the Special Period also bred nostalgia. Just as older Cubans often remembered the 1960s with fondness as a romantic era in which citizens were united with leaders in a collective project, the generation that followed frequently reminisced about the 1980s, describing this decade as a time of relative moral and material plenty that stood in stark contrast to the scarcity of the 1990s and the twenty-first century. In the 1980s, one friend recalled as we chatted in her sunroom on a Sunday afternoon, youth and children were valued and no one lacked for anything. But with the collapse of the Soviet Union and the economic crisis that ensued, she continued, people became "more individualistic" and "less communist." Even Cubans born only a few years before the collapse of the Soviet Union often waxed nostalgic to me about the 1980s. As we sat waiting for a scene change on a film set, one actor born in 1985 described how, in the 1980s, you could entrust strangers to pass your fare to the driver on a crowded bus. Now you had to be vigilant to make certain that shop attendants did not rob you, he observed: "It's a jungle out there; you have to defend yourself in order to survive." Finally, many maintained that the Special Period itself marked an important generational divide. "This is a generation that didn't grow up with the Russians, that didn't go to Silvio Rodríguez's concerts, that didn't experience the 1980s," commented one actress, describing Cubans born in the 1990s. "It's a generation that was born with the dollar, that is dollarized."[14]

Yet if Cubans generally lament what they view as the loss of a collectivist ethos and the rise of individualism in the Special Period, many also remember the 1990s as a time of new opportunities and freedoms. In addition to fostering foreign tourism and investment, in this decade, the state legalized a limited number of small private businesses, including operating taxis, renting rooms to foreigners, and running paladares (small, private restaurants). These reforms exacerbated class, racial, and generational differences, enabling some Cubans, mostly the white and the young, to flourish, while others, especially Afro-Cubans and the elderly, grew more impoverished. For some, however, the Special Period also gave rise to new hope. Observed Arturo Sotto:

Cubans need to live in peace, to avoid the constant paranoia of aggression, to concentrate a bit on ourselves and realize that you need a good sofa, a good roof. During the crisis, there was hope that we were headed somewhere, that there would be change and we would have more economic freedom, that the phenomenon of the paladares and trabajo por cuenta propia [self-employment] would expand, that this was a process that could not be reversed, because citizens need to cultivate their initiative. Like an artist painting a painting, people who have a talent for business need to express themselves this way.

In an interview conducted just prior to his death from cancer in 1996, Tomás Gutiérrez Alea observed that Cubans were "losing our values; all the values the Revolution recuperated in human beings are deteriorating" (qtd. in Chanan 2002, 51). As the above comments make clear, by the twenty-first century, this complaint had become so widespread that even Cubans who were too young to remember much about the time before the collapse of the Soviet Union often compared the fraying social values of the post-Soviet era to what they described as an earlier, more morally sound, period. Similar forms of nostalgia have been observed in many other late- or postsocialist contexts (Ghodsee and Henry 2010; Todorova and Gille 2010). As in these contexts, such nostalgia does not mean that Cubans idealize state socialism or are incapable of recognizing its failings. Rather, as Sotto's description of the excitement induced by the economic openings of the Special Period suggests, many long for a system that would combine a commitment to collective well-being with new opportunities for individual expression and material plenty.

Staying and Fighting

For many Cuban artists, a critical version of nationalism and stories of staying and fighting served to articulate this ambivalent commitment to values long associated with the Revolution along with their frustration with the socialist state and desire for change. Just shortly before his death in 2008, I asked film director Humberto Solás what solidarity meant to him. Solás, who had been active in Havana's urban underground during the struggle against Batista, answered this question with a fairly typical expression of disillusionment with state policies combined with ongoing commitment to revolutionary values and ideals: "For me, solidarity is compassion and tolerance. It is trying not to have a lifestyle that is in excess of that held by the rest of the population. It is making sure that there isn't a huge difference between social groups. I have a very critical view of the Revolution and have been against many of the decisions that have been taken. But I have never been able to renounce that condition of sensitivity to others, which is the most profound essence of the Revolution."

His next comments revealed how nationalism could work to reconcile such views. "The Revolution exists thanks to José Martí," he continued, referring to the poet, journalist, and politician who in the nineteenth century was one of the figureheads of Cuba's war for independence from Spain and who remains the nation's most emblematic hero. "The whole generation that sacrificed itself and fought was a *martiana* generation. Even during the era of Batista and with the dictatorship and the widespread corruption in the country, the majority of youth were martiana. We were ready to change the country through the Revolution or through some other means. This wasn't the only path it could have taken."[15] Solás's account treats solidarity and social justice as the true essence of the Revolution only to then equate these values with the teachings of José Martí. Notably, he concludes by crediting Martí and not Fidel Castro's 26th of July Movement with his generation's uprising against Batista, an uprising that, Solás intimated, might easily have had a different and even, perhaps, a more satisfactory outcome than Fidel Castro's rise to power.

Younger filmmakers likewise turned to nationalism to separate ideals of solidarity and social justice from the socialist state. Noting that he agreed with what he saw as socialism's original goal of "sharing" and "community," producer and director Ricardo Figueredo explained that he preferred the concept of nationalism:

> I believe a bit in what Martí said about the meaning of being Cuban, of being responsible toward one's country. For me, socialism and communism are words written on the wall, doctrines that you have to follow in order to represent something that someone else wants you to represent. It's that you should dress in a certain way, cut your hair in a certain way, walk in a certain way, think in a certain way—that you think as I think. No Cuban thinks the same way as another; that's impossible.[16]

For Figueredo, state socialism was a militant dogma that demanded uniformity; nationalism, by contrast, promised a collective project that might allow for individual difference.

Finally, many intellectuals framed their personal decisions to stay in Cuba as a resistance to the dichotomies that have long dominated Cuban politics. Like many Cubans, film critic and ISA professor Gustavo Arcos was born into a politically divided family. Two of his uncles went from being active in the struggle against Batista—one in the 26th of July Movement and the other in the urban underground—to becoming leading dissidents on the island. His father, by contrast, worked alongside Che Guevara and remained an important functionary in the revolutionary government well into the 1970s. When I asked Arcos how he situated himself politically given this complicated family history, he responded:

> I'm on my own side. I have questioned the Revolution publicly, in the circles I move in, anywhere I might have some influence. I have opinions about a variety of aspects of the Revolution and I have never kept them quiet. I've suffered a number of times for expressing my opinions in the media. Still, I have traveled outside Cuba, I've been abroad, I've even received job offers

abroad, but I have always returned. I love my country and I think I help my country more by staying here. I try to see what inspires the Revolution and its leaders and also to question everything that seems to me to be poorly done, but I do it from here. I won't accomplish anything by going to Spain, to France, or Miami, joining a group of Latinos or Cubans in exile, having a meeting every now and then, writing a book or publishing something in the press against Cuba and the Revolution. To speak ill of Cuba, it's best to do it here, to confront things from here. This is what I do when it seems necessary to me. In sum, whose side am I on? I'm on my own side—where I believe I can be more honest.[17]

Ricardo Figueredo concurred with the political value of staying in Cuba.

For me there's not much sense in leaving the country and, when you get to Miami or wherever, starting to criticize, to talk, to say what is happening in Cuba. It's not good enough to go and become a famous writer or a famous filmmaker by talking about the misery you lived through in Cuba, how bad the situation is in Cuba. Whatever you have to say, you should say it here so that it can be debated. This is what I admire of many young filmmakers. Many of them have made work here, have stayed here, and many have taken responsibility for what they have said and want to keep doing things.

In the Special Period, Cuban political leaders substituted a nationalism based on Cuban culture and history for a more politically oriented socialist project as a means of maintaining the government's legitimacy in the wake of the Soviet Union's disappearance (Hernández-Reguant 2009b and 2009c). Intellectuals' adoption of a critical nationalism and stories of staying and fighting cooperated with this shift, but they also articulated growing disillusionment with both traditional exile positions and with the socialist state.

Love the Nation That Loves You Back

Critical nationalism and stories of staying and fighting likewise became a mainstay of bureaucrat comedies, where a new emphasis on romance often helped convey a growing frustration with the socialist state and, more specifically, with economic crisis and ongoing demands for citizen self-sacrifice. Arturo Sotto's second feature film, *Amor vertical* (*Vertical Love*, 1997), exemplifies the new centrality of love plots and fantasies of a nation capable of materially sustaining this love in post-Soviet bureaucrat comedies.

Dedicated to Tomás Gutiérrez Alea, Federico Fellini, and Luis Buñuel, *Amor vertical* takes up where Alea's *La muerte de un burócrata* and rectification-era bureaucrat comedies left off. An early sequence in the film makes this connection explicit. Tracking over an eclectic array of characters waiting impatiently in a long queue, the camera stops on an elderly gentleman who explains his situation with some desperation to an impassive receptionist: his uncle has been buried with his work ID and must be exhumed so that his aunt can claim his pension. The once-young protagonist of Alea's *Muerte*, it seems, never did resolve his dilemma, instead aging with a bureaucracy that has itself grown exponentially in size and absurdity. As the camera pans upward, it reveals an enormous warehouse filled with rows of desks and a chaotic tangle of plaintiffs and bureaucrats whose identical grey suits and dark-tinted sunglasses erase all hope of personalized care.

Like the protagonists of Juan Carlos Tabío's *Se permuta*, meanwhile, Estela, the heroine of *Amor vertical*, is a young architectural student who dreams of improving the Cuban housing situation. But whereas in *Se permuta* Yolanda's bourgeois mother and functionary fiancé's fantasies of living in a luxurious home in the right kind of neighborhood lead to ever-more-complex housing exchanges, in *Amor vertical*, the problem is finding any home at all in a city filled with buildings on the verge of collapse. Entrusted by the bureaucracy with convincing residents to leave their dilapidated homes for inadequate state shelters, Estela soon finds herself confronting her own housing quandary. When her military office father, Faustino, catches her about to have sex with a medical assistant, Ernesto, she flees her family home with her would-be lover in search of a place to lose her virginity. The couple finally achieves this goal when they get stuck in a malfunctioning elevator in an apartment complex designed without stairs. While the police mount an elaborate operation to rescue the building's inhabitants, Estela and Ernesto experiment with a series of sexual positions until coming to a sweaty climax.

The young couple's quest to make love facilitates a series of reflections on Cuban society, the state, and filmmaking. At the most obvious level, the obstacles the protagonists face speak to the frustrations of life in a context where multiple generations often live together in cramped quarters. Adding to the film's allegorical resonances, Estela's bed in her family home is depicted as a giant crib while her father shares his bed with her uncle, a priest, and her querulous grandfather. This mise-en-scène alludes not only to Cuba's chronic housing problem but also to the infantilization of citizens by a paternalistic socialist state that, in the 1990s, began to renew its relations with the Catholic Church. Finally, Sotto's relatively explicit sex scenes themselves bespeak youthful rebellion. Pornography is illegal in Cuba while cinema and television depict sex with reserve, if at all. "We wanted to depict eroticism and sexuality in the crudest manner possible," Sotto told me. "We are the most sensual country in the world—we'll have sex anywhere and at any time—but our cinema is very prudish. It was a defense of love, of youth."

Importantly, however, the film does not end with the characters' simultaneous orgasm. During the Special Period, Sotto explained, "the biggest challenge in Cuba was not where you make love but how to sustain that love. You can make love in the cemetery, but afterward, how are you going to get by?" This question motivates the second half of the film, as the characters struggle to remain together against the wishes of Estela's family and Ernesto's previous lover, an older woman significantly named Lucía, who was once an important Cuban film actress and who provides Ernesto with lodgings in a film projection booth.[18] Leaving their former abodes behind, the young couple improvises a house out of scrap wood and abandoned furniture below the bridge over Havana's Almendares River. Here they at first get by on coconuts, herbal tea, and love. But this soon proves insufficient for Estela, who takes to reciting poetry bare-chested to passing fishermen in exchange for fish. Estela's trade of skin for food, suggestive in an era that saw a rapid rise in prostitution and hustling for tourists, also provides her with the means to keep them in their improvised home. When functionaries inform them that they have to leave their new abode because it was built in an area zoned for a long-abandoned children's playground that is highly unlikely to be rebuilt, Estela bribes one of the bureaucrats with fish to let them stay.

Estela's actions suggest the important role that women played in keeping households together throughout the scarcity of the Special Period, but Ernesto is less than pleased and returns briefly to Lucía. This initial separation is further compounded when the young couple's elders conspire with the bureaucracy to have them separated, a goal finally achieved by conscripting Ernesto into the militia and threatening to send him to an unspecified war. With Ernesto out of the way, meanwhile, Estela's family works to convince her to abandon their home and the love affair. *Amor vertical* was among the first Cuban films to venture overtly conciliatory depictions of the diaspora, a theme most clearly embodied in Ernesto's sisters, Mary and Mariana, conjoined twins who cannot agree on whether to migrate to Miami or to stay in Cuba and yet cannot be surgically separated without risk of death.[19] In a similarly conciliatory nod to the diaspora, Estela's uncle tries to separate the young couple by encouraging Estela to migrate to Spain. Handing her a stack of letters, he tells her that they are from her brother, who was shown leaving for war earlier on in the film but who, her uncle informs Estela, has fallen in love with a foreigner and is now living abroad. Estela should likewise choose emigration, he continues, presenting her with a Spanish priest who has volunteered to marry her. In Madrid, Estela's uncle promises, she can work as an architect and will never lack for "ham or wine." But Estela's father protests: "What will you do away from Havana? They say that people are dying of nostalgia in Madrid!" For her part, Estela ignores her family's squabbling, reading her brother's letters with a smile that bespeaks love for those who have chosen to leave.

The young architect's path, however, ultimately lies elsewhere—somewhere between her father's militant commitment to Cuba and her uncle's longings for material plenty. In the film's final sequences, Estela and Ernesto reconcile just as the bureaucracy arrives to tear down their improvised home. Presented with a choice between relocating to one of Havana's many crowded *albergues* (shelters for the homeless) or returning to their family homes, the young couple opts to stay together, declaring their love for one another on the bridge where they began their domestic adventure. Still, their affirmation of commitment to each other and to their city does not resolve the question of how their love will be sustained. The film's final image shows Estela and Ernesto walking hand in hand past cars and soldiers through a Havana city street as the voice of a radio announcer informs listeners of a "strange technological epidemic" that has affected the "elevators of the city's old buildings," causing them to exude a "strange smell of flowers and human sweat" (figure 4.1). "We will keep you up to date about this strange event affecting Havana, the most, most, most beautiful city in the world. Don't abandon this signal, which would be to abandon your city," the announcer concludes.

Recalling Estela and Ernesto's previous adventures making love in an elevator, this radio message at once calls on youth to stay in Cuba and reminds viewers of the unanswered dilemma confronting the couple. As such, it establishes the film as a national allegory for an era of crisis. Doris Sommer (1993, 7) argues that nineteenth-century Latin American romances linked tales of star-crossed lovers to stories of forging new nations, such that the struggle to achieve personal happiness was tied metonymically to hopes

Figure 4.1 Ernesto (Jorge Perugorría) and Estela (Sílvia Águila) walk hand in hand through Havana's streets at the end of Arturo Sotto's *Amor vertical* (1997).

for national prosperity. *Amor vertical* similarly links getting the girl/boy to committing to Cuba, but, in keeping with Cuban intellectuals' own stories of staying and fighting, its open ending highlights the importance of fighting for a nation capable of satisfying citizens' personal desires and material needs.

The Trouble with Open Endings, Reprise

As I have been arguing throughout, however, communicating such an ambivalent take on the Revolution could frequently prove challenging. As with *Alicia en el pueblo de maravillas*, conflicts in the interpretation of films' and their authors' political positions often revolved around film endings, but these conflicts took on a slightly different tone in the post-Soviet era. In the controversy over *Alicia*, recall, spectators and functionaries objected to an ending that they interpreted as a rejection of state socialism. In the post-Soviet era, by contrast, filmmakers found themselves struggling to produce endings that balanced ongoing limits to state tolerance with the demands of disillusioned audiences.

The production and reception of Juan Carlos Tabío's *Lista de espera* (*The Waiting List*, 2000) demonstrate these new difficulties. Using the crisis in transportation that plagued the Special Period as its starting point, *Lista de espera* tells the story of a group of would-be travelers who find themselves stuck in a provincial bus terminal when buses either fail to arrive or turn up full. When the station manager tries to send the passengers home, they instead take over the station against the objections of a bureaucrat, who protests this violation of regulations then sets off on foot to fetch the authorities.

The remaining passengers, meanwhile, set aside their differences and work together. Led by a young engineer by the name of Emilio, the passengers first try to repair the station's bus. When this plan falls through, they paint the bus station, fill it with plants, establish a library, rekindle a dwindling marriage, and start new romances that belie the limits imposed by the Special Period. Keeping with the centrality of love plots in many post-Soviet bureaucrat comedies, Emilio's central motivation is his desire for the attractive Jaqueline, who is engaged to a Spaniard. Whereas her wealthy and kind Spanish fiancé would be the obvious choice for many Cubans acutely aware of the opportunities such a match could provide in the midst of economic crisis, Jaqueline instead abandons him for Emilio, who had initially intended to move back to his family's pig farm because he could no longer sustain himself as an engineer in Havana. In sum, pulled forward by this central love plot, the characters create a new utopia that restores solidarity while also fulfilling individual aspirations and material needs.

If all this seems too good to be true, the filmmakers themselves would agree. Just as an ideal version of socialism takes root in the broken-down bus station, the characters wake up from what turns out to have been a shared dream. Arturo Arango, who wrote both the film's screenplay and the short story on which the film was based, explained that he and Tabío initially came up with the device of the dream to render the love story between Emilio and Jaqueline plausible. To satisfy coproduction requirements, Arango and Tabío decided to cast a Spaniard in the role of Jaqueline's boyfriend, instead of representing the character as Cuban, as he had been in the short story. While this was a logical way of resolving the need for Spanish representation in the film's artistic team imposed by the film's financing, the decision also introduced plot complications. "No sane Cuban in the year 2000 was going to believe that a pretty woman with a nice Spanish boyfriend would renounce living in Madrid for a good man who was going to raise pigs in Santiago," Arango told me flatly.[20] The dream structure helped resolve this tension.

But this device also contributed to a more idyllic and hopeful representation of socialism than what had initially been present in the short story.

In Arango's original story, utopia comes undone when the bus station's community begins to develop internal problems. In the film, by contrast, the characters wake up from a dream in which their idyllic collective was still functional. This more positive representation of socialism is then further reinforced by the film's ending. After they wake up, the characters head off in their separate directions: Jaqueline reunites with her Spanish boyfriend as Emilio looks on with disappointment, and Emilio continues his journey to the east and his family pig farm on the back of a pickup truck. The film concludes in yet another bus terminal, where Emilio and those traveling with him stop to take a washroom break. A fellow passenger points out a broken water fountain to Emilio, who begins fixing it, just as he had repaired a similarly broken fountain in the previous station in an effort to impress Jaqueline. He then hears a voice that might be hers ask for "el último" (the last person in line), as she had previously done on arrival at the last bus station. He looks up and raises his hand with a smile. This open-ended return to the beginning of the film thus restores hope that the young couple's love story and a utopian collective future might yet take root in Cuban soil. "Ultimately the theme of the short story is the impossibility of utopias," observed Arango. "The film holds out the possibility of re-creating in real life the utopia the characters dreamed."

This hopeful ending provoked bitter debate among the island's film community. Film critic Rufo Caballero was the first to suggest that *Lista de espera*'s representation of collective solidarity steered dangerously close to what he dismissed as socialist realism's political platitudes.[21] Others soon echoed this criticism. While the "collective will for change and improvement" featured in the film was "legitimate in and of itself," wrote island film critic Frank Padrón (2000), *Lista de espera* erred by depicting this solidarity in an "unproblematized and idyllic [tone] more appropriate to the utopias of the 1960s or, in the worst of cases, to socialist realism." Notably, even those who defended the film subscribed to this criticism of excess optimism. Their argument was that, contrary to the claims of its critics, *Lista de espera* struck the right balance between hope and recognition of the nation's plight. "Where fans of apocalypse have seen optimistic propaganda," argued Rolando Pérez Betancourt (2000), the regular film columnist for the Communist Party newspaper, *Granma*, "in fact one finds an incisive attempt to mix happy notes of native humor with reflections that are not free of contradiction and bitterness." Film critic Joel del Río (2000) likewise praised the film for its balance of optimism and criticism. Arango and Tabío had transformed the bus station into a "crucible and gallery, nightmare and dream, convergence and inventory of the best that saves us and the worst of our failures," he maintained (12).

Meanwhile, two of *Lista de espera*'s most established actors—Vladimir Cruz, who played the role of Emilio in the film, and Jorge Perugorría, who was cast as a man who pretends to be blind in order to receive preferential treatment—provided radically different interpretations of the film's message. For Cruz, who had previously collaborated with Tabío on *Fresa y chocolate* where he played the role of David, *Lista de espera* allegorized the need to set aside the utopian dreams that had once shaped Cuban life. He interpreted the film as a call to leave innocence behind and confront a challenging reality. "I remember my father telling me how the island would be in the year 2000 and imagining what type of country my son would live in," Cruz commented in one interview, in a statement that resonated with Sotto's and del Llano's memories of the certainty in a triumphant socialist future that had shaped their childhoods. "More than a dream, we have constructed the waiting room of the dream," Cruz continued, equating the Special Period with a time out of time, marked by the loss of belief in the teleology that had previously oriented Cuban state socialism (Belinchón 2000). In an interview with me, Cruz elaborated on this position: "We [Cubans] discovered that reality was headed in a different direction. We saw clearly that the dream was beautiful, but that it didn't correspond to reality. That film seemed important to me for that reason."[22] If Cruz's interpretation thus aligns the film with the original short story's emphasis on the failure of utopias, Jorge Perugorría, who played key roles in *Fresa y chocolate* (David), *Guantanamera* (the truck driver / main love interest), and *Amor vertical* (Ernesto), took a more optimistic view. *Lista de espera* "invited [Cubans] to stay in Cuba, to work for a better society instead of leaving," he argued, reading the film through the genre of staying and fighting. "I would like it if everyone interpreted the film as a message that solidarity can emerge as a solution in the midst of difficulties" (Belinchón 2000).

Behind these arguments over the film's meaning and its political implications, I soon learned, lay a challenging production history. Not only had coproduction requirements, as mentioned earlier, shaped the film's narrative; so had censorship. The process of getting approval for the screenplay from the ICAIC had been long and difficult. At one point, Tabío and Arango told me, they even contemplated shooting the film in Mexico. There were a number of reasons that may have provoked the ICAIC's hesitation. Production on *Lista de espera* began just after Fidel Castro denounced *Guantanamera* (see chapter 2), a scandal that had directly implicated both the ICAIC and Tabío. The ICAIC leadership may thus have been wary of attracting further political trouble. Alfredo Guevara, for his part, was clearly concerned that *Lista de espera* would cater to market demands for what analysts and Global South artists deride as "poverty porn," or stereotyped images of the economic woes of developing countries designed to appeal to audiences in the Global North.[23] In a letter written to address concerns that had clearly previously been articulated by Guevara, Tabío insisted that *Lista de espera* would not engage in "slum aesthetics" or attempt to force a "confrontation with the 'disaster of our reality.'" To ensure that the film would avoid such stereotyped depictions, the director promised to temper the depiction of "deterioration and malfunction" in its first scenes (Guevara 2008, 540).

Yet in spite of these adjustments, six days before shooting was set to begin, Arango and Tabío were informed that all but the last six pages of the screenplay had been approved. "Juan Carlos and I racked our brains trying to figure out what was in those six pages that couldn't be approved," Arango recalled. Finally, an ICAIC functionary telephoned screenwriter Senel Paz, who was helping Arango and Tabío with the final stages of writing, to explain the objection. "The problem," Arango recounted, "was that the film might be interpreted as arguing that one could only survive in Cuba by remaining within a dream." With the scheduled start date for shooting rapidly approaching, Arango, Paz, and Tabío met at Tabío's house. Just as Paz was lamenting to Arango that they had run out of solutions, Tabío emerged from the kitchen, where he had been preparing coffee, and happily declared, "the DVD player."

Arango explained: "In one of the versions we had made of the ending, the characters arrive at the second terminal like a sort of wild army that sets about fixing everything. It was like magic and within that there had been a DVD player. The way that we made clear that they didn't want to go back to sleep in the next terminal but rather to remake in reality what they had previously built in the dream was through that water fountain that Emilio fixes, with which we rewrote the previous scenes to give it an active presence throughout the film." The new ending, in other words, sided with Jorge Perugorría's interpretation and a conservative version of staying and fighting for an improved nation, bracketing the short story and Vladimir Cruz's preference for a more strident criticism of utopias.

While this strategy put the ICAIC's concerns to rest and allowed the production of the film to proceed, it left many Cuban film critics dissatisfied and sat uncomfortably with Arango and Tabío. The film received a normal theatrical release both in Cuba and abroad but, like many other Cuban films, was blocked for years from state television. Following Enrique Colina's denunciation of this situation in an email circulated during the 2007 email war (see chapter 1), the film was finally shown on state television in 2008. Suggesting his own retrospective dissatisfaction with the film, Tabío took the opportunity to create yet another version of the ending. Presenting the film as a "director's cut," he ended this version of the film at the point when the characters wake up in the terminal only to discover that their shared utopia had all been a dream. Whereas previously the film had "ended hopefully," Tabío explained, "by ending in the terminal, it finishes on a bitter note."[24]

Retrospectively, Arango and Tabío also discovered new meanings in their film. "I believe that the film vindicates the need for civil society to have its own spaces within socialism, for people to participate in solving problems themselves, free of state paternalism," Arango commented, acknowledging that this was a meaning he had discovered upon watching the finished film rather than a theme that he had contemplated while they were in the process of making it. Tabío concurred with this interpretation, suggesting that the ICAIC might have censored the film out of fear that it could be read as a declaration "that the problems in this country could only be solved through a coup d'état." "Those people take the station by assault and solve their own problems because they won't be solved from above," he told me. "True solidarity exists when you're in charge of your own life, when you're not following norms that are imposed on you."

Arango's insistence on the importance of citizen action instead of top-down solutions and Tabío's argument that "true solidarity" opposes hierarchical political authority emphasize again how, by the twenty-first century, Cuban artists' attachment to revolutionary values often went hand in hand with resistance to the state. The filmmakers' retrospective interpretations of *Lista de espera* as well as Tabío's decision to release a new cut on television can also be read as an effort to manage their own reputations in light of the controversy that erupted over the film's ending. By reading the film as an allegory for civil society and releasing a version that ended on a more pessimistic note, Arango and Tabío worked to establish themselves as critics from within the Revolution rather than as accomplices to an official state ideology out of keeping with Cuban reality.

Political Attractions

Juan de los muertos reveals how tensions between the demands of state officials and those of disillusioned spectators continued to influence the reception of Cuban films well into the twenty-first century, and how the market and entertainment aspirations of a new generation of filmmakers can sometimes inadvertently add to these dynamics. Arguably the biggest commercial success in Cuban cinema after *Fresa y chocolate*, following its release in September 2011 at the Toronto International Film Festival, *Juan de los muertos* made the circuit of both art and genre film festivals and was picked up for distribution in theaters, on television, and through video streaming services in more than thirty-five national territories. In Cuba, meanwhile, the film and its team received rock star treatment. At Havana's December 2011 New Latin American Film Festival, a reported fourteen thousand spectators showed up for the first scheduled screening alone (*Juventud Rebelde* 2011), additional screenings were programmed to accommodate the crowds, and police were called out to manage queues that took up entire city blocks. Spectators of all ages found themselves waiting in line for hours to see the film, yet the struggle to get into theaters only stoked the crowds' enthusiasm (figure 4.2). When Alexis Díaz de Villegas, who had previously worked more in theater than in cinema, was called to the stage for the film's presentation at the Yara movie theater, the audience of more than one thousand let out a roar worthy of any stadium concert. When the actor returned to the back of the theater where I was standing with the rest of the core artistic team and their life partners, his cheeks were flushed with an excitement they all shared.

This interest was generated in part by the film's novel production and promotional strategies. With a budget of more than three million dollars, up to four hundred extras on set in key scenes, and computer-generated special effects staging the apocalyptic destruction of iconic Havana landmarks, at the time of its release, the relatively low-budget film was a big budget production by Cuban standards and was also one of the most ambitious Cuban movies to be made independently of state institutions. As noted in chapter 2, the twenty-first century saw the rise of new forms of independent filmmaking spearheaded by a younger generation and aided by digital technologies. Independent production groups multiplied, bringing filmmakers together into collectives that produced documentaries, fiction shorts, and even feature-length fiction films using digital cameras, computer software editing programs, limited funds, and personal perseverance.

Figure 4.2 Crowds queue to see Alejandro Brugués's *Juan de los muertos* (2011) at the Charlie Chaplin Cinema in Havana during the 2011 New Latin American Film Festival. Many of those photographed here waited more than eight hours to see the film. Photo by author.

Nonetheless, for years the island's independent production groups functioned in a legal gray zone. Efforts on the part of filmmakers to convince state officials to legally recognize these groups, begun in earnest as of 2013, only yielded concrete outcomes in March 2019, even as the independent collectives played an increasingly important role in Cuban film production and the provision of services.[25]

Producciones de la 5ta Avenida (5th Avenue Productions), the group behind *Juan de los muertos*, was one of the first to find a way to circumvent these obstacles. Taking advantage of Alejandro Brugués's dual nationality with Bolivia, in the early twenty-first century Brugués and producer Inti Herrera established the company as a legal entity in Bolivia while setting up offices in Havana. This in turn enabled Brugués, Herrera, and producer Claudia Calviño, who took over at the helm of the company after Brugués left for Los Angeles and Herrera branched out to other projects, to negotiate a new relationship to the state. Rather than working directly under the state film institute, the team sold the ICAIC national exhibition rights to *Juan de los muertos* in exchange for technical support and shooting permits while managing their own coproduction agreement with the Andalucian company La Zanfoña Producciones.[26]

With *Juan de los muertos*, 5ta Avenida also mobilized digital technologies to put into place promotional strategies then novel within the Cuban context. Cuban filmmakers often complain that the ICAIC does little to promote their films at home or abroad. By contrast, 5ta Avenida took matters into its own hands, inviting international news organizations to conduct interviews on set while the film was still in production and plying Twitter, Facebook, and YouTube with updates on the film's progress. To get around the island's limited internet connectivity, the team asked friends and colleagues traveling outside the country to transport digital copies of promotional materials, which they then posted from abroad on prearranged dates. At home, meanwhile, the producers turned the island's rampant piracy to their commercial advantage. Cuban films are almost always leaked during or even before their initial theatrical release, leaks for which many believe that ICAIC personnel are responsible. To prevent piracy, the 5ta Avenida team distributed the film to festivals through password-protected websites and posted staff in Cuban theaters to block spectators from recording the film. At the same time, they used the island's informal distribution networks to promote the film, planting the trailer on computers in ICAIC offices used by multiple employees and distributing it to known pirates. The strategy was clearly successful. Several spectators who went to see *Juan de los muertos* during the New Latin American Film Festival told me that they had become interested in the film after seeing pirated copies of the trailer, while Cuban film critics spoke excitedly about how they had been unable to locate an advance copy of the film from any of their usual sources.

Finally, politics and Hollywood-style spectacle were also key both to 5ta Avenida's marketing strategies and to the interest generated by the film. From the beginning of the project, Inti Herrera told me, the team was clear that they were marketing two concepts: "One concept was Cuba, what could be the image of Cuba, and the other was the world of zombies."[27] Alejandro Brugués linked the film's adoption of the zombie genre to criticism and social allegory. In an interview with a live audience for Cuban television whose filming I observed, he noted that *Juan de los muertos* was driven both by his love for zombie movies and by his interest in the genre's capacity to facilitate social commentary. For their part, Cuban spectators were clearly titillated by the film's critical edge. When I asked one seventy-seven-year-old physics professor who had queued from 1:00 p.m. to 10:00 p.m. why she was so intent on seeing the film, she replied gaily from the cement pillar where she was sitting: "*Chica*, because they say that it reflects our reality and that it's really critical. And you know that we Cubans like that because we're *muy criticones* [really critical]." A Cuban film critic, meanwhile, recalled with some relish how, after he first saw the film, he told Brugués that he had made a film "against the regime."

Even the film's foreign backers appeared to have been initially drawn to the film at least in part because of its risqué political criticism. *Juan de los muertos*'s Spanish producer, Gervasio Iglesias, first learned of the project after awarding a postproduction prize at the Guadalajara Film Festival to Brugués's fiction feature *Personal Belongings* (2006). Fifteen days into completing this work at Iglesias's studio in Spain, Iglesias recalled, Brugués mentioned that he had another screenplay that might interest him. "What's it about?" Iglesias asked. "Fifty years after the Cuban Revolution, another revolution is about to start: the zombie revolution," Brugués responded, citing what later became the film's tagline. Iglesias continued:

> I told him to give me the screenplay, I read it that night, and the following morning, I said, "This is fantastic. It's amazing. I'm interested in making it but—can it be done?" And I meant it in terms of logistics and production and in terms of politics. I had never been to Cuba and I didn't know. He [Brugués] told me: "Look, as far as production is concerned, you have to come to Cuba and meet the people involved with 5ta Avenida because it is a big film. As for politics, I believe this is the moment and that we'll know how to manage things *por la izquierda* [through unofficial channels]."

When I asked Iglesias to elaborate on what caught his attention when he read the screenplay that first time, he told me that it made him laugh a lot, that it worked well in terms of genre, and that the characters were magnificent. But he also reiterated his observation that "the film was really critical and very intelligent," perhaps even "the most critical thing that has been made in Cuba." *Juan de los muertos*, he concluded, was the "perfect film to talk about Cuba, about this society and about Cubans." The Spanish television producers Iglesias approached to fund the film, he explained, shared his reaction to the screenplay. Immediately fascinated by the project, they also worried if such a large and critical production could be made on an impoverished island still under socialist rule. "Yes, yes," Iglesias recalled responding, with an assurance he perhaps did not entirely feel.[28]

In the end, of course, not only was 5ta Avenida able to carry off the project, but it did so with the cooperation of the ICAIC, one of the requirements Iglesias imposed as part of the coproduction agreement. The film's ending may well have played some role in making it palatable to state authorities. To a large extent, *Juan de los muertos* simply provides a new, if more direct, spin on themes previously addressed in post-Soviet Cuban bureaucrat comedies. Using zombies as an allegory to criticize the reification of revolutionary energies, the film concludes by calling on citizens to stay in Cuba and combat social problems.

Zombies have long been used as tools for social criticism. In the Haitian and West African folklore from whence the term derives, *zombis* are individuals whose souls or bodies have been captured by Vodou priests. As many scholars argue, this version of the myth has frequently been used to negotiate histories of slavery and the reduction of humans to commodities. Following the US marine occupation of Haiti from 1915 to 1934, zombies made their way to Hollywood, where they at first featured largely as signs of the exotic other. George Romero's classic zombie trilogy—*Night of the Living Dead* (1968), *Dawn of the Dead* (1978), and *Day of the Dead* (1985)—played an important role in remaking the Haitian tradition of zombi slaves into the self-reproducing horde that dominates the genre today (Lauro and Embry 2008; Mantz 2013; McAlister 2012).[29] In this guise, zombies have come to stand in for all sorts of social ills and, in particular, for modern capitalism. In *Dawn of the Dead*, for instance, the band of survivors takes refuge in a shopping mall and goes on a consumerist joy ride, appropriating items freely from stores. When the mall is taken over by zombies, the allegorical equation between modern consumers and the living dead is made clear. "They're us, that's all," comments Peter, the African American protagonist of the film, as the zombies lumber through abandoned stores.

If zombies, as this scene makes clear, are particularly good for thinking capitalism, then this is because they stand in for a perversion of human energies. As Chris Harman puts it, "Capitalism as a whole is a zombie system, seemingly dead when it comes to achieving human goals and human feelings, but capable of sudden spurts of activity that cause chaos all around" (2010, 12). Whether shambling about in the case of Romero's traditional slow zombies or moving at lightning speeds in Hollywood's new fast versions, zombies represent a terrifying loss of vitality and autonomy to a single and repetitive purpose: consume and make more consumers. Further social commentary is provided in zombie movies through the predicaments faced by human survivors. The real drama of these films, scholars argue, revolves around the question of whether survivors will choose a more individualistic, "every (wo)man for themselves" solution to the crisis or a more communitarian response, bringing to the fore questions of social morality and the relationship between the individual and the collective (Greene and Mohammed 2010; Mantz 2013; Murray 2010).

As this description already begins to suggest, then, what makes zombies particularly fruitful for allegorizing the alienating effects of capitalism turns out to also make them good for criticizing state socialism. Both the perverted energies of zombies and the moral dilemmas confronted by survivors resonate with concerns that, in Cuba, have long been expressed through criticism of the bureaucracy and bureaucrat comedies: namely, the fear that the affective immediacy meant to bind Cuban citizens to one another and to political leaders has become reified and corrupt and, adding to this theme, post-Soviet worries that solidarity and social justice have given way to materialism and individualism.

In *Juan de los muertos*, this perversion of collective energies comes to the fore in a scene that takes place in Havana's Plaza de la Revolución (Revolution Square) (figure 4.3). The Plaza de la Revolución occupies a key role in the Cuban political imagination. While the buildings around the plaza house the revolutionary government, the plaza itself has long been a central site for the mass rallies that Che Guevara took as emblematic of the affectively immediate governance that ought ideally to bind Cuban political leaders to citizens (see chapter 3). In Brugués's film, however, the plaza has instead become home to a shambling half-life. While traversing the plaza, the gang finds itself surrounded by zombies. They huddle together in the plaza's center, framed against the square's iconic mural of Che Guevara with its revolutionary slogan, "Hasta la victoria siempre" (Until victory always).

Belying this nationalistic cry, however, it is a foreign character with an American genealogy who finally comes to our heroes' rescue. As the gang struggles to fend off the monsters, a military-style jeep suddenly comes roaring into the square and beheads the zombies with a wire chord fired from its roof. Juan and his friends look on in amazement as their unlikely savior steps out of the vehicle: a minor character whose dubiously accented English and safari-style hat and shorts are later justified by his introduction as a humanitarian missionary by the name of "Preacher Jones." Far from delivering a nation united by collective effervescence, this scene suggests, the Revolution has reduced citizens to cannibalistic automatons while rescue comes

Figure 4.3 Zombies take over the Plaza de la Revolución in Alejandro Brugués's *Juan de los muertos* (2011).

through a comic spin-off on that agent of American imperialism himself, Indiana Jones.

Preacher Jones's triumph, however, proves short-lived. In the next scene, Lázaro accidentally harpoons the character just as he is about to reveal a plan for doing away with the zombies. But if foreign intervention remains a comically unviable solution, state socialism proves even more ineffective. As in earlier bureaucrat comedies from *Alicia en el pueblo de maravillas* to *Guantanamera*, much of the humor in *Juan de los muertos* comes from the film's satirical send-up of the state's retreat into a repetitive propaganda out of touch with reality. Throughout the film, a TV news anchor (played by director Manuel Herrera, who is producer Inti Herrera's father) repeatedly blames the zombie attacks on "antisocial behavior" fomented by "dissidents" backed by "US imperialism."[30] A sequence in which Juan teaches his neighbors to defend themselves against the zombies further satirizes the Cuban state's tendency to blame all social ills on the United States. "This is like preparation for defense," Juan explains, referring to the militia training that is a regular part of Cuban life. "Except that this time, the enemy isn't the Yankees but rather a real enemy, one that is here, among us."

Also as in previous bureaucrat comedies, then, Cuba's worst enemy lies within. But *Juan de los muertos* goes further than many earlier films, making clear that a good part of the blame for the failings of the Revolution rests not only with citizens but also with their leaders. In a gag that plays out over a number of scenes, Juan fields a series of ever-more-absurd requests for the gang's zombie-killing services from a phone attached to the wall of his rooftop apartment. The last of these calls shocks him. "Who?" he asks incredulously, after listening silently to the request issued by the caller. "No, no, compañero, that's your business," he finally answers. When he hangs up the phone, his bewildered expression bespeaks a you-know-who that spectators are meant to recognize. In another scene, Lázaro's son, Vladimir California, whose name emblematizes the nation's historically conflicted geopolitical allegiances, announces that he would like to travel the world, then explains that he will stay put in the first place where no one has ever heard of socialism or Fidel Castro. Bringing home this send-up of the state, later on in the film, the heroes watch as a bus is taken over by zombies and skids down the road on its side, crashing at last into a billboard that reads, "Revolución o muerte" (Revolution or Death). The answer to this rallying cry, it seems, is obvious: death—or at least a living death—has already won out over the Revolution, transforming political leaders and citizens into walking corpses.

While *Juan de los muertos* is thus arguably more transparent in its satire, especially of the Revolution's political leaders, than previous Cuban films, like the bureaucrat comedies that preceded it, it does not so much abandon revolutionary values and ideals as call for renewed efforts to combat social ills. This moral is conveyed most directly through the development of Juan's character. When the film first opens, Juan is an unlikely hero. As noted earlier, the character stands in for those Cubans who came of age in the midst of the worst years of the crisis and were torn between revolutionary solidarity and an individualistic ethos of survival. Survival dominates Juan's initial response to the zombie apocalypse. After he launches his zombie-killing business in an effort to transform the crisis into personal income, Juan and his gang engage in a series of comic encounters that demonstrate their commitment to their own well-being over that of their fellow citizens. In one early scene, for instance, the gang faces off against a group of paunchy, undead Spanish tourists dressed in S&M gear and accompanied by also undead Cuban *jineteras* (prostitutes), accidentally kill the woman who initially hired them for the job in the confusion provoked by a power outage, and then ransack her home for money.

Juan's questionable morality is further reinforced by one of the film's principal love stories. In a twist on the love plots of other post-Soviet bureaucrat comedies, romance in *Juan de los muertos* revolves, on the one hand, around what Gustavo Subero (2016) aptly describes as the "homosocial bromance" between Juan and Lázaro and, on the other, the relationship between Juan and his daughter, Camila. Heterosexual romance, meanwhile, is displaced onto a burgeoning love affair between Camila and California. From the beginning of the film, Juan is presented as a macho philanderer while Lázaro lives vicariously through his friend's exploits. The relationship between the two characters comes to a head in a scene toward the end of the film. In a nod to Edgar Wright's zombie comedy, *Shaun of the Dead*, Lázaro and Juan wait together on the rooftop of Havana's iconic Habana Libre Hotel for Lázaro to succumb to what he believes to have been a zombie bite. As stirring emotional music plays, Lázaro confesses his love to Juan and asks the latter to perform oral sex on him.

When Juan agrees, without, notably, all that much prompting, Lázaro bursts into laughter and accuses him of being a "tremendo maricón" (tremendous fag) and a "metrosexual," thereby affirming the two men's love for one another while also anxiously asserting their heterosexuality. La China and El Primo, meanwhile, serve as foils to this relationship. If the incorporation of these latter two characters into the gang shows some tolerance toward sexual and gender diversity, this acceptance clearly only goes so far. In a sequence midway through the film, China starts to turn into a zombie while attached to Juan by handcuffs. The two engage in an awkward salsa as Juan tries to avoid getting bitten, then finally throws China over the side of his apartment building. Upon reencountering a zombified China in the plaza scene, Juan violently beats the character to death. China's friend, El Primo, meanwhile, is the last of the gang to die, thus killing off the Afro-Cuban characters and leaving the white, heterosexual protagonists as the final survivors.

If the bromance between Juan and Lázaro asserts Juan's loyalty only to those nearest him, however, his relationship to Camila demonstrates his capacity for a broader solidarity. Even at the beginning of the film, Juan is not without a moral code. In early scenes, he helps his elderly neighbor with her groceries, warns Lázaro that California must be stopped from following in their footsteps, scolds China for stealing in their neighborhood, and insists on his commitment to staying in Cuba rather than immigrating to Miami, even if part of his reasoning is that in Miami he would have to work. But it is his relationship to Camila that provides the crucial catalyst for change. In one scene, Camila bonds with California over memories of how their fathers used to dress them in rags and bring them to Old Havana to beg from tourists. It is because of such antics that her mother decided to take her to Spain, Camila recalls, thus setting up the film's central conflict: Juan's efforts to win his daughter's affections by demonstrating his capacity for reform. If at first these efforts are generally comic, by the end of the film Juan proves himself to have more in common with the new man immortalized by Che Guevara than his initial self-interested focus on getting by suggested.

As the invasion worsens and Havana is reduced to a postapocalyptic nightmare, the gang confronts a difficult choice. "Should we retreat to the Sierra and advance from there?" inquires California, implicitly referring to the strategy adopted by the 26th of July Movement. "You're joking, but that's what we should have done in the first place," answers Juan. But Camila convinces her father that their tiny group cannot stand up to the zombies, and Juan announces a "Plan B" as iconic of post-Soviet Cuba as guerrilla tactics were of the struggle against Batista: they will find a boat and head to Miami. The gang then carries out an elaborate escape plan. They build a floating car in the basement of the Habana Libre, then Juan and Lázaro take on a crowd of zombies and drag their remains into a ramp at the foot of Havana's iconic statue to the USS *Maine* on the edge of the Malecón.[31] At this point, the two men hear a young boy cry for help. Confirming his moral makeover, Juan rescues the child from his zombified father by driving the latter into a stake (a scene that provides a pretext for more homophobic humor), while the rest of the gang sends the floating car careening up the ramp of zombies, over the Malecón, and into the ocean.

At the last moment, however, Juan decides to stay behind. After carrying the young boy into the ocean and handing him to Lázaro, Juan pushes the floating car away and backs toward the shore. "I'm a survivor," he explains, launching into lines that at once echo filmmakers' own stories of commitment to Cuba and reference the historical uncertainty that accompanied Raúl Castro's ascension to power: "I survived the Mariel, I survived Angola, I survived the Special Period and that thing that came after, and I will survive this. Maybe people will see me and join me to help. I'm good here. This is what I like." "Dad, please," Camila pleads. Tying the knot on the film's family romance, Juan smiles as he responds that it is "the first time you've called me that," acknowledges that Camila and California make an

Figure 4.4 Juan leaps into the zombie horde at the end of *Juan de los muertos* (2011).

attractive couple, and then threatens to castrate California if he touches his daughter. Finally, as the opening strains of the Sex Pistols' punk-rock version of Frank Sinatra's ballad "My Way" plays, Juan climbs back onto the Malecón. He watches wistfully as his friends and daughter drive away, then he grabs his crotch, brandishes the oar that serves as his signature weapon, and launches himself into an endless sea of zombies (figure 4.4).

Bruce Lee and the Newest New Man

By now it should be clear how this ending rehearses a genre—staying and fighting—that in the post-Soviet era became increasingly common to Cuban intellectuals' life narratives and to bureaucrat comedies. As in these other contexts, Juan's decision can be read as a form of critical nationalism: he chooses to remain in Cuba out of both a personal sense of commitment to the nation and a desire to combat the problems that plague it. Also true to the genre, the state appears more a part of the problem than a potential ally. But while some spectators interpreted the scene as an example of critical nationalism and political ambivalence, others criticized the ending for resurrecting a self-sacrificial nationalism.

Several Cuban spectators with whom I spoke interpreted Juan's choice to stay in Cuba as a patriotism that included recognizing and working to resolve the nation's internal problems. A middle-aged man who had gone to see the film at the Payret, a large movie theater in Central Havana, praised the film for its "messages" about the "revolutionary process," implying that these messages were critical, then went on to identify with Juan's decision to stay in Cuba. "I found the ending convincing," he told me. "Because I'm the same as him. I love my country and I have been part of this process since I was born and I don't want to leave. I like trying to do something good for people." A cleaning woman who watched the film from the back of the Payret concurred. She liked the ending, she explained, because Juan "stayed in his Cuba, you know? With all its problems, he stays in Cuba."[32]

Jorge Molina, who played the role of Lázaro in the film, emphasized the critical implications of Juan's nationalism: "You have to take into account what kind of hero he is. This isn't the exemplary worker or the family man who works from five in the morning to midnight. He's not an upright military man, an internationalist, or a policeman. This guy is a low-class delinquent. And so that has a tremendous connotation because it shows that the idea of *patria* [homeland] is not just ideology. That is, I might not like the government, but nobody can get me to leave here, and if there's an invasion I'll be the first to take up arms."[33] For Molina, the film's depiction of Juan as a delinquent who loves his country rather than as a more upright version of the new man establishes a difference between loyalty to the nation and allegiance to the state. Nonetheless, it is notable that in his description, critical nationalism leads to a willingness to defend the country that might well work in harmony with state interests.

For other spectators, it was this resonance of the ending with state interests and ideology that stood out. One older woman who watched the film at the Yara, a large theater located in the middle-class Vedado neighborhood, commented: "I would do the same as Juan, but I'm sixty years old. Young people may not feel the same way. They have other expectations. Life is hard for young people in Cuba. There are many good things, but because of the economic situation they also lack a lot—affordable clothing, places to go out and have fun, to live their youth the way my generation did."[34] Confirming this generation gap, a man in his twenties observed that he "liked the film because it deals with Cuban reality" but hesitated when I asked him what he thought of the ending. "Look, the film criticizes social problems," he told me. "And the ending . . . This is so as to not give so much weight to those things [the criticism], to put a lid on them. To change the film so that he stays in Cuba and '¡Cuba sí!' But the dream of Cubans is to travel."[35] For this young man, Juan's decision to stay was a strategy designed to make the film's otherwise scathing criticism of Cuba acceptable to state officials. Perhaps even more significantly, it betrayed what he believed to be the real aspiration of many Cubans and Cuban youth: the dream of leaving the country, whether to travel and return or in search of a better life abroad.

Like the friend with whom I first watched the film, still other spectators complained that Juan's decision to stay was tantamount to suicide. "He'll only wind up dead by staying on alone," commented one man on his way out of a screening of the film at the Charlie Chaplin movie theater in Vedado. "It would have been better if he had left."[36] Another spectator noted the affinity of the film's ending to official revolutionary myth. When I spoke with the seventy-seven-year-old physics professor mentioned earlier after she had seen the film, she dismissed Juan's heroism with a smile. "He thinks that with that oar he can take everyone on," she said with a laugh. "It's absurd!" But then she went on to muse that life in Cuba had always been full of such absurdities. "It's a fight against the impossible but, well, it's a fight that we've been carrying on for fifty-three years," she observed. "We've lived through extremely difficult situations like the embargo and everything and we've always come out afloat."[37]

When I ran into her in the street a few days later, she was still thinking about the ending of *Juan de los muertos*. "It's like Cinco Palmas [Five Palms]," she explained, referring to a legendary moment in Cuban revolutionary mythology. Shortly after they landed by boat on the coast of Cuba, Fidel Castro and his forces suffered a bitter defeat at the hands of Batista and were forced to separate into two groups. Upon reuniting with the group led by Raúl Castro at a farm, later renamed Cinco Palmas, Fidel Castro asked his brother how many guns he and his men had with them. "¡Ahora sí ganamos la guerra!" (Now we'll definitely win the war!), Fidel supposedly proclaimed upon learning that between them they had seven guns and a handful of men. Juan's kamikaze leap into the zombie horde, my interlocutor suggested, resonated with this David versus Goliath bravado.

In *Amor vertical* and *Lista de espera*, as I have shown, the convergence of personal romance and national passion linked hopes for the renewal of collective solidarity to demands for a nation that could sustain its citizens and fulfill their personal desires. But while love for his daughter motivates Juan's moral transformation, in deciding to stay behind, he not only sacrifices his personal relationships for the sake of the collective but also puts his own life in danger. Viewed from this perspective, the film's ending reinforces a self-sacrificial version of nationalism that, by the twenty-first century, had become increasingly unacceptable to many Cubans. Ironically, this was a connotation exacerbated by the filmmakers' aspirations to produce a new kind of Cuban cinema. His was a generation that grew up watching the films of directors like Steven Spielberg, Alejandro Brugués explained during the interview for Cuban television mentioned earlier. But when he began his studies at the EICTV, everyone was obsessed with art cinema directors like Ingrid Bergman and wanted to make anti-Hollywood films. But why should filmmakers reject Hollywood, he asked, if this was the cinema spectators wanted to see? Better to use action, entertainment, and zombies to "say things" about Cuba.[38]

In keeping with this ambition, the film is jam-packed with references to Hollywood and crossover cinema. A scene where a minor character is eaten by a shark while attempting to escape the island, Brugués told me, paid homage to Spielberg's *Jaws* (1975). Later in the film, a comically spectacular fight sequence ends with Juan leaping on a zombie's head while disgust and horror play across his face, a move that is inspired by Bruce Lee's fight against Caucasian American karate champion Bob Wall in *Enter the Dragon* (1973). Bruce Lee, whose Hong Kong films, notably, have often been celebrated as an expression of Third World solidarity and postcolonial resistance, also served as an important reference for Juan's kamikaze leap into the zombie horde.[39] From the beginning of the project, Brugués told me, he knew how he wanted the film to end. But it was the film's Spanish cinematographer who suggested that they have Juan face off against a horde instead of the smaller group of zombies that had originally been planned. "In one of the first meetings with Carlos Guzi, he said if we've already seen Juan fight against a group of zombies and we know that he wins then it doesn't make any sense," Brugués recalled. "That is, if you're going to launch him, launch him against a million zombies so that it's an impossible fight. I liked that better." The inspiration for this scene, Brugués elaborated, came from Bruce Lee's *Fist of Fury* (1972), which ends with the martial arts master jump kicking into a police lineup in an image that freezes as gunshots are heard (figure 4.5).

The overlay of this scene with the Sex Pistols' punk-rock anthem, finally, also invokes another, more obscure global reference. At the end of *The Great Rock 'n' Roll Swindle* (1980), Julien Temple's contested documentary about the Sex Pistols, Sid Vicious finishes a rendition of his version of "My Way"

Figure 4.5 Bruce Lee's final jump kick into a line of police in *Fist of Fury* (1972).

by pulling a gun on the wealthy and conservative diegetic audience and then, in a brief direct address, on the nondiegetic spectators. The film then cuts to a cartoon animation that depicts the British band as pirates tossed on a stormy sea who get eaten by sharks and ends, finally, with a collage of news headlines reporting Vicious's murder of his lover, Nancy Spungen, and his death by overdose at the age of twenty-one. The irony of this finale is only further heightened if one considers that "My Way," as originally written by Paul Anka and performed by Frank Sinatra, was meant as an ode sung by a man looking back on his long life.[40]

The references to Bruce Lee and the Sex Pistols invoke the film's crossover and antiestablishment ambitions. But their suicidal overtones also get in the way of creating an ending that conveys just the right mix of social criticism and political optimism, especially for spectators who might not catch these international references. This was an inadvertent effect that the filmmakers worked to correct. Notably, the film does not end with Juan's decision to stay on in Cuba alone. Rather, the freeze-frame that, as in *Fist of Fury*, captures Juan's leap transitions into an animated coda intercut with the closing credits, as in *The Great Rock 'n' Roll Swindle*. But whereas in the Sex Pistols documentary Sid Vicious's real-life death is anticipated by the animation, in the coda to *Juan de los muertos*, the rest of the gang returns to help Juan trounce the zombies while "My Way" plays on.

Commenting on his interest in the open endings of films such as *Fist of Fury* or even *Thelma and Louise* (1991), Brugués told me that he is the sort of "optimist who always believes that the protagonist survives." The coda, then, might be read as an attempt to ensure that spectators would walk away with a similar interpretation. "The coda reinforced the ending and gave it less of a suicidal tone," explained producer Inti Herrera. "Because the idea isn't suicide. The idea is to confront and finish off the zombies." Sadly, this was a message that most spectators at the New Latin American Film Festival missed. Reflecting, perhaps, their own concerns about how the ending of the film might be interpreted, several of the artists involved in the making of *Juan de los muertos* complained to me that spectators rushed to exit the theater the moment the film appeared to have finished, hence missing the coda with its corrective optimism.

What's Fun Got to Do with It?

My interlocutors often insisted that conciliatory representations of the diaspora in post-Soviet films indicated the triumph of a more liberal current within Cuban cultural politics. Yet well into the twenty-first century, there were still clearly limits to the depictions of emigrants and emigration that state officials were willing to tolerate. This can be seen in the scandal provoked by Cuban director Ian Padrón's documentary of Los Industriales, Havana's beloved baseball team, in *Fuera de liga* (*Out of This League*, 2008).

Fuera de liga follows Los Industriales over the course of six months, embedding the players' everyday struggles within a broader historical and political context. Toward the end of the documentary, a sequence intercuts conversations with baseball fans on the island with interviews with former Industriales players who defected to the US, recorded by Padrón while in the United States attending a film festival. Among the US-based players interviewed is legendary Orlando Hernández Pedroso, more popularly known as "El Duque," who went on to play for the New York Yankees in two World Series after he left Cuba in 1997. One interviewee explains the departure of El Duque and other Industriales players as a response to the economic crisis of the Special Period. But this reasoning does not, at least initially, convince the fans back home. An older man observes from the steps of the Capitolio that "the dollar beat them. They were defeated by the dollar." A little boy who pretends to be El Duque as he plays baseball in an abandoned lot reveals a strain in his identification with the player. "If Cuba gave him [El Duque] the opportunity to be a great player, then why did he leave?" he asks Padrón. "He should have stayed." A middle-aged man, hanging out with the fans who gather regularly to talk baseball in Old Havana's Central Park, comments that everyone has problems but not all players have left. "Some have left, but others have stayed," he notes, implicitly framing staying as heroic and leaving as morally mistaken.

As the sequence continues, however, *Fuera de liga* evokes hope for reconciliation between the US-based players and Cubans on the island. One of the fans in Central Park tells Padrón to bring them video footage of the exiled players, so that the players can explain their decision to leave to those at home. The documentary then cuts to an interview with El Duque, who insists that he remains Los Industriales' biggest fan. The fans in the park ask Padrón to let El Duque know that they are proud of him. The man who initially praised players who stayed in Cuba appears to have had a change of heart. "We Cubans who are here are proud of him and everything that he has done," he says of El Duque. "Friendship can't have frontiers," adds Rey Vicente Anglada, the manager of Los Industriales. "When you're friends, you have to respect one another's ideals even if you disagree." Finally, another defected player observes how much he would love to play an exhibition game back in Havana and to get a few beers at the Hotel Nacional. All the US-based players insist that they are not traitors and that they are, as one puts it, "100 percent Cuban," even if they no longer live in Cuba.

This message of friendship and reconciliation, however, was clearly too ambitious for state authorities. Completed in 2003, *Fuera de liga* was not officially approved for release until 2008, when it appeared on television alongside *Lista de espera* and other previously censored Cuban films in the wake of the email war. "They didn't approve the film because it includes baseball players who live in the United States," explained Padrón. "Here in Cuba, they're considered traitors. I don't believe this and so I included them, and as a result I had to wait for five years for the film to be approved."[41]

This story makes clear that spectators who saw in the ending of *Juan de los muertos* a deliberate ploy to appeal to state censors may well have had a point: staying and fighting for a better nation is a message more in line with official state discourse. At the same time, such stories are not simply progovernment. Rather, as I have shown here, from the 1990s well into the twenty-first century, artists and spectators alike often turned to critical nationalism and stories of staying and fighting as a means of reconciling revolutionary ideals of community and solidarity with growing resistance to the socialist state and, in particular, its ongoing demands for citizen self-sacrifice. Through a new foregrounding of love plots, post-Soviet bureaucrat comedies such as *Amor vertical* and *Lista de espera* offered up fantasies of a nation that would love its citizens back, combining a renewed commitment to Cuba with a demand that citizens' material needs and personal desires be met. This was a vision that the ending of *Juan de los muertos* inadvertently betrayed, in part through the filmmakers' efforts to deliver spectacle inspired by a global cannon.

In the end, however, perhaps what is most remarkable about *Juan de los muertos* is both how direct its political gags are and how much they seem to be just part of the fun. Whereas Daniel Díaz Torres publicly denied the controversial interpretations of *Alicia en el pueblo de maravillas* right up until his death in 2013, when I asked Alejandro Brugués about *Juan de los muertos's* references to Fidel Castro, he seemed primarily concerned that spectators might have missed the punch line. Admitting forthrightly that the last of the telephone calls Juan receives requesting zombie-killing services was meant to imply that Castro had become a zombie, he observed that the soundtrack of the film makes it difficult for viewers to hear the exchange, a mistake made in editing that was never resolved. This open irreverence reveals the growing impatience of a new generation of artists with the political caution of their predecessors, while also suggesting that politics may well have become just another ingredient in a new, entertainment-oriented cinema.

The real heroes of *Juan de los muertos* for both Cuban and foreign film professionals and audiences, after all, were the young filmmakers behind the project, whose deft mobilization of political humor, spectacle, and marketing savvy demonstrated the possibility of creating a commercially viable independent cinema in Cuba. In this context, the fact that the only central characters to die in the film are the sexually deviant, mixed-race and Afro-Cuban La China and El Primo acquires a further significance. *Juan de los muertos* begs the question of who will benefit from Cuba's latest round of economic reforms, resonating with the mixed feelings I encountered among my friends and interlocutors in December 2011 and subsequent trips, their skepticism and yet their hope that, this time, change might lead to a nation in which citizens could finally thrive and youth would not feel obliged to leave. I return to the ambivalence opened up by Raúl Castro's efforts to decentralize the economy and changes in the relationship between filmmakers and the state in the coda. But first, in the next chapter, I demonstrate how a new series of art films produced in the twenty-first century by young Cuban filmmakers turned to the montage and collage experiments of the 1960s to explore the post-Soviet crisis in Cuban historicity and to reconsider the legacy of revolutionary Cuban filmmaking.

CHAPTER FIVE

MONTAGE IN THE PARENTHESIS

After History

In one of the multiple interviews I carried out with Cuban film director Fernando Pérez in the modest Centro Habana apartment where he lives with his eldest daughter, he explained to me why he often insisted that his cinema is art and not politics. He had once believed in the "militant cinema" of the 1970s for which Latin American filmmakers such as Octavio Getino and Fernando Solanas advocated through montage films such as *La hora de los hornos* (*The Hour of the Furnaces*, 1968), a cinema in which "what was most important was political commitment and the immediacy of transforming society." This aesthetic commitment went hand in hand for him with a certainty that "history went in a direct line forward, that we were going to change the world, that we were going to create that new man to whom we aspired." "Today I don't think that way," he continued. "I still believe in those ideas, but I don't believe very much in ideologies. They get converted into dogmas that don't favor life and transformation."[1] A similarly ambivalent relationship to dominant revolutionary discourse often came up in my conversations with younger filmmakers. If they frequently voiced impatience with the political compromises of their elders, they also occasionally waxed nostalgic for an earlier era that they imagined as one of greater moral clarity. "In 1959 we were opposing a system that was totally unjust; it was obvious that it had to be eliminated," filmmaker Alina

Rodríguez Abreu once told me. "Today the line between what is good and what is bad is very difficult to define."[2]

As many have noted, the collapse of the Soviet Union was accompanied in Cuba, as in other state socialist countries, with a significant crisis in historicity, as citizens scrambled to reimagine the future and make sense of the present in the wake of the loss of the narratives that had previously organized their lives.[3] The life stories of filmmakers and the films touched on in the previous chapter already begin to demonstrate this post-Soviet disruption of shared moral references and understandings of Cuba's place in the world. Recall Eduardo del Llano's recollections of how the fall of the Berlin Wall shocked a generation that had grown up with the idea that "capitalism and imperialism were the bad guys and that we were on the side of good," a belief consolidated in part through the race for space that set the United States against the Soviet Union with Cuba as active ally to the Soviets; or Arturo Sotto's memories of how his generation was convinced that "socialism was the system of the future" and "waited every day for capitalism to stop existing."

Films, meanwhile, reflected a pervasive new experience of history as impasse or parenthesis. *Lista de espera*'s story of passengers unable to leave a bus station, for instance, allegorizes the present as a period of relentless waiting, a historical state of exception framed, on one end, by the collapse of the Soviet Union and, on the other, by the ongoing assumption that change must be somewhere on the horizon, even as this change never quite seems to arrive. Juan's signature line—"I'm a survivor. I survived the Mariel. I survived the Special Period and la cosa esta que vino después [that thing that came after]"—meanwhile, speaks to the interminable nature of this parenthesis. If, in this statement, the Special Period has definitively come to an end, it has done so only to be replaced by an even more ambiguous era, one not yet concretized into a name in a nation in which periods were long given designations, invoking an orderly and deliberate movement from one era to the next.[4]

As these examples show, alongside the question of whether to leave or to stay explored in chapter 4, the crisis in historicity became one of the most dominant themes of Cuban cinema and other arts in the post-Soviet era. In this chapter, I take up a series of films by young filmmakers trained at the ISA and the EICTV that take this crisis as their organizing ethos. The films examined here were released between 2005 and 2017 and, hence, in a period that spans those ambiguous years referenced in *Juan de los muertos* through the consolidation of Raúl Castro's presidency and the economic reforms launched under his presidency. As such, they demonstrate how the sense of living in a parenthesis and the frustration of waiting for change lasted well into yet another era that many at first had hoped might bring more significant reform. More specifically, if in the previous chapter one of my goals was to map the rise of a new independent and entertainment-forward commercial cinema, here I am interested in how other young filmmakers working outside the ICAIC turned to the montage experiments of the 1960s and 1970s both to challenge the teleological certainty that shaped early revolutionary filmmaking and to find tools in this work for recounting alternative histories of the Revolution and its aftermath.[5]

As I have shown, from the 1960s well into the 1980s, Cuban filmmakers adopted modernist techniques and open endings to expose social problems—sometimes engaging in far-reaching criticisms of the state and state policies—while nonetheless working to maintain socialist meanings and outcomes. Yet as Pérez's comment about the dangers of ideas that devolve into dogmas or Rodríguez Abreu's insistence on the loss of moral clarity in the present make clear, in the wake of the collapse of the Soviet Union, even such tempered attachments to socialist truth and visions of history as foreseeable became untenable. The filmmakers whose work I examine here instead recover for an uncertain present the oeuvre of Afro-Cuban filmmaker Nicolás Guillén Landrián, whose films, long censored on the island, provide an unusually early criticism of revolutionary discourse and socialist modernization, or find unexpected resonances in more canonical takes on the Revolution by French filmmakers Chris Marker and Agnès Varda and Afro-Cuban director Sara Gómez. These efforts involve a shift from earlier modernist allegories, in which experimental techniques were used in Brechtian fashion to encourage spectators to reach the socialist conclusions posited by films for themselves, to something more akin to the modern allegory theorized by Walter Benjamin, in which meaning and history are tenuous and emergent.

This challenge to the models of montage and allegory that dominated earlier revolutionary Cuban filmmaking in turn puts political paranoia and the politics of filmmaking on display. Some of the films discussed here reveal their complicity with paranoia; others counter dominant political discourses through a paranoid style that highlights the ambiguity of all narratives; and all explore the damages wrought on individual lives and personal relationships by Cold War divides. Through these tactics, these films challenge the classificatory impulses of Cold War politics and of filmmaking itself, questioning the ethics of producing definite meanings out of a contradictory reality. Yet if, in so doing, these films emphasize the need for new political options, they also leave unanswered the question of how such a project might be forged in the midst of pervasive uncertainty and what, if any, role cinema might play in this effort.

The Violence of Filmmaking

In October 2007, a group of Swedish documentarists visited the EICTV to discuss their work with the students at the school. During the question and answer period, one of these filmmakers asked the audience what documentary genres were most popular in Cuba, mentioning that in Sweden, for instance, video diaries had grown in importance. While some documentaries in Cuba were more personal, one audience member responded, most were focused on sociopolitical and economic realities. This was an emphasis promoted by Cuba's cultural institutions, another observed, noting with some disparagement the ICAIC's efforts to involve artists in documentaries about Cuban internationalist work abroad.[6]

By the end of that year, however, one young documentarist at the school had demonstrated how a turn to the personal could be used to explore and expose a political that, as the audience's comments suggested, many Cubans experienced as frustratingly overdetermined. Susana Barriga's earlier documentaries, *Como construir un barco* (*How to Build a Boat*, 2006) and *Patria* (*Homeland*, 2007), depict the impact of Cold War divides and political paranoia on individual lives and relationships, while her graduating thesis from the EICTV, *The Illusion* (2008), uses a painful encounter with her exiled father to explore how such dynamics structure her own family relationships. But her work's self-reflexive use of the gaze and of muteness also highlights the violence involved in filmmaking, begging the question of whether cinema, and especially her own ethically questionable decision to film her father without his knowledge, facilitates new understandings or simply colludes with and exacerbates existing political impasses.[7]

Barriga's attempts to trouble Cold War binaries and the ethics of filmmaking in her work owe much to the oeuvre of Afro-Cuban filmmaker Nicolás Guillén Landrián. The nephew of one of Cuba's most respected poets, Nicolás Guillén, Guillén Landrián was one of only a handful of Afro-Cuban film directors who worked at the ICAIC in the 1960s and 1970s.[8] From 1962 to 1971, he filmed twelve documentaries as well as four shorts for the ICAIC's *Popular Encyclopedia* series while running into increasingly grave political problems (Reyes 2010, 9–10). In interviews and letters written in the early 2000s, Guillén Landrián explained that he was sent to prison in the 1960s for "ideological reasons" and later to an agricultural work camp for functionaries with "improper conduct," where doctors diagnosed him with schizophrenia and arranged for his transfer to a psychiatric hospital in Havana (qtd. in Petusky Coger, Ríos, and Zayas 2005; Zayas 2010). He went back to work at the ICAIC after his release from the psychiatric hospital, but the documentaries he produced in the late 1960s and the early 1970s met with increasing censure until he was expelled from the institution in 1971. After leaving the ICAIC, he worked odd jobs and continued to paint. In 1989 he was finally allowed to depart for Miami, where he produced a documentary—*Inside Downtown* (2001)—before passing away in 2003. His death coincided with a resurgence of interest in his filmmaking in Cuba. Censored for decades on the island and excluded from studies of Cuban cinema, his films were screened at the 2002 and 2003 editions of the Muestra Joven (Youth Exhibit) to great success.[9] Many younger Cuban filmmakers recall seeing his films for the first time as a profound and moving revelation, and his work has subsequently had an important impact on the work of a new generation (Goldberg 2014; Reyes 2013).[10]

Part of the attraction of Guillén Landrián's work for a younger, more disillusioned generation of filmmakers is clearly his unorthodox approach to revolutionary politics and life in Cuba. In the 1960s, explained Guillén Landrián, "cinema about the Cuban people had to be made at least with euphoria, and I didn't have any" (qtd. in Petusky Coger, Ríos, and Zayas 2005). Setting aside revolutionary triumphalism, the documentarist's early work instead takes an ambivalent approach, adopting what Dean Luis Reyes describes as an "obsession with contrasts" (2010, 14). *En un barrio viejo* (*In an Old Neighborhood*, 1963), for instance, uses a contrapuntal montage of sound and image inspired by Eisenstein to convey a sense of the contradictions that shaped life in Old Havana in the 1960s. A series of establishing shots—the roofs of several houses seen from above, a girl perched on a rooftop who looks impassively back at the camera—leads to a long shot of a revolutionary militia marching down a narrow street. The film highlights the sounds of their march, the sharp echo of their feet striking pavement, their voices shouting "uno dos tres"—then quickly juxtaposes these sounds with the other rhythms that shape the neighborhood. A man gets a haircut; others play chess, drink, and dance to a catchy song; then the music fades as the film returns once more to the sound and visuals of the militia's march.

This ambivalent approach to revolutionary politics comes to the fore in the film's final sequence. Here the film moves from circling shots of Cuban flags, the 26th of July Movement's insignia, and posters of Camilo Cien-fuegos and Fidel Castro affixed to a wall, to images of racially diverse individu-als practicing a *palo* ritual, apparently in the same room. The camera focuses in on a black woman dancing to the persistent drumbeat, her white skirt twirling around her legs, then the film closes in a freeze-frame of this image and fades to black. "Fin" (End) read white letters superimposed on the black screen; then another line appears: "Pero no es el fin" (But it's not the end).

As I have shown, in the early decades of the Revolution, open endings were meant to invite spectators to come up with the solutions to the social problems illustrated by films for themselves, a tactic that, at least in theory, would both foster spectators' critical reason and lead them of their own ac-cord to socialist conclusions. The ending of *En un barrio viejo* casts doubt on this strategy. Julio García Espinosa registered the difficult relationship of Guillén Landrián's film to dominant revolutionary aesthetics in a review of the film that he published in *Cine cubano*:

> The documentary distances itself from simple didacticism and reflects with precision and not a little poetry the detained atmosphere of the old neigh-borhoods. This is ruptured at the end by a montage whose dialectic shows the struggle, or better yet the coexistence, between the past and the present. The documentary, nonetheless, loses force by clinging to a nostalgic vision of the old neighborhoods, similar to that of the tourists of yesteryear who re-inforced their aesthetic through images of dilapidated, poor, and static rural huts. (1964, 17)

Espinosa's praise for *En un barrio viejo*'s refusal of didacticism suggests an affinity between Guillén Landrián's work and the ICAIC filmmakers' criti-cism of the reduction of art to propaganda. But Espinosa's argument that the documentary plays to a touristic nostalgia indicates what, for him, was evidently a troubling departure from official revolutionary discourse. *En un barrio viejo*'s deliberate reference to the unfinished nature of the social processes it records, the simultaneity of local traditions with revolutionary politics, fits uneasily with the political vision of the 1960s, which took for granted, as Fernando Pérez put it, that history was proceeding in a straight line toward a new society.

Guillén Landrián's challenge to revolutionary teleology went hand in hand with a critical contemplation of the ethics of filmmaking. As theorists from Frantz Fanon (1967) through Laura Mulvey (1999) and E. Ann Kaplan (1997) have argued, cinema often privileges the gaze of white Western men, treat-ing women, people of color, and the colonized as objects to be consumed.[11]

Given Guillén Landrián's own marginal position as one of Cuba's few black film directors, it is perhaps unsurprising that *En un barrio viejo* underscores the potential violence involved in relationships of looking. At times the film adopts a voyeuristic perspective, offering spectators the illusion of an unmediated perspective on the neighborhood's residents. In one early sequence, for instance, a handheld camera records the patrons at a café, peering over their shoulders, then moving rapidly away just as it seems that they might return the filmmaker's gaze.

Later sequences, however, complicate this dynamic. In a self-reflexive scene, the film takes us for a tour of the local cinema. Spectators examine the program affixed to a wall outside the theater, a man sprawls at the entrance beside photographs and posters, then the camera ventures inside the theater itself. In a line that constitutes the film's only dialogue, a character from Vittorio de Sica's *Umberto D* asks if there will be war. If the handheld camera in *En un barrio viejo* at times recalls free cinema's ambitions to provide an unmediated look at reality, this sequence, as Manuel Zayas (2010) and Santiago Juan-Navarro (2015) observe, breaks the "fourth wall" and draws our attention to the fact that we are watching a film. In the sequence that follows, the film calls attention to the violence of the gaze. A moving shot follows two young women as they walk through the city streets accompanied by a nondiegetic drumbeat; a subsequent shot confirms their sexualization, zeroing in on their posteriors. It is perhaps significant that the two women in question are white, thus privileging the gaze of a black man looking at white women. It is certainly significant that the two shots of the young women are intercut with an image of an elderly, white-haired woman who stares impassively into the camera. The scene culminates with images of women who either glance at the camera or flash the filmmaker/spectators a knowing smile. If women here are still objects of the gaze, the film both allows them to look back and highlights the potential aggression in that relationship.

This mute return of the gaze, in fact, is a dominant trope throughout *En un barrio viejo*. In a number of the film's sequences, local neighborhood residents are shown posing for and looking back at the camera. A girl holds her doll shyly to her face as she looks at the camera; in our next glimpse of her she moves the doll away from her mouth and seems to say something to us. A boy walks across the street carrying a heavy block of ice, then turns and stares directly at us, leg cocked awkwardly to the side. Later in the film, a series of more distant framings capture older men standing in front of their stores, framed by entryways crowded with the objects of their trade.

Figure 5.1 Portrait-like shots of Old Havana residents in Nicolás Guillén Landrián's *En un barrio viejo* (1963).

This sequence concludes with an image of two men standing in front of a local Committee for the Defense of the Revolution (CDR), its paired garage doors painted with the Cuban flag and the Soviet hammer and sickle (figure 5.1). These images should not be taken as a simple assertion of the agency of the filmed. As Manuel Zayas (2010) notes, the neighborhood's residents are surely looking at the camera because the filmmaker has told them to. Moreover, the portrait-like nature of the shots resonates with nineteenth- and twentieth-century "type" photography. In Latin America and elsewhere, type photography often depicted anonymous individuals with the tools of their trade, employing a classificatory impulse that worked to reinforce colonial racial and social hierarchies (Poole 1997, 2004). At the same time, the absence of text or dialogue that might give more didactic meaning to these images suggests the limits of the filmmakers' and spectators' knowledge. Here again, then, where other Cuban films of the same era deployed modernist techniques in at least a theoretical effort to prompt spectators to independently arrive at social-ist conclusions, the mute return of the gaze in *En un barrio viejo* instead bespeaks an ineffability that resists socialist teleology and the efforts to fix the meanings of the lives documented by the camera.

Later works by Guillén Landrián continue this self-reflexive play with muteness and the gaze. *Ociel del Toa* (*Ociel of the Toa*, 1965) records the contradictions that characterize the life of peasants on the eastern coast of Cuba through a focus on Ociel, a sixteen-year-old boy who works poling cargo canoes down the river. In one much-noted sequence, intertitles present a young girl who wants to join the communist youth group but who also attends church with her aunt. As in *En un barrio viejo*, the political ambivalence highlighted by such dilemmas is accompanied by a refusal of socialist historicity. One of the first sequences of *Ociel del Toa* introduces the theme of birth through images and sounds of a woman in labor, while the closing sequence turns to the topic of death. The film, meanwhile, ends as it began, with Ociel and an unnamed companion poling their boat down the Toa River. The Revolution and its promises of a history that will proceed in a teleological line toward a new society, this narrative structure suggests, is only one component of a social world shaped by the cyclical flows of life and death.

Also as in *En un barrio viejo*, this ambivalent approach to revolutionary politics is once more accompanied by a contemplation of the role of filmmaking in the production of meaning. Adopting a portrait-style depiction of subjects who return the gaze similar to that used in *En un barrio viejo*, *Ociel del Toa* further explores the relationship between filmmaker and filmed through a play with intertitles that take the place of dialogue. At times these intertitles present the filmmaker/narrator as an omniscient and objective authority. The film's first intertitle, for instance, describes Ociel through a list of sociological details akin to the placement of characters with the objects of their trade in the earlier documentary:

ociel:
16 años
tercer grado de escolaridad
miliciano
desde los diez años trabaja en el río

[ociel:
16 years old
third grade
militant
has worked on the river since he was ten years old]

As the film continues, however, the intertitles begin to complicate the position of narrator and narrated. Taking modernist literature as one example, Benjamin Lee (1997, 277–320) observes that the presence or absence of framing devices such as quotation marks can work to either assert or to blur the boundary between narrator and character. By playing with both written and image equivalents to such devices, *Ociel del Toa* allows characters to speak for themselves while simultaneously drawing attention to the role of the filmmaker in shaping our understanding of the filmed. The complex narrational strategies of *Ociel del Toa* can be seen, for instance, in the film's closing sequence, which is presented as a dialogue. Images of campesinos traveling along the river in boats, the funeral procession, and, finally, shots of Ociel and his companion poling their boat down the river are intercut with a series of five intertitles about death.

(intertitle 1)   ¿ustedes han visto la muerte?
(intertitle 2)   ociel:
                 la muerte
                 no se puede ver
(intertitle 3)   ¿ustedes han visto la muerte?
(intertitle 4)   yo nunca he visto la muerte
(intertitle 5)   la muerte no se puede tocar
                 ni oír
                 ni sentir

(intertitle 1)   [have you seen death?
(intertitle 2)   ociel:
                 death
                 cannot be seen
(intertitle 3)   have you seen death?
(intertitle 4)   i have never seen death
(intertitle 5)   death cannot be touched
                 nor heard
                 nor felt]

The inclusion of Ociel's name followed by a colon in the second intertitle makes clear that it is he who responds to the first question, suggesting that the question itself was posed by the filmmaker. As the dialogue proceeds, however, it becomes more difficult to link statements to speakers. If the first question about death is posed by the filmmaker and answered by Ociel, who is responsible for its second iteration? Are we to assume that the filmmaker poses the question again, eliciting a response from Ociel? This seems the most likely interpretation. Close-ups of Ociel gazing into the camera in a direct address are positioned before and after the response, "yo nunca he visto la muerte" (i have never seen death), inviting us to read these shots as visual framing devices. But the remainder of the sequence confuses the issue. After the second of these shots of Ociel, the film cuts to his companion followed by close-ups of unidentified arms and torso, making it more difficult to identify a speaker for the final intertitle. Who utters these conclusions about death: Ociel, his companion, or the filmmaker? The play with written and visual framing devices and the rendering of all statements as intertitles rather than voices more easily attributed to individuals invite ambiguity.

The intertitles that follow the first introduction of Ociel up to this final dialogue, meanwhile, create an even stronger blurring between filmmaker/ narrator and filmed. One early sequence, for instance, intercuts the following four intertitles with shots of Ociel and Filín, one of the men with whom Ociel works, walking their boat through the water (figures 5.2–5.10).

(figure 5.4)	todo va al guajiro en cayuca: comida, ropa los maestros
(figure 5.6)	son horas con los pies en el agua
(figure 5.7)	con los pies en el agua
(figure 5.9)	es bueno que esto lo vean en la Habana

(figure 5.4)	[everything goes to the peasant by boat: food, clothing teachers
(figure 5.6)	it's hours with one's feet in the water
(figure 5.7)	with one's feet in the water
(figure 5.9)	it's good that they will see this in Havana]

The final intertitle draws explicit attention to how the circulation of the film might create new connections between the rural and the urban, the provinces and the capital. Like the scene that introduces the neighborhood

---

Figures 5.2–5.10 (*opposite; left to right, top to bottom*) The repetition of the line "con los pies en el agua" in Nicolás Guillén Landrián's *Ociel del Toa* (1965), the second time in larger font, adds emotional coloring, while shots of Ociel looking directly into the camera toward the beginning of the sequence (5.2) and the end (5.8) suggest that some of these statements may have been voiced by him. But the inclusion of close-ups of Filín in the sequence (5.3 and 5.5), the shift between more sociological (5.4) and more emotional description (5.7), and the predominant use of the third person in the intertitles render voicing ambiguous.

todo va al guajiro
en cayuca:
comida, ropa
los maestros

son horas
con los pies en el agua

con los pies en el agua

es bueno que esto lo vean
en la habana

cinema in *En el barrio viejo*, it also serves as a self-reflexive reference to the movie that we ourselves are watching.[12] The repetition of the line "los pies en el agua" (with one's feet in the water), the second time in larger font, meanwhile, adds a crucial emotional coloring. The intimacy with which these intertitles recount life in the countryside as well as the framing of the sequence by shots in which Ociel looks into the camera suggest that some, at least, of these statements might be attributed to him. Indeed, Reyes (2010, 44) argues that one might interpret the bulk of the intertitles in the film as the voice of the film's protagonist, a reading justified by Ociel's clear protagonism and repeated gaze into the camera, the personal nature of many intertitles, and the occasional slip into the first person. But the first set of intertitles following the initial introduction of Ociel in the film in fact uses the first person to describe the life history not of Ociel but rather of his mother, both introducing the possibility of reading the intertitles as statements made by the people recorded in the documentary and opening up the question of who voiced them. More crucially, the predominant use of the third person in intertitles that, as in the sequence just described, vary between objective and emotional description begs the question of whether statements should be attributed to the filmmaker or to the filmed. The end result of this ambiguous voicing is to invite viewers into an intimate glimpse of the lives and feelings of the recorded while also drawing our attention to the role of the filmmaker and filmmaking in shaping their interpretation.

The influence of Guillén Landrián's films on Susana Barriga's work can be seen most clearly in her first two documentaries, *Como construir un barco* (2006) and *Patria* (2007). *Patria* provides a portrait of a young campesino who, as a woman tells us in the only spoken dialogue in the short film, wants to leave the countryside for Havana. Depicting his work "fixing the same road for the last five years," as a closing intertitle explains, the film returns repeatedly to close-ups of the young man, including a medium shot in which he seems to stand in wait for something, gaze turned toward the camera.

Como construir un barco, for its part, combines intertitles with portrait-style shots in which subjects return the gaze to reveal the impact of Cold War binaries and revolutionary politics on the lives of Cuban citizens. The documentary depicts everyday life in Santa Cruz del Norte, a fishing town where state prohibitions intended to stop the migration of Cubans to Florida have prevented the residents from building or repairing the fishing boats necessary to ply their trade. The film opens with images of a middle-aged man laying out boards in the shape of the boats that can no longer be built, then, in a clear homage to *Ociel del Toa*, cuts to an intertitle that describes the character just introduced through a series of sociological details.

Gilberto Falcón:
Pesca desde los 9 años
Construyó barcos hasta el 94
En Cuba prohibieron la construcción
de los barcos

[**Gilberto Falcón:**
Has fished since he was 9 years old
Built boats until 94
In Cuba the construction of boats is forbidden]

This introduction sets up a sequence that describes Falcón's dilemma. A series of intertitles explaining Falcón's desire to repair his boat and the lengthy bureaucratic process involved in obtaining permission to do so are intercut with shots of a boat being hauled onto land, close-ups of Falcón's work tools lying in disrepair, and images of Falcón. The sequence concludes with the following two intertitles, framed by a long shot of Falcón seated at the end of his boat, gazing impassively into the camera, and a close-up of the bow of the boat bumping up against a dock.

(intertitle 1)   Si uno quiere reparar su barco es para no mojarse
(intertitle 2)   Es para no mojarse

(intertitle 1)   [If one wants to repair one's boat it's to not get wet
(intertitle 2)   It's to not get wet]

Later sequences vary this use of the third person with the first, as different characters recount their stories. Despite its clear homage, then, voicing in *Como construir un barco* ultimately remains more stable than in *Ociel del Toa*, with the third person more clearly aligned with the filmmaker/narrator. Nonetheless, like Guillén Landrián's documentary, *Como construir un barco* employs techniques that blur the lines between filmmaker and filmed, sociological description and emotional experience: the substitution of intertitles for voice; the use of repetition and a larger font to invoke emotion even in intertitles using the third person, a tactic employed in the second intertitle referenced above and elsewhere in the documentary; and the repeated return to images of characters gazing into the camera.

Also as in Guillén Landrián's work, this relationship between filmmaker and filmed is not without violence. When I asked Barriga about her work's reliance on the mute return of the gaze, for instance, she suggested that such expressions sometimes "explained things better than could any verbal expression."[13] Yet she also acknowledged the formative influence of film-making, arguing that such moments do not merely reflect the feelings of those who are documented but also what a filmmaker induces in the people with whom they are working. "When you're filming someone, this return of the gaze is a look that contains that person and you as well," she explained. "They're talking to someone and that someone is you with everything that you provoked in them previously and in that moment." Intertitles that blur the positions of filmmaker and filmed and images of characters looking back at the camera, to put this otherwise, draw attention to the ways in which filmmaking itself, like revolutionary and Cold War political dis-course, often attributes meanings and interpretations to subjects that may or may not cohere with their sense of self or the desires that led them to consent (or not) to being filmed.

If Guillén Landrián's signature techniques are most evident in Barriga's earlier documentaries, it is her 2008 film, *The Illusion*, that provides her most poignant exploration of the relationship between filmmaking and the personal effects of revolutionary politics and Cold War divides. Produced as Barriga's graduating thesis from the EICTV while she was on an exchange with the University of Salford in Manchester, England, *The Illusion* records the filmmaker's thwarted attempt to reconnect with her father, who moved to England in 1994. Barriga did the filming for this documentary herself, using a lightweight HDV camera with onboard microphone that her father could see but did not know was turned on. The opening sequence of *The Illusion* establishes the film's key themes and aesthetic tactics: the daughter's dream of reconciliation with her father, frustrated by paranoia; an explora-tion of the gaze; fragmented and obstructed images of the London tube and of the film's principal characters; and the filmmaker's own participation in the paranoia and violence she documents.

A long shot reveals a man standing on a street corner, his features in-discernible in the night. He moves out of the camera's line of vision, but the filmmaker, persistent, moves with him while the jostling of the camera registers her steps. As we soon learn, the man in the distance is Barriga's father—and this is the clearest image of him we will have. As she follows him, Barriga intones in Spanish: "Sometimes I try to remember his face and I see this image, the only image I have of him. I wanted to make a film about happiness but all I have are diffuse memories whose significance I still don't understand." Suddenly, a British man demands angrily that she cease filming. "I definitely understand who you are!" he shouts. "What is she doing filming people? It's illegal to film people!" Barriga protests in heavily accented English, "He is my father!" Glimpses of her father are followed by blurred images as the camera spins rapidly over surfaces while we hear shouts that suggest that the man has attacked Barriga and is being hauled away. The image cuts to black. A new male voice asks in carefully spaced-out words if Barriga would like him to call the police. When she does not respond immediately, he speaks louder, as though volume could compensate for the language difference. The unknown British man's paranoia about surveillance, a paranoia within reason given the use of CCTV and other surveillance cameras in the UK, combines with Barriga's own inability to communicate her intentions effectively in English to render her a less-than-innocent victim of unfamiliar social conventions and laws.

This disruption of longed-for intimacy by paranoia, as well as the suggestion of Barriga and her film's complicity with this violence, sets the tone for the remainder of the film. After the opening sequence, the film loops backward to recount the events that led to this dénouement. The confrontation in the tube station is followed by shots of individuals traveling through London's underground transit system and by images of a door, stairwell, and cars parked outside an apartment building. The camera moves shakily to the door, suggesting Barriga's approach, then the film cuts to the shadowy outline of a man seen from the perspective of the camera evidently lying on a table. We hear Barriga and her father's voice as he greets her with surprise, affection, and suspicion. Asking to see her passport to verify that she is who she claims to be, he reduces her to this citizenship when he learns of her intentions to return to Cuba. Barriga protests that the fact that the government has allowed her to leave the country does not necessarily mean that she is "with the government," but her father insists. Fidel Castro's people will know that she has visited him "within a few minutes if you're with them, and within a few days if you're not with them," he tells her. And when they find out that she "came but not to stay, they will throw a party."

Just as the angry unknown British man in the opening sequence perceives in Barriga the threat of surveillance and the man who helps her reduces her to the status of foreigner, her father "knows who she is"—and this identity has more to do with politics than with the status of daughter for which she longs. Yet the film also does not dismiss Barriga's father's paranoia. Before their encounter goes entirely wrong, he tells her that although he trusts no one and Cubans even less, he has to trust her, his own daughter. In voice-over, she intones: "I was thinking about the camera. I never told him I was filming." The admission complicates attempts to attribute guilt or innocence. Both Barriga and her father appear simultaneously as agents and victims of Cold War binaries and political paranoia, suggesting just how difficult it would be to overcome the cumulated history of resentment, fear, and suspicion that has led to what her father terms at one moment in the film as the "division of the family" that has taken place under the Cuban Revolution.

The aesthetic techniques in *The Illusion* further reinforce this painful interruption of familial intimacy. Because Susana filmed the encounter in secret, we do not see either her or her father clearly. Instead, their voices are heard over obscured and handheld images of her father's apartment and the shadowy outlines of his body as the camera rests on tables or hangs by her side. These images of the film's principal characters are complemented by similarly fragmented and obstructed shots of individuals traveling through London's underground transit system: a close-up of a woman's hands, criss-crossed as they grasp the overhead rail of a car; the face of a young woman gazing back at the camera, both the car's window and its red pole obstruct-ing the frame (figure 5.11); and the pages of a newspaper left lying on a seat blowing open in the wind, accompanied by the ambient hum of trains mov-ing through stations.

At the level of narrative, the fragmented and obstructed shots of Barriga and her father function as an index of her physical presence, emphasizing the first-person and highly intimate nature of this documentary. Depict-ing individuals who travel together but alone, isolated from one another in the crowd, the shots of the London tube, meanwhile, indicate the physical journey through the foreign city that Barriga takes to find her father and act as a metaphor for the seemingly unbridgeable emotional distance that ultimately separates them. Importantly, however, both sets of images have a further connotation, one that brings the limits of filmmaking into view. At moments of particular emotional intensity, such as when Barriga's father asks her to confirm the death of her sister, the film returns to images of the tube and shots of the stairwell and door. Just as the fragmented images of their reunion deny viewers the privilege of an omniscient access to their en-counter and remind us of Barriga's questionable decision to film her father in secret, these repeated cuts bring into view the limits to our knowledge of the history and dynamics that have gone into this impasse.

Figure 5.11 Obstructed and fragmented image of a London tube passenger in Susana Barriga's *The Illusion* (2008).

The strain of history on personal relations and the question of whether filmmaking contributes to new understanding or merely exacerbates such divides is further reinforced by the film's ending, which circles around to its beginning. After Barriga and her father leave one another at the tube station, Barriga picks up her camera and focuses from a distance on her father's obscured silhouette. He returns her gaze. In voice-over, she explains: "This was the last time I saw my father. We watched each other for a long time, a time that would never fit into this documentary. I will never know if this wait was a gesture of love or was only because of what he was seeing. This is my last image of him. And his? A woman who was filming him with a camera?" The obstructed and jostling handheld image that opens and closes this documentary is a far cry from the static portraits and mute return of the gaze in Guillén Landrián's or Barriga's early documentaries. But, as her voice-over suggests, it partakes in their ethical challenge. As in these films, *The Illusion*'s play with the gaze gives expression to a longing for intimacy frustrated by the aggression and classificatory impulses of Cold War politics and Barriga's own filmmaking.

Counterhistories of Modernization

Where Barriga's documentaries turn to Guillén Landrián's early work to explore the lasting damages of Cold War politics on Cubans' personal lives and relationships, including her own, other young Cuban filmmakers took inspiration in his later films to produce open-ended counterhistories that expose the devastating consequences of state socialist modernization projects. In the late 1960s, Guillén Landrián's oeuvre moved from the lyrical style characteristic of earlier works such as *En un barrio viejo* and *Ociel del Toa* to dense collages of images and sounds in *Coffea arabiga* (*Arabian Coffee*, 1968) and *Desde la Habana ¡1969! recordar* (*From Havana 1969! Remember*, 1969). As analysts such as Dylon Robbins (2009) and Amelia Duarte and Ariadna Ruiz (2011) suggest, *Desde la Habana 1969, recordar* in particular uses a collage aesthetic to reveal Cuba's complicity in the violence of modernization.

The film's opening sequence emphasizes the achievements and the costs of modern science and technology. Discordant noises are followed by dynamic intertitles announcing, in Spanish, the Beatles song "Mother Nature's Son," followed by the sound and image of a nuclear explosion. Further reinforcing these themes of nature and science, life and destruction, the images and intertitles that follow depict the devastation of World War II, malnutrition, Girón (the Bay of Pigs), Vietnam, the Ku Klux Klan, a sign that reads "No Viet Cong ever called me 'nigger,'" a New Orleans parade, and poverty. These are intercut with shots announcing the invention of artificial hearts in the United States and the arrival of Americans on the moon, accompanied by a soundtrack that interweaves the Beatles song with a radio broadcast of the moon landing. Then the song comes to a sudden halt and intertitles compare the dream of reaching the moon to the history of colonial conquest. "La luna es un sueño" (The moon is a dream), announces one frame, followed quickly by a number of dynamic intertitles that together read, "Colón es el descubridor" (Columbus is the discoverer). This analogy announces the transition from an account of American and Western European modernity to a contemplation of revolutionary Cuba. As Fidel Castro's voice overlaps and competes with ominous noises, intertitles and a close-up of hands planting coffee plants allude to the Cordón de la Habana (Havana Greenbelt Project), then the film cuts to the opening credits.

The criticism of American and Western European versions of modernity in this opening sequence is clear. Achievements such as artificial hearts and the arrival on the moon are undermined by the death and destruction brought on by colonization and twentieth-century developments in science and technology. While the white American astronauts Neil Armstrong and Edwin "Buzz" Aldrin become the first men to walk on the moon, back on Earth, African Americans protest ongoing racism and the United States spearheads military invasions of Cuba (the Bay of Pigs reference) and Vietnam. To this point, Guillén Landrián's documentary remains safely within the realm of the internationalist Third World discourse that dominated Cuban politics and filmmaking in the 1960s and 1970s. But the quick transition at the end of the sequence to Cuba's agricultural plans is more ambiguous. The Cordón de la Habana, as it was known in Cuba, was an ambitious plan launched in 1966 to render the metropole agriculturally self-sufficient. Involving significant investments of money, equipment, and volunteer labor, the Cordón proved a spectacular failure when crop yields in 1968 failed to measure up to projections, foreshadowing the equally unsuccessful 1970 project to harvest ten million tons of sugar cane.[14] The reference to the Cordón at the close of Desde la Habana ¡1969! recordar's opening sequence, then, could be read either as proposing the Revolution as antidote to colonialism and its aftermath, or as suggesting a parallel between American and Western European plans of modernization and the Cuban socialist alternative.

This challenge to official Cuban revolutionary discourse is further developed throughout the film, which can be divided roughly into five thematic sequences, including the prelude described above. In the sequence immediately following the credits, images of Havana—its streets, vehicles, signs, and inhabitants during the day and at night—are rhythmically cut to the tune of a cha-cha-cha and interspersed with meditations on production, such as a bizarre instructional soundtrack comparing the importance of keeping tractors clean to personal cleanliness, punctuated by rhythmic close-ups of this machine and its components. Opening with a close-up of a poster announcing "100 años de lucha" (100 years of struggle), the second sequence offers a revisionist history of Cuba. As Robbins (2009) argues, this sequence draws attention to the failure of Fidel Castro and other political leaders to address Cuba's history of racism in the commemorative celebrations of 1968, which cast the 1959 Cuban Revolution as the natural outcome and fulfillment of Cuba's first war for independence against Spain (1868–1878).

The fourth sequence revolves around a conversation between Nicolás Guillén Landrián and a woman named Milagros. Intercut with family photographs of Milagros, her husband, and her child, Milagros recounts her dreams of becoming a model to avoid ruining her nails. The sequence culminates with a rapid collage of images from fashion magazines and Cuban women cutting sugar cane or driving a tractor, cut to the rhythm of the Beatles song "Everybody's Got Something to Hide except Me and My Monkey." The film's final sequence interweaves the cha-cha-cha from the film's earlier city sequence; Nicolás Guillén's recital of his poem "Elegía a Jesús Menéndez" (Elegy to Jesús Menéndez), written after the assassination of this Afro-Cuban labor activist in 1946; texts from Che Guevara's Bolivian diary in which he describes his struggles with asthma; and three blurred photographs of a young Che Guevara. Castro's voice gradually triumphs over the conflicting soundtracks, and the film ends with his emblematic declaration, "Patria o muerte" (Fatherland or death). But Castro's "patria o muerte" is here stripped of the usual conclusion to this phrase, "venceremos" (we will win), replaced instead by a sudden cut to blackness and an echoing clanging. Combined with Guillén's eulogy and Che Guevara's mundane concerns about his asthma, the conclusion once more seems to question whether this aggressive patriotism is truly in service of a future utopia or, like the aspirations to modernity described in the first sequence, complicit with death and destruction.

The film can thus be read as a counterhistory that takes on and criticizes socialist modernization. Importantly, this is a message that is conveyed through a self-reflexive contemplation of the difficulties and challenges involved in making out such meanings. In his essay "On the Concept of History" (1940), Walter Benjamin argues that dominant historical narratives are tales told by the victors, a "triumphal procession in which current rulers step over those who are lying prostrate." Progress, meanwhile, is depicted as a storm piling wreckage at the feet of the angel of history, as pictured in Paul Klee's painting *Angelus Novus* (Benjamin [1940] 2003, 391–92). Benjamin counters what he terms the dialectical image against this destructive version of history and progress. In *The Arcades Project* (1940), he describes this method as follows: "It's not that what is past casts its light on what is present, or what is present its light on the past; rather, image is that wherein what has been comes together in a flash with the now to form a constellation. In other words, image is dialectics at a standstill. For while the relation of the present to the past is a purely temporal, continuous one, the relation of what-has-been to the now is dialectical: it is not progression but image, suddenly emergent" ([1940] 1999, 462, Convolute N2, A3). The counterhistory revealed by the dialectical image is antiteleological and evanescent. Emerging only in a flash, elements of the past recombine in light of the present to reveal new meanings that might disturb dominant historical narratives, opening up alternative histories and visions of the future for the victims of the storm called progress.

A similar search for an elusive meaning that might pierce through the teleological histories of the victors characterizes not just the thematic content of *Desde la Habana ¡1969! recordar* but also its aesthetic method. As a number of analysts have noted, the conversation between Guillén Landrián and Milagros begins with a parable that sheds light on the film's aesthetic strategies (Duarte and Ruiz 2011; Ramos 2013; Robbins 2009). Here, the filmmaker relates the encounter between Milagros and a blind man. Catching sight of the man walking with his cane, Milagros pities him and calls him a "poor thing." But the blind man responds by saying, "No hay peor ciego que aquel que no quiere ver" (there is no worse blind person than the person who doesn't want to see), and they laugh. To add to the joke, this anecdote is told over still photos of a young white woman, presumably Milagros, and of Guillén Landrián himself as the blind man, dressed in a white suit and dark sunglasses, which he lifts with a smile to reveal his eyes as the story comes to an end. This exchange establishes an ambiguous relationship between blindness and sight, appearance and truth, which is further reinforced by the introduction soon after of the Beatles refrain "everybody's got something to hide except for me and my monkey," visualized for the spectator in an intertitle where the line appears in Spanish translation.

We might thus read this sequence as an injunction to a hermeneutics of suspicion: if everyone has something to hide, then our task is to see past these confused surfaces to the truth, just as Guillén Landrián does by shedding his sunglasses to reveal sighted eyes. But the bewildering layering of sounds and images that characterizes the film also suggests the difficulty of moving beyond surfaces with any certainty. As described above, the film's sound design frequently incorporates several different audio samples at once, making it challenging to follow any one of them without great effort; images and intertitles are cut to privilege rhythm over meaning, moving by at such a velocity that it is often difficult to make out their details; and a dense layering throughout of capitalist advertisements, socialist propaganda, and other archival footage, occasionally obstructed by white-and-black flecks, further contributes to the elusiveness of meaning. Indeed, a repeated intertitle, "de la radio" (from the radio), and a cut immediately after the opening credits to the image of a radio sonar suggest that the film's message is as much about the challenge of piecing together historical accounts out of the barrage of information that inundated both twentieth-century capitalism and socialism as it is a criticism of modernization. If the film adopts a paranoid style, piecing together a new narrative by uncovering hidden linkages between disparate materials, then this is a version of political paranoia in which the challenges of producing meaning and the ambiguity of all narratives are made readily apparent.[15]

Esteban Insausti's *Existen* (*They Exist*, 2005) might likewise be described as deploying a paranoid style to highlight the ambiguity of reality and narrative. Dedicated to Nicolás Guillén Landrián, this short intercuts archival footage and mass media images with present-day interviews with, as the film's credits put it, "algunos de los locos mas notables de la ciudad" (some of the city's most prominent crazy people), shot using a variety of different cameras and formats.[16] *Existen* opens and closes with archival images of a 1960 Soviet exhibit of technology and culture that took place in Havana. Mannequins display Soviet furs, miniature models demonstrate Soviet prowess in construction, a sign behind a tractor touts the Soviets' achievements in the construction of these machines, and women test state-of-the art 1960s automatic exercise machines. These shots are in turn intercut with a series of seemingly random color images ranging from a woman's hands covering her breasts to others that go by so quickly that it is impossible to make them out. A narrator from the footage of the Soviet exhibition explains that, "given the ideological characteristics of the exhibiting nation," it is important to specify that the display of these products "does not necessarily imply that we have to incorporate this ideology." But the cut at the conclusion of this sequence belies this assertion of national autonomy. A shot of a woman on one of the exercise machines, significantly taken from between her spread legs, cuts to the image of an unidentified blonde, eyes clenched and mouth opened in a scream. Statistics attesting to the rising numbers of mental illness in the world follow.

This sequence lays out the film's central theme. As Antonio José Ponte argues, Cuba is "in danger of remaining outside itself, given into a destiny that is not its own, driven crazy" (2006; see also Loss 2014, 186). As the film continues, this alienation of the nation is clearly linked to the drive toward modernization and internationalism that characterized the early decades of the Revolution and was motivated both by Soviet influence and by the nation's own political ambitions. One early sequence loosely organized around food highlights official film and radio broadcasts touting Cuba's achievements in agriculture, replete with impressive statistics. This found footage is intercut with images of elderly Cubans practicing tai chi in a park, their slow exercises interrupted by the occasional yawn; more mass media images, which once again flash by so quickly it is difficult to make them out;

and speeches by two of the city's mentally disturbed. A man with chipped coke-bottle glasses decries the lack of quality in the food of La Pelota, a state-run cafeteria in Havana's middle-class Vedado neighborhood. "There are days where they give things that are bad," he explains, pausing with finger on mouth as he collects his thoughts. "The *croquetas* are stale, the food is stale; they don't give enough ham, cheese, mayonnaise; and the croquetas come out badly. This is not correct. We have to resolve this problem as quickly as possible."

This decisive denunciation of La Pelota both contradicts official declarations of abundance and parodies official state discourse. The sequence then cuts to found footage from a 1960s black-and-white documentary celebrating record numbers in pig cultivation and to an interview with a second mentally disturbed resident of Havana. "To be Cuban is completely the back part of what is the fourth third ninth of the ideological causes that have to do with the process of the third part of the intensification of nature," he observes, looking into the camera. Ann Marie Stock (2009, 211) interprets this statement as an expression of the complexity of Cuban identity following the collapse of the Soviet Union and its new position in a global world. Read in connection with the 1960s black-and-white documentary footage celebrating record numbers in pig cultivation with which it is immediately juxtaposed, however, it can also be interpreted as a criticism of official rhetoric. Alexei Yurchak (2006) argues that late Soviet political discourse increasingly emphasized the performative over the constative dimensions of language, copying authoritative styles with little regard to referential or constative meaning. This reified discursive context in turn gave rise to specific forms of humor such as *stiob*, which imitated the style of authoritative discourse so closely it was difficult to discern whether the resulting performance was sincere or a parody. In *Existen*, the man's seemingly nonsensical iteration of numbers takes the exaggerated drive toward statistics that dominates state media to its logical extreme. It works, in other words, as a true reflection of Cuban state rhetoric, revealing its emphasis on performance over an accurate description of reality.

Later sequences further unfold the damaging effects of revolutionary militancy. A sequence on war opens with a cartoon animation of a helicopter, photographic negatives of a man holding a rifle, and an intertitle that reads, "Enrique eloqueció en la guerra" (Enrique went crazy in the war). Black-and-white shots of cemetery monuments rhythmically cut to the staccato of gunfire pay possible homage to the work of Cuban experimental documentarist Santiago Álvarez, who used similar play with gunfire, rhythmic montage, and the photographic negative in early documentaries such as *Now* (1965) and *79 primaveras* (*79 Springtimes*, 1969). Then the film cuts to rapid hand-held moving shots through the aisles of the cemetery. Superimposed on these shots are the names of the many countries in which Cubans have fought as soldiers under the Revolution: Angola, Ethiopia, Nicaragua, Namibia, El Salvador, Mozambique, Congo, Vietnam, Libya, and Republic of Yemen. These images culminate with a close-up of a blindfolded angel of justice, a fallen soldier embraced in its arms, and the words "descansen en paz" (rest in peace).

This moving testament to the cost of Cuba's internationalism is followed by an exploration of the consequences of the embargo and the ongoing standoff between the United States and Cuba. Anticipating accords that finally seemed to be coming to fruition with the normalization of relations announced by Presidents Barack Obama and Raúl Castro in December 2014, the man with the coke-bottle glasses calls for Fidel Castro and George W. Bush to end the confrontation between the two countries: "Fidel should say to Bush, 'I don't want any more wars and let's get along and let's have loans.' And that's it. That's how the war ends—one president reaching an agreement with the other president." Once again, images that range from the seemingly random shot of a human tongue to an elderly man dressed as Uncle Sam interrupt and underscore this speech in rapid rhythm. Other sequences explore post-Soviet emigration, frustrations in individual and national romance, and cinema and television before and after the Revolution. Then the film returns to the 1960 Soviet exhibition with which it began. A narrator justifies the exhibit by explaining that Cuba welcomes all nations that come to it with "good intentions" while also insisting that Cuba's celebration of the "progress exhibited by the products" and the "technical capacity of its workers" demonstrated by the Soviet exhibit remain rooted in the "nationalist feelings" that inform the Cuban Revolution. The film, however, makes clear its ironic take on this nationalist declaration. The narrator concludes by citing José Martí—"mi patria para el mundo; no el mundo para mi patria" (my homeland for the world, not the world for my homeland)—then the film cuts to an image of a woman screaming.

As in Guillén Landrián's *Desde la Habana ¡1969! recordar*, *Existen*'s exploration of the painful consequences of Cuba's modernizing aspirations is closely tied to its aesthetics. Esteban Insausti explained:

> The thesis of *Existen* starts from chaos theory. That is, the film attempts to find an answer within incoherence, among those crazy people who walk through the city . . . . In all that incoherence that one confronts every day, I

tried to find a possible coherent answer. It seems like a paradox, but that's what it's about. And what I was most interested in finding out was how the crazy person saw the world and who the crazy people are in reality: them or us. Or which is the most interesting world.[17]

As suggested by Insausti's comment, the film's juxtaposition of found footage, interviews with Havana's mentally disturbed, and contemporary media images have a number of significations. On the one hand, the constant interruption of the dominant image track by seemingly random images, which often go by at such a velocity that the viewer does not have time to puzzle them out, itself acts as a metaphor for the alienation and trauma that the film suggests characterizes individual and national experience. But these mass media materials also occasionally form more meaningful associations with the footage with which they are juxtaposed, as in the cut from the archival image of the woman on the exercise machine to the blonde woman's scream or the juxtaposition of the seemingly incoherent description of what it means to be Cuban with found footage describing record numbers of pig cultivation. It is this sudden emergence of meaning that best describes the film's method. Through unexpected juxtapositions of archival and found footage and contemporary interviews, *Existen* seeks out an alternative account of Cuba's past and its possible future. As in Guillén Landrián's collage films, however, such truths emerge only in momentary flashes, evanescent glimpses of a repressed collective unconscious or counterhistory that resists easy formulation into a coherent, singular meaning, even as it highlights the inadequacies of dominant national narratives and political discourse.

Death, the Index, and the International

At one point in *Existen*, an older Afro-Cuban man gazes softly into the camera and comments, "I know Harlem, the Bronx, Queens, Harlem . . . Central Park, with all its provinces. The Colorado Canyon, the Thailand Cave, Niagara Falls—*todo eso es mío. Pero . . .* [all of that is mine. But . . .]." He shakes his head, then continues, "*Mi Cuba es mi Cuba*" (My Cuba is my Cuba). At first glance, the man's statement seems inchoate. Yet it might also be read as utopian, a wishful assertion of ownership over both the iconic city of New York and the world at a time in which Cuba's own international importance appeared to have faded. The next short film discussed in this chapter—Yan Vega's *Memorias de una familia cubana* (*Memories of a Cuban*

Family, 2007)—articulates a similarly poignant reflection on Cuba's strained historicity and its place in the world, reappropriating the early montage experiments of French filmmakers who traveled to Cuba in the early 1960s to recount the personal impact of the demise of utopian revolutionary aspirations.

Memorias de una familia cubana uses still photographs from the director's own family album (animated through zooms, pans, close-ups, superimpositions, and other cinematic techniques), voice-overs provided by his relatives, and archival images and sounds documenting key events in Cuban history to recount the story of a fictional Cuban family. The film opens with a sepia-tinted image of adults and children around a birthday cake, replaced through a dissolve by a hand-colored photograph of a morose little girl whose dress—a Cuban flag—calls on viewers to interpret the story as national allegory. As these images go by, voices sing "Happy Birthday" to "Tatiana," warping the song's lines as traditionally occurred in Cuba to the nonsensical "happy baby you you." The song is supplanted by a news radio broadcast as the film cuts to a shot of Tatiana, beaming out at the photographer from her perch on a brand-new bicycle in front of a Christmas tree. "¿Papi, quienes son los revolucionarios?" (Papi, who are the revolutionaries?), she asks. Her father stumbles over an answer while her mother dismisses the question as inappropriate for little girls. The film, meanwhile, depicts the conversation by intercutting the image of Tatiana with her bicycle with photographs of her father and mother.

This naïve question, in a sense, occupies the rest of the film, which in sixteen minutes covers the major transitions and events that marked Cuban history from the 1959 overthrow of Fulgencio Batista through the collapse of the Soviet Union and mass emigration during the Special Period. A new exchange between Tatiana, now pictured as a young woman, and her father suggests just how quickly cultural references were transformed for those whose lives were swept up by the fervor of the Revolution. Tatiana tells her father that she wants to join the literacy campaign to teach people in the mountains to read. He responds with pride, his previous hesitation over whether discussing revolutionaries is an appropriate topic for little girls seemingly forgotten. The scenes that follow depict Tatiana's growing involvement in the Revolution, her encounter with and marriage to revolutionary fighter and government official Pedro Suárez, her pregnancy, and the birth of their two children.

This last sequence emphasizes how childhood is transformed from Tatiana's era to that of the next generation. Demonstrating the growing influence of the Soviet Union on Cuban culture, Tatiana explains that she named her daughter Valentina after the first woman astronaut in space, Valentina Tereshkova, a Soviet citizen. In case the referent for Tatiana's son's name, Ernesto, is not sufficiently clear, the sequence moves from a wedding march announcing Tatiana and Pedro's union to a speech by Fidel Castro calling on youth to be like el Che. Shots of Valentina's birthday party are accompanied by the Spanish-language "Feliz cumpleaños" (Happy Birthday), indicating the rejection of earlier American influences. The sequence closes with an ironic reflection on the revolutionary aspirations of the new generation that resonates with the ending of Guillén Landrián's *Desde la Habana ¡1969! recordar*. Ernesto declares his desire to be "asthmatic like el Che" when he grows up. Valentina notes that she wants to "travel to all of the countries in the world—but not the United States, obviously." Tatiana tells her children that for the moment all they need to do is concentrate on their studies. Pedro, revealing his militant orientation, warns them that the only things they cannot become are "counterrevolutionaries, marijuana users, *maricones*, or, in the case of women, *invertidas*."[18]

As viewers of the film already know, however, the future will not turn out to be as straightforward as anticipated by these hopes and dreams. *Memorias de una familia cubana*'s critical take on the Revolution is apparent from the outset. Over the opening credits to the film, we hear Fidel Castro explain to a foreign reporter his willingness to step down from power if this is what is necessary to ensure the future of the nation. "Sincerely I don't ambition power money nothing, only to serve my country," Castro says in halting English. The irony of this statement is clear to present-day viewers and emphasized in a sequence that follows shortly thereafter where men's voices praise the leader as "un caballo" (literally, a horse, meaning a great man) and "a poet." A later sequence pokes fun at the state socialist practice of distributing vehicles and other major goods as rewards for labor and political service. Photographs of Pedro in an official meeting; cultivating cane; as a delegate to the Soviet Union, East Germany, and Vietnam; and as a revolutionary fighter are accompanied by a voice declaring that, in reward for his service, the Communist Party has decided to "award Pedro Suárez Ramírez the opportunity to buy a car." This statement comes to a finale with the sounds of cymbals crashing, a cuckoo clock, and close-ups of Pedro himself, eyes wide open in a look of comic surprise, transforming what might otherwise have been a joyful event into parody.

But the film's most moving criticism of the Revolution and its damaging aftereffects comes later in the film. A photograph of an aging Tatiana and

Pedro and their friends at the beach is transformed into the anticipation of crisis. As the film closes in on the individuals in the image one at a time, they voice their concerns about the current state of the Soviet Union and the consequences for Cuba if it should collapse. "I have no doubt that the Revolution and Fidel will come out on top," Tatiana says. "He knows what he's doing." But Pedro, previously a staunch defender of the Revolution, has lost all such certainty. Head stooped and looking down over his belly, he replies: "Yo, realmente, no sé qué pensar" (I don't even know what to think). A weighty pause follows, then we hear the first intonations of a speech. Fidel Castro's declaration that "Cuba and the Revolution will continue to fight and to resist" even if the Soviet Union collapses is interwoven with the ominous sound of a heart monitor, as the film cuts first to an image of a reflective Pedro at an official meeting; then to Tatiana lying on a bed, arm covering her eyes; and finally to portraits of Pedro at increasingly older ages. The last of these portraits gives way to a doctor's voice informing Tatiana that the "patient Pedro Suárez is not responding" to treatment. The only thing left to do is wait, he tells her. Then the heart monitor flat lines, the screen cuts to black, and portraits of the couple at various ages are shown to the tune of a traditional love song.

In the sequence that follows, Ernesto declares to his remaining family that his childhood friend, Yunieski, is gay, while a radio announcer notes that the Russian movie *Burnt by the Sun* (1994) has won out over *Fresa y chocolate* for the Oscar for best foreign film, thus linking global fascination with the demise of state socialism to Cuban cinema and changes in Cuban sexual politics. Other scenes depict the migration of Valentina and her husband to Miami; Ernesto's brief stint as a cab driver using his father's car; and, finally, Ernesto's own marriage to a French citizen and migration to France. In the film's closing sequence, Tatiana receives a phone call from Ernesto. "Aquí nada cambia" (Here nothing changes), she tells her son, repeating the pervasive and plaintive refrain that, in the post-Soviet period, emblematized the sense of living in an interminable parenthesis. As she hangs up the phone, she hums, "Porque te vas" (Because you are leaving). The film closes with shots of the car that Pedro was awarded for his service, now rusting on blocks. Like Tatiana's melancholy solitude, the car allegorizes the abandonment of the country by a younger generation forced to pursue their lives and dreams elsewhere.

As in the previous films examined in this chapter, in *Memorias de una familia cubana*, the dashed hopes and promises of the Revolution as well as the new realities forged through emigration are, significantly, recorded not just through the film's themes but also by its aesthetic form. Vega frequently cites Santiago Álvarez as well as French filmmakers Chris Marker and Agnès Varda as inspirations for *Memorias de una familia cubana*. The influence of these filmmakers can be seen in the film's animation of still photographs, an approach that is mobilized in different ways in Álvarez's early documentaries as well as in Chris Marker's science fiction short, *La jetée* (*The Jetty*, 1962), and Agnès Varda's documentary, *Salut les cubains* (*Hello Cubans*, 1963).

Vega also takes from Marker and Varda's work a powerful exploration of memory, death, and their relationship to the photographic image. Providing a suggestive precedent for *Memorias de una familia cubana*'s exploration of a present in ruins, Marker's *La jetée* tells the story of a man who finds himself a prisoner in an underground camp in the aftermath of an imagined World War III. Forced by guards to draw on his own memories to travel in time in search of help to rebuild the earth, he discovers that the image of a man dying that marked him as a child—an image with which the film both begins and ends—was in fact the moment of his own death. In Varda's *Salut les cubains,* which uses photographs shot by Varda while visiting Cuba to document the Revolution, death comes to the fore in a sequence directly cited in *Memorias de una familia cubana*. As the opening credits of *Memorias de una familia cubana* come to a close, chants of "Fidel!" give way to the conga refrain "¿Dónde está Teresa?" and a photograph of Pedro in revolutionary uniform is made to dance. The soundtrack in this sequence obviously invokes the iconic opening of *Memorias del subdesarrollo*, with that scene's contemplation of violence. But Pedro's dance also references a particularly moving scene from *Salut les cubains*. As part of that documentary's exploration of a revolution "set to the march of a conga," Varda introduces us to Cuban musician Benny Moré, described by the monikers often used to refer to him in Cuba—the "King of Rhythm" or the "Barbarian." Via the animation of still photographs, the famous musician sings and dances a *son montuno* for the viewer, but the joyful moment soon turns mournful.[19] Over shots of Moré, now without music, we hear Varda's voice bid farewell to the musician "sadly lost between these images and this film." "Salut au roi qui est mort" (Goodbye to the king who is dead), she concludes.

Benjamin once linked photography to an uncanny temporality imbued with death. Contemplating a picture of the photographer Karl Dauthendey and his wife, the latter of whom would commit suicide six years after the photograph was taken, the theorist argues that the viewer is tempted to seek in that image some trace of a future that could only be grasped from the present: "No matter how artful the photographer, no matter how carefully posed his subject, the beholder feels an irresistible urge to search such a picture for the tiny spark of contingency, of the here and now, with which reality has (so to speak) seared the subject, to find the inconspicuous spot where in the immediacy of that long-forgotten moment the future nests so eloquently that we, looking back, may discover it" ([1931] 1999, 510). As Miriam Hansen (2012, 107) notes, Benjamin's experience of this photograph is marked "not just by circumstantial knowledge of its posthistory or that of its subject" but also by what he brings to its viewing and by what we, knowing that Benjamin himself will eventually commit suicide, bring to our reading of his encounter with the image: "The futurity that has seared the photographic image . . . emerges in the field of the beholder's compulsively searching gaze." This urge to place pressure on images from the past such that they yield presentiments of a tragic future resonates with the final demise of the time traveler in Marker's *La jetée*, narrated through a photograph whose full significance is unfolded at the end of the film, and with Varda's solemn homage in *Salut les cubains* to Benny Moré, "the dead king," a moment that interrupts her otherwise celebratory documentary of the Cuban Revolution with a statement that, from the perspective of the early twenty-first century, acquires broader allegorical significance.

Looking back on the history of the Revolution and that of his own family from the vantage point of the present, Vega's *Memorias de una familia cubana* makes this insistent, tragic vision its centerpiece. Vega's father, photographs of whom are used to represent the fictional character of Pedro, was an important figure in the revolutionary government before he passed away in May 2002. While Vega himself was openly critical of the Castro government during the time I spent with him, he also often reminisced with a mixture of fondness and bewilderment about his father's staunch support for the Revolution and his sometimes-frustrating adherence to its laws. Vega's use of images of his father thus acts as a sign for two overlapping disasters: the death of his own father; and the demise of the dream of the Revolution, emblematized through Pedro/Vega's father's death and the closing image of the character's ruined car. Finally, *Memorias de una familia cubana*'s homage to the work of Chris Marker and Agnès Varda also invokes a moment in Cuban history in which international artists descended on the island and uncovers its unanticipated afterlife.[20] Vega made *Memorias de una familia cubana* after he emigrated from Cuba to France to marry the woman (a French EICTV graduate) pictured in the film as Ernesto's wife. Vega himself, meanwhile, appears briefly as Ernesto's childhood friend, Yunieski, while

Vega's mother appears as Tatiana. *Memorias de una familia cubana* thus merges Vega's own family's story with that of the nation through a fictionalized take on personal photographs that also pays homage to the French filmmakers who traveled to Cuba in search of utopia. In so doing, the film emphasizes the personal consequences of Cuba's lost revolutionary dreams for the future and reclaims an international aesthetic heritage for a nation in which the diaspora must also be included.

Memory and the Material

If *Memorias de una familia cubana* ends with an image of an island abandoned by its youth, Vega's personal trajectory speaks to the transition from an era in which emigration meant exile to a period in which many Cubans, especially those from younger generations, began to move with greater ease back and forth between the island and locations abroad. Upon returning briefly to Cuba in 2013, Vega worked as an editor for Carlos Machado Quintela's feature-length fiction film *La obra del siglo* (*The Project of the Century*, 2015), before migrating first to Miami and eventually to New York. Like Vega's short, one of the greatest strengths of *La obra del siglo* is its recovery of a neglected archive. Like Insausti's and Guillén Landrián's documentaries, the film mobilizes this archive to reflect on the personal impact of Cuba's stalled plans for modernization. Finally, *La obra del siglo* emphasizes the sensory and material dimensions of the archival images and sounds it includes in ways that allow these objects themselves to become important sites for recalling and reworking the past and Cuba's lost dreams of modernity in the present.

La obra del siglo was filmed and set in La Ciudad Electro Nuclear (CEN, The Electro-nuclear City), itself an important feat. Previously, directors Arturo Sotto and Enrique Colina had both tried and failed to secure permission to shoot films in this location. The CEN was constructed to house the Soviet and Cuban workers recruited to take part in an ambitious plan to build two nuclear reactors in the province of Cienfuegos. Work on this project began in 1983 but was suspended in 1992 after the withdrawal of funds and personnel following the collapse of the Soviet Union, and the project was definitively terminated in 2000. As Quintela recounted the story to me, the idea to film in the CEN first occurred to him when he was completing his studies in screenwriting at the EICTV. After attending a screenwriting workshop held by the school in the CEN, he returned to the city while scouting locations for a different project and was struck by the strange appearance of the reactor. "When you look at it, it doesn't seem to have anything to do with Cuba—it's like a UFO," he observed.[21] Around the same time, Abel Arcos, with whom Quintela had previously collaborated on his first feature-length film, *La piscina* (*The Swimming Pool*, 2011), wrote a story about three generations of men living together in an apartment building in Havana. Another filmmaker showed some interest in the screenplay but then moved on to other projects, so Quintela and Arcos began adapting the story to the setting of the CEN.

It was during this initial stage of work that Quintela first learned of the existence of the Tele-Nuclear archive that he would eventually incorporate in the film. He explained:

> This archive was supposed to have been destroyed, but it had been abandoned in the closet of the CEN's cultural center and a resident of the CEN told me about it. They were somewhat nervous about what to do with this archive, and so what they did was to exclude all of the images in which Fidel appeared, which didn't really matter to me. Anyway, they gave me the archive, I took it back with me to Havana and had it digitized, and afterward returned it to the city. We researched the rights to this archive and discovered that Tele-Nuclear had been a video group that belonged to the Ministry of Heavy Industry, a ministry that produces rice and has no legal precedent to deal with audiovisual images. The group itself, meanwhile, ceased to exist twenty years earlier.

The discovery of this archive proved fortuitous. While Quintela and his team filmed the screenplay as it had originally been written, difficulties during the production weakened the story. With the collaboration of Yan Vega, this story was then enriched during editing through the incorporation of the archival footage, which significantly transformed the film's aesthetic and its affective impact.

La obra del siglo uses the strained relations between three generations of men to explore the crisis in historicity that followed the collapse of the Soviet Union. As the opening credits roll, we hear the sounds of fighting and a male voice comments with some irritation that they have destroyed a rocking chair that he owned for forty years. The following images introduce us to the film's protagonists: Otto, the grandfather and owner of the apartment who made the comment about the rocking chair; his son, Rafael, who once worked as a nuclear engineer and now raises pigs; and his grandson, Leo, recently returned to the apartment after a falling-out with his girlfriend. No specific reason is given for the physical altercation between Rafael and

Leo, but as the film continues, their differences soon take on generational and national connotations. In a later scene in the film, the gold medal win of eighteen-year-old Cuban boxer Robeysi Ramírez at the 2012 Olympics provides a pretext to explain the professional and moral crisis that characterizes Rafael's generation—those who, like Juan in *Juan de los muertos*, confronted the collapse of the Soviet Union and the crisis that ensued in the midst of their professional lives or as these were just getting started. Cuban television footage announcing Ramírez's win cuts to Otto and Leo, drinking beer at a picnic table outside a gas station. "They're embarrassed that we're still here," Otto mutters, noting how the television announcer named Cienfuegos as Ramírez's birthplace when in fact he had been born in the CEN. "When I was a kid, the champions were always focused on the money," he continues. "Then they were told it wasn't about that. And they accepted it. . . . That's how your father grew up: with all of that shit they stuffed his head with. Poor guy—he got more punches than he deserved. Now it turns out that money is what people want after all." Acknowledging that Leo will not stay in the CEN, Otto tells him that before he leaves he needs to spend some time with his father. Leo agrees.

This conversation sets the stage for a rapprochement between father and son. In a scene soon after, archival footage of the arrival of the nuclear reactor's vessel in the CEN on January 3, 1989, is intercut with images of Rafael and Leo playing inside the now-abandoned vessel. In a voice-over addressed to Leo, Rafael recalls his arrival in Russia in 1982, his studies in that country, and his return to Cuba to work on the reactor: "I came here to work from dawn until dusk because I hoped this reactor would light up the island. And what happened? The Berlin Wall fell. The Soviet bloc collapsed. And Fidel arrived here one day in the pouring rain to tell us that even though nature was crying, we mustn't cry because if we cried it should be out of pride and not from cowardice because we must face our problems." He pauses while archival images depicting the installation of the reactor's vessel continue to unfold. "But I was the first to cry," he observes, his calm voice bespeaking the tragic consequences for his generation of the collapse of the Soviet Union.

If Rafael and Leo achieve greater understanding of one another through dwelling on the personal effects of history, however, no such rapprochement seems possible for Rafael and Otto. The film's fictional story ends, in many ways, as it begins, only this time the intergenerational conflict takes place between Otto and Rafael. In one of the film's final scenes, Otto overhears Rafael having sex in his room with his girlfriend, played by Damarys Gutiérrez, an

Eastern European immigrant who is one of the amateur actresses of the CEN whom Quintela met on his first trip to the city. Otto pounds on the door, yelling that Rafael knows that he is not allowed to have women in the house and that she is trying to steal his apartment. Rafael bursts out of his room, accuses his father of being jealous because he cannot get an erection, and amid much talk of dicks, they pull theirs out and shake them at one another while Leo tries to pry them apart.

This testosterone-filled confrontation, meanwhile, brings to a head the film's exploration of masculinity at both the individual and the national level. *La obra del siglo*'s opening sequence revolves around a different sort of machista showdown. Archival images of the CEN seen from a helicopter circling the city cut to a black-and-white shot of Otto's living room. The doorbell rings and Otto answers, letting in two men who have arrived to fumigate the house as part of the Cuban state's long-standing efforts to prevent the spread of dengue. As one of the two men begins spraying in Otto's bedroom, Otto and the chief fumigator, played by actor Jorge Molina, take refuge on the balcony. Molina reminisces about the Cold War. "That was a golden era," he muses. "It was a competition to see who had the bigger dick: the Russians or the Americans."

As Molina recounts the history of the space race between the two superpowers, the film cuts to color archival images depicting Yuri Gagarin, the Soviet astronaut who in 1961 was the first human to travel to space. Molina gestures toward a stark Soviet-style apartment building standing in the middle of a bare terrain. "Doesn't it look like a rocket about to take off?" he asks Otto. "I would have liked to have gone to space," he adds. "What about you?" A close-up of Otto's face, looking dreamily up into the sky as he quietly mutters, "el cosmos" (space), provides his own nostalgic response to the lost dream of the future that motivated both the race for space and the construction of Cuba's electro-nuclear reactors. A jaunty, 1980s electro-synth music further evokes the excitement of this era, and the sequence cuts to an interview with Lieutenant Colonel Arnaldo Tamayo Méndez, who, in 1978, was the first Cuban in space. The film then returns to a shot of the apartment building and a voice begins counting down in Russian. The sequence closes with an image of Molina leading a crew of suited fumigators through a smoke-filled basement while the sound of a rocket taking off gives way to an urgent throbbing noise as of a nuclear alarm.

This sequence's nostalgia for the grandeur of the space race thus also sets up an ambivalent account of Cuba's nuclear project. Combined with the insistent alarm, the billowing smoke that envelops Molina and his fumigators at once invokes space travel and the dangers of radiation. This danger is further reinforced throughout the film as fictional characters and archival sequences make clear that, given the faulty nature of the equipment sent from the Soviet Union, Cuba might well have experienced a nuclear disaster similar to that of Chernobyl had the plant ever become operational. At the same time, the repeat references to Chernobyl and radiation throughout the film combine with the story of the characters' frustrated ambitions to suggest that the residents of the CEN are the victims of a different sort of nuclear disaster. The dream of space, just like the dream of nuclear power, has given way to an abandoned city, whose cold, modernist lines stand as desolate testaments to an era when Cuba's future seemed bright and it could claim, if only by association, an important position on the world stage.

Molina's comparison of the Cold War to a competition between the United States and the Soviet Union to see who had the bigger dick, meanwhile, suggests that this is a loss that went hand in hand with a crisis in masculinity. *La obra del siglo* pays homage to Sara Gómez's only feature-length fiction film, *De cierta manera* (*One Way or Another*, 1974), which combines fiction with archival footage and documentary to explore the efforts of its two protagonists to adapt to the social and moral transformations instituted by the Revolution. Yolanda, a light-skinned, middle-class mulata, struggles to navigate the challenging conditions of the lower-class neighborhood Miraflores, where she has been sent as a schoolteacher. Her lover, Mario, a darker-skinned mulato from this same neighborhood, works to reconcile local codes of honor and masculinity with the new values of the Revolution. This conflict is brought to a head for Mario when his friend and fellow factory worker Humberto confides his decision to miss several days of work to visit a lover in Santiago de Cuba, a trip that he excuses as a visit to care for his dying mother. The film opens with Humberto's trial by his fellow factory workers, during which Mario reveals his friend's duplicity, then repeats the scene again toward the end of the film. The film's final sequence depicts Mario's ongoing struggle to reconcile himself to his decision to expose Humberto as well as an interview with a group of factory workers who debate the ethics of the two men's actions. This Brechtian sequence thus at once depicts an onscreen audience debating the questions posed by the film about class, race, and masculinity in the new society and, in theory, prompts spectators to take up these questions for themselves.

In *La obra del siglo*, the character of Otto is played by a now-much-older Mario Balsameda, the same actor who decades before performed the role of Mario in Sara Gómez's film. Taking advantage of this unplanned coincidence,

La obra del siglo incorporates a sequence from *De cierta manera* in which Yolanda makes fun of Mario's swaggering public machismo, while Mario himself confesses to an overwhelming fear. If the two characters performed decades apart by Balsameda share a fear tied to masculine codes in common, however, the sources of this dread are markedly different. In Gómez's movie, Mario struggles to adapt to new values that prioritize loyalty to work and the Revolution over the bonds between friends. The protagonists of *La obra del siglo*, by contrast, must struggle to determine what it means to be a man or, more generally, how to give meaning to their lives, after the demise of the revolutionary collectivism that Gómez's film endorses.

This dilemma is further reinforced by Rafael's mournful relationship to the power plant. Following the standoff between Rafael and Otto, a news report about the disruption of work on the power plant gives way to archival images of women planting coconut trees in the fields in 1996, the reactor visible in the distance. Over these images, Cuban musician Vicente Rojas croons romantically of his nostalgia for a lost lover in his hit song from the 1980s "Me quedé con ganas" (I Was Left with Desire). Shortly after this sequence, the film shows Rafael seated in the reactor, gazing with a casual melancholy at the camera (figure 5.12). The image begins to shake as we hear the sounds of a spaceship taking off, then the film cuts to its final shot: a rocket soaring through space. Under Soviet socialism, notes Susan Buck-Morss (2000, 195–96), intimate relations were at least ideologically transferred from the domestic realm of the family to the public realm of the factory, a transition also reflected in Cuba through films like *De cierta manera*.[22] *La obra del siglo* records the devastation for those whose affective investments in their sites of production, in this film also linked to the race for space and dreams of a new technological future for the nation and humanity, were ultimately disappointed.

Finally, as this play with archival images and the music of Vicente Rojas suggests, the film's engagement with a vanishing sociohistorical context depends not just on narrative but also on a sensory experience closely linked to nostalgia. The film's present-day fictional scenes are shot in black and white while the archival footage is shown in its original color, suggesting a past characterized by an optimism lost to the present. This nostalgic effect is reinforced by the film's soundtrack. After watching *La obra del siglo* at the Miami International Film Festival in 2015, a Cuban immigrant who was working in Miami television at the time commented on how kitsch Vicente Rojas's music was, then noted that listening to his music had prompted her own nostalgic memories of her childhood and early adolescence in Cuba in

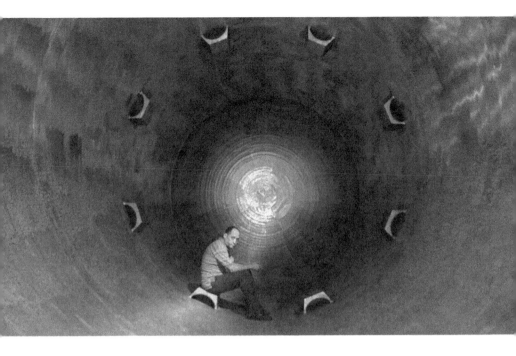

Figure 5.12 Rafael gazes at the camera as Cuba's failed nuclear reactor begins to shake in Carlos Machado Quintela's *La obra del siglo* (2015).

the 1980s. At times, the sounds and textures of the 1980s worked in the film at even more subliminal levels. As I learned through observing Quintela and Vega as they edited *La obra del siglo*, the 1980s electro-synth music that accompanies Molina's expression of his desire to go to space in the opening sequence is in fact the theme music from an East German cartoon of that era, *Röschens Abenteuer*, or, as it was known in Cuba, *Rosita la cosmonauta* (*Rosita the Cosmonaut*).

Indeed, for filmmakers such as Quintela, arguably too young to fully comprehend the events occurring around them in the late 1980s, these sensory experiences may well be the most tangible remnants of an earlier era. When I asked him about his own memories of the 1980s, Quintela recalled the toy planes that his father used to bring him from Eastern Europe and that you had to put together yourself through months of labor, toys that he felt contributed to his desire to become a filmmaker; the disappearance of apples from the markets; the books about astronauts that his mother used to bring him, and that provoked a repeat nightmare about being lost in space;

the harsh response of school administrators when a schoolmate brought his lunch to school wrapped in the pages of a newspaper that featured an image of Gorbachev; and the Eastern European cartoons known in Cuba as *muñequitos rusos* (Russian cartoons), which, he explained, had a different rhythm than the American cartoons that replaced them and frequently emphasized the suffering of the characters. Drawing on Walter Benjamin and Ernst Bloch, Nadia Seremetakis (1996, 10–12) argues that sociocultural identity and a collective historical unconscious are tied up with sensory experience and material culture, such that engagements with material objects can reanimate "once valued" and "now inadmissible" lifeworlds, making them available for imaginings of a different present and future. In *La obra del siglo*, archival images in their original color, Vicente Rojas's "kitsch" music, and the music of one of the Eastern European cartoons that shaped the childhood of those Cubans born from the 1960s through the 1980s provide viewers with sensual and material prompts through which to reconsider the legacy of Cuba's lost dreams of the future in the present. Arguably, this holds a particular importance for a generation for whom this Soviet past remains an essential and yet, especially for its youngest members, often a diffuse memory of childhood.

The Parenthesis, Still

In December 2017, when I returned to Havana for the New Latin American Film Festival, the first time my teaching schedule had allowed me to do so in years, a couple of films caught my attention. One of these was Alejandro Alonso's *El Proyecto* (*The Project*, 2017), a docufiction merging film footage, graphic animation, and archival materials to reflect on the history and aftermath of Cuba's *escuelas en el campo* (schools in the countryside). As part of the state's efforts to ensure universal education and to socialize younger generations into "new men" and "women," in the late 1960s, the Cuban government established programs through which schoolchildren were sent to live in the countryside, where they both studied and performed agricultural labor. Such experiences lasted from forty-five days for those who went to school in town to full academic years for those who attended boarding schools in the countryside, primarily during preuniversity, which, in Cuba, follows high school for students aged fifteen through eighteen. Alonso, who studied at the same *pre en el campo* that his mother had attended before him, just outside his hometown of Pinar del Río, recalled how he and his classmates would invent illnesses and countless other excuses to try to avoid the long hours of cutting through tall weeds with a machete in the orange fields, and how his parents would travel with great difficulty to the countryside to bring him food to supplement the school's less-than-adequate diet.[23]

In the midst of his formal studies in the documentary stream at the EICTV, some years after the government closed down the majority of these schools around 2011, Alonso took an interest in this history and began visiting abandoned schools with an eye to producing a documentary. According to his account, he visited more than twenty such establishments, accidentally walking into some that had been transformed into light security prisons (thus reversing, he observed to me, the revolutionary government's original declaration that it would transform prisons into schools) and visiting others whose utopian names and abandoned premises—La Comuna de Paris (The Paris Commune), for instance—poignantly encapsulated for him the failure and abandonment of this utopian project. But one school in particular, situated near the EICTV in the province of Artemisa, captured his interest. Here he found ruined premises that had taken on new life, as teachers recruited from the Eastern part of the island took up residence in the classrooms in which they had once taught, raising their children and establishing an improvised community. Following several months of research at the school—including taking a small amount of test footage, which Alonso shot himself—Alonso and his team began filming in earnest. When they arrived at the school in Artemisa, however, they were met by the police, who told them that 'their application for permits to film at the school had been irregular (Alonso explained that the address initially given to him by the director of the school had been erroneous), and their request was ultimately denied.

After some weeks of attempting without success to gain support from the island's cultural institutions, including the Asociación de Hermanos Saíz and the UNEAC, Alonso constructed a film out of what he had initially intended as research materials, using the fictional conceit of an aged filmmaker looking back on the materials of a work that had been censored. The finished film demonstrates the continued creative use of several of the techniques explored in this chapter. In one sequence, archival images of architectural plans, grainy newspaper photographs of construction work on the schools, and images of happy schoolchildren moving through the finished buildings go by while a voice—the only voice to be heard in the film—intones in repetitive detail the plans for the new schools, returning repeatedly to declarations of their key role as a basis for the future society.[24] The monotone delivery of these statements belies their declaration of utopia, as does the equally repetitive return to lists of numbers and measurements ("3,100 kg; 635,750 kg") and to seemingly nonsensical declarations: "el hombre nuevo debe tener la piel curtida para prevenir los ataques futuros" (the new man should have tanned skin to prevent future attacks). This imitation of authoritative state discourse resonates with the stiob strategy used by Esteban Insausti to satirize state agricultural production in *Existen*, as well as with the work of Nicolás Guillén Landrián that inspired both young directors.

The combination of Alonso's documentary footage and the film's fictional conceit, meanwhile, highlights the human costs of these utopian aspirations. The film opens with graphic animations of modernist school plans floating through a white space while the text that provides the dominant narration in the film presents the disparate thoughts of the aged filmmaker as he contemplates his ongoing efforts over the years to "piece together the fragments of this film that they didn't let me finish." The first reference to *citrus tristeza* (sad citrus), an actual virus that infects and kills off citrus fruit in Cuba and elsewhere, appears in this sequence, presented here as a mysterious plague. The apocalyptic overtones of this scene are reinforced in the images that follow. A young boy crawls through a cobweb-infested basement, a sack of oranges slung over his shoulder. Another boy peers up through foliage as men dressed in yellow sterilization suits take Polaroid pictures and spray dead trees. Close-ups reveal rotten fruit and damaged leaves.

Later sequences use Alonso's test footage to attest to the current ruined state of the school in Artemisa as well as to the difficult living conditions of those who occupy it. Clothing flutters from a clothesline on the school's rooftop. Two young men watch a television that we cannot hear in a homey environment invented out of a classroom through chairs, a lamp, a pink velvet curtain, and a plant. A young man pulls a skull-tight net over his hair, scratches some numbers onto a wall, then sits in front of a wrought iron headboard and plays a mournful tune on a guitar, the edges of an oil painting of Marilyn Monroe just visible in the frame. A little girl goes cartwheeling down an immense and emptied corridor as the last of these notes fade away, the sign "Comedor" (Lunchroom) over a door to the left the only indication of this desolate space's former use. And in footage that Alonso went back to shoot surreptitiously after he was denied a permit, the school's inhabitants gaze into the camera.

Combined with the repeat references to citrus tristeza and the visuals of the yellow-suited men, these documentary images present the school's real-life inhabitants as postapocalyptic survivors, achieving an effect similar to that obtained in *La obra del siglo*. The shots of the ruined school's inhabitants gazing into the camera, meanwhile, bear an obvious affinity with the play with portraiture and the gaze that characterizes Guillén Landrián's early documentaries and Susana Barriga's *The Illusion*, the latter of which Alonso first saw in 2009 when he was still living in Pinar del Río and was just beginning to explore filmmaking. Finally, like all the works examined in this chapter, Alonso's film returns repeatedly to the lived consequences of revolutionary aspirations and to the contingency and violence involved in the production of meaning. In this film, however, such challenges are tied not only to the relationship between filmmaker and filmed but also to the specific paranoia induced by the threats of surveillance and censorship. "Le digo a Didier que se pare frente a la cámara y que camine si no lo estuviera mirando, como si nadie nos estuviera mirando" (I tell Didier to walk in front of the camera as though no one were watching him, as though nobody were watching us), a text reads over the initial images of the young boy walking through the cobweb-filled basement of a school. Lines such as these invoke both the film's fictional conceit and, at least for those viewers aware of the story behind the film's production, the difficulties faced by Alonso and his team.

By 2017, the year in which Alonso's film was released, the hopes that were initially sparked by Raúl Castro's declaration of plans for extensive economic reforms in 2010 and the 2014 efforts to normalize diplomatic relations between Cuba and the United States had faded into a renewed sense of history as parenthesis. Donald Trump's election in 2016 put a halt to the reforms begun under Barack Obama, a change confirmed by the 2017 evacuation of personnel from the only recently reopened American embassy amid renewed conspiracy theories and accusations that the Cuban state had engaged in sonic attacks on American and Canadian diplomats. Combined with Alonso's own experience of state censorship, it is not surprising, then, that his film supplies the most direct version of both the demand for change and skepticism about its possibility implicit in the works examined in this chapter. "A todos nos asustan los comienzos" (We are all afraid of beginnings), a text states over the silhouettes of two young men playing ping-pong—without rackets—in stylized, dancelike movements, against a clouded sky in a scene from *El Proyecto* (figure 5.13). The text continues: "Hoy me sigo preguntando frente a estos sacos de imágenes que no pude terminar porque tuvimos miedo a empezar, cambiar, romper el estado de inercia" (Today I keep asking myself, faced with these sacks of images that I was unable to complete, why we were afraid of beginning, changing, breaking with this state of inertia).

Read allegorically, the image of these two young men bespeaks a new generation's hopes for change, as they struggle to make their own lives and

A todos nos asustan los comienzos.

Figure 5.13 Two young men play a game of ping-pong without rackets in Alejandro Alonso's *El Proyecto* (2017).

meanings out of the ruins left by their predecessors' utopian dreams. Yet their engagement in a game that, by its stylized nature, can have no end also invokes the impasse that continues to characterize Cuban politics and public debate. By returning to the montage experiments of the 1960s and 1970s, as I have shown in this chapter, young filmmakers challenge Cold War divides and register the need for new political options. But, faced with Alonso's query about the fear of beginnings, I cannot help but wonder if the return to earlier revolutionary filmmaking also betrays a certain nostalgia, a yearning for an era where some artists at least still believed that meaningful social and political change was possible and that experimental aesthetics had a central role to play in bringing it about.

"CUBA ESTÁ DE MODA"

Symptomologies of a Détente

In December 2013, while I was visiting a filmmaker friend of mine at his apartment in Havana, his brother returned home with curious news: Barack Obama and Raúl Castro had shaken hands at Nelson Mandela's memorial service. A furtive handshake in 2000 between Fidel Castro and Bill Clinton was the only precedent for such an exchange since diplomatic relations had been cut off between the two nations in the early 1960s. The international press and the Cuban blogosphere exploded in speculation. Some wondered if this more recent encounter signaled a move toward reconciliation between the United States and Cuba. Most cautioned that it probably meant nothing at all.[1] Like good symptomologists, my friend and I joined excitedly in the speculations, wondering what subterranean political movements this small gesture might index. But the furor over the incident soon died down and our own and others' interest moved on to other matters.

As it turned out, the handshake at Mandela's funeral did portend significant change. In December 2014, this same Cuban friend came to visit me in Chicago, having entered the country using his European passport with the intention of eventually returning using his Cuban documents in order to immigrate. On the morning of the seventeenth, however, our holiday plans hit a snag. Turning on the television to catch a daily dose of news, we found ourselves watching with both hope and anxiety as Barack Obama and Raúl Castro announced the renewal of diplomatic relations between the United

States and Cuba. This agreement, as it turned out, was the result of months of secret negotiations. But the announcement, when made, took everyone by surprise. My friend scrambled to get across a border and back into the country, joining hundreds of others who took advantage of the wet-foot/dry-foot policy in the following months, anticipating (correctly) that allowances for Cuban immigrants would soon be canceled in this changed political climate.[2] Meanwhile, a steady stream of American diplomats, journalists, entrepreneurs, artists, and filmmakers flooded into Cuba, looking to take in the sights and pleasures of the once-forbidden island and to take advantage of new economic openings. As Cuban reggaetón singer Yulien Oviedo put it in a 2016 song, Cuba was, once more, "de moda" (in style), with all that might entail for cultural production, politics, and the economy.[3]

In the discussion that follows, I outline some of the major events that shaped Cuban cultural politics and the relationship between artists on the island and in the diaspora, the state, and foreign production companies between the announcement of the renewal of diplomatic relations in December 2014 and the New Latin American Film Festival in December 2017, a year after Donald Trump was elected to the American presidency and Fidel Castro passed away. The events described here, including several new censorship scandals, Cuban filmmakers' struggles to secure a cinema law, and Hollywood's first big-budget ventures onto the island, reveal ever-more-forceful demands for political and economic reform on the part of artists and intellectuals on the island, facilitated in part by digital technologies. But these events also suggest a certain nostalgia for older forms of political patronage. Even as Cuban artists and intellectuals grew increasingly resistant to the state and state censorship, I contend, they also worried about what change might bring in a context where legal status for independent producers was slow in arriving and the cultural institutions that had once supported and protected critical and experimental art—if always within limits—seemed to have lost the political capital they once held.

From Détente to Censorship

The announcement of the détente brought cautious hope for change in Cuba. But when it came to cinema and the arts, if anything, state officials appeared to be resorting to ever-more-openly repressive tactics—or, at the very least, such tactics were being given unprecedented publicity. The months leading up to December 2014 and the days immediately following were marked by two censorship scandals that riveted the Cuban film community: the December 2014 censorship of French filmmaker Laurent Cantet's movie *Regreso a Itaca* (*Return to Ithaca*, 2014) and the removal of Cuban dissident blogger and EICTV graduate Boris González Arenas from his position as coordinator of the school's humanities department on January 5, 2015.

Based on a screenplay by Cuban novelist Leonardo Padura, Cantet's *Regreso a Itaca* gathered together some of Cuba's most important actors from the generation born in the 1960s, many of whom have been previously mentioned in this book. Néstor Jiménez from *Monte Rouge* (2005) and Eduardo del Llano's Nicanor series; Jorge Perugorría of *Fresa y chocolate* (1993), *Guantanamera* (1995), *Amor vertical* (1997), and *Lista de espera* (2000); and Isabel Santos from *Se permuta* (1985) all had starring roles in this story about a group of middle-aged artists and intellectuals. Gathered together to celebrate the return to Cuba of a friend, played by Jiménez, who has been in exile for sixteen years, the characters reminisce about the past that led to their disappointed present, unveiling stories of censorship, corruption, and frustrated artistic dreams. Iván Giroud, who took over the presidency of the New Latin American Film Festival after Alfredo Guevara passed away in May 2013, programmed *Regreso a Itaca* for the international showcase of Havana's festival in December 2014 after seeing the film at the Toronto International Film Festival in September of that year. While *Regreso a Itaca* was primarily a French production, it was filmed in Havana using services provided by the ICAIC, whose officials had therefore read and approved the film's screenplay. Nevertheless, the ICAIC and the Ministry of Culture blocked the screening of the film at the Havana festival based, at least according to my interlocutors, on the belief that the film was an indictment of the Castros.

A group of filmmakers quickly organized to try to stop the censorship of the film. They met with officials at the ICAIC and the Ministry of Culture and organized a screening of *Regreso a Itaca* at the German-Cuban cultural institution Fundación Ludwig in an attempt to quell doubts about the film's content and political implications. In the short term, however, these efforts were in vain and the film remained banned from the New Latin American Film Festival. The filmmakers who had organized against its censorship released a statement denouncing the film's ban from the festival on December 22, 2014. They justified their delay in releasing this statement as an effort to not interfere with the success of the New Latin American Film Festival, whose president had, after all, worked to have the film shown. *Regreso a Itaca* was finally screened in Havana as part of the annual Festival de Cine Francés (French Film Festival) in May 2015, while Cantet was invited to form part of the jury of the 2015 New Latin American Film Festival. One film director who had organized against the film's censorship described these gestures as a belated attempt to rectify the mistake that the ICAIC and the Ministry of Culture had committed in banning the film in the first place. More cynically, another filmmaker observed that while the French Film Festival in Havana is an important and generally well-attended event, it does not have the same international or national reach as the New Latin American Film Festival.

The scandal over Cantet's film was quickly followed by another case of censorship that was arguably even more painful and personal for many in the Cuban film community. Following the December 17 announcement of the restoration of diplomatic relations between Cuba and the United States, internationally renowned Cuban artist Tania Bruguera, who by this point had been living and working primarily in the United States for a number of years, wrote an open letter to Barack Obama, Raúl Castro, and Pope Francis proposing to restage her performance art piece *Tatlin's Whisper #6* in the Plaza de la Revolución. In *Tatlin's Whisper #6*, a microphone is made available to audience members, who are invited to speak for one minute. Actors dressed in military uniform place a white dove on the shoulder of each speaker, a reference to the bird that landed on Fidel Castro's shoulder during his first speech in Havana following the triumph of the July 26th Movement and the urban underground against Batista, and which was interpreted by many as religious confirmation of Castro's leadership. When the sixty seconds are complete, the actors escort the speaker off the stage and invite the next speaker forward. Bruguera had previously staged this piece on the patio of Old Havana's Wilfredo Lam Contemporary Art Center during the 2009 Havana Biennale, an event that the organizers of the biennale later denounced due to the participation of dissident bloggers in the performance.[4]

On December 26, 2014, Bruguera flew to Havana to carry out this project. In the days that followed, cultural officials and the Cuban police denied Bruguera's request to stage the performance piece in the Plaza de la Revolución. Suggesting the ongoing logic of a repressive tolerance that prefers to manage dissent by providing it with a limited outlet, the president of the Consejo Nacional de Artes Plásticas (National Council of Fine Arts), Rubén del Valle, reportedly proposed that she instead hold the performance in an alternative venue, such as a school or a factory.[5] But Bruguera persisted in her plans, sending out an invitation via Facebook for Cubans to join her at the Plaza de la Revolución on December 30. That morning, she was arrested at her home, along with several other dissidents and bloggers who had either made clear their intentions to join her in the performance or were intercepted at the plaza itself.

Bruguera was released on December 31, but her passport was confiscated and she was placed under house arrest. During the eight months that she remained in Cuba, she was detained several times more: once while guiding a one-hundred-hour-long reading of Hannah Arendt's *The Origins of Totalitarianism* during the 2015 Havana Biennale, which was "conveniently" disrupted by state construction work across the street from her house; and again in June 2015 as she was exiting a Mass that she attended with the long-standing Cuban dissident group the Ladies in White, founded by the wives and other female relatives of the independent journalists and other political dissidents who were jailed in 2003 and released into exile in Spain under Raúl Castro. In July 2016, Bruguera's passport was finally returned to her and she left Cuba, apparently after obtaining a written letter from the Cuban government stating that she would be allowed to return to the country.

These events also had direct repercussions in the Cuban film community. Among those detained during Bruguera's initial protest was Cuban blogger and filmmaker Boris González Arenas. On January 5, 2016, three days after his release from prison, he was called into a meeting headed by Jerónimo Labrada, director of the EICTV, where González worked as a coordinator within the school's humanities department. In the company of the heads of the other school's departments, including two filmmakers who had been involved in attempting to overturn the censorship of *Regreso a Itaca*, Labrada dismissed González from his position and presented him with an official document to this effect, which made clear that the reason for his expulsion was his criticism of the Castros in his blog, *Probidad (Honesty)*.[6] González took to Facebook, the Cuban blogosphere, and international newspapers to call attention to his dismissal and the political reasons behind it, questioning the legality of the proceedings and threatening a lawsuit that never came to fruition. Graduates of the EICTV and the Cuban film community, meanwhile, engaged in heated debates over the ethics of his dismissal and its consequences for the school.

Criticism as Complicity, Reprise

These two events bring to the fore dynamics I have examined throughout this book and suggest their ongoing relevance well into the late 2010s. In both cases, suspicion that criticism deals in stereotypes of life in late socialist Cuba converged with accusations that island filmmakers do not go far enough in resisting censorship. As these reactions make clear, efforts to promote freedom of expression continue to go hand in hand with a paranoia that, while reasonable, also often reinforces well-worn political positions.

While some Cuban artists and intellectuals both on and off the island went on record condemning Bruguera's arrest, her efforts also provoked concerns that, in this case, art had once more been reduced to a marketing technique.[7] One of the few island artists to publish extensively about the piece, Lázaro Saavedra (2014), observed that Bruguera knew the "rules of the game" perfectly well. That is, knowing full well that she would be stopped and arrested but that her high-profile status would protect her from more serious repercussions, Bruguera went forward with her actions for the benefit of her international reputation. Her disrupted performance merely made evident the repressive tactics of which all Cubans were already well aware, noted Saavedra. A more interesting option would have been to look for "effective and real strategies to 'open the microphones' so that 'all voices' could be heard," a tactic that would have required Bruguera to "evade censorship and formal structures of social control." Cuban American artist and intellectual Coco Fusco's (2014) more sympathetic reading of Bruguera's piece took Saavedra's position into consideration. Summarizing his argument, she concurred that limitations on internet access in Cuba meant that the primary audience for the performance was the outside world rather than citizens on the island. But she also defended this move, observing that Bruguera's performance reminded foreign artists and arts professionals that they must think carefully about whether or not to collaborate with state-sponsored artists and institutions in a context where the government continues to resort to "draconian measures to enforce its hegemonic control over public space and discourse."

Reactions to *Regreso a Itaca* were arguably less inflamed but equally mixed. One thirtysomething friend of mine who worked at the time in the Cinemateca de Cuba told me that *Regreso a Itaca* accurately represented the disillusionment and despair of older generations of Cubans. When I asked another friend around the same age what he thought of the film, he noted that the film voiced two or three criticisms that might have been important to older generations but that he himself did not think much of it. A number of those filmmakers who were active in combatting the censorship of *Regreso a Itaca* expressed their dissatisfaction with the film. Film director Enrique Álvarez observed:

It seemed to me that the film makes the same mistake as many Cuban films. When they treat some aspect of Cuban reality that merits criticism, they overemphasize this and make it the center of the story. This has impoverished a lot of Cuban films and does so in this case as well. Instead of playing characters, the actors end up performing stereotypes because they are more concerned with delivering critical speeches about Cuban reality than with recounting a personal experience. But in spite of this, it always seemed to me that the film needed to be shown, that this film shouldn't be censored, because to do so would also mean giving more importance to a film that, in my opinion, wasn't all that important.[8]

Acknowledging that the stories depicted in *Regreso a Itaca* might be more accurate for older artists, those who, born in the 1950s, launched careers in the midst of the militant censorship of the 1970s, Álvarez nonetheless questioned the film's relentlessly defeatist tone. *Regreso a Itaca*, he concluded, reduced what it meant to be an artist and intellectual in Cuba to stereotypes, sacrificing subtleties of character and narrative to political diatribe. Nonetheless, Álvarez and others insisted that the film ought to be shown, arguing that to censor it would only help promote a work that might otherwise go unperceived.

If, in this case, filmmakers on the island took a strong public stance against censorship, however, the expulsion of Boris González Arenas from the EICTV emphasized the ongoing limits to the dissent that Cuban filmmakers were able or willing to defend. Following González's dismissal, the EICTV released an official document explaining the decision, which included the following statement: "Boris González Arenas has published articles that oppose the Cuban state. These articles are not merely the expression of a critical dissent whose right to exist the EICTV defends and will continue to defend to the last, but rather are frontal attacks on the [Revolution's] humanist values, values in which the school shares, and against the institutions and leaders of this nation that houses the school. His ideas differ from and oppose the principles on which the work of the EICTV is based."[9] This declaration of the EICTV's support for criticism in a document that justified the dismissal of a filmmaker for publicly expressing his political views, as this book has demonstrated, is more than simply hypocritical. Rather, the statement insists once more on island filmmakers' commitment to criticism from within, while also specifying the ongoing limits to what forms of criticism could be tolerated from this position.

In spite of the language of "humanism" folded into this declaration by the EICTV, the real sticking point that led to González's dismissal was clearly his open opposition to the Cuban state and to the Castros, an opposition that was rendered uncomfortably visible for the school because of his participation in Bruguera's high-profile performance and his subsequent arrest.

Dissidents and exiles, unsurprisingly, were quick to denounce González's dismissal as signs of Cuban filmmakers' ongoing complicity with a repressive regime. Two of the filmmakers who had earlier participated in the denunciation of the censorship of *Regreso a Itaca* were also present at the meeting in which González was dismissed from his position at the school. Drawing attention to this fact, exiled author Antonio José Ponte (2015) asked how intellectuals could legitimize criticizing the Ministry of Culture, the ICAIC, and the UNEAC for their exercise of censorship, while reserving that right for themselves: "If they are going to justify [this action] with the game of within the Revolution and against the Revolution that Fidel Castro inaugurated in 'Palabras a los intelectuales' (Cantet and Padura are within; González Arenas is against) what guarantee do they have that the Ministry of Culture and the ICAIC won't respond to their petition with precisely the same argument?"

In more conciliatory terms, González circulated a letter via Facebook in which he argued that the meeting in which he was fired was an affront not only to his own dignity but also to that of his colleagues: "Some of my ex-colleagues were at the meeting where my dismissal from the school was communicated. I am aware that this spectacle was mounted also against them, against their social and intellectual prestige. For 'el Castrismo' there are no differences with respect to dissent. Even dissent that declares some revolutionary or Castro affiliation is permanently humiliated. People whose critical postures I have sincerely valued were brought to that meeting not to expel me but rather to humiliate them."[10] Ponte's statement dismissed arguments for criticism from within as hypocritical. González's statement, by contrast, paid greater respect to the critical postures of his former work colleagues and mentors. In the end, however, both comments treated Cuba as a totalitarian regime in which meaningful debate was by definition impossible. Any stance that fell short of directly targeting the Castro government, from this perspective, could only lead to a shameful and humiliating complicity with the socialist state.

Many of the filmmakers on the island with whom I spoke, meanwhile, questioned the wisdom of the timing of González's dismissal. Some observed that the EICTV staff should have demonstrated greater solidarity with González after his arrest. Others noted that the timing of his dismissal damaged the international reputation of the school and divided EICTV alumni at a time when their support was desperately needed. Such comments, however, generally went hand in hand with understanding for why Labrada and others had felt compelled to take the action that they did. In 2012, Cuban state security had tried to convince Guatemalan filmmaker and EICTV graduate Rafael Rosal, who was then serving as director of the school, to fire González. González claimed that it was Rosal who fought to retain him; others attributed this earlier defense of the filmmaker to Labrada.

Later that same year, however, Rosal himself was dismissed from his position as director of the EICTV on charges of corruption and financial irregularities, including revelations of a black-market beer trade that had long been floating the finances of students, workers, and the school as a whole. The effects on the school were immediate and dire. Labrada temporarily took over the leadership of the EICTV while a new director was sought, the school delayed the entry of the new class of 2013 in order to reduce costs, and salaries in CUC were reduced or cut for much of the school's staff. An institution that had historically enjoyed a certain degree of independence from government directives as well as relatively good labor conditions suddenly found both forms of stability under threat. Those who participated in the expulsion of González, my interlocutors explained, were not acting out of their own beliefs so much as out of a desire to protect the already vulnerable position of the school. "The school has a certain independence or freedom that also includes the responsibility of deciding just how far we can go," one young filmmaker told me over Facebook Messenger shortly after González's dismissal. "If I as a student make a documentary where I speak openly against Fidel and the school promotes it, the authorities will block our ability to make work outside of the school." For many, as this statement suggests, defending the school's ability to operate trumped protecting a dissident blogger.

Such arguments frequently reflected ongoing belief that more effective change in Cuba will ultimately come from attempting to carve out a political position between the extremes of unquestioning support for the Cuban government and dissident challenges to the government's authority. Enrique Álvarez was one of the two filmmakers who was both active in efforts to resist the censorship of *Regreso a Itaca* and present at González's dismissal. When I asked him about the latter event, he replied:

I believe that the great majority of Cubans are in agreement that the country needs to change and evolve, socially, politically, and economically, but we don't all see this in the same way nor do we confront it in the same way. This is a very complex situation where you can't always understand what game people are playing at. There are opposing positions that don't want to dialogue but rather to always keep relations tense. At a certain moment, both sides start to seem like one another, and you can't tell if they're playing the same game; they're like two sides of the same face. This is a society that has reached a level of neuroticism where it has become difficult for people to look one another in the eye and to speak with clarity. This country is too—I wouldn't say politicized, but rather ideologized. That is, there's an extreme ideological confrontation, which gets painted as black and white. I believe that this society needs to evolve and advance without more traumas than those that it has already experienced and that it has to do this through a dialogue with everyone, not by closing itself off into positions of any type, because this will only tighten the noose and cause further ruptures.

As the censorship of *Regreso a Itaca* and the dismissal of Boris González Arenas reveal, the boundaries of what can and cannot be expressed in Cuba continue to be hotly contested. For many dissidents and exiles, to accept ongoing limits to criticism is to block meaningful change. For others, it is a compromise that enables them to keep making art in Cuba and to fight for new outcomes. The mutually exclusive logic of these two positions reveals just how fraught establishing a new dialogue among Cubans continues to be.

Nostalgia for Patrons

If, by 2016, a number of Cuban filmmakers on the island remained committed to working from within the Cuban political system, the censorship scandals described above also reveal a growing disaffection, even among older artists, with the cultural institutions that they felt had once protected them. Such concerns can be seen in a growing nostalgia for the patrons of yore that, somewhat paradoxically, went hand in hand with filmmakers' efforts to establish new and more democratic methods of cinema production. Many of the filmmakers who mobilized to try to counter the censorship of *Regreso a Itaca* were also involved in efforts begun in 2013 to establish a new cinema law. Among the most important goals involved in this project were the legalization of the independent production groups that, by the 2010s, were playing ever more central roles in promoting national film production and in providing services to foreign filmmakers; and the establishment of a national cinema fund to which filmmakers might apply to fund their projects and to which they would return a portion of their profits.

Ideals of democracy, transparency, and freedom from censorship figured largely in the conversations among the filmmakers who met to discuss and work on these plans on a regular basis from 2013 to 2016 at Fresa y chocolate, the bar and cultural venue across the street from the ICAIC's offices in Vedado. At a meeting I attended on May 30, 2015, several months after the censorship of *Regreso a Itaca* from the New Latin American Film Festival and a few weeks after it was screened during the French Film Festival, filmmakers hotly debated several items on a draft of a proposal for the national cinema fund. One film director objected to the use of the term *único* (sole), used to designate the fund as the mechanism that should be used for the distribution of national financing to film productions. Filmmakers' subjugation to governance by a singular institution with a monopoly over production, he noted, was a major source of their problems in the present. One of the authors of the proposal made a note to rethink this language but also observed that the term had been introduced to prevent the Ministry of Culture and the ICAIC from using other mechanisms that would be less transparent than the proposed cinema fund.

Other comments revealed similar efforts to ensure a new transparency and democracy in cinema production. A clause specifying that the head of the fund should have the right to review the first cuts of films raised concerns that this would enable censorship. A clause specifying that films must be screened in Cuban theaters provoked the objection that theaters were controlled by the state. What happened, the filmmakers asked, if state theaters decided not to screen a film? Would the filmmakers be punished for this act of censorship and blocked from applying to the cinema fund in the future? Finally, concerns were raised about what qualified a film as Cuban and, hence, as eligible for funding, especially since so many films that involved significant work by Cubans received financing from foreign investors.

The model of cultural production called for by filmmakers in meetings such as this differed in important ways from the centralized and paternalistic rule that many recalled as having characterized the ICAIC under Alfredo Guevara. When Guevara left his position as director of the ICAIC for the second and last time to take on the leadership of the New Latin American Film Festival in 2000, he called the ICAIC filmmakers together to announce his departure. Film director Manuel Pérez recalled: "Alfredo held a meeting with us to tell us that he was leaving the ICAIC. He recommended a few things that we should do with this project and he told us: 'Now you'll have to learn how to defend yourselves on your own.' It was like a father who tells his children and his nephews and nieces, look—before I defended you, now it's up to you."[11] For Pérez, Guevara's statement reeked of a paternalism that infantilized the ICAIC filmmakers, many of whom, by the time of Guevara's departure, were themselves well into their later years. The functionary's transfer from one institution to the next, meanwhile, bespoke ongoing tendencies to secret political negotiations that left the general citizenry struggling to discern the motives of those in power. Pérez speculated that Guevara's reassignment had been a backroom deal arranged between Fidel Castro and Guevara following the scandals—*Fresa y chocolate*'s release; the controversy over *Guantanamera*—that had accompanied Guevara's return to power at the ICAIC in the 1990s.

Yet even as Cuban filmmakers criticized such paternalism and secrecy, by the late 2010s some had also begun to remember Guevara's ICAIC with a certain nostalgia. The ICAIC and the Ministry of Culture's refusal to cede in the censorship of *Regreso a Itaca*, argued some filmmakers, was motivated in part by a desire to reassert authority over artists, a move that some believed demonstrated the inability of the current ICAIC leadership to exercise the same kind of independence that had been possible for Guevara. Enrique Álvarez explained:

In its first forty or so years the ICAIC was under the leadership of founders who were polemical intellectuals. You might agree with them and you might not, but these were people who had standards. They were capable of defending those standards under any circumstance. And when they made mistakes, they were also capable of confronting those mistakes and discussing them. There is a whole tradition of the ICAIC as independent at key moments in the history of the Revolution, of acting independently of the directives that operated in other Cuban cultural institutions.

Filmmakers have also historically confronted the cultural and political authorities of the country on a regular basis. This is what is occurring now with the G20 [the group leading the push for the establishment of a cinema law], but in every previous instance the leaders of the ICAIC have aligned themselves with the filmmakers and this hasn't occurred now. The most that the current leadership of the ICAIC has done is to try to dialogue with us, to listen to us, but no more than this. We have been putting forward a series of petitions for over three years that the leadership of the ICAIC could have taken on for itself and hasn't, which to my mind is a clear demonstration that they don't have the intellectual or the political independence to confront a series of decisions.[12]

Even younger filmmakers sometimes concurred with these sentiments. In 2014, a year after Guevara's death, one young Cuban film director lamented that the cultural officials who had had personal relationships with Fidel Castro and could therefore pressure political leaders into preserving Cuban cinema were all dying. Those who replaced them, he concluded, were functionaries without the same political capital as their predecessors, leaving artists with even less protection than in earlier decades.

As to the cinema law, agreement was reached during the VII Congress of the Communist Party of Cuba in 2016 that national cinema production should be reformed. In the summer of 2018, discussion of what these changes might look like was discretely under way among a small group of filmmakers and functionaries. Possible plans fell short of legalizing independent production companies but did include the establishment of a national cinema fund; the creation of a national registry of artists working in a variety of roles in independent filmmaking, which would thus give artists some legal standing; and changes designed to facilitate financial investment in independent cinema projects. At a meeting at the UNEAC in October 2018, the president of the ICAIC reportedly announced that these changes were being debated in the Council of Ministers, the highest executive body of Cuba, and would soon be approved. And on March 25, 2019, the government finally approved a new cinema law. Filmmakers received the news with a mix of cynicism and hope, waiting to see what concrete changes would be made.[13]

Fast and Furious in Havana

Like most forms of postsocialist nostalgia, reminiscences about Guevara's ICAIC do not signal the desire of Cuban filmmakers to return to the systems of the past. Indeed, the mounting confrontations between artists and government officials can also be chalked up to artists' efforts to take advantage of new forms of freedom. As an increasing number of films are produced either partly or entirely independently of state institutions, there are fewer opportunities for officials to censor works as they are in the process of being made, leading to more intense confrontations when officials try to control films that are already completed. Nostalgia for Guevara's rule, however, can also be linked to filmmakers' concerns about what will happen to national cinema in the midst of economic change. Just as the collapse of

Eastern European socialism required filmmakers to adapt to the demands of the global market, the restoration of diplomatic relations with the United States opened up new, albeit ultimately short-lived, economic opportunities and challenges.

If, as I mentioned at the end of chapter 4, many Cubans hope for a day when youth will not feel obligated to seek their futures in another country, that moment has clearly still not arrived. Laimir Fano, Susana Barriga, and Esteban Insausti, the young filmmakers whose shorts I discuss in chapters 2 and 5, all eventually emigrated from Cuba to other countries. Alejandro Brugués, director of *Juan de los muertos*, left shortly after that film's release for Los Angeles, where he carved out a US-based career for himself, including, for instance, directing short films for horror anthologies *ABCs of Death 2* (2014) and *Nightmare Cinema* (2018). Others joined the exodus in the months following the 2014 announcement of the normalization of relations between Cuba and the United States. Ian Padrón, director of the baseball documentary *Fuera de liga* (2003) (see chapter 4), was among them. In an interview with CNN in February 2015, Padrón explained his decision to move to the United States by citing "exhaustion with fighting and with complications in his work." His next statement demonstrated how stories of staying and fighting in Cuba, long used, as I show in chapter 4, to articulate a critical commitment to the nation, might also be mobilized in a more conciliatory fashion. "I always wanted to live in Cuba because I felt a responsibility, a duty to fight to improve my country," he stated. But then he continued: "We have to respect those who for many years have been in Cuba fighting to improve things and we have to respect those who want to change things and who live outside of Cuba" (CubaNet 2015).

While some filmmakers left, however, others who had emigrated in previous years began returning to the island either permanently or temporarily, bringing with them new skills and professional connections. While in Havana for a few months in the summer of 2016, I commented to a filmmaker friend, "Cada vez que vengo a Cuba" (Every time I come to Cuba), a sentence whose sentiment is so well understood that he completed it for me, "hay menos gente" (there are fewer people). The next day, however, I ran into a sound engineer whom I had first met when he was still a student at the EICTV. After years of trying and failing to find employment abroad, he was moving back to Havana. Cinema, meanwhile, continued to benefit from an increasingly fluid movement of artists between Cuba and other countries. Carlos Machado Quintela, for instance, shot his film *Higashi no Okami* (*The Wolves of the East*, 2017) in Japan, carried out the editing with

Yan Vega partly in Miami and partly in Havana, and completed the film's sound design in Brazil, where Cuban sound engineer Rúben Valdés, with whom Quintela had also worked in the past, was then residing. As he was completing the film, Quintela himself finally left Havana for Madrid. In 2019, with the long-distance collaboration of many of the artists with whom he had worked previously, he released a new web series, *El sucesor* (*The Successor*), in which actor Alberto Pujol plays Cuba's new president in an unabashed satire of Miguel Díaz-Canel.

Others succeeded in taking advantage of the economic opportunities opened up by Cuba's new economic reforms while staying on the island. Inti Herrera, one of the original members of Producciones de la 5ta Avenida, the independent production company behind *Juan de los muertos*, found a new career as a producer for the state-private business enterprise Fábrica de Arte Cubano (Cuban Art Factory). The highly successful venture operates as a nightclub and showcase for Cuban arts ranging from industrial and graphic design through theater, cinema, photography, and music, demonstrating how economic openings could be turned into opportunities to cash in on national cultural production. Still others took advantage of the new distribution opportunities presented by the paquete semanal, finding paid work in the independent advertising industry enabled by the paquete (Humphreys 2017b). Claudia Calviño, the third member of the production team behind *Juan de los muertos*, took over at the helm of 5ta Avenida and has since become one of the most recognized and prolific of independent Cuban film producers on the island.

At the same time, many artists worried that the state's long delay in ratifying a cinema law combined with what they viewed as the ICAIC leadership's political disinterest was leaving filmmakers defenseless in an increasingly open market. These concerns came to a head when two Hollywood film franchises, *The Fast and the Furious* and *Transformers*, became the first big-budget American productions to film in Cuba. When I arrived in Cuba at the beginning of May 2016, my friends and acquaintances were deeply engaged in the controversy provoked by the filming of *The Fate of the Furious*, informally known as *Fast and Furious 8*. Several of the Cuban artists and technicians hired via the ICAIC to work on *The Fate of the Furious* were pleased with the salaries they earned, my friends explained, which were higher than what they would be paid for work on Cuban films. Others were excited by the opportunity to work with technologies to which they otherwise would not have access or to catch a glimpse of Hollywood stars. But many of those involved in the production complained about the markedly different treatment of workers from Cuba versus those from the United States or other countries, noting that Cubans earned much lower salaries and that the food they were provided through a catering company contracted by the ICAIC was inadequate. Citizens, meanwhile, objected to the disruptions to transit throughout the city and argued that the production caused damage to already fragile buildings. Others wondered why the ICAIC was supporting the sorts of commercial films and stereotyped visions of Cuba that the institute had been founded to combat. Exacerbating these frustrations, many argued that the ICAIC had been insufficiently transparent about the finances of the project, failing to specify how much money had been received from the Americans and how this money would be spent.[14]

As *The Fate of the Furious* was wrapping up in Havana, the president of the ICAIC, Roberto Smith, gave an interview to the state newspaper *Juventud Rebelde* in an obvious attempt to quell these concerns (Fonticoba Gener 2016). The decision to allow *The Fate of the Furious* to be filmed in Havana in spite of the fact that it "does not correspond to the type of cinema that we defend," Smith explained, had been made with an eye to the publicity that the movie could provide as well as the income that it would ensure the Cuban film industry. "Beyond the question of their artistic quality," he explained, "these films are screened the world over. . . . The promotion of Havana and Cuba on a global level was thus also an element to consider." The ICAIC, he noted, had also made every effort to ensure that improvements to city infrastructure, such as road repairs and the restoration of buildings in areas where the film was shot, were folded into the production plan. As to the money that the ICAIC earned for services provided, while Smith declared himself unable to provide exact figures, he insisted that this would be reinvested in Cuban cinema, especially in expanding the island's digital postproduction capacities. But in the ongoing absence at that time of clear legal support for independent production, many Cuban filmmakers continued to worry that national cinema would be sold out to foreigners to line the pockets of the Cuban oligarchy.

Waiting for a Beginning

Concerns about how state institutions would manage American investment, however, soon proved to be the sort of problem that many Cuban artists longed to have again. Toward the end of 2016, Cuban artists found themselves embroiled in yet another censorship scandal, just as a significant hitch was thrown into the newly developing relationship between the

United States and Cuba. Directed by Cuban filmmaker Carlos Lechuga and produced by Claudia Calviño of Producciones 5ta Avenida, *Santa y Andrés* (2016) recounts the friendship between Andrés, a gay Cuban writer who resides in isolation in the Cuban countryside in the early 1980s following the Mariel exodus, and Santa, a rural woman sent to surveil him to prevent him from causing disturbances during a local political event.

The film has clear antecedents in Néstor Almendros and Orlando Jiménez Leal's *Improper Conduct* (1984), which was one of the many documentaries that the filmmakers used to research the censorship of gay artists, as well as in Tomás Gutiérrez Alea and Juan Carlos Tabío's *Fresa y chocolate* (1993). It did not, however, share this latter film's political good fortune. As had previously occurred with *Regreso a Itaca*, *Santa y Andrés* was selected by Iván Giroud to compete in the New Latin American Film Festival after he saw the film at its premiere in the Toronto International Film Festival. But the film was blocked from exhibition during the festival by the ICAIC and the Ministry of Culture. Also as with *Regreso a Itaca*, Cuban filmmakers organized to try to counter the film's censorship, gathering to support the young filmmakers at meetings held with the ICAIC leadership and the Ministry of Culture, and posting their objections to online blogs and magazines.

These efforts, however, were to no avail. The initial move to block the film from exhibition at the December 2016 New Latin American Film Festival was confirmed and compounded by the death of Fidel Castro on November 25, 2016, which occurred shortly after the last of the meetings about the film. In one deeply emotional scene in the film, a local communist leader pressures Santa and other town residents to denounce Andrés as a counter-revolutionary. They sing the national anthem, shout, "¡Viva la Revolución!" "¡Abajo la gusanera!" (Down with the worms!) and "¡Viva Fidel!" then the communist leader forces a tearful Santa to pelt Andrés with eggs. Andrés tries to escape into his house, but he is dragged back to confront his accusers. At this moment, he cries out to Cuba's most iconic nationalist hero: "¡Viva Martí!" Demonstrating the ongoing importance of conflicts over allegory and textual interpretation to censorship and public debate, retrospectively at least, state functionaries interpreted this scene as an attempt to represent José Martí's teachings as in opposition to Fidel Castro's leadership and legacy. As the country went into mourning for its decades-long leader, Roberto Smith, in a letter published online that referred implicitly to this and other moments of the film, defended the state film institute's decision. *Santa y Andrés*, Smith argued (2016), "used our patriotic symbols irresponsibly and made unacceptable references to *el compañero* Fidel."[15] *Santa y*

Andrés suffered further censorship when it was withdrawn from competition at New York's Havana Film Festival as a result of pressure by island officials. Lechuga and Calviño, meanwhile, were blocked from participating as jury members at a Cuban film festival in Gibara, Cuba, and endured several months of surveillance and home visits by state security. In addition to the stress provoked by this surveillance, the filmmakers deeply lamented losing the opportunity, Calviño told me, of watching the film in a Havana theater with its intended public.

Since it was an independent production, however, state officials could do nothing more to block *Santa y Andrés*, and the film had a normal international circulation. Some distributors also used its censorship as a promotional strategy. The first line of the summary of the film on Amazon's streaming services, for instance, describes *Santa y Andrés* as a film that was "banned in its home country of Cuba." In Cuba, meanwhile, as with *Regreso a Itaca* before it, the film eventually circulated via the paquete semanal. The conflict over *Santa y Andrés* demonstrates once more Cuban intellectuals' growing impatience with censorship and their desire for change, as well as the ways in which digital technologies are transforming the relationship between artists and state officials. The circulation of the film through the paquete and intellectuals' protests of the film's censorship via blogs and social media show how digital technologies enable intellectuals to circumvent state censorship to some degree and, at the very least, to give acts of censorship more publicity than ever before. Gone are the days when clashes between filmmakers and officials were confined to rumors circulated in the hallways of the ICAIC, as was still the case, for instance, as late as the censorship of Ian Padrón's *Fuera de liga* from 2003 to 2008.

Nonetheless, the concerns expressed during the 2007 email war (see chapter 1) about the reliance of such debates on digital technologies still cannot be set aside. Roberto Smith's online criticism of *Santa y Andrés* shows how state officials, too, are turning to digital technologies in an effort to sway public opinion. More significantly, while connectivity in Cuba was much improved by the end of the 2010s, thanks in part to the state's establishment in 2015 of Wi-Fi hotspots in parks and other locations and to the inauguration of a new 3G data service for smartphones in December 2018, the ongoing expense and inconvenience involved in getting online help to ensure that many citizens connect for other reasons than to read about the latest censorship scandal. Under these circumstances, then, banning films from state theaters may still work to confine debates to elite and international spheres, while uses of such crises for advertising purposes (as in the case of Amazon's promotion of *Santa y Andrés*) flatten the debate's nuances. One can only hope that the mounting efforts to combat censorship by Cuban intellectuals, many of whom are committed to staying on the island, might yet succeed in opening up a broader public conversation that could advance new political options.[16]

The need for new options, meanwhile, was brought to the fore by other events. The censorship of *Santa y Andrés* coincided not only with Fidel Castro's death but also with Donald Trump's election to the presidency of the United States. Fears that the new president would roll back the reforms that had briefly brought hope to many young artists and entrepreneurs in Cuba were confirmed in the months that followed. In the summer of 2017, the Cuban state put a temporary freeze on cuentapropista licenses as government officials worked to reorganize the licensing and taxation system. Compounding the anxieties provoked by this decision, in November 2017, Trump renewed restrictions in the American embargo, imposing a lengthy list of rules designed to block American businesses from dealing with the Cuban military and limiting the auspices under which Americans could legally travel to Cuba.[17] Tourism to Cuba dropped, as did the influx of American and foreign artists and companies interested in filming or coproducing work in Cuba. When Trump was elected, for instance, Alejandro Brugués had only just completed negotiations with the American television network Starz to produce *Santería*, a TV series that proposed to depict a secret war between opposing sects of Afro-Cuban religion and was set to be filmed in Cuba. In the wake of the sudden political shift, plans for the series came to a halt.

In August 2017, meanwhile, diplomatic relations between the two countries reached a new low as they became embroiled in a controversy over alleged sonic attacks. When some employees of the American and Canadian embassies in Cuba reported adverse health effects after experiencing "nausea, dizziness, and headaches accompanied by strange sounds compared to loud insects or metal dragging across the floor," nonemergency staff were withdrawn from the only recently reopened American embassy and the state department warned against travel to Cuba (Cohen 2017). The closure of the American embassy forced Cubans to travel at great expense to third countries in order to secure visas to the United States, effectively making legal entry into the US even more difficult for Cubans than it had been prior to 2014 and efforts to normalize relations between the two countries. In October 2017, Trump declared his certainty that Cuba was behind the sonic attacks. But well into 2019, controversy still swirled around the incident. Arguments raged over whether or not the attacks had occurred in the first place, who was responsible for them, what weapon might have been involved, and, in a real-life echo of *Monte Rouge*'s absurdist send-up of the material limitations that plague the work of the Cuban secret police (see chapter 3), if the sounds the US and Canadian diplomats were subjected to might have emerged from malfunctioning surveillance equipment.[18]

Thoughts of this controversy played a role in my reaction to one Cuban film released at the December 2017 New Latin American Film Festival. Produced in part by American actor Ron Perlman, Cuban director Ernesto Daranas's *Sergio y Serguéi* (2017) was one of the first and, potentially, given Trump's policies, one of the last major feature-length Cuban American coproductions. In this film, a Cuban professor of Marxist philosophy and amateur radio ham who is struggling to make ends meet makes radio contact with Serguéi, a Soviet astronaut who has been abandoned in space following the collapse of the Soviet Union. Over the course of the film, illicit radio communications lead to a bond not only between these two men but also between Sergio and Peter (played by Perlman), an American radio aficionado and conspiracy theorist who is obsessed with revealing the Apollo 11 moon landing as a hoax. In a poignant conversation with Sergio, whom the film presents as a critical intellectual who is nonetheless committed to socialism, Peter explains that, as a Polish Jew whose family was massacred under Stalin, he is adamantly anti-communist. By the end of the film, however, Peter and Sergio overcome their political differences and collaborate to get Serguéi returned to Earth, in part by making use of Peter's "connections" at NASA. ("Doesn't everybody?" Peter responds, when Sergio asks him if he has contacts in the American space agency.) The Cuban official who tries throughout the film to spy on and interfere with Sergio's efforts, meanwhile, finds himself magically spinning out into space, while Peter gives the finger to an FBI agent who helps the three men, adamantly refusing the agent's suggestion that the two might continue to cooperate in the future.

In this film, then, political paranoia and surveillance are countered by ordinary citizens who use their own conspiratorial connections to manipulate the authorities while building a friendship that traverses geopolitical divides. This melodramatic message is clearly naïve and commercial. The differences and suspicions that shape relations between Cubans on and off the island, as well as artists' simultaneous eagerness for American investment and their concerns that such exchanges will only benefit the oligarchy, make clear that there is no easy solution to the political impasse and

Cold War tensions that continue to shape everyday life and public debate in and about Cuba. Nonetheless, watching *Sergio y Serguéi* with my friends' worries about their futures in mind, I was struck by what, in the tense political climate of the late 2010s, seemed like the utopianism of its efforts to imagine new alliances. If "we are all afraid of beginnings," as a line in Alejandro Alonso's *El Proyecto* (2017), also shown at Havana's film festival that December, suggested (see chapter 5), surely such a beginning is more pressing than ever.

NOTES

INTRODUCTION

1   All translations of field notes, recorded interviews, films, and other primary documents in Spanish quoted in this book are my own.

2   In Cuba, the terms *la Revolución cubana* (the Cuban Revolution) or, more simply, *la Revolución* (the Revolution) and even *el proceso* (the process, for the revolutionary process) are used to refer to all events following 1959. This use of the terms thus ties a historical period to a set of values and ideals that include solidarity, social justice, national sovereignty, and a commitment to public health care and education, although, as I point out throughout this book, many Cubans contest whether or not the actions of the state have in fact always lined up with the values and ideals associated with the Revolution. I capitalize Cuban Revolution and Revolution to reflect standard practice in Cuba and to indicate where I mean to refer to these historical and conceptual uses of these terms.

3   Cuba, of course, is in fact an archipelago, not an island. Throughout this work I adopt the more conventional term *island*, which is how most Cubans I worked with refer to Cuba.

4   José Esteban Muñoz notes a similar ambivalence at work among the Cuban American Left and describes this position beautifully: "This ambivalence is not a passive ambivalence. It is more nearly a passionate investment in Cuba that sees the promise of the revolution, its potential, and its various failures and shortcomings" (2000, 258).

5   For key accounts of Cuban film and cultural history, see Amiot and Berthier (2006); Balaisis (2016); Burton (1997); Chanan (2004); Fehimović (2018); García (2015); Miller (2008); Paranagua and Cobas (1990); Stock (2009); and

Venegas (2009). For analyses of Cuban cinema within the broader continental context of the New Latin American cinema, see King (1990); López (1997); and Pick (1993).

6   I take this general definition of allegory from Fletcher ([1964] 2012, 2–3). For other incisive overviews of allegory, see Copeland and Struck (2010) and Xavier (2004).

7   There is some debate over when to date the end of the Special Period. While some take the custody battle over Elián González in 2000 as a significant bookend to this era (Hernández-Reguant 2009c, 9–10, 17), others identify the end of the Special Period with the official removal of the US dollar from circulation in 2004 and Fidel Castro's suggestion in a speech given on International Women's Day in 2005 that the Special Period might finally be coming to a close (Whitfield 2008, 2, 159). My periodization here, shifted slightly from an earlier version (Humphreys 2017a), attempts to highlight that pervasive sense of uncertainty that characterized the years following Fidel Castro's withdrawal from public office due to illness in 2006 through to the first definite announcements of economic decentralization in 2010, as Cubans waited to see what direction Raúl Castro's new government would take.

8   The decisive announcement of the beginning of the Special Period was made in the international edition of the Communist Party newspaper, *Granma*, on December 30, 1990, after several months of mixed statements about the possibility that Cuba might be forced to adopt wartime economic measures in order to survive the dissolution of the Soviet Union (Hernández-Reguant 2009c, 4). See the essays collected by Ariana Hernández-Reguant (2009a) for changes in cultural production during the Special Period.

9   For a similar argument about openings made for social criticism in the arts in the 1990s, see Baker (2011); Fernandes (2006); and Hernández-Reguant (2006, 2009c).

10   My engagement with Marcuse and Haraszti warrants some clarification. What I find insightful in their arguments is the notion that the tolerance of divergent positions or artwork may sometimes work to consolidate the political status quo. Suspicions that this is the case, as this book will show, often shape debates in Cuba, reinforcing political divides. Contrary to their arguments, however, I believe that criticism articulated within the framework of existing political systems does sometimes result in important change, no matter how incremental. I also depart from their understanding of what motivates participation in dominant systems. Marcuse adopts a strong false consciousness theory of ideology, arguing that citizens acquiesce to repressive tolerance because they are steeped in the ruling political discourse and incapable of autonomous thought. In Haraszti's text, meanwhile, artists and intellectuals are primarily motivated by cynical self-interest. My emphasis on ambivalence offers an alternative to false consciousness or cynical reason theories of ideology, allowing us to recognize how individuals may continue to support or at least fail to directly rebel against the existing political system

in the hopes that the values, promises, and ideals with which they have vested it might yet come true, even as they recognize its shortcomings and failures. In addition to José Esteban Muñoz (2000), for this argument I am inspired by Lauren Berlant's (2011) account of cruel optimism, in which individuals remain attached to narratives of the good life in spite of repeated disappointment, and Alexei Yurchak's (2006, 93–98) description of how citizens in late socialist Russia separated the state and its practices from the original ideals of socialism. As elaborated in the next section, I also depart from Yurchak's argument in important ways. For seminal accounts of cynical reason, see also Sloterdijk (1987) and Žižek (1989).

11   Originally named the Instituto de las Artes or National Arts Institute, the ISA was later renamed the Universidad de las Artes or the Arts University while retaining the original acronym.

12   See Stock (2009) for a comprehensive summary of the state and nonstate organizations that played an increasingly active role in Cuban film production as of the 1990s, which also include the Asociación Hermanos Saíz (Sáiz Brothers' Organization), a state organization founded in 1986 to promote the work of artists under the age of thirty-five; the Movimiento Nacional de Video (National Video Movement), a state organization founded in 1988 with the goal of promoting video work; and the Fundación Ludwig de Cuba, a nongovernmental organization backed by German philanthropists that aims to promote the work of young Cuban artists. Since 2014, the Norwegian Embassy in Havana has become one of the main sources of funding for independent Cuban cinema (Reyes 2017).

13   For writings on the paquete and the debates it provoked in Cuba, see, for instance, Humphreys (2017a); Pertierra (2012); and Rodríguez (2016).

14   I discuss early suspicions of the Muestra in chapter 1. The Muestra subsequently faced censorship scandals in 2008, 2009, and 2018, when films previously approved by the organizing committee were ultimately excluded from exhibition following conflicts with ICAIC officials. In 2009 this led to well-known filmmaker Fernando Pérez's public decision to leave his position as director of the Muestra. For a report of Pérez's decision and its motivation by censorship, see Inter Press Service en Cuba, "Fernando Pérez renuncia como director de la Muestra Joven," March 15, 2012, http://www.ipscuba.net /cultura/fernando-perez-renuncia-como-director-de-la-muestra-joven/.

15   One of the first certain signs of the new era of economic reforms was the announcement of state plans to move 500,000 workers from the state to the private sector. "Pronunciamiento de la Central de Trabajadores de Cuba," *Granma*, September 13, 2010, http://www.granma.cu/granmad/2010/09/13/nacional /artic01.html. In October 2010, municipal offices began processing applications for business licenses. Other significant events included the release in draft forms of the plans for reform, the "Lineamientos de la Política Economíca y Social," in November 2010, and the official adoption of this document in May 2011. For an overview and a timeline of the reforms, see Peters (2012a, 2012b).

16 New cuentapropista regulations were announced in July 2018, to be put into effect in December of that year. These regulations, which included the restriction of licenses to one per individual and new taxation and banking requirements, were justified by the government in the name of limiting tax evasion and preventing excessive income disparity. But they also immediately provoked much controversy both on the island and among international observers.

17 While Fidel Castro quickly became the most internationally known figurehead of the new Cuban government following the 1959 defeat of Batista, he did not officially step into the presidency until 1976. Prior to this, Castro served as prime minister and as first secretary of the Communist Party of Cuba, while the presidency was held by a former lawyer, Osvaldo Dorticós Torrado.

18 Hernández-Reguant (2016) provides a compelling analysis of Miami-based Cubans' support for Donald Trump in the 2016 elections.

19 For this account of how commercial public spheres, including cinema, have historically provided opportunities to articulate the life experiences of those marginalized by the bourgeois public sphere, see especially Hansen (1990, 1991); Negt and Kluge ([1972] 1993); and Stewart (2005).

20 Yurchak has elaborated on these arguments and their relevance for late liberalism in the Global North in conjunction with Dominic Boyer (Boyer and Yurchak 2010).

21 I deliberately use the term *alternative public sphere* rather than the more common *publics* and *counterpublics* (Warner 2002) or, in relation to the publics that formed in late Soviet Russia, *deterritorialized publics* (Yurchak 2006). The type of public sphere that Cuban intellectuals theorized and attempted to bring into being in the early 1960s shared many characteristics with the political and literary bourgeois public spheres described by Habermas ([1962] 1989), including an emphasis on critical rational debate among citizens coming together as equals to debate matters of public import. However, in the early decades of the Revolution, Cuban intellectuals challenged the assumption that the public must be autonomous from the state and adopted a different addressee: revolutionaries instead of humans as such. Cuban intellectuals' reconceptualization of the public sphere thus cohered with a broader attempt at the time to articulate an alternative modernity opposed to liberalism and capitalism. As I show, intellectuals' efforts to articulate an alternative public sphere were nonetheless plagued by anxieties about autonomy from the first. These anxieties were then exacerbated in the late socialist era.

22 The debate over paranoid or symptomatic readings has been elaborated in two special issues of *Representations*: Best and Marcus (2009) and Freedgood and Schmitt (2014). Several scholars object to the alternatives proposed to paranoid readings on the grounds that these methods often adopt an acritical notion that the text means just what it says it means (Rooney 2010; Weed 2012). Here I do not so much abandon interpretation as alter its locus. As described in the next section of this introduction, I approach films as archives to be analyzed alongside other forms of archival and ethnographic material in

order to determine signs of the debates and struggles that have gone into film production, circulation, and reception.

23 In addition to Hofstadter and Sedgwick, I also draw my understanding of political paranoia from the rich anthropological engagement with the concept since the 1990s. For this work, see, for instance, Boyer (2006); Comaroff and Comaroff (1999); Lepselter (2005, 2016); Marcus (1999); Ryer (2015); Walton (2010); and West and Sanders (2003). This scholarship has often involved compelling accounts of how the marginalized or disenfranchised may turn to political paranoia either to make sense of global systems of power whose workings are otherwise abstract and obscure (Comaroff and Comaroff 1999) or, conversely, to destabilize dominant histories by drawing out the ambiguity inherent in all narratives (Lepselter 2005, 141). My own sense is that the uses and consequences of political paranoia vary greatly depending on how it is mobilized and under what circumstances. Like the anthropological literature on the topic, I take paranoia to be an entirely reasonable response to the ambiguity and indirection often deliberately at play in Cuban art and politics, and one that may on occasion produce its own insights or even open up fissures in dominant narratives. Nonetheless, much of this book is concerned with demonstrating the ways in which political paranoia can limit public debate. Not only is political paranoia equally a tool of those in power—a fact that is especially evident in a context shaped by Cold War politics—in Cuba, paranoid speculations frequently end in resurrecting the political binaries that have long plagued national politics and that the work of artists might otherwise put into question.

24 Scholars have long maintained that artists and spectators turn to allegory and other tactics of aesthetic indirection to communicate illicit meanings in contexts shaped by censorship. A smaller number of works show how a growing orientation to the global market in Global South and postsocialist contexts can spark concerns that art plays into stereotyped representations of the nation or acts as propaganda for authoritarian states. My emphasis on allegory as a contested social process draws attention to how artists both capitalize on and attempt to interrupt such suspicions in an effort to articulate more ambivalent takes on social and political dynamics. For work on the importance of aesthetic indirection under conditions of censorship, see Fernandez and Huber (2001); Humphrey (1999); Jacobs (1988, 1997); Loseff (1984); Maltby (1996); Rofel (2007); Taruskin (2000); Wedeen (1999); and Yurchak (2006). For analyses of the effects of the global market on art from the Global South and late- or postsocialist contexts, see Larkin (2009); Ong (2012); Ross (2011); Whitfield (2008); and Winegar (2006).

25 See Briggs and Bauman (1992) and Silverstein (2004) for this definition of genre.

26 If we adopt a more expansive and flexible definition of genre, then the distinction between genre and mode might best be viewed as a categorization issue, with the more encompassing concept of mode designed to capture the ways in which meaningful aesthetic and narrative patterns recur across forms

that we might otherwise want to categorize as separate genres (Gledhill 2000, 229). For simplicity's sake and with the exception of paranoia (traditionally referred to as a style) and allegory (which I label as a mode to distinguish it from the more specific subsets of allegory also relevant here, e.g., modernist vs. modern allegory), I default in this book to *genre* as the label for these socially meaningful discursive patterns.

1. SYMPTOMOLOGIES OF THE STATE

1 Cuban writer and intellectual Ambrosio Fornet coined the term *quinquenio gris* to describe the period of heightened censorship of the 1970s, using it in his book *Las máscaras del tiempo* (1995, 56, 62). See Fornet (2008) for a discussion of this term and an analysis of Cuban cultural politics in the late 1960s into the 1970s.

2 For accounts of the Mariel exodus and memories of homophobia in the Revolution more broadly, see Hamilton (2012, 117–48) and Lumsden (1996, 78–80).

3 See Navarro (2008) and Ponte (2010) for summaries of the email war from opposing political views.

4 Paranoia is neither exclusive to state socialism, nor did it begin in Cuba with the Revolution, but it certainly acquired a specific structure and pervasiveness in this era. Paul Ryer (2015) traces political paranoia in Cuba back to the nineteenth century, discussing in particular the various conspiracy theories that surrounded the 1898 explosion of the USS *Maine* in the Havana harbor during the Cuban war for independence from Spain. As he notes, this incident was varyingly attributed either to Spanish loyalists or to the Americans themselves, who were suspected of blowing up the ship in order to justify US intervention in the war and, subsequently, in Cuban politics.

5 For analyses of the CDRs and the ways in which they have fomented suspicion, see Fagen (1969, 69–103) and Routon (2010, 19–38).

6 This interpretation of these events was suggested to me, for instance, by Ambrosio Fornet, interview by the author, Havana, November 15, 2003. Older intellectuals described other famous cultural conflicts, such as the debate between Blas Roca and Alfredo Guevara over cinema (see chapter 2), as motivated as much by specific political and aesthetic commitments as by a struggle for control over the cultural field between different factions of intellectuals. Manuel Pérez, interview by the author, Havana, September 21, 2008.

7 See Chanan (2004, 133–43); G. Muñoz (2011); and Robbins (2009) for accounts of the censorship of *P.M.* and analyses of the aesthetic style and politics of this documentary. Guevara provided a retrospective explanation of his decision to censor *P.M.* in an interview for the December 1992 issue of *La Gaceta de Cuba* (reprinted in A. Guevara 1998, 85–99).

8 An expanded number of intellectuals' interventions during the sessions at the Biblioteca Nacional have been made available in recent decades. Alfredo

Guevara published a statement he made during the conference (see A. Guevara 1998, 181–200). Fragments of the broader debates that took place, including statements by intellectuals such as Virgilio Piñera, have been published in Jiménez Leal and Zayas (2012).

9 Castro does not specifically name socialist realism in his speech, but the fact that this is what he was referring to is made clear through the recollections of intellectuals who participated in the meetings. Cuban intellectual and cultural functionary Roberto Fernández Retamar (2001), for instance, recalls the widespread concern about the possible imposition of socialist realism in a retrospective analysis of "Palabras a los intelectuales" published in the UNEAC's official cultural magazine, *La Gaceta de Cuba*.

10 Miklós Haraszti (1988, 42–45) argues that intellectuals willingly accepted the restrictions imposed on them by state socialism in the Soviet Union in part because it freed them from the vagaries and demands of the market, providing them not only with material support but also with the promise of social utility and ready audiences. Castro's speech makes clear that such possibilities were also part of the seductive promise of the Cuban Revolution for many Cuban intellectuals. Such aspirations also came through in intellectuals' recollections of the 1960s. As Ambrosio Fornet put it to me in our 2003 interview, "What we wanted to do was create a modern culture for everyone." Interview by the author, Havana, November 15, 2003.

11 Retrospective accounts of this conference argue that Castro's reference to "honest" intellectuals who were nonetheless not revolutionaries was a response to concerns raised by Cuban author and playwright Virgilio Piñera about whether Catholicism would be tolerated. Ambrosio Fornet, interview by the author, Havana, November 15, 2003.

12 See Kapcia (2005, 132–34) and Kumaraswami (2009) for analyses of "Palabras." Both authors conclude that the speech guaranteed expansiveness in the arts. My point is that to understand the speech's political and social effects analysts need to examine how it was interpreted and deployed rather than focusing on what may or may not have been Fidel Castro's original intentions.

13 Fernández Retamar's arguments in the 1969 debate among intellectuals clearly resonate with and most likely refer to Che Guevara's position in "El socialismo y el hombre en Cuba." Cuban intellectuals were also aware of and in dialogue with the work of Herbert Marcuse. While I do not know if they had access to Marcuse's (1965) essay on repressive tolerance, at least one of his essays on aesthetics was translated and published in no. 49/50 of *Cine Cubano*, alongside writings by other foreign theorists, such as Marshal McLuhan. Thanks to Nicholas Balaisis for drawing my attention to this reference.

14 In the passage in "El socialismo y el hombre en Cuba" that Fornet refers to, Che Guevara decisively dismisses socialist realism. A number of older Cuban intellectuals insisted to me that Guevara's rejection of socialist realism helped ensure that the style was never adopted in Cuba. At the same time, Che Guevara's stance on Cuban intellectuals was ambiguous. Further on in the

same essay he laments what he refers to as the "original sin" of Cuba's artists and intellectuals, arguing that they are "not authentically revolutionary" and that political leaders must prevent the current generation from "perverting" the new. This statement was subsequently often mobilized to discredit intellectuals ([1965] 1967, 635–36).

15 An *oportunista* is someone who aligns oneself with current political trends for the sake of personal advantage. To have *doble moral* means to say or think something other than what one secretly believes or does. Accusations of oportunismo and doble moral are commonplace in Cuba, reflecting the pervasive concern with hidden political intentions. Many Cuban intellectuals insisted to me, for instance, that hardliners of the 1970s were themselves oportunistas, citing as evidence the fact that several emigrated after the collapse of the Soviet Union.

16 Cuban film editor Nelson Rodríguez recalled the misery that followed in the wake of the 1968 Ofensiva Revolucionaria as follows: "All of a sudden you went to Havana and you didn't have anywhere to drink water, to eat, to have a soft drink, to go to the bathroom. The misery in this country at that time was impressive. They closed all the bars, they closed all the cabarets, they closed everything. That place that is in front of the ICAIC that used to be a ten-cent store for the American chain Woolworths had only busts of Martí and [Antonio] Maceo and a few little Cuban flags. There was nothing. We had already lived the Special Period of the 1990s." This statement suggests the disillusionment with state policies that began to set in during that period, even among intellectuals who continued to largely support the Revolution. Interview by the author, Havana, October 26, 2008.

17 See Scarpaci, Segre, and Coyula (2002, 140–41) for an account of the Havana Greenbelt Project and the Ten Million Ton Sugar Harvest.

18 Similar to arguments made about the ICAIC, the Casa de las Américas' ability to survive the quinquenio gris is often chalked up to the political prestige of its director, Haydée Santamaría, who was one of two women active in the attack on the Moncada Barracks in Santiago de Cuba on July 26, 1953.

19 Arturo Sotto, interview by the author, Havana, November 20, 2008.

20 Daphne Berdahl and Sheila Fitzpatrick note similar tendencies to communicate through ambiguous signals by Soviet and East German states. Fitzpatrick (2000, 24–28) attributes Stalin's reliance on such tactics both to the ways in which mystery and ambiguity help reinforce an impression of power and to the fact that such maneuvers allowed policy directions to be strategically denied. Berdahl (1999, 44–71) argues that the East German state derived its power in part through its ability to shroud its actions in mystery. The knowledge that the state was conducting surveillance of its citizens' activities along with the mystery that surrounded such activities, she notes, encouraged citizens in the small border village where she conducted her fieldwork to attribute greater control to the state than what it actually exercised, which in turn helped secure citizens' compliance. A similar play between deliberate

ambiguity on the part of state officials and citizens' attempts to interpret these signs is clearly at work in Cuban politics, as indicated by this story of the Congreso Nacional and, as discussed later in this chapter, the declaration published by the UNEAC in the Communist Party's newspaper, *Granma*, in response to the email war. My interest here is in pointing out how such dynamics are exacerbated by the state's adoption of repressive tolerance as well as how citizens' paranoid responses, no matter how reasonable, can limit political debate by reinscribing polarizing views of Cuban politics.

21 Navarro's position during this debate was in keeping with his earlier work. In a 2002 essay, Navarro defended the importance of criticism within the Revolution, listing and criticizing the various rationales that had historically been used to limit public debate.

22 Navarro, "Indignación intelectual I," *Encuentro de la cultura cubana*, January 9, 2007, http://www.cubaencuentro.com/cultura/temas/tema-la-exaltacion -de-ex-comisarios-politicos/indignacion-intelectual-i-29430. The emails exchanged during the email war were initially archived on the website of the Cuban blog *Consenso*, "Polémica intelectual," http://www.desdecuba.com /polemica/. I downloaded and archived them on August 1, 2010. Emails that were obtained from this source are cited subsequently in this text by email author and the title of the original *Consenso* dossier, "Polémica intelectual." As of 2019, many of these emails can be found on the website of the Cuban exile journal *Encuentro de la cultura cubana*, www.cubaencuentro.com, in the thematic section "La exaltación de los comisarios politicos." Links to individual emails cited in this chapter that are available on *Encuentro* are included in endnotes.

23 Navarro, "Indignación intelectual I."

24 Arango, "Indignación intelectual I."

25 Coyula, "Polémica intelectual."

26 Ambrosio Fornet, interview by the author, Havana, February 25, 2009. Subsequent comments by Fornet quoted in this chapter are from this interview.

27 Arturo Arango, interview by the author, Havana, October 1, 2008.

28 See this book's introduction and chapter 4 for an account of efforts in the post-Soviet period to incorporate the diaspora and diasporic cultural production into the Cuban national corpus.

29 Arango, "Polémica intelectual."

30 Valle, "Polémica intelectual."

31 Portela, "Indignación intelectual I."

32 Gustavo Arcos, interview by the author, Havana, May 26, 2008.

33 For analyses of the paquete in both its full and incipient forms, see Humphreys (2017b); Pertierra (2012); and Rodríguez (2016).

34 "Declaración del Secretariado de la UNEAC," *Encuentro de la cultura cubana*, January 19, 2007, http://www.cubaencuentro.com/cultura/temas/tema-la -exaltacion-de-ex-comisarios-politicos/declaracion-del-secretariado-de-la -uneac-30014.

35 Félix Sánchez, "Acerca de la Declaración del Secretariado de la UNEAC," *Encuentro de la cultura cubana*, February 14, 2007, http://www.cubaencuentro .com/cultura/temas/tema-la-exaltacion-de-ex-comisarios-politicos/acerca-de -la-declaracion-del-secretariado-de-la-uneac-31085.

36 Jiménez Pérez, "Polémica intelectual."

37 Menéndez, "Polémica intelectual."

38 Miranda, "Polémica intelectual."

39 Padura, "Polémica intelectual."

40 Jorge Luis Arcos, "Según imagen: A propósito de la declaración del secretariado de la UNEAC," *Encuentro de la cultura cubana*, January 23, 2007, http://www .cubaencuentro.com/cultura/temas/tema-la-exaltacion-de-ex-comisarios -politicos/segun-imagen-30129.

41 Desiderio Navarro, interview by the author, Havana, March 4, 2009. Subsequent comments by Navarro referred to in this chapter are from this interview.

42 "Betty," "Polémica intelectual."

43 Hernández, "Polémica intelectual."

44 Sánchez, "Polémica intelectual."

45 Reynaldo González, "Una pesadilla sin perdón ni olvido," *Encuentro de la cultura cubana*, February 7, 2007, http://www.cubaencuentro.com/cultura/temas /tema-la-exaltacion-de-ex-comisarios-politicos/una-pesadilla-sin-perdon-ni -olvido-30833.

46 Valle, "Polémica intelectual."

47 Valle, "Polémica intelectual."

48 Cuza Malé, "Polémica intelectual."

49 Duanel Díaz, "Crítica y memoria," *Encuentro de la cultura cubana*, January 10, 2007, https://www.cubaencuentro.com/cultura/temas/tema-la-exaltacion -de-ex-comisarios-politicos/critica-y-memoria-29437. Duanel Díaz has subsequently published several books on art and intellectual politics in the Cuban Revolution, with a special emphasis on literature. See, for example, Díaz (2009).

50 José Prats Sariol, "La izquierda masoquista se pavonea," *Encuentro de la cultura cubana*, January 10, 2007, https://www.cubaencuentro.com/cultura/temas /tema-la-exaltacion-de-ex-comisarios-politicos/la-izquierda-masoquista-se -pavonea-29447.

51 Haroldo Dilla Alfonso, "El establo de caballos finos," *Encuentro de la cultura cubana*, February 12, 2007, https://www.cubaencuentro.com/cultura/temas /tema-la-exaltacion-de-ex-comisarios-politicos/el-establo-de-caballos-finos -30978.

52 Eliseo Alberto, "Mi punto de vista," *Encuentro de la cultura cubana*, January 12, 2007, https://www.cubaencuentro.com/cultura/temas/tema-la -exaltacion-de-ex-comisarios-politicos/mi-punto-de-vista-29577.

53 Enrique Colina, "Una opinión," *Encuentro de la cultura cubana*, January 29, 2007, https://www.cubaencuentro.com/cultura/temas/tema-la-exaltacion-de

-ex-comisarios-politicos/una-opinion-30435. Colina's demand that Cuban films that had never been shown on state television be released by the ICRT may well have been instrumental in breaking with this censorship. As discussed in Chapter 4, Juan Carlos Tabío's *Lista de espera* (*The Waiting List,* 2000) and Ian Padrón's *Fuera de liga* (*Out of this League,* 2003) were shown on state television in 2008. *Lista de espera* had previously been censored from state television while the ICAIC leadership had refused to release *Fuera de liga* because of its conciliatory treatment of Cuban baseball players who defected to the United States. Colina's demand that political leaders face journalists on television found ironic, albeit coincidental, culmination during Barack Obama's historic visit to Cuba in March 2016. Obama and Raúl Castro appeared in a televised press conference where the latter stammered in his attempt to answer questions posed by journalists about political prisoners and human rights issues.

54 Manuel Herrera, interview by the author, Havana, February 11, 2008.

55 Nelson Rodríguez, interview by the author, Havana, April 28, 2008.

56 Alina Rodríguez Abreu, one of the young filmmakers recruited to participate in the project, acknowledged that the ICAIC leadership likely hoped that the opportunity would convert those involved to more official positions. But she also insisted that the filmmakers resisted creating a merely propagandistic depiction of Cuba's literacy programs. In her short for the documentary, she explained, she depicted both how the program opened up new opportunities for the Aymara, an indigenous group in Bolivia, and how it threatened the survival of their own language. Alina Rodríguez Abreu, interview by the author, Havana, June 25, 2008.

57 Yoani Sánchez, one of the most visible members of the Cuban blogger movement, recounted that it was her frustration with being locked outside the doors of the first of the quinquenio gris conferences that prompted her to start her blog, *Generación Y* (*Generation Y*). Bernardo Gutiérrez, "Yoaní, la blogera cubana de la Generación Y," *Público,* March 16, 2008, https://www .publico.es/internacional/yoani-blogera-cubana-generacion-y.html. She has since become a renowned international figure, winning human rights awards and engaging in dialogue with celebrities from Barack Obama to Julia Stiles. Sánchez herself has also been the subject of the sort of political paranoia that plagued the email war. When she terminated her contract with the Italian newspaper *La strada*, her translator, Gordiano Lupi, argued that she worked in self-interested pursuit of financial gain rather than out of an idealistic attempt to facilitate freedom of expression in Cuba. "I began to wonder if Yoani was not so much an agent of the C.I.A.—as her detractors say—as [an agent] of the Castro family, paid to blow smoke in people's eyes," wrote Lupi. "Yoani Is Denounced by Her Italian Translator," *Progreso Weekly,* May 13, 2014, https://progresoweekly.us/yoani-denounced-italian-translator /). This sort of complex and seemingly contradictory suspicion is not unusual in Cuba. Like Lupi, my interlocutors would occasionally speculate as to

whether artist *x* who had produced critical work *y* was an agent of the CIA or of the Castros, in a tone that could vary between serious concern and good humor. These sorts of comments reveal the ways in which the openings for public debate in the late socialist period combined with an awareness of the potential of capitalizing on criticism have made it increasingly difficult to discern freedom of expression from complicity.

58 Following the censorship of playwright and filmmaker Juan Carlos Cremata's production of Eugène Ionesco's play *El rey se muere* (*The King Dies*) and further interference in his work in 2015, prominent Cuban intellectuals, many of whom had been active in the email war, published articles denouncing the censorship of Cremata's work to Cuban blogs. At a meeting held by intellectuals to discuss the conflict, playwright Norge Espinosa reportedly invoked the 2007 guerra de los emails as an earlier instance in which intellectuals had rallied against censorship. See Luz Escobar, "Cuban Filmmakers Mobilize against Censorship," *14ymedio*, December 4, 2015, https://translatingcuba.com/category/authors/polemica-the-little-email-war/.

2. PARANOID READINGS AND AMBIVALENT ALLEGORIES

1 The censorship faced by Luis Alberto García and Néstor Jíménez for their work in *Monte Rouge*, García told me, was "the worst kind of censorship: a veiled censorship." Neither he nor Jíménez were directly told that they had been banned from working in state television or by whom. Rather, various directors in the ICRT informed the actors that they had been told not to hire García or Jíménez or had been asked to cut scenes already filmed with the two actors. This continued for eleven months, when the minister of culture, Abel Prieto, intervened on the actors' behalf. At the time of our interview, García was still clearly angry about the ban. Notably, however, he was also concerned to convey to me, a foreigner, that his experience both demonstrated ongoing censorship in Cuba and showed that Cuba was not the totalitarian and repressive society it is often depicted to be. "¡Ojo!" (Pay attention!) he observed. "I was never called in by state security; they didn't send me to jail; they didn't threaten me by phone—nothing like that. . . . The usual thing is to say that 'Cuba is a closed society; it's a total dictatorship' and it's not like that either. Things get debated here. Sometimes it takes a while to reach a solution to a specific problem, but things get debated and they get debated a lot. Because look at how a problem like mine was solved." García was also careful to note that the ban had emerged from the ICRT and not from the ICAIC, reiterating the common sentiment among artists that the ICAIC has at least historically allowed for greater freedom of expression than state television or journalism. In addition to demonstrating how the Cuban state—like all states—is not a singular monolith but rather is composed of different agencies and individuals who may often be at odds with one another (Abrams 1988), this story provides a salient example of artists'

growing frustration with censorship in the twenty-first century; the ongoing belief among some artists that such problems might still be resolved from within the Cuban Revolution; and the ways in which combatting censorship often depends on a patronage system whereby controversial artists receive protection from "enlightened" state officials. The ban also did not prevent García or Jíménez from making the art they wanted to make. Following the initial controversy, Eduardo del Llano and the two actors continued on to produce a series of short films revolving around the Nicanor character that lampooned various social and political problems in Cuba. Luis Alberto García, interview by the author, Havana, March 12, 2008.

2 Cuban sound engineer, informal conversation with the author, San Antonio de los Baños, March 17, 2008.

3 Del Llano's distinction of his film from a "pamphlet" here is notable for the ways in which it repeats and shifts the meaning of a term that has long had weight in Cuban cultural politics. As noted in the previous chapter, the term *pamphlet* was repeatedly invoked in the 1960s to describe the reduction of art to propaganda for the state. By the late socialist period, it was also being used to refer to work that abandoned aesthetic nuance for what was perceived as political diatribe against the state. Quotes from del Llano are taken from an interview by the author, Havana, February 1, 2008.

4 See Clark (2000); Condee (2000); and Schmelz (2009) for analyses of the transformations that took place in the arts in the Soviet Union during the Khrushchev Thaw.

5 As mentioned briefly in the introduction to this book, in its initial years, the ICAIC drew for its staff on intellectuals involved in the radical cultural society, Nuestro Tiempo, and the film club, Cine-Club Visión. Of the founding generation, only Tomás Gutiérrez Alea, Julio García Espinosa, and Néstor Almendros had formal training, having studied in Rome's Centro Sperimentale di Cinematografia. Much of the staff of the fledgling film institute thus learned filmmaking through practice, including, importantly, by collaborating with well-known filmmakers—such as Mikhail Kalatozov (Russia), Joris Ivens (Holland), and Chris Marker and Agnès Varda (France)—who came to witness the new revolution firsthand. Cuban filmmakers were also active in the foundation of New Latin American cinema, engaging in conferences and festivals with filmmakers from across the continent.

6 Many of the older filmmakers with whom I worked argued that this debate was motivated by a power struggle between Blas Roca and Alfredo Guevara, who left the PSP in the 1950s. For an account of the relationship between the PSP and the 26th of July Movement, see Farber (1983). Regardless of the motivations that sparked the debate, it also clearly provided an opportunity for the ICAIC filmmakers to develop and fight for their vision of revolutionary art and cinema.

7 Reactions against US cultural imperialism moved to the fore among both Left-leaning intellectuals and politicians in the 1960s and 1970s. Ariel Dorfman

and Armand Mattelart's *How to Read Donald Duck* ([1971] 1991) provides a classic example of these arguments.

8 The equation of socialist realism with dogmatism and the infantilization of spectators was frequently repeated. In a debate between ICAIC filmmakers and University of Havana professors a few months before the polemics between Blas Roca and Alfredo Guevara, for instance, Julio García Espinosa argued that "dogmatic[s]" treated the public as "a sort of newborn to whom one has to provide everything premasticated" ([1963] 2006, 91).

9 Similar concerns about the influence of cinematic images on the masses—and especially on women, the lower classes, and others deemed excessively vulnerable to the medium's affective force—have pervaded debates over cinema in contexts ranging from the early twentieth-century United States to contemporary India (Grieveson 2004; Mazzarella 2013). William Mazzarella (2015, 92–93) links such anxieties to tensions in the liberal imaginary between aspirations to self-determination and the threat of influence by the social. As discussed in chapter 1, Cuban intellectuals challenged liberal aspirations to autonomy in the early years of the Revolution, theorizing an alternative public sphere that would combine political commitment with critical rational debate. Cuban filmmakers' adoption of modernist allegories aimed to advance this project by simultaneously promoting spectators' commitment to the Revolution and training citizens in the use of critical reason. As my discussion of *Memorias del subdesarrollo* in this chapter suggests, however, even Cuban intellectuals committed to the Revolution did not entirely succeed in overcoming anxieties about the threat that crowd affect might pose to reason. These debates thus suggest how tensions between autonomy and the social also shaped socialist imaginaries, even as artists and intellectuals strove to prioritize collectivity and relatedness over autonomy and self-determination.

10 Guevara also insisted that the ICAIC had to participate in the Revolution in a more direct fashion. Thus, in the 1962 speech to the National Congress of Culture cited here, he noted that the film institute had devised certain forms such as the newsreel and informative documentaries to fulfill the immediate political and pedagogic needs of the revolution. Fiction and artistic documentaries, he argued, must be preserved from such a demand ([1962] 1998, 47).

11 I deliberately use *modernist* instead of *modern* as a description of the specific genre of allegory theorized and adopted by Cuban filmmakers in the early decades of the Revolution. As Ismail Xavier (2004, 345–48) notes, modern allegory, as theorized by Walter Benjamin in *The Origin of German Tragic Drama* ([1928] 2009) and later essays, questioned a teleological vision of history and foregrounded the opacity of language or the gap between experience and its expression. As I discuss in chapter 5, in the early twenty-first century, young Cuban filmmakers increasingly turned to forms of allegory more akin to the tactics theorized by Benjamin, exploring new versions of Cuban history and questioning the politics and ethics of the production of meaning. With the notable exception of Nicolás Guillén Landrián, the version of allegory

adopted by the majority of Cuban filmmakers on the island in the early decades of the Revolution, by contrast, took a more teleological and positivist approach to history and to meaning, using modernist and open-ended techniques in an attempt to guide spectators through their independent use of critical reason to the "correct" socialist conclusions posited by films.

12 The term *mulato/a* comes from the Latin *mulus*, or mule, the sterile hybrid of a horse and donkey, and thus bespeaks a racist colonial history in which the offspring of white colonizers and enslaved Africans were viewed with suspicion. The term *mulato/a* also remains a commonly invoked racial category in Cuba, typically referring to individuals with lighter dark skin and a combination of other features (nose, hair, eyes) that mix traits deemed typically African versus European. As is typical of Latin America, Cuba operates with a racial classification system that is performative and context-driven, in which individuals are racially categorized depending on a combination of their phenotypical features as well as modes of dressing and behavior. This fluid system nonetheless remains racist, with white at the top and black at the bottom, in spite of the Revolution's official claims to have done away with racism. In this book, I employ the terms *mulato/a* in order to invoke the allegorical role historically played by mixed-race characters. For overviews of the Cuban racial classification system and race in the Revolution, see, for instance, de la Fuente (2001); Roland (2013); Sawyer (2006). For the origins of the term *mulato/a*, see Fraunhar (2005, 162–63). For accounts of the use of the mulata as allegory for the nation in Cuban cinema and art, see Benamou (1994); D'Lugo (1997); and Fraunhar (2005, 2018).

13 The ending thus invokes official arguments that the Revolution would do away with sexism, even as it presents this problem as one that is still ongoing. Addressing ongoing sexism remained a viable and prevalent topic in a number of key Cuban films, including, for instance, Pastor Vega's *Retrato de Teresa* (*Portrait of Teresa*, 1979).

14 In the passage cited by Sergio, Ortega y Gasset argues that animals "do not live according to themselves but rather according to the other . . . which is the equivalent to saying the animal lives in a constant state of inconsistency and alienation, that [the animal's] life is pure inconsistency" (Ortega y Gasset ([1939] 1964, 299).

15 *Memorias del subdesarrollo* is critical of Sergio's reduction of women to ciphers for his own fantasies. At the same time, the film does not so much resolve these dynamics as deploy them to new allegorical ends in order to analyze Sergio's own alienation.

16 Nelson Rodríguez, interview by the author, Havana, October 26, 2008.

17 In one scene in *Memorias del subdesarrollo*, Sergio attends a roundtable conference in which Edmundo Desnoes, the author of the novel on which the film is based, discusses how North Americans commonly view Latin Americans as "blacks" while an Afro-Cuban waiter silently pours water for the light-skinned panel. As Catherine Benamou (1994, 51) points out, in this scene, the film

clearly means to highlight the contradiction between the panelists' claim to radicalism and their ongoing racism. As with its portrayal of gender relations, however, the film itself does not entirely escape these contradictions.

18 To give reason to Rodríguez's view, it is worth recalling again that the sequence is a metatextual moment designed to prompt the spectator how to read the film. In this sense, the ongoing anxiety that it also conveys about the threat posed to individual reason by crowd affect only works to confirm the need for spectators to internalize its lesson.

19 Nelson Rodríguez's description of Tomás Gutiérrez Alea in his interview with me picked up on and resonated with wording Che Guevara once used to describe the new man. As discussed in greater detail in chapter 3, in a 1962 speech to the Union of Communist Youth, Che Guevara called on the gathered youth to remain resolutely nonconformist, alert to all problems and injustice, quick to question "lo que no está claro" (what isn't clear), and ready to protest "cada vez que surge algo que está mal, lo haya dicho quien lo haya dicho" (every time something occurs that is wrong, no matter who has said it) ([1962] 1967, 364).

20 In an article published a few months before the film's release, Alea criticized Sergio with a vehemence that Hector Amaya (2010, 110–11) reads as an attempt to ward off interpretations that would see the film as sympathetic to the bourgeoisie. Alea's presentation of the film at the 1968 Karlovy Vary Film Festival indicates an even more explicit concern with potentially uncomfortable political interpretations of the film. He closed his speech with a resounding declaration: "It is a painful film, a critical film. And if the enemy believes that he can take advantage of criticism, we are convinced that we can take even more advantage of it, because our weapons are sharpened with pain and criticism, because we make ourselves more solid, more authentic, and we come even closer to the truth" (Gutiérrez Alea [1968] 1998, 73).

21 Cuban film editor, interview by the author, Havana, October 26, 2008.

22 As mentioned in the introduction and Chapter 1, Orlando Jiménez Leal codirected *P.M.* with Saba Cabrera Infante. Néstor Almendros and Guillermo Cabrera Infante had also been embroiled in that conflict, as intellectuals aligned with the group involved in the production of the journal *Revolución* and its weekly cultural supplement, *Lunes de Revolución*. The debate between these intellectuals and Tomás Gutiérrez Alea thus continued a long-standing and clearly personal conflict. See Ana M. López (1993) for an analysis of *Improper Conduct* and the ways in which the documentary denies the possibility of debate and historical change within Cuba. She notes, for instance, that after introducing the topic of the UMAP, the documentary fails to mention that they were closed.

23 Néstor Almendros (1984) wrote an initial letter in response to the *Village Voice* interview with Alea in which he argued that Alea was acting as a propagandist for the Cuban state because he had recently encountered political trouble in the production of his latest film, *Hasta cierto punto* (*To a*

Certain Point, 1983). Alea's follow-up letter acknowledged that *Hasta cierto punto* had provoked controversy, but he denied the accusation that his criticism of *Improper Conduct* was motivated by an attempt to ingratiate himself to Cuban political leaders. This exchange then also provides an early example of how suspicion can be mobilized to dismiss Cuban artists' claims of commitment to the Revolution as a mere cover for their actual counterrevolutionary intentions.

24 Juan Carlos Tabío, interview by the author, Havana, November 12, 2008.

25 Joel del Río noted that he eventually regretted making his criticism of *Guantanamera* public, in light of the fact that Alea passed away from cancer soon after. Although he insisted that his criticism did not play into Castro's reaction to the film, pointing to the gap between this incident and the release of his own film review, the scandal also contributed to his regret. This and other events, he told me, taught him to be cautious about publicly criticizing critical or controversial films for fear of contributing to political repercussions for filmmakers. Joel del Río, interview by the author, Havana, December 20, 2011.

26 Pavel Giroud, interview by the author, Havana, February 8, 2008.

27 Cuban film director and producer, interview by the author, Havana, June 19, 2009.

28 Arturo Infante, interview by the author, Havana, 16 January 2008.

29 Pavel Giroud, interview by the author, Havana, 8 February 2008.

30 See Robbins (2009) for an astute analysis of this sequence's ambivalent treatment of Afro-Cuban popular culture.

31 See Livon-Grossman (2016) and Zayas (2010) for discussions of Guillén Landrián's participation in the making of this sequence.

3. FAITH WITHOUT FIDEL

1 As employed in Cuba, the term *dirigente* generally refers to someone who has acquired their leadership role by rising through the ranks of the political bureaucracy. Here I translate this term as "apparatchik" to capture this more specific meaning of the term. For simplicity's sake, I generally refer to the character referenced here by Daniel Díaz Torres as the director of the town sanatorium, but readers should bear in mind the more specific connotation implied by the term dirigente. As Díaz Torres himself acknowledged, the character clearly stood in for an important political leader; what was at dispute in the scandal over *Alicia* was whether or not the character represented Fidel Castro himself.

2 See chapter 2 for a discussion of the satirical short film, *Monte Rouge* (2005), that Eduardo del Llano would later go on to write and direct. He is also a prolific short story writer and has written the screenplays for several Cuban feature films.

3 Information about the reception of *Alicia en el pueblo de maravillas*, including the circulation of VHS copies and the specific allegorical readings that circulated

at the time of its release, was obtained through interviews and conversations with Daniel Díaz Torres, Manuel Pérez, Enrique Colina, Eduardo del Llano, Arturo Sotto, Joel del Río, and several anonymous film workers and spectators.

4 Joel del Río recalled applauding the film when he went to see it at a local neighborhood cinema. Interview by the author, San Antonio de los Baños, March 21, 2008. A worker at the Cinemateca de Cuba who helped me obtain copies of several key films recalled witnessing a party member hit a man when he laughed out loud at the film in a movie theater. Informal conversation with the author, Havana, January 23, 2009.

5 For excellent accounts of the controversy over the film and the contextual factors that led to it, see Redruello Campos (2007) and Soles (2005, 58–96).

6 Eagleton terms these dynamics *aesthetics*, taken in its broadest sense, but in the parlances of current critical theory, they might also be termed *affect*, and also bear a resemblance to what early social theorists such as Émile Durkheim termed *mana*. See Mazzarella (2017, 10–11) for this explanation and for a compelling argument about how concepts such as mana can open up new thinking about affect and aesthetics.

7 Of interest to the arguments in this book, in *The Social Contract*, Rousseau justifies censorship as a means for cultivating the sorts of citizens who would have the tastes and habits necessary to govern themselves adequately, a move that thus relates censorship to this desire to instill social order through imprinting it on the hearts of citizens. See Rousseau (2001, 167–68).

8 My discussion of Tomás Gutiérrez Alea's *Memorias del subdesarrollo* in chapter 2 demonstrated how the crowd figured as a threat to individual capacities for reason even for filmmakers committed to the Revolution; modernist allegories were meant to counter such threats by training spectators to be critical socialists who could think for themselves. In this chapter, anxieties about the crowd show up in a different way. Here I track how fear about the evanescence of crowd energies characterized political and intellectual discourse and films and was sometimes used to justify quite far-reaching social criticism.

9 As noted in chapter 1, while "El socialismo y el hombre en Cuba" was ostensibly focused on the role of the individual in the new revolutionary society, the essay also included a lengthy consideration of art and an explicit rejection of socialist realism. This suggests the importance that aesthetics played in at least some political leaders' efforts to think through questions of individual freedom and social order in the new society.

10 For classic analyses of Fidel Castro as a charismatic leader, see Valdés (1976, 2008). Kenneth Routon provides a compelling overview of the links between Afro-Cuban religion and popular views of Cuban state power. See Routon (2010, 51) for a discussion of the doves incident.

11 Stephan Palmié (2004, 258–59) also notes the resonance between Émile Durkheim's description of collective effervescence and Che Guevara's image of Fidel Castro and the crowd.

12 Anthropologist Katherine Verdery (1995) observes that the legitimacy of actually existing state socialist societies rests on their *capacity* to redistribute or allocate goods, an orientation that is generally independent of the *actual* distribution of these goods to consumers. As a result, there is a drive among the different bureaucratic organizations that compose the state and which, with the nationalization of industry and retail, take over the society's central economic and productive functions to increase the resources over which they have control without necessarily increasing production, which in turn leads to the endemic shortages for which state socialism is notorious (1995, 72–83). Guevara and other political leaders' repeated return to concerns about the growth of bureaucracy under state socialism reveals that they recognized this dilemma, but they tended to locate the problem and its solution in consciousness and social energetics rather than in the institutional structure put into place under state socialism.

13 Hart was an important leader in Fidel Castro's 26th of July Movement and at the time that he wrote these editorials was the organization secretary of the Communist Party of Cuba. He would later become the Minister of Culture when this institution was formed in 1976 (see Chapter 1).

14 See Pérez-Stable (1999, 153) for an explanation of the differences between rectification in Cuba and perestroika and glasnost in the Soviet Union.

15 Arturo Arango, interview by the author, Havana, October 1, 2008.

16 Some analysts argue that the rectification campaign was motivated more by economic than by political factors and included a combination of putting an end to some of the market openings that had been promoted in the 1970s while promoting others, such as foreign investment and tourism (Eckstein 2003, 60–87). Indeed, by the mid-1980s, the Cuban state was facing important economic challenges, including increasing foreign debt, a drastic drop in the price of sugar, and diminishing aid from the Soviet Union, to which the renewal of a centralized economy can be seen as a response (Pérez-Stable 1992, 15). For accounts of rectification and debates over the relative weight that economic versus political factors played in the policies of the era, see Azicri (2000, 49–68); Eckstein (2003, 60–87); and Pérez-Stable (1992; 1999, 153–73).

17 Cuban film director, interview by the author, Havana, November 20, 2008.

18 There were a number of feature-length films that dealt with contemporary themes in a critical manner released during and especially toward the end of the 1970s, including Manuel Octavio Gómez's *Ustedes tienen la palabra* (*It's Your Turn to Speak*, 1973); Sara Gómez's *De cierta manera* (*One Way or Another*, 1974) (discussed in greater detail in chapter 5); and Tomás Gutiérrez Alea's surrealist account of a bourgeois family that isolates itself in its mansion amid the Revolution, *Los sobrevivientes* (*The Survivors*, 1978). But this was also the decade that saw the emergence of a number of important historical films, including Sergio Giral's slavery trilogy and Alea's *La última cena* (*The Last Supper*, 1976), also on the topic of slavery (although some at least read *La última cena* through a contemporary lens, taking it as an allegory of power

in a period of increased control). Other significant films in this decade were more action oriented, recording the heroic efforts of Cuban spies working undercover among rebel groups supported by the CIA in the Escambray (Manuel Pérez's *El hombre de Maísinicu* [*The Man from Maísinicu*, 1973]) and the efforts of a young urban teacher to resist counterrevolutionaries and teach literacy to rural people in a small town near Playa Girón (Octavio Cortázar's *El brigadista* [*The Teacher*, 1977]). By comparison, the output of the 1980s is often viewed as having a more contemporary and critical focus, although the decade also saw a rise in lighthearted social and romantic comedies.

19 Enrique Colina, interview by the author, Havana, June 11, 2009. Subsequent comments by Enrique Colina quoted in this chapter come from this interview.

20 For an impressive and detailed documentation of the *Noticiero ICAIC*, including interviews with many of the principal artists involved, see Álvarez Díaz (2012).

21 See Chanan (2004, 388–94) for a discussion of *Cecilia* and the controversy it provoked.

22 The censorship of *Techo de vidrio* has traditionally been explained as at least in part the consequence of its supposedly less than satisfactory aesthetic result (Chanan 2004, 398–99). Giral implicitly referenced this argument when he noted García Espinosa's argument that the film was "not that important anyway," but his account of events also challenged this theory for why the film was censored. Giral told me that he later learned that the decision to ban the film had come directly from Fidel Castro. Although he did not specify his source "because this person is dead and I don't like to disturb the dead," Giral reported that he was told that the controversy over the film "got to Fidel Castro" who "called a meeting with members of the Communist Youth League who worked in the area of culture so that they could see the film and give him their opinion. He [Fidel Castro] saw it [*Techo de vidrio*] and said, 'I believe that this film does damage to the Revolution.' The person who told me [about these events] said that there was a big debate because many people said, 'no, that's reality, that's what is happening.' And other people said, 'no, no, it's not happening. This [story] should not be told.' And so there you have it. I have the honor of having a film that was censored by Fidel Castro and not by Alfredo Guevara or the Ministry of Culture." Sergio Giral, interview by the author, Miami, March 6, 2015. Subsequent comments by Sergio Giral quoted in this chapter are from this interview.

23 *Modern Times* opens with a lengthy sequence depicting Charlie Chaplin at work in a factory where he is subjected to surveillance and a rapidly increased work pace on the assembly line, gets drawn into the cogs of the machine, and finally gets carted away by an ambulance. Portions of this opening sequence were also featured in Octavio Cortázar's 1967 documentary, *Por primera vez* (*For the First Time*), which depicts rural peasants watching *Modern Times* as their first experience of cinema, provided through the

ICAIC's mobile film unit. See Balaisis (2014) for an excellent analysis of Cortázar's documentary.

24   As I elaborate in chapter 4, the bureaucrat comedy, which came to the fore during rectification, extended into the Special Period and the twenty-first century, with the difference that later examples of the genre increasingly revolved around romance and emigration. In addition to the films discussed in the two chapters of this book focused on bureaucrat comedies (chapters 3 and 4), Juan Carlos Tabío and Tomás Gutiérrez Alea's *Guantanamera* (1995), discussed in chapter 2, also arguably belongs to the genre, as does Juan Carlos Cremata's *Nada* (*Nothing*, 2001). These directors all acknowledge the influence of *La muerte de un burócrata* on their work, but the grouping of these films as bureaucrat comedies is my own device.

25   See Hendrix (1996, 61–71) for a summary of housing laws under the Cuban Revolution.

26   Juan Carlos Tabío, interview by the author, Havana, November 12, 2008. Subsequent comments by Juan Carlos Tabío quoted in this chapter come from this interview.

27   Notably, *Plaff*'s beginning echoes the opening sequence of *Chapucerías*, a 1987 documentary directed by Enrique Colina that satirizes workplace inefficiency. *Chapucerías* opens with an intertitle explaining that any deficiencies in the documentary have resulted from the workers' efforts to "over-fulfill our Technical-Economic plan by 102%," an announcement that is then followed by the disintegration of the film stills themselves as voices call frantically for the projector to be stopped. This scene arguably turns to comic effect the more serious play with disintegrating film stills and film negatives in which Santiago Álvarez engaged at the end of his 1969 documentary about Ho Chi Minh, *79 primaveras* (*79 Springtimes*).

28   Practicing members of the Regla de Ocha religion, commonly grouped together with other Afro-Cuban syncretic religions as *santería*, have a *madrina* (godmother) or *padrino* (godfather), who is responsible for their initiation into the religion.

29   A Cuban press release dated November 23, 1964, reported that Fidel Castro "offered a demonstration of his ability as a baseball pitcher" in a game just outside Havana. After the game, according to this same report, Fidel Castro engaged in conversation with the crowd. He "reiterated that, in January, the people will enjoy the magnificent results of the plan of 60 million eggs monthly he proposed several months ago" and also defined bureaucracy as "an excess of personnel who are not performing a certain function and are not in production" (Castro Ruíz 1964). Like Armando Hart's editorials three years later, this news item presents Fidel Castro's direct engagement with leisure and even the most minute aspects of production as an antidote to bureaucracy. It also ties the image of the charismatic leader in at least a curious way to the eggs-baseball-bureaucracy motif of *Plaff*.

30   Ambrosio Fornet, interview by the author, Havana, November 15, 2003.

31 Gerardo Chijona, interview by the author, Havana, February 7, 2009.

32 Castro's attack on the corruption of functionaries during the rectification campaign eventually led to the execution in 1989 of several high-ranking officials, including General Arnaldo Ochoa, on charges of drug smuggling and treason. These executions provoked shock and disillusionment for many Cuban intellectuals. These are the technocrats to which Colina referred in his interview. Sergio Giral noted that the execution of Ochoa was one of the factors that led to his eventual decision to leave Cuba.

33 Erick Grass, interview by the author, Havana, January 14, 2008.

34 Daniel Díaz Torres, interview by the author, Havana, July 28, 2003.

35 Daniel Díaz Torres, interview by the author, Havana, July 8, 2009.

36 This development has interesting resonance with *Plaff* and demonstrates both *Alicia* and *Plaff*'s use of the grotesque to illustrate the problem of social energetics. In both films, excrement signals the detrimental effects of bureaucracy on society (the Ministry of Excrement in *Plaff*; the animation of the bird happy in a pile of cow dung in *Alicia*) and serves as a tool through which characters attempt to get society's energies flowing smoothly again (Clarita's use of excrement to make an affordable polymer in *Plaff*; Omar and the children's use of excrement to enable Alicia's escape and, metaphorically, to refuse the conformity emblematized by the animation in *Alicia*).

37 Daniel Díaz Torres, interview by the author, Havana, July 8, 2009.

38 Cuban filmmaker, interview by the author, Havana, October 26, 2008.

39 Enrique Colina's letter circulated during the email war provides an excellent example of how intellectuals began drawing on a discourse of revolutionary commitment in order to demand greater accountability from political leaders in the twenty-first century. As discussed in chapter 1, in that email Colina demanded that political leaders give televised press conferences where journalists could ask them challenging questions.

40 Daniel Díaz Torres, interview by the author, Havana, July 28, 2003. Pérez's *Madagascar* recounts the story of Laura and Laurita, a university professor and her teenaged daughter, as they attempt to make sense of their lives and their place in society after the collapse of the Soviet Union. For many Cuban artists, this film was exemplary in its depiction of the disorientation that arose as a result of the crisis in historicity that characterized the early 1990s. For analyses of *Madagascar*, see Fowler (1996); Mejía (2006); Podalsky (2011); and Serra (2006).

4. STAYING AND SUSPICION

1 *Travesti* is a term used throughout Latin America to refer to biological males who adopt feminine modes of dress and affect. I leave the term in Spanish here because both possible translations—transvestite and transgender—have slightly different connotations. See Stout (2014, 26) for an explanation of this term and the difficulties with translation.

2   Questions of emigration do make an appearance in a few earlier Cuban films. Tomás Gutiérrez Alea's *Memorias del subdesarrollo*, for instance, shows middle-class Cubans, including Sergio's own parents and ex-wife, leaving for the United States in the first years of the Revolution. Sergio's conflict, meanwhile, revolves around his inability to adapt to changed circumstances in spite of his decision to stay (see chapter 2). One of the first Cuban films to make emigration its focal point was Jesús Díaz's *Lejanía (Parting of the Ways*, 1985), which depicts the reunion between Rey and his mother, Susana, who abandoned her son for Miami and has now returned for a visit, and his cousin, Ana, who lives in New York and tearfully speaks of how she was "taken away" from Cuba by her parents. See Johnson (2014) for an excellent analysis of *Lejanía* and how it anticipates the growing centrality of the question of whether to stay or to go in post-Soviet Cuban films.

3   See Ariana Hernández-Reguant (2009b) for a compelling overview of how art, intellectual conferences, and official political discourse in the Special Period reenvisioned the nation as bound by culture rather than a specific political ideology, a move that allowed for the inclusion of diasporic cultural production as part of the national cannon so long as emigrants did not explicitly or directly challenge the Cuban state. As she notes, this shift both paralleled similar transformations in European postsocialist nations and supported the state's need to establish more conciliatory relationships with moderate expatriate communities in light of the loss of its socialist allies and the need for both remittances and international support. Here, I add to this argument and, more specifically, to debates over the significance of representations of emigration in post-Soviet Cuban films, by showing how, for many Cuban intellectuals, stories of staying and fighting stand in for political ambivalence and are part of efforts to push state institutions and leaders to more expansive views. Controversies over these stories and their ideological implications can thus be seen as reflecting tensions between their status as criticism from within for some Cubans and foreign observers and arguments by others that they do not go far enough.

4   Alejandro Brugués, interview by the author, Havana, December 21, 2011. Subsequent comments by Alejandro Brugués quoted in this chapter are from this interview.

5   Hernández-Reguant (2009c, 9–10, 17) uses the Elián González controversy as an endpoint, while also noting that the Special Period was never officially declared over. In her analysis of Special Period literature, Esther Whitfield (2008, 2, 159) uses the removal of the US dollar from circulation and Fidel Castro's reference to the possibility of an end to the Special Period in his 2005 International Women's Day speech.

6   Rumors that Cuba might be entering another Special Period began to circulate as of late June 2016. During the National Assembly meeting on July 8, 2016, Raúl Castro assured the population that the Cuban economy and the nation's international trading partners were more diversified than they had been

in 1990, when 80% of the nation's trade was with the Soviet Union. This greater diversification, the Cuban government insisted, would allow the nation to avoid economic collapse regardless of declining trade relations with Venezuela. For the Cuban state's response to the rumors, see Randy Alonso Falcón, "Cuba y los interesados presagios: ¿Por qué la situación de hoy no es la de los 90?," *Granma*, July 22, 2016, http://www.granma.cu/cuba/2016-07 -22/cuba-y-los-interesados-presagios-por-que-la-situacion-de-hoy-no-es-la -de-los-90-22-07-2016-22-07-49. For a report of the discussion held in the National Assembly, see Oscar Sánchez Serra, "Después de la Asamblea Nacional," *Granma*, July 10, 2016, http://www.granma.cu/cuba/2016-07-10 /despues-de-la-asamblea-nacional-10-07-2016-22-07-38.

7   The idea of "la lucha" or "the struggle" has been a core symbol in Cuban revolutionary rhetoric since the beginning of the battle against Fulgencio Batista in the 1950s, with the state repeatedly calling on citizens to overcome various obstacles in order to preserve and advance the Revolution (Fagen 1969, 11). The use of the word *luchar* to refer to struggles to get by and make ends meet in an economy of scarcity thus transforms a term that once implied personal sacrifice for the sake of the collective to one that gives new weight to the efforts of individuals to survive and thrive.

8   For an overview of the 1994 rafter crisis, see University of Miami Digital Library Program, "The Cuban Rafter Phenomenon," http://balseros.miami.edu/, accessed February 2, 2019. Barack Obama suspended the wet-foot/dry-foot policy in January 2017, shortly before the end of his term in office.

9   Manuel Herrera, interview by the author, Havana, February 11, 2008.

10   Julia Yip, interview by the author, Havana, March 12, 2008. Yip's story resonates with Serguei Alex Oushakine's (2009) account of reactions to the collapse of socialism in Russia. When the political rituals and daily routines that organized life under the Soviet Union disappeared, he contends, individuals turned to narratives of national loss and trauma to connect their private experiences with new modes of belonging.

11   All Eastern European cartoons were referred to as *muñequitos rusos* by Cubans, reflecting the predominance of Russia in Cubans' understanding of their relationship with the Soviet bloc. See Jácome (2012) for the use of the phrase "la generación de los muñequitos rusos." Dissident blogger Yoani Sánchez consolidated the use of the term *Generación Y* with the establishment of her blog by that same name in 2007, following the email war.

12   Eduardo del Llano, interview by the author, Havana, March 11, 2008.

13   Arturo Sotto, interview by the author, Havana, November 20, 2008. Subsequent comments by Arturo Sotto quoted in this chapter are from this interview.

14   Mayling Gómez, interview by the author, Havana, September 16, 2008.

15   Humberto Solás, interview by the author, Havana, June 2, 2008.

16   Ricardo Figueredo, interview by the author, Havana, June 19, 2009. Subsequent comments by Ricardo Figueredo quoted in this chapter are from this interview.

17 Gustavo Arcos, interview by the author, Havana, May 26, 2008.

18 The choice of Lucía for this character's name alludes to Humberto Solás's *Lucía* (1968), adding to the film's abundant references to early revolutionary Cuban cinema.

19 As Désirée Díaz (2000, 38–39) argues, Mary and Mariana's dilemma suggests that, for all their political differences, Cuba and Miami are inextricably bound together, a united nation whose separation damages both halves.

20 Arturo Arango, interview by the author, Havana, October 1, 2008. Subsequent comments by Arturo Arango quoted in this chapter are from this interview.

21 Arturo Arango and film critic Joel del Río both cited Caballero as the source of this criticism. Joel del Río, interview by the author, Havana, December 20, 2011.

22 Vladimir Cruz, interview by the author, Havana, December 18, 2007.

23 See Ross (2011) for an argument about how Global North funders such as the Netherlands' International Film Festival Rotterdam via their Hubert Bals Fund often encourage an emphasis on poverty in Latin American and Global South cinema.

24 Juan Carlos Tabío, interview by the author, Havana, November 12, 2008. Subsequent comments by Juan Carlos Tabío quoted in this chapter are from this interview.

25 Agreement was reached at the VII Congress of the Communist Part of Cuba in 2016 that there should be legal changes made in cinema on the island. In the summer of 2018, discussions of what these changes might look like were discretely under way among a small group of filmmakers and functionaries. Possible plans fell short of legalizing independent production companies but did include the establishment of a national cinema fund; the creation of a registry of individuals working in various roles within independent filmmaking, which would thus give artists some legal standing; and changes designed to facilitate investment in independent film projects. At a meeting held with intellectuals at the UNEAC in October 2018, the president of the ICAIC, Ramón Samada Suárez, reportedly announced that these changes were under debate in the Council of Ministers, the highest executive body of Cuba, and would soon be ready to be launched. At the time of this writing, however, these plans had yet to be implemented. See the coda for a discussion of the debates that took place among filmmakers during the efforts to create a new cinema law and legalize independent production companies. See Rosa Miriam Elizalde, Jorge Legañoa Alonso, and Ismael Francisco, "Aprueban resoluciones del VII Congreso del Partido," Cubadebate, http://www .cubadebate.cu/noticias/2016/04/18/presentan-dictamenes-de-trabajo-de -las-comisiones-en-el-vii-congreso-del-partido/#.XGL-ddF7k_U, April 18, 2016, for reference to the discussions that took place about changes to cinema during the VII Party Congress. See Celia Medina, "'No vamos a cansarnos': Notas desde las asambleas de cineastas para asomarnos al campo periodístico en Cuba," *Cuba posible*, November 17, 2016, https://cubaposible.com/notas

-asambleas-cineastas-prensa-cuba/, for a detailed overview as of 2016 of the efforts to gain a new legal standing for independent cinema. See Brian Ramírez Val, "Sorpresa en el ICAIC: Nuevas medidas para el cine cubano," *Diario de Cuba*, October 26, 2018, http://www.diariodecuba.com/cultura /1540569484_42643.html, for a report of Ramón Samada Suárez's announcement at the UNEAC.

26 Other filmmakers have also adopted this model. Director Carlos Machado Quintela, whose feature film *La obra del siglo* (*The Project of the Century*, 2015) I discuss in chapter 5, cofounded an independent production company called Uranio Films with fellow EICTV graduate Kate Hartnoll. The company was established as a legal entity in the United Kingdom, where Hartnoll is a citizen.

27 Inti Herrera, interview by the author, Havana, December 19, 2011. Subsequent comments by Inti Herrera quoted in this chapter are from this interview.

28 Gervasio Iglesias, interview by the author, Havana, December 7, 2011.

29 Alejandro Brugués and Inti Herrera recounted that the title of *Juan de los muertos* (*Juan of the Dead*) first occurred to Brugués in English and pays homage both to Romero's *Dawn of the Dead* and to British director Edgar Wright's zombie comedy, *Shaun of the Dead* (2004), the title for which also clearly references Romero's *Dawn of the Dead*.

30 *Juan de los muertos* features numerous well-known and well-established Cuban actors and directors in small roles such as this one, while using lesser-known actors and, in the case of El Primo, a nonprofessional actor, for its principal characters. For the Cuban film community and those knowledgeable about Cuban cinema, this tactic also helped frame the film as a declaration of the rise of a new generation of filmmakers and actors.

31 The explosion of the USS *Maine*, an American naval ship, in the Havana harbor in 1898 helped popularize US intervention into the Cuban-Spanish civil war, which in turn led to American intervention into Cuban national politics. After the triumph against Batista, so goes the story, Cuban citizens spontaneously pulled down the American imperial eagle from the top of this monument, leaving only the pedestal. The statue thus stands in for the threat of American imperialism and for Cubans' nationalist response, making it a significant location for the characters' escape to Miami and Juan's nationalist decision to stay. See also chapter 1, note 4, for a discussion of the relationship between the USS *Maine* and the history of conspiracy theory and political paranoia in Cuba.

32 Cuban film spectators, interview by the author, following screening at the Payret movie theater in Centro Habana, Havana, December 6, 2011. Interviews with spectators of *Juan de los muertos* were obtained both through brief interviews with spectators as they were leaving screenings of the film during the December 2011 New Latin American Film Festival and by taking their contact information and arranging for later, lengthier discussions.

33 Jorge Molina, interview by the author, Havana, December 7, 2011.

34 Cuban film spectator, interview by the author, following screening at the Yara movie theater in Vedado, Havana, December 12, 2011.

35 Cuban film spectator, interview by the author, following screening at the Payret movie theater in Centro Habana, Havana, December 6, 2011.

36 Cuban film spectator, interview by the author, following screening at the Charlie Chaplin movie theater in Vedado, Havana, December 9, 2011.

37 Cuban film spectator, interview by the author, Havana, December 15, 2011.

38 *Juan de los muertos*'s adoption of genre film has precedents in Cuba in Juan Padrón's animated vampire comedies, *Vampiros en la Habana* (*Vampires in Havana*, 1985) and *Más vampiros en la Habana* (*More Vampires in Havana*, 2003), as well as in a series of low-budget erotic horror films that Jorge Molina began making in the late 1990s. Building on these earlier efforts, *Juan de los muertos* represents a novel attempt to fuse Cuba's auteurist and art cinema legacy with Hollywood and crossover-style spectacle and action.

39 For this interpretation of Bruce Lee's films, see Prashad (2003). Along with classic Hollywood films like *Jaws*, Bruce Lee was widely popular among Cubans in the 1980s. The references in *Juan de los muertos* thus speak to transnational media flows that played an important role in Cuban film reception and filmmaking but have yet to be thoroughly documented. Indeed, Bruce Lee and his popularity throughout the "Third" or socialist world has come to stand in for such untold transnational cinematic histories, so much so that a recent artistic and scholarly project dedicated to the experiences and work of African and Middle Eastern filmmakers who trained in Moscow was titled "Saving Bruce Lee." Koyo Kouoh and Rasha Salti, curators, "Saving Bruce Lee: African and Arab Cinema in the Era of Soviet Cultural Diplomacy," January 19–21, 2018, https://www.hkw.de/en/programm/projekte/2018/saving _bruce_lee/saving_bruce_lee_start.php.

40 The ending of Martin Scorsese's *Goodfellas* (1990) also provides a possible reference point for the ending of *Juan de los muertos*. In the final scene of *Goodfellas*, the protagonist, Henry King, who had previously been a high-flying mobster, laments his relegation to a boring suburban life. The film then cuts to an image of an already deceased gangster, Tommy, who shoots his gun directly into the nondiegetic audience while Sid Vicious's "My Way" plays. See Stern (1995, 1–3) for a discussion of this scene.

41 Ian Padrón, interview by the author, Havana, February 5, 2008.

5. MONTAGE IN THE PARENTHESIS

1 Fernando Pérez, interview by the author, Havana, June 8, 2008.

2 Alina Rodríguez Abreu, interview by the author, Havana, July 25, 2008. The difficulty of making moral distinctions also makes a comical appearance in *Juan de los muertos*. As the zombie apocalypse sets in, Lázaro takes aim with a rock at what he thinks is a zombie in the street below Juan's rooftop apartment. When Lázaro hits his target, however, he discovers that the man is still alive or, at the very least, was alive up to that moment; the man yells when struck by the rock, drawing the attention of nearby zombies, who crowd about and

begin to attack him. "¿Coño, Lázaro, no sabes diferenciar entre los buenos y los malos?" (Fuck, Lázaro, can't you tell the difference between the good ones and the bad ones?), asks Camila. "Niña, en este país siempre ha sido muy difícil hacer eso" (Girl, it's always been difficult to do that in this country), Lázaro replies as he calmly watches the young man get devoured by zombies.

3   See Quiroga (2005) for an exploration of the politics of memory in Cuba and its diaspora in the wake of the collapse of the Soviet Union. Loss (2014); Loss and Prieto (2012); and Reyes (2011) examine how contemporary Cuban literature and cinema represent the legacy of the nation's relationship with the Soviet Union.

4   I take my description of post-Soviet and early twenty-first-century experiences of history as parenthesis or impasse in Cuba from Lauren Berlant. In her book *Cruel Optimism*, she argues that the fraying of the welfare state and increasing economic precarity in post–World War II United States and Europe from the 1990s into the twenty-first century gave rise to an experience of the present as impasse, as previous versions of the "good life" became unattainable, crisis was rendered ordinary, and older political alternatives were deemed unworkable (2011, 3–5).

5   These efforts to question teleological visions of history through montage and collage aesthetics resonate with international aesthetic tactics and trends in the latter half of the twentieth century. See Skoller (2005) for an analysis of European, American, and Latin American work in this vein. By montage, I mean the juxtaposition of images and sounds in ways that highlight the constructed nature of meaning.

6   This comment may have referred to the ICAIC's recruitment of young Cuban filmmakers to produce *La dimensión de las palabras* (*The Dimension of Words*, 2008), a documentary about the nation's literacy programs abroad, which was in production at the time of the Swedish documentarists' visit to the EICTV. As discussed in chapter 1, this project provoked some controversy, as rumors circulated that it had originated as part of an effort to recruit critical young artists to positions more in line with official state politics.

7   This analysis builds on my earlier review of Susana Barriga's *The Illusion* (Humphreys 2010). For other discussions of Barriga's work, see Danae C. Diéguez's (2012) reflections on Barriga's work in the context of other emerging work by young Cuban women filmmakers; Susan Lord and Zaira Zarza's (2014) discussion of depictions of emigration and exile by young women Cuban filmmakers; and Joel del Río's (2014) analysis of what he describes as the melodramatic tendencies in Barriga's documentaries.

8   Afro-Cuban directors who worked at the ICAIC prior to the 1990s included Sergio Giral, whose work I discuss in chapter 3, and Sara Gómez, whom I discuss later in this chapter. Since the early 1990s the numbers of Afro-Cuban directors have been very slowly increasing and now include such significant filmmakers as Ernesto Daranas (see coda), Karel Ducase Manzaro, Damián Sainz, and Jorge Luis Sánchez.

9   Ernesto Livon-Grosman (2016) notes that there was a growing interest in Guillén Landrián's work on the island as of the late 1990s. Guillén Landrián's oeuvre began to have direct influence on the work of a younger generation of filmmakers once it was revived during the Muestras in the early 2000s.

10   One student at the EICTV in particular, Manuel Zayas, has played a key role in reviving interest in Guillén Landrián's work. In 2003 Zayas presented a documentary on the filmmaker titled *Café con leche* (*Coffee with Milk*) as his graduating thesis from the EICTV and has subsequently continued his exploration of Guillén Landrián's work in a number of articles and blog posts, including several cited in this chapter. In addition to the works cited in this chapter, for analyses of Guillén Landrián's oeuvre, see "Dossier: Especial Nicolás Guillén Landrian,"*La Fuga*, spring 2013, http://www.lafuga.cl/dossier /especial-nicolas-guillen-landrian/15/.

11   Corinn Columpar (2002) provides a good overview of literature on the gaze in cinema.

12   In an interview with Manuel Zayas, Guillén Landrián explained that the final intertitle in this sequence—"es bueno que esto lo vean en la Habana"—was suggested to him by the people with whom he worked in the community, further contributing to the complexity of voicing in the documentary (Petusky Coger, Ríos, and Zayas 2005).

13   Susana Barriga, interview by the author, San Antonio de los Baños, March 9, 2009.

14   The production of coffee involved in this plan was the subject of Guillén Landrián's earlier, controversial documentary *Coffea arabiga* (1968).

15   The tactics employed in *Desde la Habana ¡1969! recordar* thus more closely resemble the effects of conspiracy theory as described by Susan Lepselter (2005, 2016), who argues that political paranoia can undermine dominant historical and political discourses by highlighting the ambiguity inherent in any narrative. In this sense, this film and Esteban Insausti's *Existen* stand apart from other versions of political paranoia described in this book, in which paranoid readings tend to rely on and reinscribe predetermined meanings and political binaries.

16   Guillén Landrián's history of hospitalization for mental health reasons and Esteban Insausti's use of interviews with Cubans with mental health concerns complicate the comparison of their aesthetic style to paranoia. As a result, it is worth reiterating that I continue to invoke the term in its political and not in its clinical meaning.

17   Esteban Insausti, interview by the author, Havana, February 6, 2008.

18   *Maricones* and *invertidas* are pejorative terms in Spanish for, respectively, gay men and lesbians.

19   The son montuno is a subgenre of the Cuban son.

20   Like Varda and other French intellectuals and filmmakers, including Simone de Beauvoir, Jean-Paul Sartre, and Jean-Luc Godard, Chris Marker also traveled to Cuba in the early years of the Revolution. Marker's trip resulted

in his documentary about the Cuban Revolution, *Cuba sí* (1961), which is referenced in Varda's *Salut les cubains*.

21 Carlos Machado Quintela, interview by the author, Miami, March 10, 2015. Subequent comments quoted from Quintela in this chapter are from this interview.

22 A similar exploration of the transfer of familial relations from the domestic realm to the public place of work can also be seen in Pastor Vega's *Retrato de Teresa* (*Portrait of Teresa*, 1979), which depicts one woman's efforts to negotiate her husband's expectations that she take responsibility for the home along with her own ambitions to find fulfillment through her responsibilities at the textile factory where she works.

23 Alejandro Alonso, interview by the author, Havana, December 19, 2017.

24 Alonso obtained these archival images from the Oficina del Historiador (the Office of the Historian), which is headed by Cuban architect Eusebio Leal.

CODA

1 For examples of such reports, see, for instance, "Obama Shakes Hands with Raúl Castro for First Time at Mandela Memorial," *The Guardian*, December 10, 2013, https://www.theguardian.com/world/2013/dec/10/obama-shakes-hands -raul-castro-mandela-memorial; Uri Friedman, "Just How Big a Deal Is the Obama-Castro Handshake?," *The Atlantic*, December 10, 2013, http://www .theatlantic.com/international/archive/2013/12/just-how-big-a-deal-is-the -obama-castro-handshake/282200/.

2 It took longer than we and many others initially feared for the wet-foot/ dry-foot policy that allowed Cubans who made it to US soil to remain in the country and apply for permanent residency to be cut, but the policy was eventually canceled. Barack Obama suspended the policy in January 2017 as one of his last acts in office. For reports on this decision, see, for instance, Julie Hirschfield Davis and Frances Robles, "Obama Ends Exception for Cubans Who Arrive without Visas," *New York Times*, January 12, 2017.

3 See Yulien Oviedo, "Cuba está de Moda," YouTube, March 14, 2016, https:// www.youtube.com/watch?v=kfiMYAd8kXw.

4 For a description of *Tatlin's Whisper #6*, see the Guggenheim website, https:// www.guggenheim.org/artwork/33083; and Bruguera's own explanation of the work, http://www.taniabruguera.com/cms/112-0-Tatlins+Whisper+6+Havana +version.htm. For the declaration by the 2009 Biennale Organizing Committee, see "Declaración del Comité Organizador de la Décima Bienal de La Habana," *La Jiribilla*, March 28, 2009, http://epoca2.lajiribilla.cu/2009/n412_03/412_50 .html.

5 For reports of this alternative proposal made by Rubén del Valle, see "El régimen avisa a Bruguera que enfrenterá 'consecuencias legales y personales' por su 'performance,'" *Diario de Cuba* December 28, 2014, accessed September 29, 2018, http://www.diariodecuba.com/cultura/1419762275_12047.html.

6   Boris González Arenas's blog is available at http://probidadcuba.blogspot.ca/.
7   For reactions from Cuban artists residing both abroad and within Havana
     to Bruguera's arrest, see "Artistas e intelectuales cubanos condenan la
     represión del régimen contra Tania Bruguera," *Diario de Cuba*, Decem-
     ber 31, 2014, http://www.diariodecuba.com/derechos-humanos/1420029258
     _12088.html.
8   Enrique Álvarez, interview by the author, Havana, July 21, 2016. Subsequent
     comments quoted from Álvarez in this chapter are from this interview.
9   I cite this passage from the copy of the document released by Boris González
     Arenas and circulated via Facebook by Manuel Zayas.
10   This letter by Boris González Arenas was also circulated via Facebook in
     January 2015. It is reproduced in its entirety in Enrique del Risco's blog:
     "Cuando se reprime en nombre de la humanidad," *enrisco* (blog), January 14,
     2015, http://enrisco.blogspot.com/2015/01/cuando-se-reprime-en-nombre-de
     -la.html.
11   Manuel Pérez, interview by the author, Havana, July 20, 2016.
12   Interestingly, prior to his passing, Alfredo Guevara himself apparently supported
     the filmmakers' efforts to legalize and gain new grounds for independent
     cinema. In a 2013 article, Guevara was quoted as saying that the ICAIC had
     become obsolete and production should be taken over by the independent
     groups. Victoria Burnett, "A New Era's Filmmakers Find Their Way in Cuba,"
     New York Times, January 4, 2013. For this quote by Alfredo Guevara in its
     original Spanish, see Celia Medina, "'No vamos a cansarnos': Notas desde
     las asambleas de cineastas para asomarnos al campo periodístico en Cuba,"
     Cuba posible, November 17, 2016, https://cubaposible.com/notas-asambleas
     -cineastas-prensa-cuba/.
13   See Rosa Miriam Elizalde, Jorge Legañoa Alonso, and Ismael Francisco,
     "Aprueban resoluciones del VII Congreso del Partido," Cubadebate, http://
     www.cubadebate.cu/noticias/2016/04/18/presentan-Dictamenes-de-trabajo
     -de-las-comisiones-en-el-vii-congreso-del-partido/#.XGL-ddF7k_U, April 18,
     2016, for reference to the discussions that took place about changes to cinema
     during the VII Party Congress. See Medina, "'No vamos a cansarnos,'" for
     a detailed overview as of 2016 of the efforts to gain a new legal standing for
     independent cinema. See Brian Ramírez Val, "Sorpresa en el ICAIC: Nuevas
     medidas para el cine cubano," *Diario de Cuba*, October 26, 2018, http://www
     .diariodecuba.com/cultura/1540569484_42643.html, for a report of Ramón
     Samada Suárez's intervention at the UNEAC.
14   These comments are taken from conversations in May and June 2016 with
     several Cuban filmmakers who were either directly or indirectly involved
     in the production of *The Fate of the Furious*. Numerous articles in foreign
     newspapers and blogs also reported similar concerns. See, for example, Joel
     del Río, "Efecto Fast and Furious: Gentío, tranques, despliegue y algún din-
     erito," *CiberCuba*, April 26, 2016, https://www.cibercuba.com/noticias/2016
     -04-26-u80279-efecto-fast-and-furious-gentio-tranques-despliegue-y-algun

-dinerito; Sergio Alejandro Gómez, "Chanel no tiene problemas políticos," *Medium*, May 4, 2016, https://medium.com/@sergioalejandrogmezgallo /chanel-no-tiene-problemas-pol%C3%ADticos-d87fb56be131#.s5gwb482v; Ramón Peralta, "Rápido y Furioso 8," *Progreso Semanal*, May 7, 2016, http:// progresosemanal.us/20160506/rapido-furioso-8/.

15   One of the reasons given by officials for the film's censorship was a text that opens the film by describing the imprisonment and ostracism of many gay artists and writers in the early decades of the Revolution. The filmmakers agreed to eliminate this text, but this was clearly not sufficient to secure the film's theatrical release in Cuba. According to Claudia Calviño, Roberto Smith's letter was the first occasion on which state officials accused the film of mocking Fidel Castro. The timing of this accusation and of the letter itself thus suggests a strategic attempt to mobilize public support for the state's position. Information from Calviño is from an interview by the author, New Orleans, May 12, 2018. Roberto Smith's letter was initially published on the online portal *Cubarte*, which is dedicated to Cuban art. It can also be found, along with the other letters published by intellectuals about the censorship of *Santa y Andrés*, in two dossiers collected by the blog site *El cine es cortar*, which is focused on Cuban cinema and audiovisual production. "Nueva polémica cultural en Cuba: Filme 'Santa y Andrés (I)," *El cine es cortar*, December 4, 2016, http://www.elcineescortar.com/2016/12/04/nueva -polemica-cultural-el-filme-cubano-santa-y-andres/; "Nueva polémica cultural en Cuba: Filme 'Santa y Andrés (II)," *El cine es cortar*, January 14, 2017, http://www.elcineescortar.com/2017/01/14/nueva-polemica-cultural -cuba-filme-santa-andres-ii/.

16   The years since the announcement of the détente between Cuba and the United States have been marked, it seems, by a continuous stream of censorship scandals. In addition to the confrontations documented in this chapter, the 2018 Muestra Joven was rocked by scandal when Yimit Ramírez's film *Quiero hacer una película* (*I Want to Make a Film*, 2018) was ultimately excluded from the showcase on the grounds that it was disrespectful of José Martí. Luz Escobar, "El ICAIC relega un filme de la Muestra Joven por considerarlo irrespetuoso con Martí," *14 y Medio*, March 14, 2018, https://www.14ymedio .com/cultura/ICAIC-Muestra-Joven-irrespetuoso-Marti_0_2399760007.html. From July 2018 into the fall of that year, a number of Cuban artists engaged in protests against Decree 349, the clause designed to manage artistic production and performance in the new Cuban Constitution, which was released in July 2018, approved by the Cuban National Assembly in December 2018, and was scheduled to be voted on in a national referendum on February 24, 2019. Artists argued that the clause, which included numerous controls on independent artistic production and performance as well as a stipulation allowing government officials to regulate works deemed to include "contents that are damaging to ethical and cultural values," would enable far-reaching censorship. In December 2018, government officials attempted to reassure artists

that the decree would only be used to restrict the circulation of pornography and homophobic, sexist, racist, and otherwise discriminatory contents. These interventions included an interview with Alina Estévez, director of human resources at the Ministry of Culture, published in the Communist Party's newspaper, *Granma*, on November 29, 2018 (Alexis Triana, "El 349, un decreto en torno a la circulación del arte," *Granma*, http://www.granma.cu/cultura/2018-11-29/el-349-un-decreto-en-torno-a-la-circulacion-del-arte-29-11-2018-22-11-31) and a televised interview with Fernando Rojas, the vice minister of the Ministry of Culture, on December 6, 2018. When I visited Havana in December 2018, a number of intellectuals with whom I spoke interpreted these interventions as a concession on the part of government leaders to artists. Others remained skeptical about the reach that the clause would give officials over art. For a summary of early reactions to the clause, see "Cuban Artists and Intellectuals Denounce 'Decree 349,'" *E-Flux Conversations*, September 25, 2018, https://conversations.e-flux.com/t/cuban-artists-and-intellectuals-denounce-decree-349/8344. For a summary of debates about the decree in December 2018, see Redacción IPS Cuba, "¿Qué ha pasado con el polémico decreto 349 en Cuba?" Inter Press Service en Cuba, January 14, 2019. https://www.ipscuba.net/cultura/que-ha-pasado-con-el-polemico-decreto-349-en-cuba/.

17   Trump rolled back allowances that, under Obama, had opened up the category of people-to-people travel to Americans traveling to Cuba outside of an organized tour. While tourism did slow, several Americans with whom I spoke made use of the category of "support for the Cuban people" in order to visit Cuba. A good summary of the amendments to the Department of the Treasury's Office of Foreign Assets Control (OFAC) can be found on the website of the travel agency Authentic Cuba Tours, http://www.authenticubatours.com/us-legal-cubatravel.htm, January 11, 2019.

18   For speculations that these symptoms might have been caused by malfunctioning Cuban spyware, see Nora Gámez Torres, "Computer Scientists May Have Solved the Mystery behind the Sonic Attacks in Cuba," *Miami Herald*, March 2, 2018.

REFERENCES

Abrams, Philip. 1988. "Notes on the Difficulty of Studying the State." *Journal of Historical Sociology* 1, no. 1: 58–89.

Acosta, Nirma. 2005. "Entrevista con Eduardo del Llano: No se me ocurriría nunca atacar a la Revolución." *La Jiribilla: Revista digital de cultura cubana*, February. http://www.lajiribilla.co.cu/2005/n199_02/199_29.html.

Adorno, Theodor W. 1977. "Commitment." In *Aesthetics and Politics*, edited by Fredric Jameson, 177–95. New York: Verso.

Adorno, Theodor W., and Max Horkheimer. (1944) 1987. "The Culture Industry: Enlightenment as Mass Deception." In *Dialectic of Enlightenment: Philosophical Fragments*, edited by Gunzelin Schmid Noerr, translated by Edmund Jephcott, 94–136. Stanford, CA: Stanford University Press.

Ahmad, Aijaz. 1987. "Jameson's Rhetoric of Otherness and the 'National Allegory.'" *Social Text*, no. 17 (October): 3–25.

Allen, Don. 1969. "*Memories of Underdevelopment*." *Sight and Sound* 38, no. 4: 212–13.

Almendros, Néstor. 1984. "'An Illusion of Fairness': Almendros Replies to Alea." *Village Voice*, August 14, 1984, 40.

Álvarez Díaz, Mayra. 2012. *El Noticiero ICAIC y sus voces*. Havana: Ediciones La Memoria.

Amaya, Hector. 2010. *Screening Cuba: Film Criticism as Political Performance during the Cold War*. Urbana: University of Illinois Press.

Amiot, Julie, and Nancy Berthier, eds. 2006. *Cuba: Cinéma et révolution*. Lyon: GRIMH-LCE-GRIMIA.

Azicri, Max. 2000. *Cuba Today and Tomorrow: Reinventing Socialism*. Gainesville: University Press of Florida.

Baker, Geoffrey. 2005. "¡Hip Hop, Revolución! Nationalizing Rap in Cuba." *Ethnomusicology* 49, no. 3: 368–402.

Baker, Geoffrey. 2011. *Buena Vista in the Club: Rap, Reggaetón, and Revolution in Havana*. Durham, NC: Duke University Press.

Bakhtin, Mikhail. 1981. "Discourse in the Novel." In *The Dialogic Imagination: Four Essays*, edited by Michael Holquist, translated by Caryl Emerson and Michael Holquist, 259–422. Austin: University of Texas Press.

Bakhtin, Mikhail. 1984. *Rabelais and His World*. Bloomington: Indiana University Press.

Bakhtin, Mikhail. 1986. "The Problem of Speech Genres." In *Speech Genres and Other Late Essays*, 60–102. Austin: University of Texas Press.

Balaisis, Nicholas. 2014. "Modernization and Ambivalence in Octavio Cortázar's *Por primera vez*." *Cinema Journal* 54, no. 1: 1–24.

Balaisis, Nicholas. 2016. *Cuban Film Media, Late Socialism, and the Public Sphere: Imperfect Aesthetics*. New York: Palgrave Macmillan.

Baron, Guy. 2011. "Not Afraid to Search for a Critical Space: Discovering the Postmodern in Cuban Cinema; The Case of *¡Plaff!* (*o demasiado miedo a la vida*)." *Romance Studies* 29, no. 1: 54–65.

Belinchón, Gregorio. 2000. "Reunión en los origines: Entrevista a Jorge Perugorría y Vladimir Cruz." *El País*, suplemento *El Espectador*, May 21, 8.

Benamou, Catherine. 1994. "Cuban Cinema: On the Threshold of Gender." *Frontiers: A Journal of Women Studies* 15, no. 1: 51–75.

Benjamin, Walter. (1928) 2009. *The Origin of German Tragic Drama*. New York: Verso.

Benjamin, Walter. (1931) 1999. "Little History of Photography." In *Walter Benjamin: Selected Writings*, vol. 2, *1927–1934*, edited by Michael W. Jennings, Howard Eiland, and Gary Smith, translated by Rodney Livingstone, 507–30. Cambridge, MA: Belknap Press of Harvard University Press.

Benjamin, Walter. (1940) 1999. *The Arcades Project*. Cambridge, MA: Belknap Press of Harvard University Press.

Benjamin, Walter. (1940) 2003. "On the Concept of History." In *Walter Benjamin: Selected Writings*, vol. 4, *1938–1940*, edited by Howard Eiland and Michael W. Jennings, translated by Edmund Jephcott, 389–400. Cambridge, MA: Belknap Press of Harvard University Press.

Berdahl, Daphne. 1999. *Where the World Ended: Re-Unification and Identity in the German Borderland*. Berkeley: University of California Press.

Bergson, Henri. (1900) 1924. *Laughter: An Essay on the Meaning of the Comic*. New York: Macmillan.

Berlant, Lauren. 2011. *Cruel Optimism*. Durham, NC: Duke University Press.

Best, Stephen, and Sharon Marcus. 2009. "Surface Reading: An Introduction." *Representations* 108, no. 1: 1–21.

Boyer, Dominic. 2006. "Conspiracy, History, and Therapy at a Berlin Stammtisch." *American Ethnologist* 33, no. 3: 327–39.

Boyer, Dominic, and Alexei Yurchak. 2010. "American Stiob: Or, What Late-Socialist Aesthetics of Parody Reveal about Contemporary Political Culture in the West." *Cultural Anthropology* 25, no. 2: 179–221.

Brecht, Bertolt. (1930) 1992. "The Modern Theatre is the Epic Theatre." In *Brecht on Theatre: The Development of an Aesthetic*, edited by John Willett, 33–42. New York: Hill and Wang.

Brecht, Bertolt. (1949) 1992. "A Short Organum for the Theatre." In *Brecht on Theatre: The Development of an Aesthetic*, edited by John Willett, 179–205. New York: Hill and Wang.

Brecht, Bertolt. 1977. "Brecht against Lukács." In *Aesthetics and Politics*, edited by Fredric Jameson, 68–85. New York: Verso.

Briggs, Charles L., and Richard Bauman. 1992. "Genre, Intertextuality, and Social Power." *Journal of Linguistic Anthropology* 2, no. 2: 131–72.

Buck-Morss, Susan. 2000. *Dreamworld and Catastrophe: The Passing of Mass Utopia in East and West.* Cambridge, MA: MIT Press.

Burton, Julianne. 1977. "Individual Fulfillment and Collective Achievement: An Interview with Tomás Gutiérrez Alea." *Cineaste* 8, no. 1: 8–15, 59.

Burton, Julianne. 1997. "Film and Revolution in Cuba: The First Twenty-Five Years." In *New Latin American Cinema: Studies of National Cinemas*, vol. 2, edited by Michael T. Martin, 123–42. Detroit: Wayne State University Press.

Caballero, Rufo. 1996. "Te pongo el alma, y el pensamiento," *Boletín del XVII Festival* 3, December 7.

Cabrera Infante, Guillermo. 1994. "Soldado y defensor." *El País*, May 4. http://elpais .com/diario/1994/05/04/cultura/768002405_850215.html.

Callejas, Bernardo. 1991. "Sobre la película *Alicia en el pueblo de las maravillas*." *Trabajadores*, June 16.

Cancio Isla, Wilfredo. 2009. "Joven cineasta cubano se queda en Miami." *El Nuevo Herald*, May 15. http://www.elnuevoherald.com/ultimas-noticias/article1995524.html.

Casadevall, Gemma. 1994. "Con o sin embargo, la película se estrenera en Estados Unidos." *El Mundo*, February.

Casal, Lourdes. 1971. *El caso Padilla: Literatura y revolución en Cuba.* New York: Ediciones Nueva Atlantida.

Castro Ruíz, Fidel. (1961) 1980. "Palabras a los intelectuales." In *Revolución, letras, arte*, 3–33. Havana: Letras Cubanas.

Castro Ruíz, Fidel. 1964. "Castro at Ball Game." LANIC (Latin American Network Information Center), *Castro Speech Database*. Accessed September 29, 2018. http://lanic.utexas.edu/project/castro/db/1964/19641123.html.

Castro Ruíz, Fidel. 1986. "Statement at 3rd Congress of Cuba's Communist Party." LANIC (Latin American Network Information Center), *Castro Speech Database*. Accessed September 29, 2018. http://lanic.utexas.edu/project/castro/db/1986 /19861201-2.html.

Cavanaugh, Joanne. 1995. "Oscar Nomination Focuses Attention on Cuban Director." *Miami Herald*, March 23.

Chanan, Michael. 2002. "We Are Losing All Our Values: An Interview with Tomás Gutiérrez Alea." *Boundary 2* 29, no. 3: 47–53.

Chanan, Michael. 2004. *Cuban Cinema.* 2nd ed. Minneapolis: University of Minnesota Press.

Clark, Katerina. 2000. *The Soviet Novel: History as Ritual*. Bloomington: Indiana University Press.

Cohen, Zachary. 2017. "New Audio Adds to Mystery of Attacks on US Diplomats." *CNN*, October 14, 2017. https://www.cnn.com/2017/10/13/politics/cuba-us -diplomats-acoustic-weapons/index.html.

Columpar, Corinn. 2002. "The Gaze as Theoretical Touchstone: The Intersection of Film Studies, Feminist Theory, and Postcolonial Theory." *Women's Studies Quarterly* 30, no. 1/2: 25–44.

Comaroff, Jean, and John L. Comaroff. 1999. "Occult Economies and the Violence of Abstraction: Notes from the South African Postcolony." *American Ethnologist* 26, no. 2: 279–303.

Condee, Nancy. 2000. "Cultural Codes of the Thaw." In *Nikita Khrushchev*, edited by William Taubman, Sergeï Khrushchev, and Abbott Gleason, 160–76. New Haven, CT: Yale University Press.

Copeland, Rita, and Peter T. Struck. 2010. *The Cambridge Companion to Allegory*. Cambridge: Cambridge University Press.

CubaNet. 2015. "El realizador Ian Padrón se queda en EE.UU." *CubaNet Noticias*, February 16. https://www.cubanet.org/noticias/el-realizador-cinematografico -ian-padron-se-queda-en-estados-unidos/.

Dalton, Roque, René Depestre, Edmundo Desnoes, Roberto Fernández Retamar, Ambrosio Fornet, and Carlos María Gutiérrez. 1969. *El intelectual y la sociedad*. Mexico City: Siglo veintiuno editores.

de la Fuente, Alejandro. 2001. *A Nation for All: Race, Inequality, and Politics in Twentieth-Century Cuba*. Chapel Hill: University of North Carolina Press.

del Río, Joel. 2000. "Restauradora de sueños." *Juventud Rebelde*, May 7, 12.

del Río, Joel. 2014. "Afinidades tácticas entre el melodrama y el documental cubano contemporáneo." *Enfoco* 7, no. 46: 20–23.

del Valle, Sandra. 2010. "Definirse en la polémica: *PM*, *Cecilia* y *Alicia*." In *Conquistando la utopía: El ICAIC y La Revolución 50 años después*, 63–92. Havana: Ediciones ICAIC.

Díaz, Désirée. 2000. "El síndrome de Ulises: El viaje en el cine cubano de los noventa." *La Gaceta de Cuba*, no. 6: 37–40.

Díaz, Désirée. 2001. "La mirada de Ovidio: El tema de la emigración en el cine de los 90." *Temas*, no. 27: 37–52.

Díaz, Duanel. 2009. *Palabras del trasfondo: Intelectuales, literature e ideología en La Revolución Cubana*. Madrid: Editorial Colíbri.

Diéguez, Danae C. 2012. "¿Ellas miran diferente? Temas y representaciones de las realizadoras jóvenes en Cuba." *Cinémas d'Amérique latine*, no. 20: 150–62.

D'Lugo, Marvin. 1997. "'Transparent Women': Gender and Nation in Cuban Cinema." In *New Latin American Cinema*, vol. 2, *Studies of National Cinemas*, edited by Michael T. Martin, 155–66. Detroit: Wayne State University Press.

Dorfman, Ariel, and Armand Mattelart. (1971) 1991. *How to Read Donald Duck: Imperialist Ideology in the Disney Comic*. New York: International General.

Duarte, Amelia, and Ariadna Ruiz. 2011. "El collage de la nostalgia: Una mirada desde la colina; Rasgo postmodernos de la obra documental de Nicolás Guillén Landrián." *Cine Cubano*, no. 20 (January/March). http://www.cubacine.cult .cu/sitios/revistacinecubano/digital20/articulo14.htm.

Durkheim, Émile. (1912) 1995. *The Elementary Forms of Religious Life*. New York: Free Press.

Eagleton, Terry. 1990. *The Ideology of the Aesthetic*. Malden, MA: Blackwell.

Eckstein, Susan. 2003. *Back from the Future: Cuba under Castro*. 2nd ed. New York: Routledge.

Fagen, Richard R. 1969. *The Transformation of Political Culture in Cuba*. Stanford, CA: Stanford University Press.

Fanon, Frantz. 1967. *Black Skin, White Masks*. Translated by Charles Lam Markmann. New York: Grove Weidenfeld.

Farber, Samuel. 1983. "The Cuban Communists in the Early Stages of the Cuban Revolution: Revolutionaries or Reformists?" *Latin American Research Review* 18, no. 1: 59–83.

Fehimović, Dunja. 2018. *National Identity in 21st-Century Cuban Cinema: Screening the Repeating Island*. Basingstoke, UK: Palgrave Macmillan.

Fernandes, Sujatha. 2006. *Cuba Represent! Cuban Arts, State Power, and the Making of New Revolutionary Cultures*. Durham, NC: Duke University Press.

Fernandez, James, and Mary Taylor Huber. 2001. *Irony in Action: Anthropology, Practice, and the Moral Imagination*. Chicago: University of Chicago Press.

Fernández Retamar, Roberto, ed. 1967. *Obra revolucionaria*. 2nd ed. Mexico City: Ediciones Era.

Fernández Retamar, Roberto. 2001. "Cuarenta años después." *La Gaceta de Cuba*, no. 4: 47–53.

Fitzpatrick, Sheila. 2000. *Everyday Stalinism: Ordinary Life in Extraordinary Times*. New York: Oxford University Press.

Fletcher, Angus. (1964) 2012. *Allegory: The Theory of a Symbolic Mode*. Ithaca, NY: Cornell University Press.

Fonticoba Gener, Onaisys. 2016. "Rápido y furioso, trás su paso por la Habana." *Juventud Rebelde*, May 10. http://www.juventudrebelde.cu/cultura/2016-05-10 /rapido-y-furioso-tras-su-paso-por-la-habana.

Fornet, Ambrosio. (1968) 1980. "El intelectual en la Revolución." In *Revolución, letras, arte*, 315–19. Havana: Letras Cubanas.

Fornet, Ambrosio. 1995. *Las máscaras del tiempo*. Havana: Letras Cubanas.

Fornet, Ambrosio. 2008. "El quinquenio gris: Revistando el término." In *La política cultural del período revolucionario: Memoria y reflexión*, edited by Centro Teórico-Cultural Criterios, 25–46. Havana: Centro Teórico-Cultural Criterios.

Fowler, Víctor. 1996. "Identidad, diferencia, resistencia: A propósito de *Madagascar* y *Reina y Rey*." *La Gaceta de Cuba*, no. 3: 22–26.

Franco, Jean. 2002. *The Decline and Fall of the Lettered City: Latin America in the Cold War*. Cambridge, MA: Harvard University Press.

François, Anne-Lise. 2008. *Open Secrets: The Literature of Uncounted Experience.* Stanford, CA: Stanford University Press.

Fraunhar, Alison. 2005. "*Mulata Cubana*: The Problematics of National Allegory." In *Latin American Cinema: Essays on Modernity, Gender, and National Identity,* edited by Lisa Shaw and Stephanie Dennison, 160–79. Jefferson, NC: McFarland.

Fraunhar, Alison. 2018. *Mulata Nation: Visualizing Race and Gender in Cuba.* Jackson: University of Mississippi Press.

Freedgood, Elaine, and Cannon Schmitt. 2014. "Denotatively, Technically, Literally." *Representations* 125, no. 1: 1–14.

Fusco, Coco. 2014. "The State of Detention: Performance, Politics, and the Cuban Public." *E-Flux,* no. 60 (December). http://www.e-flux.com/journal/the-state -of-detention-performance-politics-and-the-cuban-public/.

Gallardo, Emilio J. 2009. *El martillo y el espejo: Directrices de la política cultural cubana (1959–1976).* Madrid: Consejo Superior de Investigaciones Científicas.

García, Enrique. 2015. *Cuban Cinema after the Cold War: A Critical Analysis of Selected Films.* Jefferson, NC: McFarland.

García Borrero, Juan Antonio. 2001. *Guía crítica del cine cubano de ficción.* Havana: Editorial Arte y Literatura.

García Espinosa, Julio. (1963) 2006. "Galgos y podencos." In Pogolotti, *Polémicas culturales de los 60,* 86–94.

García Espinosa, Julio. 1964. "Nuestro cine documental." *Cine cubano* 4, nos. 23–24–25: 3–21.

Ghodsee, Kristen, and Laura A. Henry. 2010. "Redefining the Common Good after Communism: Beyond Ideology." *ASEES NewsNet* 50, no. 4: 1–7.

Gledhill, Christine. 2000. "Rethinking Genre." In *Reinventing Film Studies,* edited by Christine Gledhill and Linda Williams, 221–43. London: Arnold.

Goldberg, Ruth. 2014. "Under the Surface of the Image: Cultural Narrative, Symbolic Landscapes, and National Identity in the Films of Jorge de León and Armando Capó." In *New Documentaries in Latin America,* edited by Vicinius Navarro and Juan Carlos Rodríguez, 59–74. New York: Palgrave Macmillan.

Goldstein, Richard. 1984. "¡Cuba sí, macho no! Persecution of Gays in a Leftist Land." *Village Voice,* July 24, 42–44.

Greene, Richard, and K. Silem Mohammad. 2010. *Zombies, Vampires, and Philosophy: New Life for the Undead.* Chicago: Open Court.

Grieveson, Lee. 2004. *Policing Cinema: Movies and Censorship in Early-Twentieth-Century America.* Berkeley: University of California Press.

Guevara, Alfredo. (1962) 1998. "Informe y saludo ante el primer congreso nacional de la cultura." *Cine cubano,* no. 140: 46–50.

Guevara, Alfredo. (1963) 1998. "El cine cubano 1963." *Cine cubano,* no. 140: 30–36.

Guevara, Alfredo. (1963) 2006. "Alfredo Guevara responde a las 'Aclaraciones.'" In Pogolotti, *Polémicas culturales de los 60,* 169–74.

Guevara, Alfredo. (1969) 1998. "El cine cubano: Instrumento de descolonización." *Cine cubano,* no. 140: 41–43.

Guevara, Alfredo. 1998. *Revolución es lucidez*. Havana: Ediciones ICAIC.

Guevara, Alfredo. 2003. *Tiempo de fundación*. Madrid: Iberautor Promociones Culturales S.L.

Guevara, Alfredo. 2008. *¿Y si fuera una huella?* Madrid: Ediciones Autor S.R.L.

Guevara, Ernesto ("Che"). (1962) 1967. "Que debe ser un joven comunista." In Fernández Retamar, *Obra revolucionaria*, 356–66.

Guevara, Ernesto ("Che"). (1963) 1967. "Contra el burocratismo." In Fernández Retamar, *Obra revolucionaria*, 545–50.

Guevara, Ernesto ("Che"). (1965) 1967. "El socialismo y el hombre en Cuba." In Fernández Retamar, *Obra revolucionaria*, 627–39.

Gutiérrez Alea, Tomás. (1968) 1998. "Presentación en Karlovy Vary." In *Alea: Una retrospectiva crítica*, edited by Ambrosio Fornet, 72–73. Havana: Letras Cubanas.

Gutiérrez Alea, Tomás. 1982. *Dialéctica del espectador*. Havana: Ediciones Unión.

Gutiérrez Alea, Tomás. 1984. "¡Cuba sí, Almendros no!" *Village Voice*, October 2, 46.

Habermas, Jürgen. (1962) 1989. *The Structural Transformation of the Public Sphere: An Inquiry into a Category of Bourgeois Society*. Cambridge, MA: MIT Press.

Hamilton, Carrie. 2012. *Sexual Revolutions in Cuba: Passion, Politics, and Memory*. Chapel Hill: University of North Carolina Press.

Hansen, Miriam. 1990. "Adventures of Goldilocks: Spectatorship, Consumerism and Public Life." *Camera Obscura* 8, no. 22: 51–71.

Hansen, Miriam. 1991. *Babel and Babylon: Spectatorship in American Silent Film*. Cambridge, MA: Harvard University Press.

Hansen, Miriam. 2012. *Cinema and Experience: Siegfried Kracauer, Walter Benjamin, and Theodor W. Adorno*. Berkeley: University of California Press.

Haraszti, Miklós. 1988. *The Velvet Prison: Artists under State Socialism*. London: I. B. Tauris.

Harman, Chris. 2010. *Zombie Capitalism: Global Crisis and the Relevance of Marx*. Chicago: Haymarket Books.

Hart Dávalos, Armando. 1967. "La lucha contra el burocratismo." In *Cuba: Una revolución en marcha*, edited by Francisco Fernández-Santos and José Martínez, 168–87. Paris: Ruedo Ibérico.

Hendrix, Steven E. 1996. "Tensions in Cuban Property Law." *Hastings International and Comparative Law Review* 20:1–101.

Hernández-Reguant, Ariana. 2006. "Havana's Timba: A Macho Sound for Black Sex." In *Globalization and Race: Transformations in the Cultural Production of Blackness*, edited by Kamari Maxine Clarke and Deborah A. Thomas, 249–78. Durham, NC: Duke University Press.

Hernández-Reguant, Ariana, ed. 2009a. *Cuba in the Special Period: Culture and Ideology in the 1990s*. New York: Palgrave Macmillan.

Hernández-Reguant, Ariana. 2009b. "Multicubanidad." In Hernández-Reguant 2009a, 69–88.

Hernández-Reguant, Ariana. 2009c. "Writing the Special Period: An Introduction." In Hernández-Reguant 2009a, 1–20.

Hernández-Reguant, Ariana. 2016. "Miami Cubans 4 Trump and the Battle for the Nation." *Cuba Counterpoints*, November 7. https://cubacounterpoints.com/archives/4399.

Hofstadter, Richard. 1965. "The Paranoid Style in American Politics." In *The Paranoid Style in American Politics and Other Essays*, 3–40. Cambridge, MA: Harvard University Press.

Humphrey, Caroline. 1999. "Remembering an 'Enemy': The Bogd Khaan in Twentieth-Century Mongolia." In *Memory, History, and Opposition under State Socialism*, edited by Rubie Watson, 21–45. Santa Fe, NM: School of American Research Press.

Humphreys, Laura-Zoë. 2010. "Film Review—*The Illusion* by Susana Barriga." *E-Misférica* 7, no. 1. http://hemisphericinstitute.org/hemi/en/e-misferica-71/laura-zoehumphreys-.

Humphreys, Laura-Zoë. 2017a. "Paranoid Readings and Ambivalent Allegories in Cuban Cinema." *Social Text* 35, no. 3: 17–40.

Humphreys, Laura-Zoë. 2017b. "Utopia in a Package? Digital Media Piracy and the Politics of Entertainment in Cuba." Hot Spots, *Cultural Anthropology* website, March 23. https://culanth.org/fieldsights/1090-utopia-in-a-package-digital-media-piracy-and-the-politics-of-entertainment-in-cuba.

Jacobs, Lea. 1988. "The Censorship of 'Blonde Venus': Textual Analysis and Historical Method." *Cinema Journal* 27, no. 3: 21–31.

Jacobs, Lea. 1997. *The Wages of Sin: Censorship and the Fallen Woman Film, 1928–1942*. Berkeley: University of California Press.

Jácome, Aurora. 2012. "The Muñequitos Rusos Generation." In *Caviar with Rum: Cuba-USSR and the Post-Soviet Experience*, edited by Jacqueline Loss and José Manuel Prieto, 27–36. New York: Palgrave Macmillan.

Jameson, Fredric, ed. 1977. *Aesthetics and Politics*. New York: Verso.

Jameson, Fredric. 1981. *The Political Unconscious: Narrative as a Socially Symbolic Act*. Ithaca, NY: Cornell University Press.

Jameson, Fredric. 1986. "Third-World Literature in the Era of Multinational Capitalism." *Social Text*, no. 15 (October): 65–88.

Jiménez Leal, Orlando, and Manuel Zayas, eds. 2012. *El caso P.M.: 14 minutos que duran medio siglo*. Madrid: Editorial Colibrí.

Johnson, Mariana. 2014. "Staying Home: Cuban Exile Film from Within." In *Cinematic Homecomings: Exile and Return in Transnational Cinema*, edited by Rebecca Prime, 129–46. New York: Bloomsbury.

Juan-Navarro, Santiago. 2015. "'En el vórtice de la enajenación': Nicolás Guillén Landrián y la implosión del documental científico-popular cubano de los 60." *Studies in Latin American Popular Culture* 33, no. 1: 3–26.

Juventud Rebelde. 2011. "Protagonistas de filme cubano *Juan de los Muertos* dialogaron con nuestros lectores." *Juventud Rebelde*, December 11. http://www.juventudrebelde.cu/cultura/2011-12-06/protagonistas-de-filme-cubano-juan-de-los-muertos-dialogaron-con-nuestros-lectores-fotos-y-video.

Kapcia, Antoni. 2005. *Havana: The Making of Cuban Culture*. New York: Berg.

Kaplan, E. Ann. 1997. *Looking for the Other: Feminism, Film and the Imperial Gaze.* New York: Routledge.

King, John. 1990. *Magical Reels: A History of Cinema in Latin America.* London: Verso.

Kumaraswami, Par. 2009. "Cultural Policy and Cultural Politics in Revolutionary Cuba: Re-reading the Palabras a los intelectuales (Words to the Intellectuals)." *Bulletin of Latin American Research* 28, no. 4: 527–41.

Larkin, Brian. 2009. "National Allegory." *Social Text* 27, no. 3: 164–68.

Lauro, Sarah Juliet, and Karen Embry. 2008. "A Zombie Manifesto: The Nonhuman Condition in the Era of Advanced Capitalism." *Boundary 2* 35, no. 1: 85–108.

Lee, Benjamin. 1997. *Talking Heads: Language, Metalanguage, and the Semiotics of Subjectivity.* Durham, NC: Duke University Press.

Lefort, Claude. 1986. *The Political Forms of Modern Society: Bureaucracy, Democracy, Totalitarianism.* Edited by John B. Thompson. Cambridge, MA: MIT Press.

Lepselter, Susan. 2005. "The License: Poetics, Power, and the Uncanny." In *E.T. Culture: Anthropology in Outerspaces*, edited by Debbora Battaglia, 130–48. Durham, NC: Duke University Press.

Lepselter, Susan. 2016. *The Resonance of Unseen Things: Poetics, Power, Captivity, and UFOs in the American Uncanny.* Ann Arbor: University of Michigan Press.

Leyva Martínez, Ivette. 2005. "Vídeo satírico contra la seguridad del estado causa furor en Miami." *Encuentro de la cultura cubana*, February 28. http://arch1 .cubaencuentro.com/cultura/noticias/20050301/b714541307f109449d0e0cfba 4fdb134.html.

Livon-Grossman, Ernesto. 2016. "Inside/Outside: Nicolasito Guillén Landrián's Subversive Strategy in *Coffea Arábiga*." In *The Essay Film: Dialogue, Politics, Utopia*, edited by Elizabeth A. Papazian and Caroline Eades, 237–55. New York: Wallflower.

López, Ana M. 1993. "Cuban Cinema in Exile: The 'Other' Island." *Jump Cut*, no. 38 (June): 51–59.

López, Ana M. 1997. "An 'Other' History: The New Latin American Cinema." In *New Latin American Cinema: Theory, Practices, and Transcontinental Articulations*, vol. 1, edited by Michael T. Martin, 135–56. Detroit: Wayne State University Press.

Lord, Susan, and Zaira Zarza. 2014. "Intimate Spaces and Migrant Imaginaries: Sandra Gómez, Susana Barriga, and Heidi Hassan." In *New Documentaries in Latin America*, edited by Vinicius Navarro and Juan Carlos Rodríguez, 199–218. New York: Palgrave Macmillan.

Loseff, Lev. 1984. *On the Beneficence of Censorship: Aesopian Language in Modern Russian Literature.* Munich: Sagner.

Loss, Jacqueline. 2014. *Dreaming in Russian: The Cuban Soviet Imaginary.* Austin: University of Texas Press.

Loss, Jaqueline, and José Manuel Prieto, eds. 2012. *Caviar with Rum: Cuba-USSR and the Post-Soviet Experience.* New York: Palgrave Macmillan.

Lumsden, Ian. 1996. *Machos, Maricones, and Gays: Cuba and Homosexuality.* Philadelphia: Temple University Press.

Maltby, Richard. 1996. "'A Brief Romantic Interlude': Dick and Jane Go to 3 1/2 Seconds of the Classical Hollywood Cinema." In *Post-Theory: Reconstructing Film Studies*, edited by Noel Carroll and David Bordwell, 434–59. Madison: University of Wisconsin Press.

Mantz, Jeffrey W. 2013. "On the Frontlines of the Zombie War in the Congo: Digital Technology, the Trade in Conflicted Minerals, and Zombification." In *Monster Culture in the 21st Century: A Reader*, edited by Marina Levina and Diem-My T. Bui, 177–92. New York: Continuum.

Marcus, George E., ed. 1999. *Paranoia within Reason: A Casebook on Conspiracy as Explanation.* Chicago: University of Chicago Press.

Marcuse, Herbert. 1965. "Repressive Tolerance." In *A Critique of Pure Tolerance*, edited by Herbert Marcuse, Barrington Moore Jr., and Robert Paul Wolff, 81–118. Boston: Beacon.

Mazzarella, William. 2013. *Censorium: Cinema and the Open Edge of Mass Publicity.* Durham, NC: Duke University Press.

Mazzarella, William. 2015. "Totalitarian Tears: Does the Crowd Really Mean It?" *Cultural Anthropology* 30, no. 1: 91–112.

Mazzarella, William. 2017. *The Mana of Mass Society.* Chicago: University of Chicago Press.

McAlister, Elizabeth. 2012. "Slaves, Cannibals, and Infected Hyper-Whites: The Race and Religion of Zombies." *Anthropological Quarterly* 85, no. 2: 457–86.

Mejía, Glenda. 2006. "*Madagascar*: Un viaje interno." *Studies in Hispanic Cinemas* 3, no. 2: 101–8.

Miller, Nicola. 2008. "A Revolutionary Modernity: The Cultural Policy of the Cuban Revolution." *Journal of Latin American Studies* 40, no. 4: 675–96.

Mulvey, Laura. 1999. "Visual Pleasure and Narrative Cinema." In *Film Theory and Criticism: Introductory Readings*, edited by Leo Braudy and Marshall Cohen, 833–44. New York: Oxford University Press.

Muñoz, Gerardo. 2011. "La política de los gestos: La actualidad de '*PM*.'" *Encuentro de la cultura cubana*, June 3. http://www.cubaencuentro.com/cultura/articulos/la -politica-de-los-gestos-la-actualidad-de-pm-263679.

Muñoz, José Esteban. 2000. "Performing Greater Cuba: Tania Bruguera and the Burden of Guilt." *Women and Performance: A Journal of Feminist Theory* 11, no. 2: 251–65.

Murray, Leah A. 2010. "When They Aren't Eating Us, They Bring Us Together: Zombies and the American Social Contract." In *Zombies, Vampires, and Philosophy: New Life for the Undead*, edited by Richard Greene and K. Silem Mohammad, 325–42. Chicago: Open Court.

Navarro, Desiderio. 2002. "In Medias Res Publicas: On Intellectuals and Social Criticism in the Cuban Public Sphere." *Boundary 2* 9, no. 3: 187–203.

Navarro, Desiderio, ed. 2008. *La política cultural del período revolucionario: Memoria y reflexión.* Havana: Centro Teórico-Cultural Criterios.

Negt, Oskar, and Alexander Kluge. (1972) 1993. *Public Sphere and Experience: Toward an Analysis of the Bourgeois and Proletarian Public Sphere*. Minneapolis: University of Minnesota Press.

ONE (Oficina Nacional de Estadisticas). 2010. "Tecnologías de la información y las comunicaciones: Uso y aceso en Cuba, enero–diciembre 2009." September. http://www.one.cu/publicaciones/o6turismoycomercio/TIC/2009%20 TIC%20Uso%20y%20Acceso%20en%20Cuba.pdf.

Ong, Aihwa. 2012. "'What Marco Polo Forgot.'" *Current Anthropology* 53, no. 4: 471–94.

Ortega y Gasset, José. (1939) 1964. "Ensimismamiento y alteración." In *Obras completas*, vol. 5, 291–378. Madrid: Ediciones Castilla.

Oushakine, Serguei Alex. 2009. *The Patriotism of Despair: Nation, War, and Loss in Russia*. Ithaca, NY: Cornell University Press.

Padrón, Frank. 2000. "Espera aún no lista." *Trabajadores*, June 19.

Palmié, Stephan. 2004. "Fascinans or Tremendum? Permutations of the State, the Body, and the Divine in Late Twentieth-Century Havana." *New West Indian Guide* 78, no. 3/4: 229–68.

Paranagua, Paulo Antonio, and Roberto Cobas. 1990. *Le cinéma cubain*. Paris: Centre Georges Pompidou.

Parmentier, Richard J. 1994. *Signs in Society: Studies in Semiotic Anthropology*. Bloomington: Indiana University Press.

Pérez Betancourt, Rolando. 2000. "El humor crítico del cine cubano y Malkovich independiente." *Granma*, December 15.

Pérez-Stable, Marifeli. 1992. "Charismatic Authority, Vanguard Party Politics, and Popular Mobilizations: Revolution and Socialism in Cuba." *Cuban Studies* 22:3–26.

Pérez-Stable, Marifeli. 1999. *The Cuban Revolution: Origins, Course, and Legacy*. New York: Oxford University Press.

Pertierra, Anna Cristina. 2012. "If They Show *Prison Break* in the United States on a Wednesday, by Thursday It Is Here: Mobile Media Networks in Twenty-First-Century Cuba." *Television and New Media* 13, no. 5: 399–414.

Peters, Philip. 2012a. *Cuba's Entrepreneurs: Foundation of a New Private Sector*. Arlington, VA: Lexington Institute.

Peters, Philip. 2012b. *A Viewer's Guide to Cuba's Economic Reforms*. Arlington, VA: Lexington Institute.

Petusky Coger, Lara, Alejandro Ríos, and Manuel Zayas. 2005. "El cine postergado." *Encuentro de la cultura cubana*, September 2. http://arch1.cubaencuentro.com /entrevistas/20050904/74540a9e00385c591a45bac12d946245/1.html.

Pick, Zuzana M. 1993. *The New Latin American Cinema: A Continental Project*. Austin: University of Texas Press.

Podalsky, Laura. 2011. *The Politics of Affect and Emotion in Contemporary Latin American Cinema: Argentina, Brazil, Cuba, and Mexico*. New York: Palgrave Macmillan.

Pogolotti, Graziella, ed. 2006. *Polémicas culturales de los 60*. Havana: Letras Cubanas.

Pollo, Roxana. 1991. "*Alicia, un festín para los rajados.*" *Granma*, June 19.

Ponte, Antonio José. 2006. "'Existen': ¿Nación que es locura?" *Encuentro de la cultura cubana*, April 18. http://www.cubaencuentro.com/cultura/articulos/existen -nacion-que-es-locura-15315.

Ponte, Antonio José. 2010. *Villa Marista en plata: Arte, política, nuevas tecnologías.* Madrid: Editorial Colibrí.

Ponte, Antonio José. 2015. "Censura y G-20." *Diario de Cuba*, January 15. http://www .diariodecuba.com/cultura/1421361592_12337.html.

Poole, Deborah. 1997. *Vision, Race, and Modernity: A Visual Economy of the Andean Image World.* Princeton, NJ: Princeton University Press.

Poole, Deborah. 2004. "An Image of 'Our Indian': Type Photographs and Racial Sentiments in Oaxaca, 1920–1940." *Hispanic American Historical Review* 84, no. 1: 37–82.

Prashad, Vijay. 2003. "Bruce Lee and the Anti-Imperialism of Kung Fu: A Polycultural Adventure." *Positions* 11, no. 1: 51–90.

Prieto, Val. 2005. "Finally: Monte Rouge (UPDATED)." *Babalú: An Island on the Net without a Bearded Dictator* (blog), March 1. http://babalublog.com/2005/03 /finally-monte-rouge-updated/.

Quiroga, José. 2005. *Cuban Palimpsests.* Minneapolis: University of Minnesota Press.

Ramos, Julio. 2013. "Los archivos de Guillén Landrián: Cine, poesía y disonancia." *La Fuga*, September. http://www.lafuga.cl/los-archivos-de-guillen-landrian/659/.

Redruello Campos, Laura. 2007. "Algunas reflexiones en torno a la película *Alicia en el pueblo de Maravillas.*" *Cuban Studies* 38, no. 1: 82–99.

Reyes, Dean Luis. 2010. *La mirada bajo asedio: El documental reflexivo cubano.* Santiago de Cuba: Instituto Cubano del Libro Editorial Oriente.

Reyes, Dean Luis. 2011. "Ostalgie caribeña: Saudade pos-soviética en el audiovisual Cubano contemporáneo." *ArtCultura* 13, no. 22: 61–70.

Reyes, Dean Luis. 2013. "Exhumaciones de Nicolás Guillén Landrián." *La Fuga*, September. http://www.lafuga.cl/exhumaciones-de-nicolas-guillen-landrian/660/.

Reyes, Dean Luis. 2017. "Tres años del fondo noruego para el cine cubano." *On Cuba*, August 16. https://oncubamagazine.com/columnas/republica-de-imagenes /tres-anos-del-fondo-noruego-para-el-cine-cubano/.

Robbins, Dylon. 2009. "On the Margins of Reality: Fiction, Documentary, and Marginal Subjectivity in Three Early Cuban Revolutionary Films." In *Visual Synergies in Fiction and Documentary Film from Latin America*, edited by Miriam Haddu and Joanna Page, 27–48. New York: Palgrave Macmillan.

Roca, Blas. (1963) 2006. "Preguntas sobre películas." In Pogolotti, *Polémicas culturales de los 60*, 145–51.

Rodríguez, Fidel A. 2016. "Cuba: Videos to the Left—Circumvention Practices and Audiovisual Ecologies." In *Geoblocking and Global Video Culture*, edited by Ramon Lobato and James Meese, 178–88. Amsterdam: Institute of Network Cultures.

Rodríguez Parilla, Bruno. 1991. "La suspicacia del rebaño." *Juventud Rebelde*, June 16.

Rofel, Lisa. 2007. *Desiring China: Experiments in Neoliberalism, Sexuality, and Public Culture*. Durham, NC: Duke University Press.

Roland, L. Kaifa. 2013. "T/racing Belonging through Cuban Tourism." *Cultural Anthropology* 28, no. 3: 396–419.

Rooney, Ellen. 2010. "Live Free or Describe: The Reading Effect and the Persistence of Form." *Differences* 21, no. 3: 112–39.

Ross, Miriam. 2011. "The Film Festival as Producer: Latin American Films and Rotterdam's Hubert Bals Fund." *Screen* 52, no. 2: 261.

Rousseau, Jean-Jacques. 2001. *Du contrat social*. Paris: Flammarion.

Routon, Kenneth. 2010. *Hidden Powers of the State in the Cuban Imagination*. Gainesville: University Press of Florida.

Ryer, Paul. 2015. "The *Maine*, the *Romney* and the Threads of Conspiracy in Cuba." *International Journal of Cuban Studies* 7, no. 2: 200–211.

Saavedra, Lázaro. 2014. "Tania gana, los dereches civiles continúan perdiendo." *Enrisco* (blog), December 31. http://enrisco.blogspot.com/2014/12/se-abre-el-debate.html.

Saavedra, María Cristina. 2005. "Nation and Migration: Emigration and Exile in Two Cuban Films of the Special Period." *Atenea* 25, no. 2: 109–24.

Sawyer, Mark Q. 2006. *Racial Politics in Post-revolutionary Cuba*. Berkeley: University of California.

Scarpaci, Joseph L., Roberto Segre, and Mario Coyula. 2002. *Havana: Two Faces of the Antillean Metropolis*. Chapel Hill: University of North Carolina Press.

Schmelz, Peter John. 2009. *Such Freedom, If Only Musical: Unofficial Soviet Music during the Thaw*. New York: Oxford University Press.

Schroeder, Paul A. 2002. *Tomás Gutiérrez Alea: The Dialectics of a Filmmaker*. New York: Routledge.

Sedgwick, Eve Kosofsky. 2003. *Touching Feeling: Affect, Pedagogy, Performativity*. Durham, NC: Duke University Press.

Seremetakis, Nadia. 1996. "The Memory of the Senses, Part I: Marks of the Transitory." In *The Senses Still: Perception and Memory as Material Culture in Modernity*, edited by Nadia Seremetakis, 1–18. Chicago: University of Chicago Press.

Serra, Ana. 2006. "La Habana cotidiana: Espacio urbano en el cine de Fernando Pérez." *Chasqui* 36, no. 1: 88–105.

Shils, Edward. 1965. "Charisma, Order, and Status." *American Sociological Review* 30, no. 2: 199–213.

Silverstein, Michael. 2004. "'Cultural' Concepts and the Language-Culture Nexus." *Current Anthropology* 45, no. 5: 621–52.

Skoller, Jeffrey. 2005. *Shadows, Specters, Shards: Making History in Avant-Garde Film*. Minneapolis: University of Minnesota Press.

Sloterdijk, Peter. 1987. *Critique of Cynical Reason*. Minneapolis: University of Minnesota Press.

Smith, Roberto. 2016. "Respuesta urgente a una provocación." *Cubarte: Portal de la cultura cubana*, November 29. http://www.cubarte.cult.cu/periodico-cubarte/respuesta-urgente-a-una-provocacion/.

Soles, Diane R. 2005. "'Within the Revolution, Everything': Civil Society, Political Critique, and the Film Industry in Cuba, 1981–2001." PhD diss., University of Wisconsin–Madison.

Sommer, Doris. 1993. *Foundational Fictions: The National Romances of Latin America.* Berkeley: University of California Press.

Stern, Lesley. 1995. *The Scorsese Connection.* Bloomington: Indiana University Press.

Stewart, Jacqueline. 2005. *Migrating to the Movies: Cinema and Black Urban Modernity.* Berkeley: University of California Press.

Stock, Ann Marie. 2009. *On Location in Cuba: Street Filmmaking during Times of Transition.* Chapel Hill: University of North Carolina Press.

Stout, Noelle. 2014. *After Love: Queer Intimacy and Erotic Economies in Post-Soviet Cuba.* Durham, NC: Duke University Press.

Subero, Gustavo. 2016. *Gender and Sexuality in Latin American Horror Cinema: Embodiments of Evil.* London: Palgrave Macmillan.

Taruskin, Richard. 2000. *Defining Russia Musically: Historical and Hermeneutical Essays.* Princeton, NJ: Princeton University Press.

Todorova, Maria, and Zuza Gille, eds. 2010. *Post-Communist Nostalgia.* New York: Berghahn Books.

Trejo, Mario (Felonius), Fausto Canel, and José de la Colina. (1963) 2006. "Eligen críticos *El ángel exterminador* y *Viridiana.*" In Pogolotti, *Polémicas culturales de los 60,* 160–63.

Valdés, Nelson P. 1976. "Revolution and Institutionalization in Cuba." *Cuban Studies* 6, no. 1: 1–37.

Valdés, Nelson P. 2008. "The Revolutionary and Political Content of Fidel Castro's Charismatic Authority." In *A Contemporary Cuba Reader,* edited by Philip Brenner, Marguerite Rose Jiménez, John M. Kirk, and William M. Leogrande, 27–40. Lanham, MD: Rowman and Littlefield.

Venegas, Cristina. 2009. "Filmmaking with Foreigners." In Hernández-Reguant, *Cuba in the Special Period,* 37–50.

Verdery, Katherine. 1995. *National Ideology under Socialism: Identity and Cultural Politics in Ceaușescu's Romania.* Berkeley: University of California Press.

Walton, Jeremy. 2010. "Hungry Wolves, Inclement Storms: Commodified Fantasies of American Imperial Power in Contemporary Turkey." In *Anthropology and Global Counterinsurgency,* edited by John D. Kelly, Beatrice Jauregui, Sean T. Mitchell, and Jeremy Walton, 105–16. Chicago: University of Chicago Press.

Warner, Michael. 2002. "Publics and Counterpublics." In *Publics and Counterpublics,* 65–124. New York: Zone Books.

Weber, Max. (1922) 1968. *Economy and Society: An Outline of Interpretive Sociology.* New York: Bedminster.

Wedeen, Lisa. 1999. *Ambiguities of Domination: Politics, Rhetoric, and Symbols in Contemporary Syria.* Chicago: University of Chicago Press.

Weed, Elizabeth. 2012. "'The Way We Read Now.'" *History of the Present* 2, no. 1: 95–106.

West, Dennis. 1993. "Alice in a Cuban Wonderland." *Cineaste* 20, no. 1: 24.

West, Harry G., and Todd Sanders, eds. 2003. *Transparency and Conspiracy: Ethnographies of Suspicion in the New World Order*. Durham, NC: Duke University Press.

Whitfield, Esther. 2008. *Cuban Currency: The Dollar and Special Period Fiction*. Minneapolis: University of Minnesota Press.

Winegar, Jessica. 2006. "Cultural Sovereignty in a Global Art Economy: Egyptian Cultural Policy and the New Western Interest in Art in the Middle East." *Cultural Anthropology* 21, no. 2: 173–204.

Xavier, Ismail. 2004. "Historical Allegory." In *A Companion to Film Theory*, edited by Toby Miller and Robert Stam, 333–62. Oxford: Blackwell.

Yurchak, Alexei. 2006. *Everything Was Forever, until It Was No More: The Last Soviet Generation*. Princeton, NJ: Princeton University Press.

Zayas, Manuel. 2010. "Nicolás Guillén Landrián: Muerte y resurección." *Cinémas d'Amérique Latine* 18, no. 1: 121–35.

Žižek, Slavoj. 1989. *The Sublime Object of Ideology*. New York: Verso.

INDEX